Advancing Multicultural Dialogues in Education

"In this time of increasing religious fundamentalism, ethno-cultural nationalism and rampant populism, there is a need for educational approaches that offer an alternative vision and the means for achieving it. This timely collection, which examines multicultural education at different levels of schooling and beyond, in both formal and informal contexts and within different national frames, provides numerous examples of effective practice and insightful critique. Its comprehensive scope makes it a significant contribution to the field and a valuable read for researchers and practitioners alike."

—Megan Watkins, *Western Sydney University, Australia*

"Richard Race and his colleagues are to be congratulated for pulling together this volume that addresses topics and issues which are relevant to global societies in the 21st century. The role of education is underlined in each chapter, as a necessary starting point and indeed as an important tool, in helping national and global societies to re-centre and to re-imagine in times of conflicting ideologies and rhetoric about what forms societies should take. Given the recent and ongoing movement of peoples through forced and other forms of migration, this book will be a critical resource for the immediate and foreseeable future, in helping those within and outside education to continue advancing multicultural dialogues."

—Paul Miller, *University of Huddersfield, UK*

"The world events associated with the late neoliberal age warrant an urgent need to initiate authentic global multicultural dialogue in education and beyond. This timely book provides an international perspective on the lingering tropes of difference and deficit that can only be diminished by dismantling the power blocs gaining advantage from them. This is a 'must read' book."

—Vini Lander, *Edge Hill University, UK*

"This text is timely, truly international and exposes the concept of multiculturalism to rigorous socio-political and cultural debate. Set across different educational contexts, 'Advancing Multicultural Dialogues in Education' offers a deconstruction of multiculturalism in global terms. This book expertly explores persistent dissonance between majority culture and minority positioning, examines critical interactions between cultural values and theoretical perspectives and promotes an impressive range of methodological approaches - all of which will benefit practitioners and students."

—Erica Joslyn, *University of Suffolk, UK*

Richard Race
Editor

Advancing Multicultural Dialogues in Education

palgrave
macmillan

Editor
Richard Race
School of Education
University of Roehampton
London, UK

ISBN 978-3-319-60557-9   ISBN 978-3-319-60558-6   (eBook)
DOI 10.1007/978-3-319-60558-6

Library of Congress Control Number: 2017951019

This Palgrave Macmillan imprint is published by Springer Nature
The registered company is Springer International Publishing AG
The registered company address is: Gewerbestrasse 11, 6330 Cham, Switzerland

FOREWORD

THE DIALOGUE SOCIETY

Dialogue and education are the two most essential concepts that are critical to our ability to tackle some of the biggest problems we are facing all around the globe in the twenty-first century, namely, ignorance and lack of dialogue. This results in antagonism, hatred and animosity towards the other. Dialogue and education are the two tools that humanity must use to challenge these ailments before it is too late as we see these illnesses spread to every corner of the world, found in the discourse of populist leaders and political actors. Fanaticism of every kind, chauvinistic nationalism, religious fundamentalism and racism are creeping ailments of mankind that need urgent treatment and rehabilitation with the remedies of education, dialogue and cooperation.

This book came about as a result of two things: the efforts of the authors who share their research on the intersections of dialogue, multiculturalism, education and representation, amongst other relevant themes, as well as the efforts of the Dialogue Society to organise two workshops on multiculturalism in 2013, which became the impetus and inspiration for this book. The book project grew larger with its wider array of authors who brought with their expertise evolving perspectives to the general theme of this volume. At the Dialogue Society, we have tried to do our best to support and contribute to this book as much as possible during its preparation.

The Dialogue Society was in fact founded on the premise of empowering people and their communities through dialogue and education—the two concepts that are reflected in the work we do, whether on the academic, grassroots or policy levels. The Society was founded in 1999 by a group of British Muslims of Turkish background to foster relations between diverse communities in the UK as well as promote dialogue—as a subdiscipline in the academy and as a catalyst to a lack of understanding and intolerance across intercultural and interfaith divides.

The Dialogue School is one example of the intersection between dialogue and education in the work of Dialogue Society. In this format, the Dialogue Society first contacts local schools and asks them whether they have disadvantaged students who may be interested in joining the Dialogue School. The Society then invites an inspiration speaker who is known for his success in his line of work, whether the speaker is an athlete, an actor or a writer. Then the inspirational speaker and the group of disadvantaged students meet at the Dialogue Society premises for an interactive session, in which first the speaker shares his or her experiences in his or her career and how s/he became successful, which is followed by a Question and Answer session, which ideally lasts about the same time as the speaker's part. The results of this type of Dialogue Society are twofold: firstly, the speaker and the students engage in dialogue; secondly, the students come out of the event more informed and inspired with increased understandings regarding attaining their own goals in their lives.

The Connecting Communities Circles is another Dialogue Society project that demonstrates how the ideas of dialogue and multiculturalism can come together to create a platform for different local communities to discuss their similarities, differences and their common concerns regarding the society they live in. The event format is an informal discussion between three to five representatives from the two local ethnic groups, participants coming from all walks of life and working in different professions. They then discuss topics on education, family, culture and language relevant to each group, which is followed by a discussion of similarities and differences in these areas. In the end, the foundations for dialogue and positive relations between the two groups are laid.

Finally, BRAVE, Building Resilience Against Violent Extremism, is an ongoing project of the Dialogue Society which tackles issues of extremism, isolation, misunderstanding and representation for the British Muslim communities, by analysing the primary sources with a view to explore texts that are considered dialogic and controversial. The project has two aims, firstly, it aims to educate British Muslim youth in their own traditions by tackling controversial verses and showing them that these cannot be understood as the extremists do (to promote violence and terrorism) by giving their proper context. Secondly, it aims to demonstrate that dialogue is, in fact, part and parcel of the primary texts of Islam, and that working towards engaging with others through dialogue is only a natural outcome of this process.

The Dialogue Society's projects are not limited to the above; there are publications, Dialogue Theories I and II being directed towards exploring the different perspectives on dialogue from world-renown dialogue thinkers, Deradicalisation by Default, a policy paper written to provide constructive ideas to tackle the issue of radicalisation in the UK, Multiculturalism I and II, which came about as a result of two workshops in Turkey on coexistence and intercultural relations in the UK and Europe. There are also seminars, conferences and roundtable discussions, which are held on a number of topics related to dialogue, community relations and reconciliation, amongst others.

The Dialogue Society is honoured to have been part of this book project from the beginning, on concepts that are at the heart of what we do. The book is a testament to the importance of dialogue and education, as well as how communities and groups are represented in the media and how this impacts on all of our daily lives. Each author displays their expertise on the topic at hand, and the book is a welcome contribution to a literature which can be benefit both academics and practitioners. The book is all the more crucial at a time when we are increasingly talking about clashes and conflict, whether on cultural, religious or ethnic lines, and lack of educational focus on these issues is a serious issue internationally. We congratulate the authors and the editor for researching and writing on such pressing issues relevant to our world today. We would like to express our thanks and gratitude to Dr Richard Race for moving this book project forward to completion and for his valuable feedback.

London   The Dialogue Society
March 2017

PREFACE

The preface to this edited collection is being written as the Prime Minister of the United Kingdom has called a general election for June 2017. In educational terms, Theresa May has talked about advancing grammar schools. As a grammar school girl herself, she has been privileged to have obtained an education in the post-1944 'Secondary Education for All' era when a tripartite system of grammar, technical and secondary modern schools was introduced in the post Second World War period. During the 1960s and 1970s, this system of secondary education was surpassed by a secondary system of comprehensive schooling that was not based on selection and streaming through an 11+ system of examination. Interestingly, Secretary of State for Education, Margaret Thatcher in the early 1970s, holds the distinction of opening more Comprehensive Schools than any other Secretary of State but as significantly she preserved over 140 grammar schools. As the current Secretary of State of Education, Justine Greening (DfE 2017) stated, 'I don't accept the arguments from those who critique grammars and selection whilst simultaneously ignoring the views of parents.' However, if you examine the critique of grammar school policy, 'The prime minister's grammars policy comes on top of cuts to school budgets that will hit schools with the poorest intakes the hardest. On her watch, free schools are opening disproportionately in more affluent areas with more spare school places than average' (The Observer 2017). Moreover, if you add to this the Key Stage Two test at 11 within the national curriculum in England and Wales over the last 28 years, you begin to wonder what has and what will actually change in education if Prime Minister May wins as predicted the general election.

It is important to provide context in relation to education policy because it is worth touching upon contemporary issues that concern the education system in England. Let's highlight some key facts:

£4.5bn of capital funding [was spent] for schools in 2015–16; [there was a …] 599,000 net increase in the number of school places between 2010 and 2015; £6.7bn [is the] estimated cost of returning all school buildings to satisfactory or better condition; and 420,000 [is the] number of new school places needed between 2016 and 2021. (NAO 2017)

In relation to school buildings and school places, you can see the pressure the Department for Education are currently under with the need to increase the number of school places but preserve and build new schools within the existing national school estate. If the money is not found, then existing schools will have to take on more children with larger classes. This puts everybody under pressure in schools from Headteachers through to teachers.

That leads us to a second issue, the recruitment and retention of teachers. As the HoCEC (2017) underline, the government has to improve teacher retention. The education system loses over 30% of qualified teachers within five years in England and Wales. A key driver for teachers considering leaving the profession is unmanageable workload. As I touch upon in both the Introduction and my chapter in this book, relevant continuing professional development is not only a must but will also raise the status of the teacher profession, thus improving retention for teachers. So, in relation to these two subjects, school buildings and places, alongside recruitment and retaining teachers, we come to multicultural dialogues. We simply need the teachers and the facilities within all schools to be able to deliver multicultural dialogues and education. We do have the Programmes of Study to achieve this in several subjects within the current national curriculum, but we need teachers who are not only trained but are also comfortable and confident to do this. I continue to advocate an international curriculum rather than a national curriculum for England and Wales, but this seems even further away when you consider the United Kingdom leaving the European Union. This Brexit reality feels more national than international.

This edited collection moves beyond the nation and national towards the international and global where multicultural dialogues have to be given the space to develop and evolve. My current research is examining the relationship between integration and education policy-making. Integration remains an important part of general policy making, let alone education policy-making. I remain interested in the responses to policy at all levels; in education one of the policies that will not be examined during the current seven-week election campaign are the numbers of children who are home educated and not educated in state-maintained schools. Interestingly, it is not only the state who is paying for the system, it is the parents who are responding and in some cases resisting the requirement of educating their children in schools that need to be further examined in education research. Why are parents unhappy with the current system of education? This two-way conditional integrationist relationship with, on the one hand, the state creating policy and on the other hand, individuals and communities responding on the other—either complying or resisting—can be applied to other areas of education, that is, the national curriculum, inclusive education and citizenship education. It is the conditional nature of integration that I continue to examine. If Katwala (2016) argues that integration matters, I will argue that *multiculturalism matters more*. This edited collection advances the call for continued multicultural dialogues in education, within the wider social sciences, but as importantly within national and international politics where more multicultural voices need to be heard.

London   Richard Race
April 2017

REFERENCES

Department for Education (DfE). (2017). Justine greening: Education at the heart of our plan for Britain. Retrieved April 19, 2017, from https://www.gov.uk/government/speeches/justine-greening-education-at-the-heart-of-our-plan-for-britain

House of Commons Education Committee (HoCEC). (2017). Recruitment and retention of teachers. Fifth Report of Session 2016–17.Retrieved April 19, 2017, from https://www.publications.parliament.uk/pa/cm201617/cmselect/cmeduc/199/199.pdf

Katwala, S. (2016). The Casey review and the need for an integration strategy. Retrieved March 31, 2017, from http://www.britishfuture.org/articles/the-casey-review-and-the-need-for-an-integration-strategy/

National Audit Office (NAO). (2017). Capital funding for schools. Retrieved April 19, 2017, from https://www.nao.org.uk/wp-content/uploads/2017/02/Capital-funding-for-schools.pdf

The Observer. (2017, April 16). Comment—'Our school are failing the poorest pupils. Politicians have no answers, only soundbites', p. 32.

Contents

LIST OF FIGURES AND TABLES

Introduction

Richard Race

The idea for this edited collection came out of the launch of the second edition of *Multiculturalism and Education* (Race 2015). The launch itself took place at the Dialogue Society's headquarters in North London in April 2015. There was a demand by the attendees to keep the multicultural dialogues discussed evolving. The cultural diversity of the people who attended the event was truly global, as were the comments that were made to the papers presented by colleagues on the day. The majority of the contributors to this edited collection attended the event. The intention of this book is to keep the dialogues of that event audible and visual to a wider audience. This becomes even more significant when we consider the current political and global landscape. The rationale for more dialogue on cultural diversity and multicultural education looks even more important when we consider the presidential election result in the USA (November 2016), the UK leaving the European Union in March 2017 to be followed by a referendum in Turkey in April 2017 and presidential elections in both France and Germany in 2017. When we consider political slogans (i.e. 'policing our borders' and 'building walls between countries or within countries'), then we have to reflect on the need to continue to highlight the importance of both multiculturalism and multicultural

R. Race (✉)
Roehampton University, London, UK

© The Author(s) 2018
R. Race (ed.), *Advancing Multicultural Dialogues in Education*,
DOI 10.1007/978-3-319-60558-6_1

1

dialogues (Banks 2016b). It's the response to these policies and politics and the increasing influence of the media which again justifies this project and the chapters in this collection. In important respects, the creation and evolution of critical race theory has allowed the opportunity for not only black and minority voices to be heard—see Coles and Hassan's chapter in this book—but a much more cultural spread of voices to allow more multicultural dialogues to take place (Taylor et al. 2009; Aleman and Gautan 2017; Johnson and Bryan 2017). This method is very important when considering a conceptual movement away from multicultural, anti-racist and anti-discrimination policy and ideas towards more integrationist and assimilationist agendas and the consequent separation of alienated communities. But this is nothing new as Banks (2016b: 29) highlights when he states: 'Modern education systems were established in order to build social cohesion through homogenization and maintain social control. The assimilationist ideology was used in nations around the world to "maintain social control" and to attain "social cohesion".' Therefore, we need to reverse this process back to more socially inclusive and equitable debates that address contemporary issues within education. Moreover, the need and requirement of this text is to offer this space for the authors in this book to develop their own multicultural dialogues which will hopefully inspire readers of this text to do the same.

MULTICULTURALISM AND MULTICULTURAL EDUCATION

The focus of the book is not only on multicultural education but the wider multicultural dialogues within the social sciences, not just in England or Europe but beyond to global recognition of the issues addressed in this edited collection (Crowder 2013). However, before we begin, an appropriate examination of the concept of multiculturalism and the evolution of multicultural education will be insightful into providing a wider context in relation to the material that follows within this book. As Joppke (2017: 153) argues, multiculturalism 'means different things to different authors and their respective learnings, from communitarian to radical and liberal, It has different implications according to the markers accommodated by it, from sexual orientations to language, religion, and race. It also takes different forms in different parts of the world, one major distinction being between New World countries, which subscribe to multiculturalism as a nation-integrating formula, and Europe, where multiculturalism is exclusively a property of minorities, with immigrants holding a central but ambiguous and increasingly contested role in it'. Tarozzi and Alberto Torres (2016: 169–170), while acknowledging how elusive the term multiculturalism can be, argue that cultural diversity and difference still count in contemporary societies. They both argue for a constructive multiculturalism in global citizenship education whereby 'culture is not the only dimension which constitutes identity, because identities are by definition multifaceted and plural. There is a process of learning of our multiple identities, which is historically contextualized, and connects with our learning and recognition'.

This history and politics of the story of multiculturalism and its impact on education provides important context for multicultural dialogues and has been discussed elsewhere (Race 2015: 15–40, 127–142; Boronski and Hassan 2015). On the one hand, Ali (2016: 10) highlights, '[to] ... understand the emergence and rise of multiculturalism ... the particular economic and political conjuncture of the decade of the 1970s binds the demise of social citizenship with the effervescence of multicultural citizenship, in other words as one was inexorably on the wane, the other was on the ascendant'. On the other hand, Banks (2016b: 3) has also addressed the Cameron, Sarkozy and Merkel debates on 'The Death Multiculturalism' which occurred in Europe in the early 2010s (McGhee 2008; Vertovec and Wessendorf 2010; Williams 2013). As a respondent clearly stated in the data collection for Race (2015), you cannot kill a phenomenon, meaning a phenomenon cannot die. However, as Banks (ibid.) shows: 'The heated discourse on multicultural education, especially in the popular press and among writers outside the field ... often obscures the theory, research, and consensus among multicultural education scholars and researchers about the nature, aims and scope of the field ... Several multicultural scholars in Germany and the United Kingdom stated that multiculturalism could not have failed in Germany and the United Kingdom because it has never been effectively implemented in policy or practice.'

Banks (2016a, b) is a key author here that links multiculturalism and multicultural education. His advocacy of both has allowed many students and researchers to develop and reflect upon their own and other multicultural dialogues (Mils and Ainscow 2011; Modood 2013; Bolton 2014; Pollard et al. 2014; Meer 2015; Miah 2015; Fook et al. 2016). For Banks (2016a: 1): 'A major goal of multicultural education ... is to reform schools, colleges, and universities so that students from diverse racial, ethnic and social class groups will experience educational equality.' If, as Banks (2016a) continues, 'multicultural education is to become better understood and implemented in ways more consistent with theory, its various dimensions must be more clearly described, conceptualized, and researched'. Banks (2016a: 4–17) has formulated the following five dimensions: content integration, the knowledge construction process, an equity pedagogy, prejudice reduction and an empowering school culture, and social structure. Those dimensions are a starting point in a pedagogy that can promote and advocate multicultural education. As Neito (2017: 2) implies, 'at its core, multicultural education is a direct challenge to public education's Eurocentric focus and curriculum, as well as to the starkly uneven outcomes of education that have been particularly onerous for children whose race, ethnicity, native language, and social class differ from the majority group'. It's that challenge that Shirley Steinberg's chapter addresses in this book. The challenge, as Neito (2017: 3 continues, shows, '*how* education was done, and who benefited and *why*. It was, in a word, a direct affront to the notion of White supremacy'. The challenge to this notion comes through as Grant (2015: 43) underlines through ideas and people. As he poses: 'What is the relevance … to education that is multicultural? Simply this: organization is essential to the survival of education that is multicultural. No idea, no cause can be sustained without organization.' The application of ideas and the continuing professional development of people then theoretically allows teachers and lecturers to become multicultural educators. Howe and Lisi (2014: 51–57) have devised a model of personal development in multicultural education which involves: 'Knowledge, Awareness, Skills and Action'. Race (2015: 96) argues that to continue to advance and advocate multicultural dialogues and multicultural education, we need to focus on 'method, depth and reach'. Multiculturalism and multicultural education is about ideas and people, but we need the tools to teach and develop the ideas surrounding cultural diversity (Banks 2016a).

If we have these tools and continue to promote and develop multicultural dialogues, we can have a more equitable focus on teachers and children within education. In relation to teachers, Ball (2006: 148) highlighted: 'I am hopeful that the voices of teachers are being heard, that teachers are teaching for social justice, and that the voices of these teachers are making an impact on educational reform movements and efforts for social change.' A continuing theme in the literature within the history of multicultural education is, as Neito (2017: 2) repeats, 'teachers who were poorly prepared to teach students of diverse backgrounds'. This criticism is not directed at teachers per se, it's about the opportunities, or lack of opportunities, that all and especially white teachers are given to develop knowledge and skills around cultural diverse issues and teaching (McAndrew 2013; Banton 2015; Shepherd and Linn 2015). This unfortunately has consequences for all children. Having personally taught a postgraduate course in a school in Slough (England) where fifteen-year-old children were acting as teaching assistants to translate curricula from English into Polish for younger students, you begin to increase understandings of the complexity of cultural diversity and its effects on schools, teachers and all pupils. Howard (2016: 9) sums up the main issue with the following question: 'Why are they sending these kids to our school?' Projected onto the larger educational scene, the answer to this question is simple: 'They live here. The growing presence of diversity in our public school population is the current reality in our classrooms and will become even more prominent in the face of our future.' This applies not only in the USA and England but globally.

What is therefore needed is educational change, and the concept of multiculturalism and the methods of multicultural education provide a change agenda that is equitable in a growing, globalised world. Neito (2017: 3) sums up the demographic changes in the USA: '[The] US population has changed considerably from one that was overwhelming European American to one that is increasingly multi-ethnic, multiracial and multicultural ... new immigrants are coming not from Europe but mostly from Mexico, the Caribbean, Central and South America, and several Asian and South Asian nations ... Moreover, the U.S Census Bureau estimates that by 2043, people of color will outnumber Whites, and that by 2060, one in three residents will be Hispanic.' It's these simple facts which have to be reacted too in a positive, culturally diverse way. We need more international curriculum in schools and universities and we can no longer rely on national curriculum to educate our children. Programmes of study in England and Wales do provide opportunities for teachers in state-maintained schools to deliver culturally diverse curricula. The question is, how many teachers, for majority and minority communities, have the training, knowledge, pedagogy and confidence to deliver a more contemporary and relevant curriculum that encompasses cultural diversity in all subjects at all levels within education? Race (2015) has shown through empirical data analysis the need for more continuing professional development through diversity training to allow more professional practitioners to not only survive in the culturally diverse classroom and lecture theatre but thrive as a professional practitioner. By researching power (i.e. the structure and institutional policies and practices that control education), we will move towards a more culturally diverse educational curriculum (Neito 2015, 2017). The book builds on existing evidence and literature to advocate that movement and highlights how important and significant multiculturalism and multicultural education remains. All of the contributors to this edited collection prove that statement through the method of advancing multicultural dialogues in education (Burn and Pratt-Adams 2015; Brown and Calderon 2016; Race and Lander 2016).

ADVANCING MULTICULTURAL DIALOGUES IN EDUCATION

Blundell addresses the theme of multicultural dialogues by proposing that behind the uncritical assumption of universality and naturalness found in developmentalist theories of childhood, there lurks a historically referenced Eurocentric provenance. The author argues that the idealised 'child' at the heart of developmentalism offers a largely invisible 'stage-setting' upon which essentialised social and cultural differences can be projected without reference to the complex entanglements of actual children's lives as social actors. Blundell argues that the curriculum might embrace a multicultural commitment to diversity and difference but this idealised 'child', as an embodiment for liberal individualism is problematic and a recondite anachronism that all too frequently frustrates attempts to recognise, respond to and embrace difference. This chapter ends by suggesting that multicultural dialogues can be advanced both through acknowledgement of the Eurocentric assumptions sustaining the concept of 'the Child' and by pursuing an understanding of children's lives that more closely fits the facts of a world marked by diverse encounters across all levels, from the local to the global.

Chetty makes a case for revitalising multiculturalism in higher education through her own teaching and learning. She argues for a culturally sensitive pedagogy that values students' own history and reflected experiences, highlighting the power of multicultural dialogues. By drawing on her own extensive research and teaching experiences, Chetty analyses a migration module she leads within a wider sociological programme. By drawing on her own professional practice and student evaluations (i.e. a questionnaire with ten semi-structured questions), one of her aims was how to increase multicultural dialogues in lectures and seminars. Chetty raises the cultural diversity of her students, allowing enhanced learning which unlocks student cultural capital. Languages are underlined as key, or a major force, in allowing multicultural dialogues to develop. The post-2016 Brexit landscape is highlighted in relation to how diversity politics could change higher education with a reduction of international students. Chetty's chapter argues for an opening out of multiculturalism debates, giving a voice to all via culturally responsive pedagogy which promotes a sense of belonging.

Coles and Hassan explore the narratives of British Muslim pupils in two locations to examine how the media misrepresents Islam through the concepts of Britishness and British values. Based on the understanding that the participant is the sole authority of their own experience, the authors collect data in East London and Bradford (England), using an open-ended questionnaire. Critical race theory is applied to the data. Themes such as frustration and anger of misrepresentation, as well as the self-confidence of respondent identity, paint a complex picture in relation to multicultural dialogues. The authors ultimately call for greater continuing professional development, particularly in relation to the teaching of British values, to enable multi-narratives rather than a media-focused portrayal of Islam and Muslims in the media.

Diamantidaki and Carruthers aim to provide an overview of the UCL, Institute of Education, (IE) Confucius Institute (CI) for schools in promoting the teaching of Chinese in primary and secondary schools in England. The authors analyse how the IOE CI developed and evolved so that in 2016 there are 200 spoke schools working with the 42 Confucius Classrooms, three of which are based in primary schools. Both authors underline the challenges of introducing Chinese into both sectors of schooling, including introducing a Programme of Study concerning Mandarin. The potential of comparing Mandarin with European languages seeks precision of meaning through complex grammar and vocabulary. Both authors focus on the challenges of teaching and learning, offering a new Programme of Study and suggesting new strategies in the teaching of characters and presenting culture. Both authors within the CI continue their work, with informal feedback suggesting that this approach is working within a flexibility which provides the possibility for integration with other materials.

Farini presents the results of four empirical research projects concerning migrant children in Italy. Data consists of young migrants' narratives, promoted and collected in 62 focus group and 118 individual interviews. Respondents in the four projects were 17–20 years old at the moment of data collection and resident in Italy for more than one year.

Non-probabilistic and convenience sampling methods were used to select respondents and narrative analysis was used to examine the data collected. The narratives produced suggest a criticism of the idea of cultural identity as an 'essential' identity, something given and fixed. Farini's research approaches personal narratives as constructed through multicultural dialogue, that is, a social process rather than an object. Issues surrounding the complexity of cultural identities are visible in the data, and the possibilities of cultural hybridisation through multicultural dialogues is presented.

Gkofa examines the stories of educational success amongst Greek Roma. This is a chapter concerning those who are and who are not recognised. The Roma in Greece experience high dropout rates from education, but the author offers hope with empirical data suggesting this picture is far from universal. The author takes entrance into higher education as a marker of educational success of which few Roma have achieved. By applying Bourdieu's theories of cultural capital, Gkofa interviewed 20 Roma who were found through gatekeepers. The data focuses on the respondents' perceptions and experiences of success. The notion of success was understood in multiple ways, with one of the major themes being internal cultivation. The author highlights how feelings of success are complex within notions of 'othering' and gender. Furthermore, complexity is underlined in the author's conclusions, whereby some participants presented themselves as successful while others did not.

Isik and Sener examine the work of Fethullah Gülen who is the inspiration behind the Hizmet movement which has opened schools and dialogue societies across the world. Gülen's philosophy of education is examined through three perspectives: humanistic, social and global. Hizmet schools are then looked at with secondary data from a number of sources from different countries. An academic focus on the sciences and the creation of national and international Science Olympiads are analysed, with the claim that competitive events like this one strengthen education. Teachers are critical and crucial within this ideology and their commitment in many countries are underlined. The arguments are balanced between almost the total commitment of teachers to the altruist temptations of material gain. The events in July 2016 in Turkey are also covered by the authors, with the continued need to allow all dialogues to be heard in multicultural settings (Sleap et al. 2013; Sener et al. 2016).

Jamison, working for the Tony Blair Faith Foundation, provides people with practical tools to address religious extremism, prejudice and violence, and to help build open-minded and pluralist societies. His chapter examines The Generation Global programme run by the Foundation, an approach enabling young people to develop these key skills and experiences that will help them to build resilience to extremist narratives or more on education's role in building resilience against extremism. What is pertinent from a methodological point of view are the ethical considerations which touch upon security concerns, confidentiality agreements and data that is taken from refugee camps around the world. Jamison believes the Foundation has a part to play in good practice and empowering young people to develop skills to build a better world. Moreover, the author is an advocate of improving access to quality education and developing multicultural dialogues and critical thinking.

Layne et al. problematize the dreams and opportunities that immigrant students in Finland are offered for their future careers. The authors focus on the perceptions and roles of school staff (teachers, study counsellors, principals and school psychologists) in these matters by applying Ahmed's organisational anti-racism theory. They also adopt a critical race theory methodology and a reflexive constructivist approach. Their empirical data consists of interviews and observation notes relating to elementary, lower secondary and upper secondary school staff. In order to provide counter-narratives, the authors use Finnish newspaper articles published on the success of immigrants and voices from two teachers with an immigrant background. Layne et al.'s aim was to increase understandings in Finland of the structures supporting the academic and social success of immigrant children and young people in education.

McKinney seeks to increase understandings of how to reduce discrimination by examining the religious landscape in Scotland. His focus is on Jewish and Muslim communities. With a detailed exploration of the rise in anti-Semitism and Islamophobia in Scotland, the author examines Jewish and Muslim perceptions of their contemporary position and safety. He highlights a recurring narrative that Scotland has been a safer place for Jews and Muslims than England and Wales. This narrative is critiqued through a close focus of the actual position of Jews and Muslims in society by applying Koenigh's four claims of recognition. McKinney then underlines infringements concerning the human rights of both Jewish and Muslim communities. The author finally looks at communication and education and emphasises the need for authentic multicultural dialogue within and between communities.

Moncrieffe examines cross-cultural encounters through British history. He applies history curricula from Key Stage Two in England and Wales to gain greater insights and understandings about Britain's migrant past. By reflecting upon his own past and through his own empirical research, he also applies an auto-ethnography concerning his identities by examining the events of the Brixton riots in London in 1981. We hear his voice, as well as his mum's reflection, which produces some fascinating insights into the contested notions surrounding the events of 1981, which were nation-wide and not centred only in Brixton. Moncrieffe then provides a comparison between Viking and Black histories and the historical content that shapes teaching and learning but also past and contemporary issues concerning cultural diversity which continues to shape historical curricula.

Odena's chapter develops his previous empirical education work in Northern Ireland and Cyprus. The opening section outlines the meanings of the main concepts used throughout the chapter, including multicultural education, ethnicity and integration. In the second and third sections, Odena discusses recent international developments and his advocacy for increased research is highlighted in post-conflict contexts if we are to increase understandings of the potential of music education research and practice for building genuine multicultural dialogues in conflict-affected settings. The concluding section offers implications for policy leaders, practitioners and community organisers, comprising nine principles for the design of pedagogies of multicultural education in post-conflict environments.

Race argues that Australia offers important lessons into how multiculturalism and multicultural policy can be implemented educationally. The objective is to advance multicultural dialogues not only within Australia but globally, which is the ultimate intention of this edited collection. This chapter uses Australian state policy documents as well as education empirical data as evidence bases to argue that in adopting a clear, explicit positive stance on multiculturalism, Australia allows its teachers to theoretically prepare their pupils for the evolving nature of cultural diversity within the country. The article also discusses the 'cultural literate dialogue' idea of Soutphommasane and how it fits within his wider idea of Australian citizenship through patriotism. It offers an assessment of these ideas within wider multicultural dialogues and the possibility of their application in a way that would allow for further positive consequences for multiculturalism and multicultural education in Australia and potentially in other countries.

Robertson reflects on her research with university students, teachers and researchers. She underlines comments and negative phrases which are being made by teachers in England and internationally. The author analyses the word 'culture' and her aim is to show how the use of 'culture' as a construct has become an acceptable tool to drive a wedge between groups of people and how this discriminatory use has been legitimised in early years policy and normalised in everyday use. Robertson argues that 'cultural' and 'culture' have become bywords for something that is not there when education professionals discuss some children—children who are somehow perceived to be the norm and considered to be 'our' children. But when teachers draw attention to some children's cultural backgrounds, the culture in question tends to be framed in a deficit model: it requires fixing. The groups of children who are perceived in need of fixing are typically those who are from a working class background or black; or speak another language at home; or they are from a minority ethnic background; or Muslim, Gypsy, Roma, Traveller; or they are recent migrants. Robertson applies critical discourse analysis to the use of the term 'cultural' and applies early year's education policy documents to ask why we continue to minoritise certain cultures over others. In light of multicultural dialogues, Robertson asks, whose stories are we telling and who are we excluding?

Steinberg, in a continuing dialogue to create greater equity and to challenge previous assumptions, believes we must articulate, identify, name and break down the power blocs which serve to sustain an inequitable world. In her chapter and by using the work of Fiske, she continues to develop the notion of critical multiculturalism, which she had created with Kincheloe. She argues that we need to *name* the forces which fight against a democratic and diverse multicultural world. She attempts to call out the white supremacist and patriarchal power blocs which maintain a dominant cultural stance within an examination of oppression. Steinberg suggests these are two of the guiding components in governing our abilities to identify what is needed in diversity: multicultural dialogues and multicultural education.

Wischmann's considers how different modes of learning in early adolescence are interrelated and at the same time interwoven with racializing and racist practices and structures and how this impacts educational trajectories of young people. Particularly in the transition between childhood and adolescence, a modification of learning spaces and forms takes place, beyond the major contexts of schooling and family. The author highlights the differentiation between formal, informal and also non-formal learning changes which become more conscious and generates a relationship that has impact on future educational developments. Formal learning takes place in educational institutions, is highly structured, organised and related to—often certified—achievement. Non-formal learning is learning in semi-structured contexts like music schools or sport clubs; informal learning is not framed by any kind of educational intention. Wischmann argues it takes place in various contexts and is not necessarily intended and can be implicit. How the relationships between these different forms of learning are configured on the individual's experiences is underlined but also on social conditions that operate within given social structures and power relations. The chapter concludes with how formal and informal education affects multicultural dialogues.

Yan and Whitty analyse the general strategies adopted by the Chinese government to integrate its minority ethnic groups and how these strategies have shifted in accordance with changes of political climate in the central government in Beijing. Four periods are identified in this chapter according to the dominant development strategies adopted by the central government. The authors examine policy changes in minority education in China and how the changes responded to wider shifts in the political climate. The case of Xinjiang was particularly discussed as an example of policy intervention in one of China's most multi-ethnic regions. The authors argue that while these policies are presented as facilitating the integration of minority ethnic groups into Chinese society, in practice they do not always constitute genuinely multicultural education. For Yan and Whitty, this should entail intercultural dialogues that respect the cultural identities of all learners. Such an education also needs to provide them with the knowledge, skills and attitudes necessary to achieve full participation in society. Both authors urge a re-think in the construction of 'Chineseness', so that the current Han-dominant vision of China can be replaced with a new vision of multi-ethnic China.

References

Aleman, S. M., & Gautan, S. (2017). 'It doesn't speak to me': Understanding student of color resistance to critical race pedagogy. *International Journal of Qualitative Studies in Education, 30*, 128–146. Retrieved from http://www.tandfonline.com/doi/full/10.1080/09518398.2016.1242801.

Ali, A. (2016). *South Asian Islam and British multiculturalism*. New Delhi: Routledge.

Ball, A. F. (2006). *Multicultural strategies of education and social change.* New York: Teachers College Press.

Banks, J. A. (2016a). *Cultural diversity and education: Foundations, curriculum, and teaching* (6th ed.). New York: Routledge.

Banks, J. A. (2016b). Civic education in the age of global migration. In J. A. Banks, M. M. Suarez-Orozoco, & M. Ben-Peretz (Eds.), *Global migration, diversity and civic education* (pp. 29–52). New York: Teachers College Press.

Banton, M. (2015). *What we know about race and ethnicity.* Oxford: Berghahn.

Bolton, G. (2014). *Reflective practice: Writing and professional development* (4th ed.). London: Sage.

Boronski, T., & Hassan, N. (2015). *Sociology of education.* London: Sage.

Brown, A. L., & Calderon, D. (2016). *Reclaiming the multicultural roots of the U.S. curriculum: Communities of color and official knowledge in education.* New York: Teachers College Press.

Burn, E., & Pratt-Adams, S. (2015). *Men teaching children 3–11: Dismantling gender barriers.* Bloomsbury: London.

Crowder, G. (2013). *Theories of multiculturalism: An introduction.* Cambridge: Policy Pres.

Fook, J., Collington, V., Ross, F., Ruch, G., & West, L. (Eds.). (2016). *Researching critical reflection: Multidisciplinary perspective.* Abingdon: Routledge.

Grant, C. A. (2015). *Multiculturalism in education and teaching: The selected works of Carl A. Grant.* London: Routledge.

Howard, G. R. (2016). *We can't teach what we don't know* (3rd ed.). New York: Teachers College Press.

Howe, W. A., & Lisi, P. L. (2014). *Becoming a multicultural educator: Developing awareness, gaining skills, and talking action.* Thousand Oaks: Sage.

Johnson, L., & Bryan, N. (2017). Using our voices, losing our bodies: Michael Brown, Trayvon Martin, and the spirit murders of Black male professors in the academy. *Race Ethnicity and Education, 20*(2), 163–177.

Joppke, C. (2017). *Is multiculturalism dead.* Cambridge: Polity Press.

McAndrew, M. (2013). *Fragile majorities and education: Belgium, Catalonia, Northern Ireland and Quebec.* Quebec, QC: McGill-Queen's University Press.

McGhee, D. (2008). *The end of multiculturalism? Terrorism, integration and human rights.* Maidenhead: McGraw-Hill Press/Open University Press.

Meer, N. (2015). *Citizenship, identity and the politics of multiculturalism.* Houndsmills: Palgrave Macmillan.

Miah, S. (2015). *Muslims, schooling and the question of self-segregation.* Houndsmills: Palgrave Macmillan.

Mils, S., & Ainscow, M. (Eds.). (2011). *Responding to diversity in schools: An inquiry-based approach.* Abingdon: Routledge.

Modood, T. (2013). *Multiculturalism* (2nd ed.). Cambridge: Polity Press.

Neito, S. (Ed.). (2015). *Why we teach now.* New York: Teachers College Press.

Neito, S. (2017). Re-imagining multicultural education: New visions, new possibilities. *Multicultural Education Review, 9*, 1–10.

Pollard, A., Black-Hawkins, K., Hodges, C. H., Dudley, P., James, M., Linklater, H., et al. (Eds.). (2014). *Reflective teaching in schools* (4th ed.). London: Bloomsbury.

Race, R. (2015). *Multiculturalism and education* (2nd ed.). London: Bloomsbury.

Race, R., & Lander, V. (Eds.). (2016). *Advancing race and ethnicity in education*. Houndsmills: Palgrave Macmillan.

Sener, O., Sleap, F., & Weller, P. (Eds.). (2016). *Dialogue theories II*. London: The Dialogue Society.

Shepherd, T. L., & Linn, D. (2015). *Behaviour and classroom management in the multicultural classroom: Proactive, active and reactive strategies*. Thousand Oaks: Sage.

Sleap, F., Sener, O., & Weller, P. (Eds.). (2013). *Dialogue theories*. London: The Dialogue Society.

Tarozzi, M., & Alberto Torres, C. (2016). *Global citizenship education and the crises of multiculturalism*. London: Bloomsbury.

Taylor, E., Gillborn, D., & Ladson-Billings, G. (Eds.). (2009). *Foundations of critical race theory in education*. New York: Routledge.

Vertovec, S., & Wessendorf, S. (Eds.). (2010). *The multiculturalism backlash: European discourses, policies and practices*. New York: Routledge.

Williams, M. H. (2013). *The multicultural dilemma: Migration, ethnic politics, and state—Intervention*. London: Routledge.

Richard Race is Senior Lecturer in Education at Roehampton University, UK. He is author of *Multiculturalism and Education* (2nd Ed.) and co-editor with Professor Vini Lander (Edge Hill University, UK) of *Advancing Race and Ethnicity in Education* (Houndsmills, Palgrave Macmillan, 2016). He is currently working on his second monograph, *Integration and Education Policy-Making* (contracted with Palgrave Macmillan). Richard is currently a member of the British Education Research Association Council and remains co-convenor of the Postgraduate Pin within the Society of Research into Higher Education.

Eurocentrism, Modern Childhood and Children's Globalised Lives

David Blundell

INTRODUCTION

This chapter addresses the theme of this edited collection by proposing that behind the uncritical assumption of universality and naturalness found in developmentalist theories of childhood, there lurks a historically referenced Eurocentric provenance. It argues that the idealised 'child' at the heart of developmentalism offers a largely invisible 'stage-setting' upon which essentialised social and cultural differences can be projected without reference to the complex entanglements of actual children's lives as social actors. In short, the curriculum may embrace a multicultural commitment to diversity and difference, but this idealised 'child', as embodiment for liberal individualism, is problematic and a recondite anachronism that all too frequently frustrates attempts to recognise, respond to and embrace difference. This chapter ends by suggesting that multicultural dialogues can be advanced both through acknowledgement of the Eurocentric assumptions sustaining the concept of 'the Child' and by pursuing an understanding of children's lives that more closely fit the facts of a world marked by diverse encounters across all scales, from the global to local.

D. Blundell (✉)
London Metropolitan University, London, UK

© The Author(s) 2018   15
R. Race (ed.), *Advancing Multicultural Dialogues in Education*,
DOI 10.1007/978-3-319-60558-6_2

LOOKING BACK: PLOWDEN, INNOCENCE AND CHILD CENTREDNESS

The report from the Central Advisory Council for Education (CACE) (England), officially known as 'Children and their Primary Schools' but more widely identified by association with Lady Bridget Plowden as 'The Plowden Report', is widely regarded as marking the high water mark for progressivism in English and Welsh state education (DES 1967). Its intellectual and philosophical heritage can be traced to the Reports of Sir William Hadow (BoE 1931) before the Second World War that gave the phenomenon we readily identify as primary education in the UK a distinct character and paved the way for the landmark 1944 Education (Butler) Act (MoE 1944). Plowden was published as self-styled 'progressive educators' acquired a professional consciousness constructed around 'the Child' as emblem at the centre of educational endeavour and possibilities for curricular development afforded by the Butler Act became apparent. A clear expression of this child-centredness comes in the Report's much-quoted opening paragraph that acquired the status of an article of faith amongst 'progressives': '*At the heart of the educational process lies the child. No advances in policy, no acquisitions of new equipment have their desired effect unless they are in harmony with the nature of the child, unless they are fundamentally acceptable to him*' (DES 1967, paragraph 9; Blundell 2012, p. 145).

Although often understood as concerned primarily with the promotion of child-centred pedagogy, the Plowden (DES 1967) committee also embodied the concerns of the UK Labour government led by Harold Wilson, then in mid-term, to promote social mobility and institutional renewal in a nation that was undergoing rapid change. The élan attaching to the post-war victors' dividend of the 1950s had waned as Britain shed its status as an Imperial power, the cultural dominance of the USA began to be felt and the cold-war established the terms for a geopolitical status quo that would last for a quarter of a century (Blundell 2012, pp. 141–142). In the spirit of transformation, large sections of the report are devoted to exploring how education and schooling can be recruited to secure socially desirable outcomes, such as the mitigation of poverty, overcoming socio-economic disadvantage and the promotion of a more meritocratic, if not actually equal, society.

The Plowden Report (DES 1967) comes 19 years after the *Empire Windrush* had docked at Tilbury as the emblematic event marking the beginning of an economic migration to the UK of ambitious young workers from the Caribbean and newly independent Indian sub-continent. By 1967 there was abundant evidence that new Commonwealth migrants faced discrimination and that tensions around 'race' were on the rise. In response to growing concerns and threats of serious conflict, the Wilson government and Roy Jenkins as Home Secretary, introduced the first measures to address what were increasingly urgent social realities (see Race 2015, pp. 19–23). Mullard (1985) traced the genesis of these policy responses over this period from the late 1950s to the early 1970s, that included Jenkins' incumbency, and identifies successive concepts shaping their goals as 'assimilationist', then 'integrationist', followed by the concept of 'cultural pluralism'. However, despite rhetorical differences, Mullard (ibid.) suggests that there was little to choose between these positions and they could be seen as variations on the fundamental assimilationist expectations (i.e. that minority populations should accommodate themselves to majority norms), and in that, little or nothing had really changed. Furthermore, whereas the emerging policy domain began with a concern over disorder and discrimination that was openly debated and understood in terms of *'race'*, Jenkins' initiatives contributed to a shift in emphasis towards *culture* as both the arena for a policy response and, by implication, the cause of discrimination and inequality. This provoked heated debates between multiculturalists and anti-racists that continued through the late 1970s and 1980s (see Troyna and Williams 1986; Sarup 1986) and was, *inter alia*, central to the research conducted by Coard (1971, 2005) and Stone (1981) about the failure of liberal ideologies as agents for change in a schooling system shot through with racist practices.

Plowden seeks to recognise and respond to this emerging diversity in its Chapter 6 entitled 'Children of Immigrants', where the language is very much couched in terms of the 'problems' faced by teachers, not only due to the presence of what it calls the 'immigrant child'—even when these children had been born in the UK—but also, in a nod towards its Rousseauian romantic roots, to parents and adults in general:

> Most experienced primary school teachers do not think that colour prejudice causes much difficulty. Children readily accept each other and set store by other qualities in their classmates than the colour of their skin. Some echoes of adult values and prejudices inevitably invade the classroom but seldom survive for long among the children. It is among the neighbours at home and when he begins to enquire about jobs that the coloured child

(sic) faces the realities of the society into which his parents have brought him. (DES 1967, Paragraph 179)

The unreflective use of 'coloured', with its assumptions about the normativity of 'whiteness', together with the use of the male pronoun with its catch-all presumption, may strike us as anachronistic. There is an assumed opposition between the values of the 'experienced primary school teachers' and the 'values and prejudices' of adults that reeks of elitism reliant on an assumed professional neutrality amongst teachers. However, for the purposes of this chapter, it is the underlying constructions surrounding children, childhood and 'the Child' that are of interest. Although published half a century ago, these constructions of what we shall call 'Modern Childhood' (i.e. a way of seeing human biological immaturity that had been invented by philosophers and scientists since the European Enlightenment of the mid-eighteenth century) continue to shape institutional practices and realities for children. Indeed, policy initiatives such as Sure Start and Every Child Matters in the UK have reinforced them through their commitment to developmentalism through which the construction of modern human subjectivity is rationalised and understood.

NATURE/CULTURE: DEVELOPMENTALISM/SOCIAL CONSTRUCTIONISM

It would, however, be unfair to suggest that developmentalist theories found in Plowden (DES 1967)—and the contribution of Piaget in particular—were championed as conservative or as strangers to a desire for radical change (see Walkerdine 1984 for an account of how the work of the radical Piaget became inserted into the institutionalised orthodoxies of children's education and care). Plowden's (ibid.) interest in the mitigation of poverty through education and the promotion of a more meritocratic society facilitated by social mobility meant that the universalism found in the claims of developmental psychology and the experimentally underpinned genetic epistemology of Piaget were received favourably in a world that had recently endorsed the UN's human rights agenda. By establishing what appeared to be universal and natural laws governing human development, Piaget's work legitimised the desire to place 'the Child' at the heart of educational practice (Piaget 1926). Indeed, it demonstrated the folly in any attempt to work against what his predecessor Pestalozzi had confidently described as *'nature's march of developments'* (Kilpatrick 1951). Reference to nature lent both a scientific legitimacy to the claims of the progressives and the force accompanying a moral imperative to ensure that the needs it identified were met by schooling along with other agencies of welfare and care. True to the doctrines of Jean-Jacques Rousseau, adherence to the laws of nature seemed to offer confidence that the progressives' project to transform society through proper, rationally justified education was placed on a sound footing (Abegglen and Blundell in press).

Plowden (DES 1967) comes at a time of significant social change that is driven and accompanied by the decline of European imperialism, shifts in economic and cultural power and the Cold War as enveloping reality out of which new social movements, including demands for nuclear disarmament, civil rights, gay liberation, emerged along with the Women's Movement and second wave feminism. Accompanying these iconoclastic developments, there were small but significant groups advocating the principle that children and young people have a claim to particular rights and entitlements not captured by those institutionalised constructions of childhood in which they are subordinate to the imperatives of the adult world.

Influenced by feminism and post-colonial scholarship and armed with theorisation deriving from new movements in anthropology, sociology and social psychology, these advocates sought to re-imagine childhood and challenge the Platonic ideal type found in 'the Child' as an idealised type by establishing its provenance as an historical and cultural artefact (Prout and James 1997). Although, for developmentalists, 'the Child' rested on twin pillars of universality and naturalness, for these emerging critics its origins were to be found in European modernity and its construction of human nature based on the trope of the Western liberal subject. The new interest flourished in the USA and Scandinavia along with the UK, where this fledgling movement gained momentum with the publication by Richards and Light (1986) in which the case for understanding children's development in social terms was presented. This was followed by James and Prout's (1990) who comprised six propositions that have served as a credo around which much subsequent research and scholarship has cohered. It is hard to overstate the importance of their intervention because of its abiding influence across this emergent multidisciplinary field. Mayall sums up the position presented in the New Paradigm as arguing for:

> ... the importance of the child as social actor, for recognising and working with the social construction of childhood and for the central importance of ethnographic empirical research with children. (2012)

On these foundations, a broad multidisciplinary field opened out, supplementing core social sciences with human geography, histories of childhood, literature and cultural studies along with a pervasive critical interest in representation. At the heart of Prout and James' (1990) New Paradigm, as Mayall (2012) suggests, lay a commitment to social constructionism and the cultural relativism that accompanies it; here they make a distinction between biology and culture:

> [T]he immaturity of children is a biological fact of life but the ways in which this immaturity is understood and made meaningful is a fact of culture ... It is these 'facts of culture' which may vary and which can be said to make of childhood a social institution.

This is reiterated to social constructionism in the first clause of their six-point paradigm, thus:

> Childhood is understood as a social construction. As such it provides an interpretive frame for contextualizing the early years of human life. Childhood, as distinct from biological immaturity, is neither a natural nor universal feature of human groups but appears as a specific structural and cultural component of many societies. (Prout and James 1990, pp. 7, 8)

In these oft-quoted sentences, Prout and James (ibid.) challenged the naturalisation of childhood found in dominant developmental accounts and opened up spaces within which the diversity found in the lives of the biologically immature people identified as *children* could be explored. In this process they suggested that there are many ways to *do* childhood. This more relativist position was in step with what Kraftl (2016) identifies as a general 'turn' towards culture and *difference* by the social sciences during the 1980s. This was led by academic developments including the establishment of the celebrated Centre for Contemporary Cultural Studies at the University of Birmingham (see Batchelor et al. 2014 for an outline of the Centre's work).

This 'cultural turn' drew inspiration from earlier anthropological insights including those of Mead with adolescent girls in Samoa during the 1920s. The subsequent controversies surrounding this were in relation to her suggestion that Western norms were not universally encountered and that dominant theories of biological determinism might not be sufficient to account for the processes of human growth and becoming (see Mead 1928). As a current anthropologist working in this field, Montgomery offers more recent evidence than the 1920s for marked differences in children's care and upbringing (Montgomery 2013). She points to differing attitudes to early child rearing and attention from adults, to beatings and corporal punishment, to responsibility for the economic well-being of family and community, or to children's entitlement to challenge adults or express opinions. Moreover, the cultural turn revealed that these are far from confined to exotic or geographically distant societies; indeed, in diverse globalised societies 'difference' continually confronts and challenges us all (Montgomery 2013; and see Blundell 2014 for a discussion of disputes over children's responsibility for household chores). These developments were accompanied by the rise of feminist agendas whose emphasis on difference complemented and propelled the cultural turn and parted company with the sort of concern with equality through universality found in Plowden (DES 1967). These moves sought to demonstrate the links between culture, meaning and the material conditions found in everyday life—hence the commitment to ethnography found within Prout and James' (1990) New Paradigm.

Other work, following in the footsteps of Prout and James (ibid.) and inspired by post-colonial theory, has elaborated and explored this theme to identify the Eurocentric and class-bound origins of many of our ways of seeing children and young people. This is implied in assumptions about their lesser competence and location as dualistic 'other' to adults. De Boeck and Honwara (2005) express this in their exploration of children and young people's lives across sub-Saharan Africa:

> ...children and youth are often perceived through opposition to adulthood and as 'people in the process of becoming rather than being'. ... children and youth appear as pre-social and passive recipients of experience. They are portrayed as dependent, immature, and incapable of assuming responsibility, properly confined to the protection of home and school ... This concept developed amongst the middle class in Europe and North America and has been universalized in such a way that youngsters who do not follow this path are considered either to be at risk or to pose a risk to society. (De Boeck and Honwara 2005, p. 12)

Shallwani (2010) extrapolates De Boeck and Honwara's (2005) point to underline ways that 'the Child' of developmentalism is implicated in the deployment of social and political power by identifying the congruencies between human development *driven by children's biology* and political development *driven by economic doctrines*. Furthermore, that far from natural or universal, both are steeped in ideologies that support an assumed civilised superiority found in 'Whiteness':

> ... the notion of "development" as "progress" implies a linear and progressive path from "the primitive" to "the civilized" ... and is thus tied up with moral and cultural ideas of White civilized superiority ... Whether the discourse is about countries or humans, it is implied that there is one path to "development", and all entities can be ranked on this continuum (e.g. under-developed, developing, developed) ... Progress and improvement are thus conceived as the pathway from racialized and gendered Other—signified by "the under-developed/developing", "the primitive", "the child"— to the White man—signified by "the developed", "the civilized", and "the adult". (Shallwani 2010, p. 238)

It may appear that the development of a country's economy and its children share unfamiliar or unlikely commonalities, but this connection is reiterated by Aitken et al. (2007). This explores developmentalism as a culturally and politically bound ideology whose apparent rootedness in natural processes is deployed to support the reproduction of human capital on the one hand, and processes leading to the globalisation of the free market on the other. They see this as a pressing issue of concern, not least because whilst around nine tenths of the world's children live in majority-world societies (i.e. outside Europe, North America and the 'new Europes'), their education, welfare and care is increasingly calibrated and enframed by norms originating in the minority world. Furthermore, that these norms may neither be recognised by or welcomed in nor applicable to the societies in question. Kjørholt (2007) illustrates this point by reference to the experience of Mary in the Philippines, who is compelled to combine hard physical labour with schoolwork if she is to achieve her aspiration to gain qualifications and change her life. By contrast, Kjørholt (ibid.) points to a Scandinavian project entitled 'Try Yourself', designed to encourage initiative through simulated enterprise activities.

Although markedly different in their lived experiences, the presumption of children's institutional separation, diminished competence, and subordination to 'real-world' adult concerns found in Try Yourself, are certainly irrelevant to Mary's situation (and, arguably, do not serve the Scandinavian children's interests well either). On the one hand, UN (1989) initiatives inspired by Western values to limit or ban child labour might deny Mary a necessary, albeit hard-won, source of income without which her family cannot afford to educate her. On the other hand, the Scandinavian children are consigned to *playing* at life rather than living it as full social actors, with all the frustrations and discontent that can follow on from that.

A similar point contrasting ideal and actual childhoods experienced by children lies at the heart of a critique of Eurocentric conceptions of 'needs' and 'rights' presented by Stainton-Rogers (2009). She proposes that these resemble the taxonomies found in natural history designed to categorise and frame all living things under a single rationalising logic. For Stainton-Rogers (ibid.), these offer a normative checklist for a universally conceived 'good childhood' that may, on the one hand, serve as a challenge to abuse, indignity and exploitation. On the other hand, the risk in achieving this comes at the cost of rendering children as passive subjects of biologically determined drives that necessarily requires them to be subject to adult-world institutional oversight and imperatives rather than full social actors in their own right. Furthermore, the obverse to any *normative* listing is that this offers a checklist by which to identify those who are deemed *abnormal* or a cause for concern. This taxonomic approach to norms expressed as needs and rights is congruent with the observation made by Rose that modern childhood has become:

> ... the most intensively governed sector of personal existence. ... The modern child has become the focus of innumerable projects that purport to safeguard it from physical, sexual, or moral danger, to ensure its 'normal' development, to actively promote certain capacities of attributes such as intelligence, educability, and emotional stability. (Rose 1997, p. 124)

This state of almost total government and the passivity it expects may seem unexceptional and acceptably beyond debate for us, but it is historically (and still in many cases, culturally) peculiar.

Stainton-Rogers' (2009) critique of this taxonomic approach is mindful of the dominant position occupied by the United Nations Convention on the Rights of the Child (UNCRC) (1989) and its rootedness in the assumptions found in Modern Childhood. The Convention was first endorsed in 1989 and ratified almost immediately by Ghana and then by the UK in 1991. This document set out 54 articles addressing aspects of children's rights in line with the following four 'guiding principles': (1) a right to non-discrimination, either against a child *per se* or because of his or her parents' actions or beliefs; (2) concern for the best interests of the child must always the primary consideration; (3) the right to life, survival and development; and (4) the right to participation in expressing views on matters concerning them and in judicial and administrative proceedings. However, this is not to say that its expectations are universally accepted or welcomed—even in Ghana. In important field research Twum-Danso (2009) explored the responses of Ghanaians to some of the articles found in the UNCRC and their implications for children and their place in the life of their communities. Signally, she found little support for the idea that children had rights as an abstract or *a priori* principle independent of responsibilities (Twum-Danso 2009). Indeed, she reports frequent rejection by interview respondents of what they saw as the cultural and political premises of the UNCRC when they stated tellingly: '*we do not want Western children here in Ghana*'. Furthermore, the sort of children versus adults dualism that is frequently presumed to exist in Western contexts and shapes many aspects of institutional life and professional practice was not wholly endorsed through the comments children themselves made. In a reversal of this formula, some children championed the *right to be able to respect* elders and parents because of the way that this is embedded in a complex web of social obligations and expectations:

> ... because if you do not respect your mother she will take you out of school or kick you out of the house ... if you are on the streets and you are respectful you could get someone to send you to school or help you in some way ... if you are disrespectful and you need help, you won't get it ... (Twum-Danso 2009, pp. 426–429 and in Montgomery 2013)

This evidence suggests that a different set of values about children, adults and relations between them are at play in the communities researched by Twum-Danso (2009) and that these could even be said to be at odds with those of the UNCRC. This sense that these were an alien imposition led many countries in sub-Saharan Africa to frame a different document in the African Charter on Human and People's Rights (ACHPR) wherein children and young people's rights are conflated with those of more mature community member. The principles of '*duty, respect for one another and social solidarity*' expressed in the concept of *Ubuntu-Hunhu* are embedded (Chinouya and O'Keefe 2003).

As a cross-cultural example, the work of Twum-Danso (2009) appears to validate the social constructionist stance adopted by Prout and James in their New Paradigm and that is further underlined in their second proposition, namely that:

> Childhood is a variable of sociological analysis. It can never be entirely divorced from other variables such as class, gender, or ethnicity. Comparative and cross-cultural analysis reveals a variety of childhoods rather than a single and universal phenomenon. (Prout and James 1990, 1997, p. 8)

However, the extent to which the Paradigm itself is consistent in its intersectionality and follows through on the implications of cultural relativism is questionable because of the way in which it goes on to assert propositions that seem to deny the legitimacy of the views. This is expressed in the Ghanaian research by Twum-Danso (2009); for example, in propositions 3 and 4 (cited above) not only do the authors endorse the view that children's lives are worth studying in their own right *'independent of the perspectives and concerns of adults'*. Moreover, *'children must be seen as active in the construction and determination of their own social lives'*. Furthermore, the Paradigm endorsed ethnographic research methods as an approach to understanding children's lives in their own terms in proposition 5. Suddenly, their rootedness in Western individualised notions of rights and entitlements that seem to reinforce Eurocentric assumptions about what are and are not appropriate responses to biological immaturity shows through. It seems that despite an intellectual commitment to cultural relativism, the social constructionism on which it is founded is, itself, culturally located, so that the Paradigm appears to be no less bound within its own social realities and cultural value settings than the members of the Ghanaian communities interviewed by Twum-Danso (2009).

This suggests that the New Paradigm that has done so much to open up the study of childhood and challenge orthodoxies through its social constructionism could itself be seen as Eurocentric in its championing of particular ways of seeing childhood as the developmentalist narratives it sought to deconstruct and replace. Indeed, that despite indicting the Eurocentrism of conventional developmentalist accounts (because of their reliance of certain culturally laden ways of seeing nature and what is natural), the concept of culture is itself as freighted with Western values and discursively constructed meanings as is 'nature'. This complex entanglement between nature and culture is explored in relation to the New Paradigm by Alan Prout himself:

> By the last two decades of the twentieth century there was widespread agreement that childhood should be understood as a historical, social and cultural phenomenon. ... This tendency was strengthened by the linguistic turn in social theory and, associated with it, the emergence of social constructionism. The impact of these moves was felt in childhood studies through the new paradigm of childhood sociology. A central feature of this view was that, while the biological immaturity of children may be a fact, the real interest and future of childhood studies lies in the study of how cultures interpret such immaturity. ... rather than questioning the opposition between 'nature' and 'culture', the claim that childhood is a social construction reproduces it. It can be interpreted as a reverse discourse. (Prout 2005, p. 84)

It was clear that the attempt to turn away from the universal and naturalised rationalities found in Modern Childhood towards a more culturally referenced understanding of biological immaturity had not only made little impression on the developmentalist position but, as Prout (ibid.) suggests, it may actually have reinforced it. So that, whilst *necessary* to wider understanding, the failure of this discourse-based understanding of children and childhood to embrace brute material realities in a convincing fashion meant that it was not *sufficient* to achieve the radical ends the New Paradigm desired. To return to Mary in the Philippines, the identification of her circumstances as socially constructed may be illuminating, but it does little in itself to address the harsh realities of her day-to-day life (Kjørholt 2007).

DECOLONIAL CHILDHOODS: LOOKING BEYOND NATURE AND CULTURE

Prout's (2005) work was concerned to explore the future of childhood. For him, this certainly entailed exploration of the thorny issues surrounding the nature/culture dualism but could not be accomplished without consideration of technology and its transformational impacts on children's lives at every scale from local to global. These impacts included: the growing engagement with electronic devices and the virtual worlds they created; bio-medical technologies including prosthetic enhancements and 'designer' performance enhancing drugs; and the implications of gene technologies for pre-natal selection. For Prout (ibid.) these developments are fundamentally altering the terms within which modernity conceived and constructed both 'nature' (and what is natural) and 'culture' (and what is artefactual). Drawing on the work of Deleuze and Guattari (1988), Prout (ibid.) proposes an understanding of childhood as comprising hybrid *assemblages* of 'natural' and 'cultural' elements whose relations are mediated, facilitated and transformed by technology—whose lifespan can be short-lived or more enduring. The Australian geographer and early childhood practitioner Taylor (2013) sees in this a potential to end what she sees as the constant 'zig-zagging' between nature and culture, discussed above, and driven by the constructions of childhood we inherit from Enlightenment modernity. Motivated by a desire to de-naturalise childhood, but also mindful of the limitations of social constructionism and the difficulty its discursively constructed account for childhood has with materiality, Taylor (ibid.) draws on feminist, ecological, post-colonial and queer theories found in the work of Haraway (1991) to explore and interpret the lives of children in remote Aboriginal Australian communities. These have borne the brunt of Western racism and imperialism since the arrival of European settlers, including attempts to impose modern childhood norms for education and care. Haraway (ibid.) charts the lives of young people whose life-worlds, sustained over the course of millennia, have neither recognised nor needed the categories 'nature' or 'culture' and find in them complex networked configurations involving their embodiment and its relation not only to other family members in conventionally conceived networks of social actors but also to domestic pets and wild creatures. These are worlds of meaning that embrace and assemble complex networks of people, places and the environmental components found in them. Furthermore, this not only includes flora and fauna, but also invests in what may to Western eyes be deemed inert, lifeless materials, such as rocks, with vital significance (see Taylor 2013; Taylor and Pacini-Ketchabaw 2015).

This may strike us as strange; however, considering the veneration afforded the (apparently) inert material known as silicon in a modern world that prides itself on adherence to secular reason, or the conjunction of organic and inorganic elements in pharmaceuticals and cosmetics that contribute to our physical health, sense of well-being and identity, this begins to look less peculiar. Indeed, by examining life-worlds that seem 'marginal' in conventional Western terms, Taylor's (2013) work 'queers' the commonplace, re-rendering it as surprising and strange; indeed, by illuminating aspects of 'modern life' that we might otherwise overlook, it suggests that most people's lives have never been truly modern in its purest most rationalising sense. Furthermore, the realisation that many children inhabit globalised and transnational worlds where they transact plural identities and lives that bring the local and global into unanticipated encounters can radically challenge many of our received assumptions about what counts as a normal childhood.

Taylor and Pacini-Ketchabaw (2015) identify the Eurocentric and colonialist origins of many of the institutions and practices through which young children are educated and cared for in what they call 'Western settler colonial societies' and seek to unsettle their discursive assumptions, material forms and practices. These 'Colonial places and spaces' include Canadian forests, Australian bush lands, Aotearoa New Zealand and the Canadian Arctic where Inuit peoples live. In line with the arguments presented here, the authors write:

> … colonialist developmental theories (cultural, economic, technological) … posit Western scientific knowledge as bringing 'progress' to the world (Burman, 2008; Castañeda, 2002). Knowingly or not, early childhood education's stock-in-trade scientific theories about the 'natural' development of the assumed-to-be universal child are part of a much larger Western epistemological project to 'lead the world forward'. With this bigger picture in mind, our efforts to unsettle early childhood education begin with the understanding that the field of early childhood education is neither culturally nor politically innocent. (Taylor and Pacini-Ketchabaw 2015, pp. 1, 2)

In this, the authors lead us back to the beginning of this chapter and with it propose an agenda not simply for the advancement of inter-cultural dialogue and exchange, but also a basis on which those dialogues can be felt to be meaningful. To challenge assumptions about the naturalness and universality of Western constructions of childhood is to unsettle a central pillar of Western modernity and its rationalising dominance in debates about human nature and the reproduction of human capital, thereby establishing standpoints from which a diversity of interlocutors can exercise an entitlement to be heard. However, as the examples in this chapter imply, genuine multicultural dialogues will often be difficult and even troubling because culturally laden presumptions—including the iconoclastic convictions of the New Social Studies of Childhood itself—cannot place themselves beyond the reach of the debates and disputes those dialogues will generate. Challenging the Eurocentric provenance of Modern Childhood and exercising greater curiosity about children and the quality of their lives' seems a good place to open up dialogues that should concern us all (Hendrik 1997; Mayall 2007; Blundell 2016).

References

Abegglen, S., & Blundell, D. (in press). Childhood and education. In S. Isaacs (Ed.), *European social problems*. London: Routledge.

Aitken, S., Lund, R., & Kjørholt, A. T. (2007). Why children? Why now? *Children's Geographies, 5*(1–2), 3–14.

Batchelor, D., Connell, K., & Hilton, M. (2014). *50 years on: The centre for contemporary cultural studies*. Birmingham: Birmingham Mac.

Blundell, D. (2012). *Education and constructions of childhood*. London: Continuum.

Blundell, D. (2014). Childhood and education. In S. Isaacs (Ed.), *Social problems in the UK: An introduction* (pp. 117–139). London: Routledge.

Blundell, D. (2016). *Rethinking children's spaces and places*. London: Bloomsbury.

Board of Education, (BoE). (1931). *The Hadow report: The primary school*. London: HMSO.

Chinouya, M., & O'Keefe, E. (2003). Young African Londoners affected by HIV: Making sense of rights. Retrieved October 2, 2010, from http://www.lshtm.ac.uk/publications/list.php?inpress=1&grouping=recent&filter=staff_id&value=105339

Coard, B. (1971). *How the West Indian child is made educationally subnormal in the British School System: The scandal of the Black Child in Schools in Britain*. London: New Beacon Books.

Coard, B. (2005). Why I wrote the SEN book. *The Guardian*. Retrieved October 25, 2016, from https://www.theguardian.com/education/2005/feb/05/schools.uk

De Boeck, F., & Honwara, A. (2005). Introduction: Children and youth in Africa. In A. Honwara & F. De Boeck (Eds.), *Makers and breakers: Children and youth in post-colonial Africa* (p. 12). Oxford: James Currey.

Department of Education and Science (DES). (1967). *Children and their primary schools, (The Plowden Report)*. London: HMSO.

Deleuze, G., & Guattari, F. (1988). *A thousand plateaus: Capitalism and schizophrenia II*. London: Athlone.

Haraway, D. (1991). *Simians, Cyborgs and Women: The reinvention of nature*. New York: Routledge.

Hendrick, H. (1997). *Children, childhood and English Society, 1880–1990: New studies in economic and social history*. Cambridge: Cambridge University Press.

Kilpatrick, W. H. (1951). *The education of man—Aphorisms*. New York: Philosophical Library.

Kjørholt, A. T. (2007). Childhood as a symbolic space: Searching for authentic voices in the era of globalisation. *Children's Geographies, 5*, 1–2.

Kraftl, P. (2016). Editorial introduction: Revisiting Denis Cosgrove and Peter Jackson's 'new directions in cultural geography'. *Area, 48*(3), 365–366.

Mayall, B. (2007). Children's lives outside school and their educational impact, Research Survey 8/1. Retrieved April 18, 2016, from http://image.guardian.co.uk/sysfiles/Education/documents/2007/11/23/livesreport.pdf

Mayall, B. (2012). An afterword: Some reflections on a seminar series. *Children's Geographies, 10*(3), 347–355.

Mead, M. (1928). *Coming of age in Samoa: A psychological study of primitive youth for Western civilization*. New York: William Morrow and Company.

Ministry of Education. (1944). *The 1944 education (Butler) Act*. London: HMSO.

Montgomery, H. (2013). Childhood: An anthropological perspective. In M.-J. Kehily (Ed.), *Understanding childhood: A cross-disciplinary approach* (pp. 161–210). London: Policy Press.

Mullard, C. (1985). *Race, power and resistance*. London: Routledge.

Piaget, J. (1926). *The language and thought of the child*. London: Routledge and Kegan Paul.

Prout, A. (2005). *The future of childhood*. London: Routledge.

Prout, A., & James, A. (1990). A new paradigm for the sociology of childhood? Provenance, promise and problems. In A. James & A. Prout (Eds.), *Constructing and reconstructing childhood: Contemporary issues in the sociological study of childhood* (pp. 7–32). London: Routledge.

Prout, A., & James, A. (1997). A new paradigm for the sociology of childhood? Provenance, promise and problems. In A. James & A. Prout (Eds.), *Constructing and reconstructing childhood: Contemporary issues in the sociological study of childhood* (pp. 7–32). London: Routledge.

Race, R. (2015). *Multiculturalism and education* (2nd ed.). London: Bloomsbury.

Richards, M., & Light, P. (Eds.). (1986). *Children of social worlds: Development in a social context*. Cambridge: Harvard University Press.

Rose, N. (1997). *Governing the soul: The shaping of the private self*. London: Routledge.

Sarup, M. (1986). *The politics of multiracial education*. London: Routledge Kogan Paul.

Shallwani, S. (2010). Racism and imperialism in the child development discourse: Deconstructing 'Developmentally Appropriate Practice'. In G. S. Cannella & L. S. Soto (Eds.), *Childhoods: A handbook* (pp. 231–244). New York: Peter Lang.

Stainton Rogers, W. (2009). Promoting better childhoods: Constructions of child concern. In M. J. Kehily (Ed.), *An Introduction to childhood studies* (pp. 141–160). Maidenhead: Open University Press.

Stone, M. (1981). *The education of the Black child: The myth of multiracial education.* London: Fontana.

Taylor, A. (2013). *Reconfiguring the natures of childhood.* London: Routledge.

Taylor, A., & Pacini-Ketchabaw, V. (Eds.). (2015). *Unsettling the colonial places and spaces of early childhood education.* New York: Routledge.

Troyna, B., & Williams, J. (1986). *Racism, education and the state.* London: Croom Helm.

Twum-Danso, A. (2009). Reciprocity, respect and responsibility: The 3Rs underlying parent-child relationships in Ghana and the implications for children's rights. *International Journal of Children's Rights, 17*(3), 415–432.

United Nations (UN). (1989). United Nations convention on the rights of the child. Retrieved October 25, 2010, from http://www.unicef.org.uk/Documents/Publication-pdfs/UNCRC_PRESS200910web.pdf

Walkerdine, V. (1984). Developmental psychology and the child-centred pedagogy: The insertion of Piaget into early education. In J. Henriques, W. Hollway, C. Urwin, C. Venn, & K. Walerdine (Eds.), *Changing the subject: Psychology and social regulation.* London: London University Paperbacks.

David Blundell is an educationist and geographer leading the Education Subject Group at London Metropolitan University. He has taught in primary schools, further education and higher education. David has a particular interest in sociocultural, historical and spatial approaches to understanding constructions of childhood in educational settings and how they shape children's experience of schooling. His other interests include the meaning of the Anthropocene and the implications of climate change for education, curricula and understandings of childhood across a culturally diverse, globalising world. David writes and teaches on these themes and seeks to facilitate students' critical understanding as they embark on professional lives.

Using Diversity to Advance Multicultural Dialogues in Higher Education

Dorrie Chetty

INTRODUCTION: MULTICULTURALISM IN HIGHER EDUCATION AS A VEHICLE OF SOCIAL COHESION

Kymlicka argues: "Talk about the retreat from multiculturalism has obscured the fact that a form of multicultural integration remains a live option for Western democracies" (Kymlicka 2012: 01). This chapter makes a case for revitalising multiculturalism in higher education through learning and teaching, employing students' cultural capital as a resource. Drawing on a range of research, cultural and educational theories and my own teaching experience, I argue for a culturally sensitive pedagogy that values student experience as a learning resource and highlights the ways in which our experiences and histories are connected, thereby helping to develop a shared sense of belonging and promote cohesion. A major objective is to demonstrate the value of advancing multicultural dialogues to address issues of diversity and social cohesion in the light of twenty-first century migration flows. Cultural diversity in relation to social cohesion is discussed within a context of a rapidly changing social, cultural and political landscape. Referring to a Year 3 sociology module

D. Chetty (✉)
Westminster University, London, UK

© The Author(s) 2018
R. Race (ed.), *Advancing Multicultural Dialogues in Education*,
DOI 10.1007/978-3-319-60558-6_3

33

on border crossings and migration at a London university, and with the aid of an extended module evaluation which included student perceptions of multiculturalism, the chapter briefly traces the path taken by multiculturalism in the UK, counters the view that it is now a redundant concept, and proposes a more dynamic mode of multiculturalism which can be fostered in higher education in the UK. In principle, this approach could be extended to wider citizenship, for instance perhaps engendering a more culturally shared ethos in the Prevent (O'Toole, 2012). Adopting a fluid approach to the concept of culture, I argue here that the experience of diversity itself can become a basis of commonality and cohesion, as cultures are not hermetically sealed, but instead historically overlap and flow into each other.

The migration module is part of a wider sociology programme, designed with the aim of teaching various sociological perspectives of migration flows, within a historical and global context. More specifically, it aims at developing students' understanding of the different motivations behind migration; the impact the process has on migrants' lives; and on the communities of origin as well as the communities of their destination. Through the design of an assessed group assignment, students are required to research and present the impact of a migrant group of their choice upon the wider society in the UK, including the responses to migrant presence. The approach to learning on the module is designed to involve students in the construction of knowledge, through their own experiences and making connections with each other's various experiences, whilst grounding their arguments within relevant theories. The students' experiences are framed within a discussion of current academic literature on diversity in education (Doyle et al. 2010; Grever et al. 2008; Howard 2003; Killick 2012; McAllister and Irvine 2002; Moncrieffe 2014; Northedge 2003; Preece 2009; Swartz 2009; Tomalin 2007). Both the mid-semester and the final assignments within the module give the students an opportunity to examine how meaning is achieved through language and how 'common sense' perceptions of migrants and migration are shaped by dominant discourses and, crucially, how power relations operate in the construction of knowledge. Furthermore, the module is drawn upon here to highlight the significance of culturally responsive pedagogy in validating student experience.

The extended evaluation was designed as a questionnaire with ten semi-structured questions and plenty of space for participants to develop their responses (Newby 2014; Robson and McCartan 2016). Consent was sought from the students and they were under no obligation to complete the questionnaire, though it was distributed to everyone. The objectives were explained and the students were reassured that their responses would remain anonymous. Aware of potential power relations, and to minimise researcher bias effect on student responses, distribution of the evaluation questionnaire was left till the last session of the year. The students completed the questionnaire after we had met for the last time, as it was a final module in their final year. A couple of students from the group volunteered to collect all the forms, put them in an envelope and post it in the lecturer's pigeon hole. As all student assignments are electronically submitted, their handwritten responses to the questionnaire were unidentifiable. Had the evaluation been started earlier, there would have been time an opportunity to improve the response rate. Using a convenience sampling method, 40 questionnaires were distributed and 28 were returned completed (Cohen et al. 2011). Though the sample is too small to generalise from, the responses gave some valuable insight into the students' perceptions of multiculturalism.

Notwithstanding policies relating to radicalisation, it is arguable that a prime forum for fostering social cohesion and advancing multicultural dialogue is the higher education sector (Killick 2012; Swartz 2009). As most UK universities are increasingly emerging as spaces where diverse groups of students are thrown together, they offer a significant opportunity where connections can be made and assumptions challenged, thereby opening rather than constricting dialogue. Students' debates can continue and extend beyond the classroom—if students' experiences and history are validated through their academic work, they are more likely to take the debates into their respective diverse communities and further develop them there. In such an approach to learning and teaching, students are centred as normative, facilitating the development of reciprocal relationships built on self-knowledge, mutual trust and respect, thereby strengthening connections between teachers, students, families and each other (Swartz 2009). Multicultural dialogues can therefore be advanced from bottom up via student experience, rather than imposed with top down authority. This approach to teaching and learning not only challenges a mono-cultural Eurocentric approach to intellectual enquiry, but importantly offers possibilities for promoting social cohesion via debates that do not shy away from issues relating to possible tensions and conflicts arising from cultural differences (Banks et al. 2001; Ngo 2010).

MULTICULTURALISM AND CULTURAL DIVERSITY: DEFINITIONS AND CONTESTATIONS

An initial overview of multiculturalism in Britain makes clear that British culture is inherently diverse and Multiculturalism isn't dead, as some have argued, but rather is developing in a way that stresses the need for interaction (Taylor-Gooby and Waite 2014). There is a need to theorise multiculturalism in history, and multicultural citizenship should be viewed as changing and responsive (Werbiner 2005) applied to policy or as a theory for understanding difference, diversity and inequalities, multiculturalism is a highly relevant and necessary perspective for understanding issues relating to integration and cohesion (Modood 2013). It needs to be understood as a process which is always contextual, with the State taking major responsibility for the successful development of diversity (Nye 2007). Home Secretary Roy Jenkins (1967) described multiculturalism as "… equal opportunity, accompanied by cultural diversity, in an atmosphere of mutual tolerance" (Jenkins 1967). This view envisages integration to be a two-way process and promotes policies of equality. A genuinely interactive process, however, never truly materialised, and the widespread view expressed by a number of politicians and commentators is that multiculturalism has in contrast led to segregated communities. To Stuart Hall, multiculturalism in the UK was not established as the result of conscious policy but evolved incrementally and unplanned, with British society 'feeling' multicultural as the presence of ethnic minority communities became more visible and began shaping national life (Hall 2000).

Whilst Britain may have drifted into multiculturalism, to use Hall's term, the points at which multiculturalism came under fire are arguably more easily identifiable. It could be said in 1989 the 'Rushdie Affair' (Asad 1990) promoted the 'clash of cultures' debate in the UK. More recently a spate of 'riots' in Burnley, Oldham and Bradford in 2001, dubbed by the popular press as the 'Northern uprisings' led to a series of reports and policy recommendations relating to community cohesion (Cantle 2001). Since these disturbances in Northern England, the events of 9/11 in the USA and the 7/7 London bombings in the UK, there has been increasing concern that diversity erodes social cohesion and destroys relations of trust and mutual help in local communities (Collier 2013; Goodhart 2004; Putnam 2007). These authors' perspectives—that too much diversity hampers social cohesion and a sense of common solidarity—has become part of some people's 'common sense' thinking, and are frequently employed by those wishing to limit immigration to the UK, leading to a strong association of immigration with security risk, re-igniting discourses of fear of the 'Other' (Bigo 2002; Cheong et al. 2007; Ibrahim 2005). The migration module, referred to above, reviews and challenges these discourses.

Nevertheless, I would argue that Britain is generally viewed by the rest of the world as a multicultural society, with its multiculturalism visible in the celebration of 'idealised' cultural difference (Fortier 2005), as evidenced, for example, by the popularity of the yearly Notting Hill carnival, South Asian cuisine on most high streets and African or African-Caribbean music resounding at garden parties and summer festivals. In the bid for the London 2012 Olympic Games London was promoted as a multicultural city, arguably playing a significant role in winning the bid (Falcous and Silk 2010). Sadly, at the height of the celebrations of the bid's success, the following day after the successful bid, London was struck by a series of terror attacks by radical Islamists, highlighting a sharp contrast between a multiculturalism that appreciates and celebrates 'easy' cultural differences and the more challenging differences in cultural values amongst some sections of British society, such as 'honour killings' and religious doctrine (Eade et al. 2008) It has been argued that the politically correct ethos behind multiculturalism may inhibit open communication and debates relating to the more challenging cultural differences (O'Donnell 2007).

The initial responses in Britain to counter racism and prejudice in the early days of ethnic minorities settlement, have been criticised by some as inadequate and enabling the development of segregated lives. Referring to Troyna, Richard Race highlights the weaknesses of cultural tourism such as the '3 Ss Multiculturalism'—saris, samosas and steel bands—which leads to superficial changes, in contrast to anti-racist strategies that can counter racism (Race 2015: 29). Alleyne refers to the focus on easy cultural differences as 'fat-free multiculturalism', and he argues that celebrating difference as good in itself does not help to redress the inequalities which continue to structure the lives of ethnic communities (Alleyne 2002). For those who fear that diversity undermines national solidarity, multiculturalism is also a source of anxiety. The way issues of multiculturalism, Britishness and national identity are debated in public and education discourses inevitably influence how teachers approach it in the classroom (Keddie 2014: 540). What is evident from my own interaction with students in seminar debates and their assignments is that students are just as likely to identify with Britishness as they are with other identity markers such as religion, ethnicity, gender and social class. For some, the mutifaceted aspects of identities (Keddie 2014: 541) mean that cohesion cannot be exclusively or mainly understood through the lens of national identity. Certain authors advocate a more complex account of diversity in debates of integration and cohesion (Olssen 2004; McGhee 2005, 2006a, b; Parekh 2002; Vertovec 2007, Vertovec and Wessendorf 2010; Bloemraad and Wright 2014). Others argue on the evidence that a long-term goal of multiculturalism has always been about an embracing and inclusive form of integration and inclusive Britishness—rather than segregation (Alleyne 2002; Modood and Salt 2011; Uberoi and Modood 2013).

The historical overview makes it clear that while feeling part of British culture may be important for social cohesion, reductionist and racialised understandings of Britishness and their associated assumptions need to be problematized. The critique of multiculturalism increasingly takes place within a context of anxieties relating to acts of terrorism and a climate of fear of 'The Other' (Abbas 2008). These anxieties are then associated with the perception of ethnic minorities' unwillingness to integrate into mainstream British culture—which furthers the argument that multiculturalism has exacerbated divisions rather than encouraged integration (Uslaner 2011). However, such a rigid and static notion of British culture and Britishness is unhelpful, since there are no evident unifying features. An understanding of the relationship between integration policies and perceptions of threats can be more illuminating (Callens and Meuleman 2016). If British culture is difficult to define, multiculturalism is equally slippery and ambiguous, but the latter is nevertheless blamed for ethnic divisions and conflicts in British society. Kymlicka discusses the rise and fall of multiculturalism (Kymlicka 2010), whilst Bloemrad and Wright (2014) disentangle the multiplicity of meanings of multiculturalism and outline them as follows: demographic diversity; political philosophy of equality or justice; a set of policies to recognise and accommodate ethno-racial and religious diversity or public discourse recognising and valorising pluralism. Given these complexities, I argue that an approach to multiculturalism that recognises multiple levels at which identities operate enables us to identify where there is potential for connecting and sharing. Moreover, it is equally important to understand how the meaning an dapplication of multiculturalism in education has been affected by a global neoliberal economy (Mitchell 2003: 391–393).

What is often neglected is the opportunity to value cultural diversity as an important resource in learning. Cultural diversity enriches the learning process by providing the opportunity for students and teachers to learn about one another, and it can also be usefully applied in an advantageous way to consolidate understanding of abstract concepts and theories. Moreover, when 'difference as deficit' is challenged, cultural diversity produces "...an emancipatory model of education that offers teachers an opportunity to engage with a broad body of knowledge that can be used to strengthen their connections with students, families and each other" (Swartz 2009: 1067).

The cultural diversity of the students on the migration module enabled students to learn about migrant communities via group work. Students taking the module understood the different perspectives on migration flows through making connections with their own and each other's histories. This approach to learning challenges power dynamics, as teachers and students develop "... reciprocal relationships built on self-knowledge, mutual trust, and respect, which they experience in the context of curriculum and instruction that are inclusive, representational, and indigenously voiced" (Swartz 2009: 1067). Although Swartz's research refers to the USA, her model of education operates within the spirit of a connective multiculturalism—giving students a sense of affirmation to their diverse identities and valuing their shared experiences as cultural capital. This chapter illustrates how diversity can be employed in the learning process, rather than seeing difference as problematic.

DIVERSITY: UNLOCKING STUDENT CULTURAL CAPITAL

For the first assessed assignment of the migration module, students are required to search material from their own and each other's communities and present contributions made by migrants. They are expected to work on the assignment together in small groups throughout the process and keep a portfolio of every group member's contribution. Some students resist this group exercise as they are accustomed to essay questions and prefer as a rule to work individually on assignments. From my close observation of students and from student evaluations, I noted that once underway, there was a positive buzz of excitement about working in groups. Bar minor disagreements amongst group members, students seem to value the opportunity of researching migrant contributions—based on their own and each other's experiences—and they are pleasantly surprised at how significant these can be. During the process of research, the students learn about each other's cultures and discuss the parallels and differences between different communities. Importantly, they are encouraged to make historical connections and understand the sociocultural, political and economic relations involved in migration flows in and out of the UK. Students' appreciation and the benefits of understanding the relationship between multiculturalism and national identity through their group assignment were apparent both through the quality of their presentation, their final individual written assignment as well as the student module evaluation forms.

When students' diverse cultures and histories are recognised and valorised in academic study, they feel integrated into a wider learning community and this sense of belonging has positive implications for cohesion. Educational researchers see learning "…as acquiring the capacity to participate in the discourses of an unfamiliar knowledge community, and teaching as supporting that participation" (Northedge 2003: 17). Perceived as an asset by educationalists, and employed to highlight and strengthen connections, cultural diversity can be capitalised upon for learning purposes, and in the process promote cohesion. Migration flows, widening participating policies and the internationalisation of degree programmes bring an increasing number of diverse students to higher education. The diversity of their different domestic and cultural backgrounds is a rich learning resource. However, a post-Brexit UK from 2016 may see a reduction in student numbers from abroad, which would impact negatively on student cultural diversity.

An element of diversity which is usefully employed on the migration module is the presence of students from overseas through study abroad programmes or student exchanges. The diverse cultural capital they bring with them is employed to gain comparative perspectives, thereby enriching seminar discussions on many levels. Thus, the students compare the different ways in which cultural diversity is dealt with in their respective countries and the impact of migration flows in their home country of study. For example, through interaction with African-American students, home students, whether from majority or minority backgrounds learn about the complexities of 'whiteness', 'gender' and 'race'. They discuss the similarities and differences of their lived experiences to understand the significance of Otherness through "intersubjective encounters [that] enables moves to identify Self with others and personalize hitherto distant places and practices" (Killick 2012: 372). As the author indicates, international mobility presents "… opportunities for multicultural/international campuses to develop spaces for similarly rich learning for the non-mobile majority" (Killick 2012: 372).

Despite initial reluctance, students on the migration module clearly enjoy interacting with the overseas students, whether or not they themselves have mobility opportunities. The benefits of cross-cultural exchanges on the migration module become evident in the cultural richness of seminar debates. Research indicates that student mobility brings with it benefits on various levels, including essential assets required for working in a global world (Resnik 2009; Doyle et al. 2010; Brux and Fry 2010; Killick 2012). However, these authors also point to potential marginalisation of those who cannot take part in exchange programmes whilst others discuss international mobility within a neoliberal global context, where increasingly host countries see international students as revenue generators. The latter highlight inequalities by pointing out that only a minority of students can take advantage of mobility opportunities to improve their skills and widen their scope for employment (Findlay et al. 2012; Altbach and Engberg 2014). Nevertheless, from my experience of the migration module, the presence of students from abroad enrich the learning experience of the whole class, especially in understanding the impact of multiculturalism on their shared daily lives.

The extended student evaluation questionnaire sought to gain the views of students on multiculturalism. For the question "Is multiculturalism important to you personally? Explain why" on the student evaluation form, every student answered positively yes, and felt that the concept enabled them to learn about cultures other than their own. Interestingly, one student showed their understanding of the complexities by qualifying their positive response: "Yes, it shows acceptance of one's culture..." and explained that it enabled them to learn about "one another's background", but this student also added to their explanation: "No, regarding emphasizing people as different. Multiculturalism is a positive concept, as long as we look at each other as equal." This particular student clearly takes into consideration that emphasizing 'difference' could be problematic. However, the majority of questionnaire responses indicate that the students value multiculturalism, viewing it as facilitating intercultural exchange.

Whether on the migration module or via the extended student evaluation, the students expressed the benefits of learning about migration through their own diverse experiences. Applied in this way, students' cultural capital facilitates cohesion and promotes a sense of belonging to a wider community. Seminar discussions and their assignments also gave the students an opportunity to understand the power relations involved in language and the construction of knowledge. For example, students analysed how language and images used in the mass media to portray migrants combine powerfully with political discourses of migration, thereby playing on the fear of the 'Other'—with the potential consequence of fuelling racism.

CULTURAL AND LANGUAGE DIVERSITY IN EDUCATION: CRITICAL REFLECTIONS

The migration module illustrates the significance of language as a major force in the construction of human subjectivities, an aspect often neglected in multicultural policies. Preece's work on linguistic diversity highlights the ways in which it is often framed as problematic, even in the design of multicultural programmes. Although her work is based on secondary education, similar analysis can be tentatively extended to higher education. She discusses a writing programme which was targeted primarily at students "…categorised as working class, from ethnic minorities, particularly British of South Asian descent, who were young, from non-selective schools in London and with non-traditional qualifications or traditional qualifications with low grades…" (Preece 2009: 22). The policy seems to be well intentioned, but as the programme assumed the linguistic diversity of the student population to be problematic it became associated with 'remedial' English and students in need of English language remediation. It isn't surprising therefore that students singled out as in need resisted being part of the programme, preferring instead to adopt slang to avoid being viewed as 'remedial'. The students' reaction hearteningly shows creative resistance on their part in response to the policy makers' lack of cultural sensitivity. Preece (2009) demonstrates a missed opportunity in recognizing the multilingual capital that the students bring with them. Linguistic diversity is viewed as an obstacle to learning rather than a resource. There appears to be a contradiction between programmes purporting to be multicultural and a higher education system that appears blind to cultural capital, including language, brought about by diverse students, hence missing the opportunity of validating their diverse identities. In higher education, Preece (ibid.) notes the failure is more a neglect of rich and diverse cultural resources rather than negative labelling which takes place.

A pedagogic framework of the kind adopted in the migration module involves critical cultural reflection by both students and teachers. This is beneficial to both groups, as it attempts to achieve equity and social justice. Tyrone Howard argues that "… the development of culturally relevant teaching strategies is contingent upon critical reflection about race and culture of teachers and students" (Howard 2003: 195). He believes that the shift in ethnic demography has important implications for students and teachers. Unfortunately, such research seems to be taking place predominantly in North America. Referring to the USA, Howard (ibid) argues that the nation needs to make the necessary adjustments "to face the changing ethnic texture of its citizens". Several researchers in the field argue that culturally relevant pedagogy needs to assert the cultural knowledge, prior experiences, frames of reference, as well as performance styles of ethnically diverse students, if they are to make learning more relevant and effective for students (Banks et al. 2001; Howard 2003; Villegas and Lucas 2002). Villegas and Lucas (2002: 30) recommend that teacher trainers use a vision of teaching and learning in a diverse society that guides teaching towards a multicultural curriculum. They argue that culturally responsive 'classroom managers' should strive to become knowledgeable about the cultures and communities in which their students live. As discussed above, there is a need to recognise students' cultural capital as an asset and be mindful of traditional teaching practices that reflect middle class Eurocentric values (Howard 2003). Furthermore, as national identity and a sense of belonging have been identified as important factors to students, I argue here for the importance of recognizing connected histories as well as differences. A dominant one-dimensional representation of ethnic communities as 'Other' and homogenous bounded groups with fixed cultural, religious, social and economic divisions obscures the multiple levels of shared common experience and connections that can promote a sense of belonging and cohesion.

DIVERSITY AND NATION: IDENTITIES IN A CHANGING LANDSCAPE

This section argues that shared diversity, far from being divisive, can bridge difference to the benefit of social cohesion. In the extended student evaluation one of the questions was: "What and how did you learn about multiculturalism on the Migration Module?", and the majority answers were along the lines of the following response: "In particular, different ways of looking at national identity, specifically problems in defining it and looking past threats of losing it and embracing a more hybrid identity, inclusive of all members." Clearly responses from this small sample must be interpreted with care, but nevertheless it is clear from the answers that an interactive multiculturalism, as experienced and understood on the module, facilitates intercultural dialogue. Crucially, students found learning about a complex but inclusive national history promoted their sense of belonging. This contrasts with history which is predominantly taught from a "master narrative that is exclusive in its presentation of a dominant Anglo-centric and nationalistic version of the past" (Moncrieffe 2014: 191).

Advocating a similar approach to the one taken on the migration module, Moncrieffe argues for developing historical inquiry from the students' and teachers' experiences. He believes that students can foster a sense of connection and belonging to each other through tracing mass migration to England. To him this approach provides "... the potential to redefine and contribute to an enriched English 'master narrative' for the twenty-first century..." (Moncrieffe 2014: 202). This connective and inclusive way of understanding history is noticeable on the migration module, and crucially is a productive way of developing a sense of belonging to the UK. Moreover, this approach highlights the myth of a unified British national identity. "First, Britain is not and never has been the unified, conflict-free land of popular imagination. There is no single white majority. Second, the 'minority' communities do not live in separate, self-sufficient enclaves, and they do display substantial difference. They too must be reimagined" (Parekh 2000: 26). That said, the Brexit campaign and voting results of 2016 have revealed the strength of nostalgic feelings, of a British nation untainted by migrant presence, amongst some sections of the British population. The political discourses and media discourses of the campaign appear to have given a licence to some people to express prejudice against the 'Other'. Given reports of a hike in hate crimes, it would be a serious mistake to disregard these as a temporary or unimportant (Travis: 2016: 1–2). Any advancement of multicultural dialogue needs to address those groups of people too and their perceptions of a more glorious and 'better' Britain prior to post-war migration. Nevertheless, I'm arguing for a move away from debating migration and social cohesion through the lens of a fixed 'imperial' national identity which sees difference as a deficit and focusing instead on the multiple levels at which communities intersect and share common ground with education being only one of them.

It is important to note that the landscape and context within which migration takes place is constantly changing. It could be argued that trans-national identities have taken over the significance of identities bound by a single national identity, if indeed this ever existed. Social relations in multiple national and wider cultural contexts have been facilitated by the continued improvement in globalised networks of communication, for example, email, Skype, mobile and various phone applications. Social cohesion needs therefore to be understood within the increasing capacity of migrants to maintain social ties with their country of origin. As transnational connections have improved and are relatively cheaper, migrants travel regularly to and from their country of origin, and in some cases send remittances to family and friends. Furthermore, cheaper and ease of travel, albeit for a minority middle to upper class group, has also facilitated connections with various parts of the world, particularly amongst young people. Migration flows may change in direction and numbers depending on national immigration policies and global geopolitics, but current trends appear likely to continue in the foreseeable future. Moreover, it is likely that patterns of transnationalism also change. There is more than one form of migrant transnationalism and there is therefore a need for continued research in this area (Vertovec 2009). In the meantime, based on my continuing interactions with students, I would argue that transnational identities do not prevent a sense of belonging to a national collective and higher education can act as an important vehicle for advancing multicultural dialogues and improving cohesion.

Conclusions: Building Bridges at Universities

The argument of this chapter based on the experience of teaching the migration module and the consequent student evaluations is that drawing on students' diverse experiences including their transnational backgrounds has the potential to revitalise the teaching of multiculturalism and even the framing of the concept itself. This approach to multiculturalism can develop and enhance social cohesion rather than diminish and threaten it. Those who blame multiculturalism for a lack of social cohesion argue that increasing ethnic diversity in a community erodes social capital. Social capital is understood in Putnam's terms, referring to "social life networks, norms, and trust that enable participants to act together more effectively to pursue shared objectives" (Putnam 1995: 2). Based on Putnam's model of social capital as a collective good, it is then assumed that increased diversity undermines the potential of integration and cohesion as differences are perceived to inhibit networking, and prevent help and trust in a community. However, some authors argue that research in this area is limited as a positive link between cultural difference and lack of integration cannot be established (Bloemraad and Wright 2014; Heath and Demereva 2014). Interestingly, even where research confirms this view, it also indicates that "...while an individual living in a diverse environment may report lower levels of social capital 'the same individual' is also likely to have more positive interethnic relations" (Laurence 2009). The implication here is that despite perceived lower levels of networking, exposure to diversity may in effect improve the potential of social cohesion.

Furthermore, I argue that a focus on linking cultural diversity with a lack of integration neglects very important issues of societal disadvantage and inequalities in society (Hooghe 2007; Gesthuizen et al. 2009; Laurence 2009; Portes and Vickstrom 2011; Uslaner 2011). Some authors consider disadvantage—with its association of intolerance—to have a stronger negative impact upon trust, social cohesion and integration than diversity (Kesler and Bloemraad 2010; Laurence 2009; Callens and Meuleman 2016; Hooghe 2007). Moreover, the findings in Laurence's study provide evidence that "...rising diversity increases tolerance by leading to more exposure to other ethnic groups, and an increasing likelihood of forming 'bridging' ties" (Laurence 2009: 16). In a global world where people are crisscrossing the globe, ties that function as bridges between communities may be more important than ties that bind people based on homogeneity. Bridging ties cut across groups and are considered essential for social cohesion and for poverty reduction in the developing world (Narayan 1999). Though the socio-political and economic context of Britain differs from that of the developing world which Narayan discusses, it is important to understand that social cohesion is multidimensional in nature and can occur at various levels of interaction. I have demonstrated above how higher education can foster bridging ties in the process of learning. As Green et al. argue, "...when it comes to promoting social cohesion, there is clearly a case for prioritising the reduction of inequalities rather than just raising average levels" (Green et al. 2003: 468).

Overall, this chapter argues that higher education is almost the ideal forum for bridging ties between diverse groups, promoting solidarity through culturally sensitive pedagogy. When considering issues of rights and equity, cultural sensitivity is essential (Parekh 2002). A more global world theoretically demands improvement in intercultural skills and has led to an increase in internationalisation of education and international student mobility. To Altbach and Teichley (2001), the international role of academic institutions offers a further layer of diversity at universities. A UNESCO report indicates, "...the number of globally mobile students increased to 3.4 million students in 2009, up from 2.1 million students in 2002" (Choudaha and Chang 2012: 7). The potential fallout of the post 2016 Brexit results, which reflected strong resistance to immigration, is not yet clear. What is evident, however, is that emotional, cognitive and socio-communicative multiculturalism are increasing realities, not least in the functioning of government and transnational corporations.

This chapter argues for an opening out of multiculturalism debates, giving a voice to both connections and singularities via culturally responsive pedagogy which promotes a sense of belonging. I do not wish to imply that universities can solve the problems of social cohesion, nor indeed that the migration module discussed above is exemplary. However, I dispute the representation of ethnic communities as hermetically sealed homogenous bounded groups and argue that social disadvantage and inequalities also need to be taken into consideration in debates of social cohesion. Nougayrede (2016: 38) quotes historian Judt who wrote "...in an age of demographic transition and resettlement, today's Europeans are more heterogeneous than ever before". She goes on to conclude that "How European societies embrace growing diversity will in many ways determine the fate of our democracies." We need to map the frontiers of the post-colonial with historical imagination and an embracing of diverse identities. A twenty-first century multiculturalism needs to take account of neoliberal globalisation and shifting diasporic and transnational flows.

REFERENCES

Abbas, T. (2008). Muslim Minorities in Britain: Integration, Multiculturalism and Radicalism in the Post-7/7. *Period Journal of Intercultural Studies, 28*(3), 287–300.

Altbach, P. G., & Teichley, U. (2001). Internationalization and exchanges in a globalized University. *Journal of Studies in International Education, 5*(1), 5–25.

Altbach, P. G., & Engberg, D. (2014). Global student mobility: The changing landscape. *International Higher Education, 77*, 11–14.

Alleyne, B. (2002). An idea of community and its discontents: Towards a more reflexive sense of belonging in multicultural Britain. *Ethnic and Racial Studies, 25*(4), 607–627.

Asad, T. (1990). Multiculturalism and British identity in the wake of the Rushdie Affair. *Politics & Society, 18*(4), 455–480.

Banks, J. A., Cookson, P., Gay, G., Hawley, W. D., Irvine, J. J., Nieto, S., et al. (2001). Diversity within unity: Essential principles for teaching and learning in a multicultural society. *The Phi Delta Kappan, 83*(3), 196–203.

Bigo, D. (2002). Security and immigration: Toward a critique of the governmentality of unease. *Alternatives, 27*(1), 63–92.

Bloemraad, I., & Wright, M. (2014). "Utter failure" or unity out of diversity? Debating and evaluating policies of multiculturalism. *International Migration Review, 48*(S1), S292–S334.

Brux, J. M., & Fry, B. (2010). 'Multicultural students in study abroad: Their interests, their issues, and their constraints. *Journal of Studies in International Education, 14*(5), 508–527.

Callens, M. S., & Meuleman, B. (2016). Do integration policies relate to economic and cultural threat perceptions. A comparative study in Europe. *International Journal of Comparative Sociology*, 1–25.

Cantle, T. (2001). *Community Cohesion*. London: Home Office.

Cheong, P. H., Edwards, R., & Solomos, J. (2007). Immigration, social cohesion and social capital: A critical review. *Critical Social Policy, 27*(1), 24–29.

Choudaha, R., & Chang, L. (2012). *Trends in International Student Mobility, Research Report 01*. New York: World Education Services. Retrieved March 15, 2016, from www.wes.org/RAS.

Cohen, L., Manion, L., & Morrison, K. (2011). *Research Methods in Education* (7th ed.). London: Routledge.

Collier, P. (2013). *Exodus: Immigration and multiculturalism in the 21st century*. London: Penguin.

Doyle, S., Gendall, P., Meyer, L. H., Hoek, J., Tait, C., McKenzie, L., et al. (2010). An investigation of factors associated with student participation in study abroad. *Journal of Studies in International Education, 14*(5), 475–490.

Eade, J., Barrett, M., Flood, C., & Race, R. (Eds.). (2008). *Advancing multiculturalism, post 7/7*. Newcastle-Upon-Tyne: Cambridge Scholars Publishing.

Falcous, M., & Silk, M. L. (2010). Olympic bidding, multicultural nationalism, terror, and the epistemological violence of 'making Britain Proud. *Studies in Ethnicity and Nationalism, 10*(2), 167–186.

Findlay, A. M., King, R., Smith, F. M., Geddes, A., & Skeldon, R. (2012). World Class? An investigation of globalisation, difference and international student mobility. *Transactions of the Institute of British Geographers, 37*(1), 118–131.

Fortier, A. M. (2005). Pride politics and multiculturalist citizenship. *Ethnic and Racial Studies, 28*(3), 559–578.

Gesthuizen, M., Van der Meer, Y., & Scheepers, P. (2009). Ethnic diversity and social capital in Europe: Tests of Putnam's thesis in European Countries. *Scandinavian Political Studies, 32*(2), 121–142. Retrieved July 18, 2016, from http://dx.doi.org/10.111/j.1467-9477.2008.00217x.

Goodhart, D. (2004). Too diverse? *Prospect, 95*(30), 7.

Green, A., Preston, J., & Sabates, R. (2003). Education, equality and social cohesion: A distributional approach. *Compare: A Journal of Comparative and International Education, 33*(4), 454–470. Retrieved July 15, 2016, from http//dx.doi.org/10.1080030579203200012757.

Grever, M., Haydn, T., & Ribbens, K. (2008). Identity and school history: The perspective of young people from the Netherlands and England. *British Journal of Educational Studies, 56*(1), 76–94.

Hall, S. (2000). Multicultural citizens, monocultural citizenship. In N. Pearce & J. Hallgartan (Eds.), *Tomorrow's citizens: Critical debates in citizenship and education* (pp. 43–51). London: Institute for Public Policy Research.

Heath, A., & Demereva, N. (2014). Has multiculturalism failed in Britain? *Ethnic and Racial Studies, 37*(1), 161–180.

Hooghe, M. (2007). Social capital and diversity generalized trust, social cohesion and regimes of diversity. *Canadian Journal of Political Science, 40*(3), 709–732.

Howard, T. C. (2003). Culturally relevant pedagogy: Ingredients for critical reflection. *Theory Into Practice, 42*(3), 195–202.

Ibrahim, M. (2005). The securitization of migration: A racial discourse. *International Migration, 43*(5), 163–187.

Jenkins, R. (1967). Address by the home secretary to the institute. *Race & Class, 8*(3), 215–221.

Keddie, A. (2014). The politics of Britishness: Multiculturalism, schooling and social cohesion. *British Educational Research Journal, 40*(3), 539–554.

Kesler, C., & Bloemraad, I. (2010). Does immigration erode social capital? The conditional effects of immigration-generated diversity on trust, membership, and participation across 19 countries, 1981–2000. *Canadian Journal of Political Science, 43*(2), 319–347.

Killick, D. (2012). Seeing-Ourselves-in-the-World: Developing global citizenship through international mobility and campus community. *Journal of Studies in International Education, 16*(4), 372–389.

Kymlicka, W. (2010). The rise and fall of multiculturalism? New debates on inclusion and accommodation in diverse societies. *International Social Science Journal, 61*(1), 97–112.

Kymlicka, W. (2012). *Multiculturalism, success, failure and the future.* Migration Policy Institute, Transatlantic Council on Migration. Last Accessed 18 July 2016.

Laurence, J. (2009). The effect of ethnic diversity and community disadvantage on social cohesion: A multi-level analysis of social capital and interethnic relations in UK communities. *European Sociological Review.* Retrieved July 16, 2016, from www.esr.oxfordjournals.org.

McAllister, G., & Irvine, J. J. (2000). Cross cultural competency and multicultural teacher education. *Review of Educational Research, 70*(1), 3–24.

McGhee, D. (2005). Patriots of the future? A critical examination of community cohesion strategies in contemporary Britain. *Sociological Research Online, 10*(3), 1–20. Retrieved July 17, 2016, from http://www.socresonline.org.uk/10/3/mcghee.html.

McGhee, D. (2006a). Getting 'host' communities on board: Finding the balance between 'managed migration' and 'managed settlement' in community cohesion strategies. *Journal of Ethnic and Migration Studies, 32*(1), 111–127.

McGhee, D. (2006b). The New Commission for equality and human rights: Building community cohesion and revitalizing citizenship in contemporary Britain. *Ethnopolitics, 5*(2), 145–166.

Mitchell, K. (2003). Educating the National citizen in neoliberal times: From the multicultural self to the strategic cosmopolitan. *Transactions of the Institute of British Geographers, 28*(4), 387–403.

Modood, T. (2013). *Multiculturalism: A civic idea* (2nd ed.). Cambridge: Polity Press.

Modood, T., & Salt, J. (2011). *Global migration, ethnicity and Britishness.* Houndsmills: Palgrave Macmillan.

Moncrieffe, M. (2014). Reconceptualising mass migration within the primary school history curriculum master narrative for a broader sense of connection and belonging to England and English History. In E. Halpin, A. Hunter, K. Murji, A. Ozwerdem, R. Race, S. Robinson, M. Demir (Eds.), *Academic workshop proceedings: Sense of belonging in a diverse Britain* (pp. 191–206). Retrieved March 15, 2016, from www.DialogueSociety.org.

Narayan, D. (1999). Bonds and bridges: Social capital and poverty. *Policy Research Working Paper 2167*, The World Bank Poverty Reduction and Economic Management Network Poverty Division.

Ngo, B. (2010). Doing "diversity" at dynamic high: Problems and possibilities of multicultural education in practice. *Education and Urban Society, 42*(4), 473–495.

Northedge, A. (2003). Rethinking teaching in the context of diversity. *Teaching in Higher Education, 8*(1), 17–32.

Newby, P. (2014). *Research methods for education* (2nd ed.). Abingdon: Routledge.

Nougayrede, N. (2016). European Muslims are not new. Nor are they all the same. *The Guardian*, Saturday 10 September 2016, p. 38.

Nye, M. (2007). The challenges of multiculturalism. *Culture and Religion, 8*(2), 109–123.

O'Donnell, M. (2007). Review debate: We need human rights not nationalism lite. Globalization and British solidarity. *Ethnicities, 7*(2), 248–259.

Olssen, M. (2004). From the Crick report to the Parekh report: Multiculturalism, cultural difference and democracy. The revising of citizenship education. *British Journal of Sociology of Education, 25*(2), 179–192.

Parekh, B. C. (2000). *The future of multi-ethnic Britain: Report of the commission on the future of multi-ethnic Britain.* London: Profile Books.

Parekh, B. C. (2002). *Rethinking multiculturalism: Cultural diversity and political theory.* Cambridge, MA: Harvard University Press.

Portes, A., & Vickstrom, E. (2011). Diversity, social capital, and social cohesion. *Annual Review of Sociology, 37,* 461–479. doi:10.1146/annurev-soc-081309-150022.

Preece, S. (2009). Multilingual identities in higher education: Negotiating the 'mother tongue', 'posh' and 'slang'. *Language and Education, 24*(1), 21–39.

Putnam, R. D. (1995). Tuning in, tuning out: The strange disappearance of social capital in America. *Political Science & Politics, 28*(04), 664–683.

Putnam, R. D. (2007). *E pluribus unum.* Diversity and community in the twenty-first century. The 2006 Johan Skytte Prize Lecture. *Scandinavian Political Studies, 30,* 137–174.

Race, R. (2015). *Multiculturalism and education* (2nd ed.). London: Bloomsbury.

Resnik, J. (2009). Multicultural education—Good for business but not for the state? The IB curriculum and global capitalism. *British Journal of Educational Studies, 57*(3), 217–244.

Robson, C., & McCartan, K. (2016). *Real world research* (4th ed.). Oxford: Wiley.

Swartz, E. (2009). Diversity: Gatekeeping knowledge and maintaining inequalities. *Review of Educational Research, 79*(2), 1044–1083.

Taylor-Gooby, P., & Waite, E. (2014). Toward a more pragmatic multiculturalism? How the UK policy community sees the future of ethnic diversity policies. *Governance, 27*(2), 267–289.

Tomalin, E. (2007). Supporting cultural and religious diversity. *Teaching in Higher Education, 12*(5–6), 621–634. Retrieved March 26, 2016, from http://dx.doi.org/10.1080/13562510701595283.

Travis, A. (2016). Lasting rise in hate crime after EU vote, figures show. *The Guardian,* Thursday 8 September 2016, p. 1–2.

Uberoi, V., & Modood, T. (2013). Inclusive Britishness: A multiculturalist advance. *Political Studies, 61,* 23–41. doi:10.1111/j.1467-9248.2012.00979.x.

Uslaner, E. M. (2011). Trust, diversity and segregation in the United Kingdom. *Comparative Sociology, 10*(2), 221–247.

Vertovec, S. (2007). Super-diversity and its implications. *Ethnic and Racial Studies, 30*(6), 1024–1054.

Vertovec, S. (2009). *Transnationalism.* New York: Routledge.

Vertovec, S., & Wessendorf, S. (2010). *The multiculturalism backlash*. New York: Routledge.

Villegas, A. M., & Lucas, T. (2002). Preparing culturally responsive teachers, rethinking the curriculum. *Journal of Teacher Education, 53*(1), 20–32.

Werbner, P. (2005). The translocation of culture: 'community cohesion' and the force of multiculturalism in History 1. *The Sociological Review, 53*(4), 745–768.

Dorrie Chetty is a senior lecturer in Sociology and Course Leader for the BA Combined (Honours) Sociology and Criminology programme at the University of Westminster. Her research, writing and teaching relate to issues of migration, gender, race and social inclusion. Dorrie is developing a Westminster Migration Network group for peer review work on migrants, integration and social cohesion, and to build a network between academics, non-governmental organisations, government agencies, journalists and migrants.

Misrepresentation: A Qualitative Study on Discourses on Islam, British Values and Identity Affecting British Muslim Pupils in Bradford and East London

Tait Coles and Nasima Hassan

This chapter explores the narratives of British Muslim pupils in Bradford and East London in order to capture how media reporting of Islam affects their self-identity and their conceptualisation of what it means to be British and their understanding of British values. Global mainstream media and social media have roused the 'them' and 'us' rhetoric, seeing Islam and its adherents as separate, foreign, homogenous, static, uncivilised and—crucially—to be feared. This chapter is based on the understanding that the participant is the sole authority of their own experience (hooks 1994), which defends the position that participants are the owners of their stories and the researcher plays a role in the transmission and interpretation of that story. The notion of ownership of knowledge (Stanley and Wise 1983) is therefore based on a shared premise of equality and mutual respect. As authors of this study, we were merely transmitters

T. Coles
Bradford Academy, Bradford, UK

N. Hassan (✉)
University of East London, London, UK

© The Author(s) 2018
R. Race (ed.), *Advancing Multicultural Dialogues in Education,*
DOI 10.1007/978-3-319-60558-6_4

of the narratives we had the privilege to hear. Applying a theoretical framework embedded in Critical Race Theory (CRT), this chapter will explore the dominant themes raised by British Muslim pupils in response to questions on media representation of Islam and Muslims, self-identity and British values

SETTING THE SCENE: LOCALITY AND SCHOOL SETTING

This chapter is located in two settings, Bradford and East London, chosen due to the professional roles and locations of the two authors. The district of Bradford is the fourth largest metropolitan district outside of London, in terms of population, in England (after Birmingham, Sheffield and Leeds). Through the Industrial Revolution of the late nineteenth century, Bradford became a centre of textile excellence; a time when various immigrant groups settled in the city, that is, Irish, German, Polish, Jewish, Ukrainian and Italian communities. The first Muslims who came to Bradford in the early 1940s were sailors from nearby seaports such as Liverpool, Middleborough and Hull, moving to Bradford to work in the local munitions factories. A larger flow of immigration began during the 1950s due to a shortage of workers needed in textiles and public transport. The majority of Muslims arriving in Bradford came from the Mirpur region of Pakistan, Kashmir, the Campbellpuri region of the Punjab, Afghanistan or Sylhet in Bangladesh. However, since the early 1990s, other Muslims have come to Bradford, not just from the Asian subcontinent, but as asylum seekers from Eastern Europe, particularly Bosnia-Herzegovina (Valentine 2006).

The school based in Bradford is referred to as 'School B' in this chapter. School B is the second most over-subscribed comprehensive in England. The ethnic composition of the school is mixed, with the largest ethnic group being from a Pakistani heritage. Currently, around 75% of the school population is from a minority ethnic group, with 23.9% of students speaking a language other than English at home. The school deprivation indicator (which is usually characterised by the percentage of students who are in receipt of free school meals) is significantly higher than the national average. Fifteen students (7 girls and 8 boys) from Years 10 and 11 took part in the study from School B.

The East London Muslim community is noted as a matrix of communities within a community including North African Arabs (Moroccan and Algerian), Somali and Yemeni groups, revert (white) Muslims communities, the well-established South Asian communities (predominantly Bengali), and Black African and Black Caribbean Muslim communities in numbers. The dominance of the Bengali Muslim community as a notable population in numbers is known to have displaced the well-established Jewish East End and is a legacy of immigration patterns and established support systems within the community, such as Madrassah education. East London has historically been and continues to be a site of fluidity and transition (Sampson 2007), and it is based on this powerful and compelling rationale that this study is located in this space. The school based in East London is referred to as 'School E' in this chapter. School E is a located in a densely populated urban setting and is a mixed 11–16 comprehensive with a non-faith ethos. Over 40% of pupils are multilingual, 48% are eligible for free school meals and 59% are eligible for pupil premium. The school offers a broad and balanced curriculum with extensive enrichment opportunities for the pupils including academic and cultural interests. Eighteen participants (10 boys and 8 girls) took part in the study from School E. Embedding this chapter in two very differing locations supports the position that our identities are inextricably linked with our experiences in a particular place and with the stories we tell of these experiences.

METHODOLOGY

The methodological approach for this chapter employed qualitative data analysis based on emerging themes (Strauss and Corbin 1990) evident in the responses of the participants. The selection of participants (aged 14–16) was a long-term project embedded in the work of the authors with School B (located in Bradford) and School E (located on East London). The preferred sampling strategy implemented was a combination of purposive and snowball sampling (Patton 2002) reflective of the complexities of selecting the appropriate participants for the study, including participants who would elicit rich data, a balanced representation of gender and ethnicity and most significantly participants who were comfortable and willing to engage with the research process. Open ended questionnaires and informal interviews (Hesse-Biber and Leavy 2004) were utilised as the preferred data collection method as this option facilitated time and space for participants to reflect on their responses, a key consideration bearing in mind the many demands on their time during school hours. Additionally, this method offered a safe avenue for self-expression and authentic re-telling of personal narratives (Delgado Bernal 2002) which took the form of storytelling. Storytelling is an established methodological approach when applying CRT and is often explored as a means of challenging the reinforced racial hegemony as expressed in dominant discourses. Importantly, storytelling captures a search for meaning (McAdams 1997) for both the researcher and the researched, or in this case, for the authors and the students.

CRITICAL RACE THEORY (CRT)

The study applied a theoretical framework that is embedded in Critical Race Theory (Delgado and Stefancic 1991). CRT is described as an approach that offers a radical lens through which to make sense of, deconstruct and challenge racial inequality in society (Rollock and Gillborn 2011). Through the investigation of the relationships between race, racism and power, Critical Race theorists and activists attempt to expose how racial inequality is sustained in society both through structures and assumptions, both of which were looked at in this study. CRT began as a legal movement in the mid-1970s after the advances of the civil rights era in the United States of the 1960s. However, more recently CRT has been implemented in the field of education, using the theoretical writings of Derrick Bell (2002). 1 (who is often credited with laying the foundation for CRT), Alan Freeman and Richard Delgado to explore ideas to help understand issues of school discipline, hierarchy and power struggles as well as looking at the influence of what and how certain knowledge and culture is 'transferred' to students.

There are central themes that underpin Critical Race Theory which are particularly prevalent in education and important to consider for the basis of this chapter. The first is the fact that racism is endemic and therefore is so extensive (not necessarily in explicit forms but often in more nuanced terms) that it is viewed as normal. This means that we need to continuously consider that institutionalised racism is always prevalent in society, including and especially in our schools. Secondly, claims of neutrality, objectivity to research, the myth of educational meritocracy and a 'colour-blindness', all act as a camouflage to what is actually happening within our schools. This is an important piece of the jigsaw that explains why race is often ignored or deliberately not chosen to be the subject of discussion or professional development in schools. The idea of CRT being an integral and invaluable part of Initial Teacher Education (ITE), for example, is one that is wholeheartedly encouraged by the authors.

Another key theme in CRT is understanding the role and influence of whiteness as a power structure which creates and reinforces racial subordination and maintains a white privilege (a socially constructed entitlement of white power and dominance that exists in everyday life). One doesn't have to look hard to find data and evidence of this. According to Steel (2015), just 7.6% of teachers in state schools in England are people of colour compared with almost 25% of students, and even more shockingly—though not surprisingly and further supporting the idea of white dominance—97% of English state school head teachers are white. Connected with whiteness is the theme of interest convergence; Derrick Bell, who is generally credited with the concept, describes it as the imbedded culture where "white elites will tolerate or encourage racial advances for blacks only when such advances also promote white self-interest" (Delgado and Stefancic 2000:23). The final key theme of CRT is Richard's Delgado's idea of a 'call to context', which challenges tradition and historical development and emphasises the importance of experiential knowledge; paying attention and highlighting the voices and experiences of students of colour. This essential 'call to context' is something that our study achieved by using the narratives and lived experience of the students we have interviewed. It is important to consider that CRT is often criticised by people with alternative perspectives who view the idea of racism as threatening to their own sense of what they view as acceptable or as 'right'. CRT continues to grow in strength and is "becoming one of the most important perspectives on the policy and practice of race inequality in the UK" (Rollock and Gillborn 2011).

DISCUSSION OF FINDINGS

An analysis of the questionnaires was conducted in order to establish dominant themes in response to open ended questions about how pupils accessed information about Muslims and Islam and how this might impact them individually and as a member of a community. The predominance of responses about pupils' experiences of misrepresentation, British values, self-identity and emancipation forms the basis of this discussion. It is pertinent to point out that in the course of gathering data, Muslim pupils' online social networking and participatory practices were noted as the main sources of accessing news about Islam and Muslims (John 2014a, b). The fact that none of the participants watched a mainstream television news channel or listened to radio stations was a clear reflection of the postmodern era and the power of new media where we can all connect on a local and global level, building support networks and communities. John (ibid.) concludes that this allows "new discursive and 'networked' spaces for young people to engage with co-citizens, form opinions and make claims in a way that bypass normative conceptions of the public sphere".

El-Nawawy (2010) concentrates on the emergence of networked, online spaces for Muslim young people as a space for social interactions and social cohesion. This is an interesting point to reflect on momentarily, as this is not the focus of this paper. Not only is this important for a new generation of young Muslims (sometimes referred to as Generation M) with respects to finding 'safe spaces' but research suggests that this new media provides a space to belong for Muslim youth (Eckert and Chadha 2013; Salvatore 2013; Aly 2012; Collins 2008) which is significant in light of their perceived exclusion from assumed spaces of belonging such as school and also as a counter-narrative in terms of empowered representations and political engagement since 9/11 (Mansouri and Marotta 2012).

MISREPRESENTATION

School B:
I despise the media for what they do as they make all Muslims seem as terrorist when in actual fact terrorists are not a part of Islam.
Adnaan, British-Pakistani, 15, male
I feel like the media is painting all of the 1.6 billion Muslims with the same brush, which I find highly disrespectful. It's propaganda [...]. It makes people think that invading Iraq and Afghanistan is okay as the Muslims are portrayed as bad people. The wars are all about oil and money and destroying Islam. Muslims are seen as being 'born to fight'. Films like *American Sniper* don't help. It's brainwashing. It's 24/7, it's everywhere. It's meant to be a trusted source, but it isn't. The media is a powerful weapon of mass destruction!
Zak, Lybian, 16, male
They just pick on us and look at us badly. But I know nobody likes Muslims. Which explains why the American and UK government didn't give any donations to the Palestinians.

Mohsin, British-Pakistani, 16, male

I get angry and frustrated that I get associated with the evil that is shown in the media about Muslims. I feel like there is a false portrayal of the religion due to the media and the way it targets Islam, therefore people aren't learning about it but they're being brainwashed into a biased view on Islam as a whole. It's definitely getting worse. It's almost like a habit for the media to portray Muslims as they do.

Akenyia, British–Muslim, 16, female

School E:

Things on the TV our parents see, news and stuff [...] my parents tell me 'don't go out [and don't go to West Ham United matches] you will be in danger'. Because of other people who act like a criminal, murders, we are in danger in Plaistow and East Ham 'cos [some] people will think we are like the ones on TV. Like, we have guns and massive knives, too and we will hurt any random. That is how we live now, always thinking the worst about ourselves.

Samie, 15, British-Algerian, male.

My beard does not mean I am a home grown terrorist.

Farooq, 16, British-Pakistani, male.

Our parents were not seen as a problem. Now, because of foreign policy...because this government supports America in their wars... we are the problem. Just look at how UKIP [United Kingdom Independence Party] talks about Islam, in public. How do you think that makes us feel? Well, we don't stay quiet like our parents, we speak out, it's our human right.

Leila, 16, British-Muslim, female

Even in creative writing, I was told writing about drone attacks (in Syria) was too political and that I need to write something about my life instead. *About my life? Are you joking me?* (Pupil K's emphasis) But, I notice when we do anything good, like we raised money for Cancer Research, my friend Saba, she's from Syria too, she is always in the picture then up on the school website and in the paper. Then, the school tells us, I mean I read about it on the website, that they are concerned about Saba's family and care for the Syrians who have lost their families. I am so confused, man.

Jannah, Syrian, 15, female

The extracts captured above speak of the frustration and angst of misrepresentation and the demands for social justice in the face of what is perceived to be biased political posturing and media misrepresentation (Solorzano and Yosso 2001). Yosso and Solórzano (2005) reinforce the notion that CRT strives to challenge dominant ideologies that perpetuate inequities at the intersections of race, class and gender, as well as substantially promoting social justice and equity. The comment from Zak, from School B, clearly displays that from someone so young, his astute thoughts and opinions are already analysing and deconstructing how powerful the media is; not only in having a negative effect on his own identity and attitude but influencing the thinking of those around him. Akenyia, again from School B, passionately spoke about the misrepresentation and how it affects her life both socially and personally. Suggested the importance of using context and details of lived experienced of minoritised people. The 'call to context'—as used in this study throughout—is a powerful tool in the counter-narrative of mainstream media.

The final extract, taken from Jannah is an exemplar of interest convergence (Bell 1980), which is understood as a conceptual tool in CRT where white people are unwilling to give up power and privilege for the overall promotion of equity and social justice. This issue of power is what interest convergence illuminates, particularly in the predominantly white world of the media. Interest convergence is a reminder that we are *given* opportunities only when our interests and those of our oppressors converge. Because our presence adds something to the multicultural dialogue of equal opportunity for all and an opportunity for privileged white people to learn from us about our communities, as if we were textbooks (Duncan 2005; Delgado and Stefancic 2001), as illustrated in Jannah's confusion about not being able to write about the first-hand experiences of her extended family in Syria, whilst at the same time reading about public statements of support for her friend's family who find themselves in a similar situation to her own.

SELF-IDENTITY

School B:
I am not entirely sure. 'Muslim' and 'British Muslim' are the same. It's about individuals. I don't care about identity. I will adapt but not fully change to suit others.

Bariah British-Pakistani, 15, female
I'm a British Muslim, but I'm not sure what British identity is!
Haaris British-Pakistani, 16, male
Personality is who you are, that's what is important. British identity? I don't know what that is!
Sarah British-Pakistani, 15, female
It's more important to be a good person rather that what I am. I am British, not British-Pakistani—my identity doesn't matter.
Akenyia British, 16, female
School E:
I have many cultures, London, East Africa, R n B, I am all of them. I would not say that they are British, though. Not like tea with milk and the Queen and say, bowling. I love Moroccan mint tea, black with lots of sugar!
Dana, Somali, 16, female
My Dad is very British, he is proud of his passport. Coming here changed his life. So he can compare the two—Pakistan and Forest Gate. I only know one place, and it causes a lot of stress [...] for me and my friends. I see the Police pick on my Black friends and it's not right. I hear monkey chants at football matches. I get called 'Taliban' and 'terrorist' on my way home from the mosque with my friends and my sister have been shouted down on the Tube because her friend wears a niqaab. No, I am not so proud to be British.
Sharaz, Pakistani-Muslim, 16, male
We are part of British history, you know the bit when we fought in the war and also when we helped rebuild in the 1950s. So, of course, we are British. That means its British to eat spicy food, to look after your family and to support England in the World Cup!
Asif, British-East African, 15, male

Many participants expressed self-confidence in their own identity and in identifying factors which might impact on their self-identity such as friendship groups, schooling experiences and faith practices. Several students talked about feeling isolated and that nobody (especially non-Muslims) was 'fighting their corner', they were made to feel like outsiders, the 'other' in spaces they should experience belonging such as their locality or even their street. For the authors this was a fascinating yet depressing thought. Perhaps the reason as to why students expressed their disappointment that no one seemed to be battling for their emancipation is in itself further indication of the several themes of CRT that are in play in their schools. The dangerous position of 'neutrality' that teachers and leaders may be forced—or choose—to hold, is one that is obviously understood by the students interviewed. Contributing to this is the fact that due to the low percentage of Black Asian Minority Ethnic (BAME) school leaders in schools may stimulate their feelings of not seeing people 'like them' or people who 'fight for them' in positions of power and authority. From this it becomes clearer why the students spoke of how they felt marginalised and "perceived through British Media fueling the nationwide discourse and hyperbole on Muslim extremism and promoting a sense of 'otherness'" (El Ella 2015:43).

The participants echoed an increasing fear that they feel that they don't belong, in places where they should feel most safe and secure: our schools. These feelings are exacerbated by the constant misguided actions of the government and their regulating body Ofsted, [Office for Standards in Education, Children's Services and Skills] who impose relentless pressure on Muslims to prove their loyalty to Britain before any notions of parental, ethnic or extended community loyalties. This pressure cooker effect creates an atmosphere where "… we are grooming untold numbers of resentful, angry, embittered and radicalized young Muslims, men and women, and they need not have been anywhere near a Muslim 'extremist'" (John 2014a, b:28).

In David Cameron's post-election speech in 2015 (where he gave a statement in the House of Commons on the National Security Strategy and Strategic Defence and Security), the then newly elected Conservative Prime Minister, highlighted the new counter-extremism bill and further promoted the rhetoric of 'Fundamental British Values' by making reference to the United Kingdom being a, "… passively tolerant society" which has helped to "… foster a narrative of extremism and grievance". This was supported by Theresa May in a Radio 4 interview—the then Home Secretary who became Prime Minister in 2016—who indicated that "the key values that underline our society…are being undermined by extremism […] things like democracy and tolerance" (May 2015). Nabulsi (2015:16) wrote that the counter-terrorism bill "represents the rise of ideological extremism masquerading as British Values…the bill itself is an extremist act".

The greatest concern for most Muslim communities and students is not that they see a conflict between Muslim values and British values but that society (through media and government strategies) now thinks there is an imaginary binary opposition against them, which explains why there was a real confusion and frustration when students were asked to articulate and explain their self-identity. This can be explored further by analysing Akenyi's (School B) comment that her "identity doesn't matter". The question that needs to be raised is why an articulate and impassioned individual would express such a matter-of-fact conclusion. This could be explained by a confusion and search for one's own identity (Modood, 2010): a search that is an essential part of growing up, but could also stem from a fear of being labelled as an 'other'. This fear, as we have read already, may stem from themes of Critical Race Theory prevalent in her society and her own school.

BRITISH VALUES

School E
When I hear about British values, I think how come? [...] they are the same as UN values, the same as American values, right? Even the same as my values and I am half Indian and half British. Calling them British values means that they are not for some people, like Polish people. So, you are not in the gang, that sort of thing.
Leila, 16, British-Muslim, female
British values are not the same as things like the countryside and scones and stereotypes like that. British vales are such a big deal these days because none of us, [...] we don't feel British. So we need the school to tell us. Even though we talk about our culture that cares for the hungry and how we look after our older generation at home, and how we share our food and even give to charity as an important rule and how we care for the earth and respect all religions. Are they not as important as your British values?
Jameel, British-Turkish, 15, male

It is important to note that only two participants (from the same school) were familiar with the notion of British values as an aspect of curriculum delivery, reflecting their own heightened political awareness and participation in election campaigning where questions on this topic were aired. This is supported by a recent survey where 250 ethnic minority pupils in one of England's most diverse cities, Peterborough, when asked, "… were generally baffled by the concept of 'British values'" (Davies 2016). Guidance on promoting British values in schools consists of non-statutory advice from the Department for Education (DfE 2014). Maintained schools have obligations under section 78 of the Education Act (2002) which requires schools, as part of a broad and balanced curriculum, to promote the spiritual, moral, social, cultural (SMSC) as well as mental and physical development of pupils at the school. Schools are also guided to promote the fundamental British values of democracy, the rule of law, individual liberty and mutual respect and tolerance of those with different faiths and beliefs. It is particularly pertinent at this point to raise the question of the possibility that a school referring a student to Channel (part of the government's Prevent initiative to support their Counter-Terrorism and Security Act of 2015 to "… prevent people from being drawn into terrorism") under false claims and a lack of evidence by the government's own admission—thousands of people have been erroneously referred to the Channel programme (NPCC 2015)—could ultimately damage a student's mental wellbeing. It may appear that the apparent safeguarding of students that schools have a duty to provide is completely in opposition with the demands that frontline staff have of monitoring and reporting students to Prevent (Cantle and Thomas 2014; Kundnani 2015). The recent Eroding Trust (2016) report from the Open Society Justice Initiative suggests that "… there are serious concerns about the treatment of children under Prevent. Although the government describes Prevent as a form of 'safeguarding' (a statutory term which denotes promotion of welfare and protection from harm), the two sets of obligations have materially different aims, particularly with respect to children".

In relation to the participant's understanding of British values, the guidance states that, through the provision of SMSC schools should "enable students to develop their self-knowledge, self-esteem and self-confidence". Jameel's conclusion from the empirical data above that "… we don't feel British" strikes at the heart of displaced self-knowledge. He goes on to express aspects of his culture which also emphasise key values including care for the elderly within the family setting and asks, "Are they not as important as your British values?" From this extract, a notion of imposed hierarchy (that British values are more important than Jameel's

British-Turkish values, as they are not the same or in some way seen as inferior) is evident. Additionally, Jameel was secure in his self-knowledge; however, this was in spite of and not because of a school-driven curriculum on British values through SMSC. Jameel spoke confidently about his culture, he was very self-aware of his own set of values (concerning family, the poor and stewardship of the earth) and expressed concern that they did not feature in the very prescriptive set of British values. He was mindful of the difference.

CONCLUSION

Using the theoretical framework of CRT, this chapter aims to create a space to hear the viewpoints and real life experiences of students as an essential step in responding to the question of misrepresentation, identity and their conceptualisation of British values. It is essential to consider that the methodology and purpose of this chapter was never to promote Derrick Bell's concept of 'interest convergence' (as discussed earlier), either for the authors or for the two schools involved. To illustrate this and the power of encouraging 'storytelling', after the informal interviews a student from School B asked, "Sir, when can we do this again?" This exemplified that the traditional hierarchical structure between a deputy head and his students was completely eradicated from the process due to the very nature of the opportunity given to students to openly articulate their opinions and thoughts. As Foucault (1984) explains, it is always essential to discover how our view of truth is influenced by power relationships and perspectives. Authority was obviously still present throughout the data collection processes; however, due to the freedom and democratic nature of the content and the explicit understanding that the interviewer was accessing knowledge that they did not have, an authoritative approach was not required. For the participants in School B, having the opportunity to speak to a white, non-Muslim teacher about their own lives was clearly an emancipatory act, as the tables were turned and a shift of power took place very early on in the interviews. As Habib (2016) reports, "Students feel empowered by having their critical counter-narratives validated and valued. Where students hear others' stories and tell their own, schools can become critical sites of opportunity for reflection, resistance and hopeful futures."

The participants—when speaking to the white non-Muslim teacher—found themselves being afforded the privilege of being able to discuss truth uncontaminated by power. Though it is not the focus of this chapter, it is important to clarify that in this scenario his whiteness did not imply hierarchy. The discussions allowed the process of '*demystifying*' to happen. Biesta's (2014) idea encourages discussion to allow a revealing of what is hidden (often overtly) from the everyday views of those being oppressed, rather than foregoing debate and pigeonholing students into a mould that society and schools have already defined for them. Only when we *demystify* the truth and encourage the ownership of knowledge from our students— as was experienced in these particular interviews—will their paths become clearer. *"Illuminate that darkness, blaze roads through that vast forest, so that we will not, in all our doing, lose sight of its purpose, which is after all, to make the world a more human dwelling place."* (Baldwin 1962)

This chapter demonstrates the essential need for open honest, safe, secure and intelligent dialogues between students and staff in our schools, colleges and universities. Only through well-designed and thoughtful delivery of school CPD (Continual Professional Development) and an investment in Initial Teacher Education focusing on Critical Race Theory will this be achieved. As educators with a duty of care for all our students, we always need to consider, respect and celebrate the authority students have as the owners of their own stories. Teachers, leaders and all staff in places of learning must listen to these stories to enable a counter-narrative to the potentially harmful and dangerous coverage and portrayal of Islam and Muslims in the media.

REFERENCES

Aly, A. (2012). Fear online: Seeking sanctuary in online forums. In A. Hayes & R. Mason (Eds.), *Cultures in refuge: Seeking sanctuary in modern Australia* (pp. 37–45). Surrey, UK: Ashgate.

Baldwin, J. (1962). *The creative process.* Creative America: Ridge Press.

Bell, D. A. (1980). Brown v. Board of education and the interest-convergence dilemma. *Harvard Law Review, 93*(3), 518–533.

Bell, D. (2002). *Ethical ambition: Living a life of meaning and worth.* New York, NY: Bloomsbury Press.

Biesta, G. J. J. (2014). *The beautiful risk of education.* Boulder: Paradigm Publishers.

Cantle, T., & Thomas, P. (2014). On Prevent. Retrieved May 8, 2016, from https://www.opendemocracy.net/can-europe-make-it/paul-thomas-ted-cantle/extremism-and-'prevent'-need-to-trust-in-education

Collin, P. (2008). The internet, youth participation poli-cies, and the development of young people's politi-cal identities in Australia. *Journal of Youth Studies*, *11*(5), 527–542.

Davies, A. (2016). *Beyond tolerance: Young British Muslims discuss ways to build community cohesion in their city, and the barriers they experience.* Maidenhead: Open University.

Delgado Bernal, D. (2002). Critical race theory, latino critical theory, and critical raced-gendered epistemologies: Recognizing students of color as holders and creators of knowledge. *Qualitative Inquiry*, *8*(1), 105–126.

Delgado, R., & Stefancic, J. (1991). Derrick Bell's chronicle of the space traders: Would the US sacrifice people of color if the price were right? *University of Colorado Law Review*.

Delgado, R., & Stefancic, J. (Eds.). (2000). *Critical race theory: The cutting edge* (2nd ed.). Philadelphia, PA: Temple University Press.

Delgado, R., & Stefancic, J. (Eds.). (2001). *Critical race theory: An introduction.* New York, NY: University Press.

Department for Education (DfE). (2014). Promoting fundamental values as part of SMSC in schools: Departmental advice for maintained schools. Retrieved January 17, 2015, from www.gov.uk/government/publications

Duncan, G. A. (2005). Critical race ethnography in education: Narrative, inequal-ity and the problem of epistemology. *Race Ethnicity and Education*, *8*(1), *93–114.*

Eckert, S., & Chadha, K. (2013). Muslim bloggers in Germany: An emerging counterpublic. *Media, Culture and Society*, *35*(8), 926–942.

El Ella, O. (2015). The suffocation of British Muslim civil society space. Retrieved January 17, 2016, from http://mediadiversified.org/2015/03/25/the-suffocation-of-british-muslim-civil-society-space/

El-Nawawy, M. (2010). Collective identity in the virtual Islamic public sphere. *International Communication Gazette*, *72*(3), 229–250.

Foucault, M. (1984). *Politics, philosophy, culture: Interviews and other writings, 1977–1984.* New York: Routledge.

Habib, S. (2016). *Teaching & Learning Britishness. Encountering and negotiating discourses of identities and belongings through critical pedagogy.* Thesis (PhD). Goldsmiths, University of London.

Hesse-Biber, S. N., & Leavy, P. (Eds.). (2004). *Approaches to qualitative research: A reader on theory and practice.* New York: Oxford University Press.

Hooks, B. (1994). *Teaching to transgress: Education as a practice of freedom.* New York: Routledge.

John, A. (2014a). Muslim young people online: "Acts of Citizenship". *In Socially Networked Spaces, Social Inclusion* (ISSN: 2183–2803), *2*(2), 71–82.

John, A. (2014b). 'Trojan Horse' brings a Packhorse of British values into every school. Retrieved May 8, 2015, from http://www.gusjohn.com/2014/06/trojan-horse-brings-a-packhorse-of-british-values-into-every-school/

Kundnani, A. (2015). Extremism and 'Prevent': The need to trust in education. Retrieved February 8, 2016, from http://www.irr.org.uk/news/counter-terrorism-policy-and-re-analysing-extremism/

Mansouri, F., & Marotta, V. (2012). *Muslims in the West and the challenges of belonging*. Carlton: Melbourne University Publishing.

May, J. (2015). Government will promote British Values, says Teresa May. *Politics Home*. Retrieved February 14, 2017, from https://www.politicshome.com/news/uk/social-affairs/politics/news/69579/government-will-promote-british-valuestheresa-may-says

McAdams, D. P. (1997). *The stories we live by: Personal myths and the making of the self*. New York: Guildford Publications.

Modood, T. (2010). *Still not easy being British: Struggles for a multicultural citizenship*. Stoke-on-Trent: Trentham Books.

Nabulsi, K. (2015). Theresa May's Prevent bill is extremism in the name of security. *The Guardian*, 4th February 2015.

National Police Chiefs' Council (NPCC). (2015). National channel referral figures. Retrieved February 14, 2017, from http://www.npcc.police.uk/FreedomofInformation/NationalChannelReferralFigures.aspx

Patton, M. Q. (2002). *Qualitative research and evaluation methods* (3rd ed.). Thousand Oaks: Sage.

Rollock, N., & Gillborn, D. (2011). Critical Race Theory (CRT), British educational research association online resource. Retrieved January 8, 2016, from https://www.bera.ac.uk/wp-content/uploads/2014/03/Critical-Race-Theory-CRT-.pdf

Salvatore, A. (2013). New media, the "Arab Spring", and the metamorphosis of the public sphere: Be-yond Western assumptions on collective agency and democratic politics. *Constellations: An International Journal of Critical & Democratic Theory, 20*(2), 217–228.

Sampson, N. (2007). Speaking of home: Bangladeshi women in London's East end reflect on belonging. *Rising East, 7*, 19–28.

Singh, A. (2016). *Eroding Trust The UK's Prevent Counter-Extremism Strategy in Health and Education*. Open Society Justice Initiative. Retrieved September 17, 2016, from https://www.opensocietyfoundations.org/sites/default/files/eroding-trust-20161017_0.pdf

Stanley, L., & Wise, S. (1983). *Breaking out again: Feminist ontology and epistemology*. London: Routledge.

Strauss, A., & Corbin, J. (1990). *Basics of qualitative research: Grounded theory procedures and techniques*. Newbury Park, CA: Sage.

Steel, S. (2015). *Race to the Top 2: Diversity in Education*. Elevation Networks. Retrieved July 8, 2016, from http://www.elevationnetworks.org/wp.../Race-to-The-Top-2-Diversity-In-Education1.pdf

Solorzano, D. G., & Yosso, T. J. (2001). Critical race and LatCrit theory and method: Counter-storytelling: Chicana and Chicano graduate school experiences. *International Journal of Qualitative Studies, 14*(4), 471–495.

Storm, I. (2015). Why are Muslims less accepted than other minorities in Britain? Retrieved January 17, 2016, from http://blog.policy.manchester.ac.uk/featured/2015/04/why-are-muslims-less-accepted-than-other-minorities-in-britain/

Valentine, S. R. (2006). *Muslims in Bradford*. Paper for COMPAS, Oxford, Oxford University Press. Retrieved January 2016, from https://www.compas.ox.ac.uk/fileadmin/fileadmin/files/publications/research/resources/urban/Bradford.Background Paper.05065.pdf

Yosso, & Solorzono (2005) is Solorano, D. G., & Yasso, T. J. (2001). Critical race and LatCrit theory and method: Counter-storytelling in Chicana and Chicano Graduate School experiences. *International Journal of Qualitative Studies, 14*(4), 471–495.

Tait Coles is a teacher, vice principal in a Bradford Academy and an educational speaker. He is a skilled and highly regarded classroom practitioner and a respected radical of modern teaching. Previously, Tait has been assistant head teacher at a comprehensive school in Leeds and was Head of Science in one of the many challenging schools in Bradford. He has also been a teaching and learning consultant for Bradford's Local Education Authority (LEA). He is also a specialist leader of education and an accredited facilitator. Tait is the author of *Never Mind the Inspectors; Here's Punk Learning*, a manifesto that challenges the orthodoxy and complacency of teaching, allowing students to be central to a critical educational culture where they learn how to become individuals and social agents rather than merely disengaged spectators who have their 'part to play' in the neoliberal ideology of modern schooling.

Nasima Hassan, originally from Lancashire, has worked in secondary school teaching humanities, in teacher training and in strategic management in higher education. She has worked extensively overseas, supporting teachers' professional development in India (Bangalore), South Africa (Kwazulu Natal) and most recently in conjunction with the United Nations High Commissioner for Refugees (UNHCR) in Malaysia. She has published chapters on the education system in South Africa, on Islamophobia and on the schooling experience of British Muslims, and in 2015 co-authored *Sociology of Education*, published by SAGE. Her doctoral thesis explored the concept of 'Muslim consciousness' through a philosophical and political exploration of identity construction. She is currently working on her second co-authored book entitled *Critical Pedagogy and Contemporary Issues*.

The Teaching and Learning of Chinese in Primary Schools in England: Developing a New Learning Approach to Support Intercultural Understanding

Fotini Diamantidaki and Katharine Carruthers

INTRODUCTION

The aim of this chapter is to provide an overview of the state of the field with respect to the activity of the UCL Institute of Education (IOE) Confucius Institute (CI) for Schools, in promoting the teaching and learning of Chinese in secondary schools. After consideration of the state of the field in the secondary sector, the focus will be shifted to the new strand of work of the IOE Confucius Institute in primary schools in England (IOE CI 2014: 1), as this is an emerging opportunity for further growth and expansion of the teaching and learning of Mandarin Chinese. More specifically, the chapter will discuss the work of the IOE Confucius Institute with regards to implementing a new Programme of Study for primary schools with the aim of raising cultural awareness and intercultural understanding, through the inclusion of Chinese characters as an integral part of language learning at an early age. In order to support our argument on

F. Diamantidaki (✉) • K. Carruthers
Institute of Education, University College London, London, UK

© The Author(s) 2018   71
R. Race (ed.), *Advancing Multicultural Dialogues in Education*,
DOI 10.1007/978-3-319-60558-6_5

developing intercultural understanding, we shall draw on theories on the role of culture in foreign language learning (Brooks 1968; Byram 1989, 1997a, b, Kramsch 1993, 2001; Zarate 1993; Abdallah-Pretceille 2003; Dervin and Suomela-Salmi 2010). This chapter will finally seek to highlight areas of further development in regards to the creation of high quality resources and the training of non-Chinese speaking primary classroom teachers.

THE CONTEXT IN WHICH THE IOE CONFUCIUS INSTITUTE FOR SCHOOLS DEVELOPED AND HOW ITS ACTIVITY IS NOW SUSTAINED

The first National Annual Conference on Chinese Teaching in Schools took place in Cambridge, UK, in the spring of 2004 with around 65 delegates; it was held in collaboration with the Association for Language Learning and the UK Federation of Chinese (Community) Schools. At this point, only a very small number of schools in England were offering any kind of Chinese provision, but those who were, were keen to share experiences and talk to each other. As an outcome of this first conference, a small e-forum for teachers of Chinese was set up at the time and some web pages were created to act as a 'virtual' staffroom, so that teachers of Chinese, many of whom felt rather isolated in their schools and localities, would be able to communicate with each other.

The conference marked a turning point in the development of Chinese teaching in schools. Although Chinese has not been widely taught in schools in England, interest has continued to grow dramatically. Political and business leaders have recognised the rise of Asia as one of the central facts of the twenty-first century. China, with its economic growth and emergence as a cultural and political leader, is integral to this shift of focus. Quah (2010) talks about the global economy's shifting centre of gravity and maintains that '... extrapolating to 2050 the global economy's centre of gravity will continue to shift east to lie between India and China'. Clearly, increasing the number of British students who can speak Chinese proficiently and can demonstrate an understanding of Chinese culture is crucial.

Alongside economic change, came the rise of coverage about China in the media and in TV programming. Chinese films, such as *Raise the Red Lantern* (1991) and *Crouching Tiger Hidden Dragon* (2000), exhibitions about China, such as the British Museum's Terracotta Warrior Exhibition (2007) and the Royal Academy's Ai Weiwei exhibition (2015), Chinese novels in translation, including the Chinese Nobel prize winner, Gao Xingjian's *Soul Mountain* (2000) and the Beijing Olympics (2008) all added to increased awareness of China in the first decade of the twentieth century. Less expensive airfares to China enabled people to go and see the country for themselves. Parents doing business in China began to ask about opportunities for learning Chinese for their children. To meet this demand globally, the Office of Chinese Language Council International (Hanban) was developing ways to support the growth of the teaching of Chinese as a foreign language and the first Confucius Institute was opened in 2004 in Seoul. Confucius Institutes are set up abroad (i.e. outside China) to support the learning of Chinese as a foreign language.

By the autumn of 2006 when the IOE Confucius Institute (IOE CI) for Schools first began, about 7–8 % of all maintained secondary schools (around 230 schools) in England offered some form of Chinese provision with about 40 % of this being off curriculum. Only 31 % of schools had trained teachers teaching Chinese. This was set against the backdrop of September 2004, when the study of a foreign language became non-compulsory in Key Stage 4 in England (i.e. for 14–16-year-olds) (Carruthers 2012).

In July 2006, the Department for Education and Skills signed a Memorandum of Understanding with the Office of Chinese Language Council International (Hanban) in Beijing around measures to expand the teaching and learning of Mandarin Chinese throughout the English education system. At the same time, the Specialist Schools and Academies Trust (SSAT) also signed an agreement with Hanban to set up a schools-based Confucius Institute; the SSAT Confucius Institute was formally launched in July 2007. The SSAT Confucius Institute transferred to the Institute of Education, University of London in June 2012 to become the UCL Institute of Education Confucius Institute for Schools (IOE CI). In its early days and from personal day to day work experience the IOE CI focused its attention on working to remove the three barriers to the teaching and learning of Chinese in schools, namely, lack of appropriate, localized teaching materials; lack of trained teachers; issues around accreditation. This work went alongside supporting and developing teachers and schools teaching Chinese.

The IOE CI is a bilateral project with Peking University and Peking University High School and is supported by the Office of Chinese

Language Council International, Hanban. As well as a small team of specialists in London, the IOE CI has established a network of 42 Confucius Classrooms across England, schools which have both Chinese firmly embedded in their own curriculum and which give advice, support and taster classes to other schools in their region looking to start offering Chinese, for instance, Kingsford Community School in Newham, London, and Archbishop Sentamu Academy in Hull. The Confucius Classroom network originally consisted of five leading Confucius Classroom schools or 'hubs', where Mandarin Chinese teaching was already strongly established; each of these 'hub' schools reached out to and worked with five 'spoke' schools delivering Chinese language lessons both on curriculum and at taster level, with a view to encouraging these schools to invest in their own Chinese teacher and develop the teaching and learning of Chinese within school. This network was extended by a further seven Confucius Classrooms in 2008 and a further 22 in 2010. In 2016 there were more than 200 spoke schools working with the 42 Confucius Classrooms, 3 of which are based in primary schools.

The IOE CI has also worked, in partnership with Pearson on the development of teaching materials for Chinese with three student books (for 11–14-year-olds and GCSE Chinese for 14–16-year-olds) together with two workbooks and three teachers' books, all under the series name: 进步一、二 Jìn bù. This was the first time that textbooks for teaching Chinese were published by a mainstream publisher in England and they have brought Chinese more closely into line with provision for other languages.

GROWTH OF CHINESE LEARNING IN PRIMARY SCHOOL CLASSROOMS

With the growth of the IOE Confucius Institute and its continuous sustainable work in the secondary school sector, the opportunity arises to implement a plan to introduce Chinese in the primary school sector in England. The Mandarin Chinese for Primary Schools Programme has been made possible thanks to support from the Hong Kong and Shanghai Banking Corporation (HSBC) and the recent changes in England with regards to the national curriculum, whereby the learning of a foreign language is a compulsory subject across all KS2 year groups (age ranges from 7 to 11) starting from September 2014. In this respect, the Department for Education (DfE) guidance on KS2 Modern Foreign Languages (MFL) identifies a series of skills in listening, speaking, reading and writing that young learners should develop. The four following attainments targets as featured in the KS2 subject content for languages (DfE 2013: 194) are representative of the range of skills to aim for:

- *Listen* *attentively to spoken language and show understanding by joining in and responding*
- *Speak* *in sentences, using familiar vocabulary, phrases and basic language structures*
- *Read* *carefully and show understanding of words, phrases and simple writing*
- *Write* *phrases from memory, and adapt these to create new sentences, to express ideas clearly*

Studying more closely the KS2 subject content for languages and the rest of the attainment targets as presented in the DfE (2013: 194–196) KS2 programme of study, it can be observed that there is a focus mainly on speaking and listening, where pupils explore sounds through songs, listen to the target language, start developing accurate pronunciation and intonation with the view to speak to an audience in full sentences and engage in simple conversations. The reading and writing skills are less targeted at primary school level, but the learners are still expected to show understanding on what they read and write phrases from memory as listed above in the last two bullet points.

All the attainment targets listed and discussed above are generic for all languages taught in primary school including Mandarin. The DfE (2013) gives no specific guidance on how to achieve the attainments above, nor does it suggest any process for assessing levels of attainment. The instruction, therefore, that 'by the end of each key stage, pupils are expected to know, apply and understand the matters, skills and processes specified in the relevant programme of study ... ' implies a freedom to create such a programme of study and apply reasonable assessment criteria relevant to it for the language in question, in our case Mandarin.

In the meantime, Mandarin is being introduced in primary schools as a new language, where initially all pupils (in Years 3, 4, 5 and 6) will be learning the same material at the same time. The challenge is that if Mandarin is introduced as a new language it can result in a 'staggered' progression over the first four years, with unequal levels of attainment by the end of Year 6 (last class of primary school), until the September 2014

Year 3 cohort reaches Year 6 (Trapp 2013: 3). To address such a challenge and enhance attainment, this chapter suggests the implementation of a new programme of study which is designed to be sufficiently flexible to be adapted to any level of learning ability and appropriate to each year group. In particular, the suggested programme of study is aimed at extending elements of cultural awareness as part of an integrated language learning programme with the ambition to develop an intercultural understanding between the children's own culture and the culture of China.

THE NEW PROGRAMME OF STUDY FOR KS2 MANDARIN

Trapp (2014) has written, in this respect, an outline Programme Of Study (PoS) for KS2 Mandarin which involves 30 teaching hours per year and a new revised version of the same document (Trapp 2016) with inclusion of greater cultural content. The generally positive reception of the original programme of study (Trapp 2014) has encouraged the creation of a new version (Trapp 2016) in which the central language content and its approach have been retained, but they have been surrounded by more extensive and sophisticated cultural material designed both to emphasise the linguistic-cultural interface and to make more explicit opportunities for cross-curricular integration. The new version is based on 14 units and they are knowledge about language; China, Chinese and saying hello; about me: names and questions; parts of the body; numbers and age 1–10; numbers 11–99 and measure words; family; countries and colours; pets and animals; food and drink; time—sun, moon and stars; time and timetables; colours; going places.

The new PoS, follows on from the old Framework for KS2 languages in England (DfE 2014) and addresses the two key strands of oracy and literacy, with suggestions to explore elements of culture and intercultural understanding for Chinese Mandarin.

From the simple enumeration of the units above, two things can be observed: first that the units are in line with the units addressed in other mainstreamed languages in England such as French and can be easily verified in any online schools' scheme of work such as the one from Roding Valley (2015), but at the same time the distinctiveness of Chinese culture is at the heart of the language teaching. To illustrate the latter, we share one snapshot of the objectives on speaking from 11th unit in the series on 'time—sun, moon and stars', whereby we attempt to illustrate the direct link between the teaching of Chinese characters, Chinese culture and intercultural understanding (please observe the highlighted comments):

From the highlighted parts, we can assert that in the new programme of study there is a continuous encouragement to make links with own culture and other languages and cultures the children may know and therefore practising ways of striving to achieve intercultural understanding and positioning themselves in the world. Another observation which is clear is that language and culture in Chinese are one. The suggestion for the example above, that in order for the children to be able to say the date they will need to know the character for moon 月, sun 日 and star 星期, is an excellent illustration of the unique nature of Chinese language and culture that they function as one and a very beautiful and intriguing aspect of the Chinese language from an outsider's view of the world. A final observation in the figure above is the different colours the characters have; red, blue, green, black, brown. This is a very significant detail in relation to the teaching of tones and how teachers can instil memory skills in their pupils, with the aim of learning correct pronunciation, without the help of pinyin. An added advantage of the entire programme of study is that 'the units are not designed as single lessons, rather as groups of lessons that can be spread over several sessions, depending both on time available and depth of content' (Trapp 2013: 3); a distinctive feature which addresses the necessity for creating a new flexible programme of study tailored to pupils' and teachers' needs.

Developing Intercultural Understanding

A vital characteristic of Mandarin, as also observed in Fig. 1 above, which is at the heart of the language's potential for opening up new ways of thinking, understanding and communicating for the young learner, is its essentially conceptual nature. In comparison with European languages which seek precision of meaning through complex grammar and precise vocabulary, Mandarin essentially uses context to refine a broader concept into a specific meaning (ibid). Whilst there are many words/characters with precise meanings and functions as parts of speech (noun, verb and so on), in many cases in Mandarin a single word/character may embody a concept which only acquires its specific meaning and/or function through its particular context. As an illustration, the common word '快kuài': in terms of function, it illustrates the Chinese stative verb in its meaning 'to be quick' as well as being a simple adjective (e.g. 快车kuài chē express

- Tongue twisters: ask the class if they know any English tongue twisters and/or share some of your own. Tell the class that Chinese has tongue twisters too and try out: 老师四十四岁，是不是？and/or 妈妈赶马，马慢，妈妈骂马
- Start by talking about how the calendar works and use previous knowledge about Chinese New year to discuss the difference between the solar and lunar calendars. Do they know that our word "month" actually comes from the word "moon" and goes back to a time when we too used the lunar calendar.
- Explain that although Chinese festivals are based on the traditional lunar calendar, for everyday life China uses the same solar calendar as we do; and the way you say the date in Mandarin uses the words for both sun 日and moon 月
- Introduce 天，今天，明天，昨天;
- Revise numbers 1-31 and then introduce month/day format x月 y 日. Explain that in Mandarin big comes before little and that this will be a useful pattern to remember – look at how this is different in English and give examples: we say 21st January 2014 but the Chinese say 2014 January 21st; when we give addresses we say 21 Happy Lane, Funtown, Laughtershire, UK, but if you look at a Chinese letter, the address is written China, Laughter Province, Funtown, Happy Lane 21 (http://www.chinasnippets.com/2005/11/06/chinese-address-formats-western-addresses/)
- N.B. YCT uses 号 for dates, so introduce it here as an alternative, mentioning it is also used in addresses for house/flat numbers. If you put the date in characters on your whiteboard, use 号.
- With the children work out today's date, day and month, write it on the whiteboard in characters and model the phrase 今天是x月y日. Highlight 明天 and 昨天 and with the class work out 昨天是。。。明天是。。。n.b. highlight that 是doesn't change, whereas in English we say "yesterday was" and if appropriate consider use of tenses in other languages the children know. Explain how Mandarin uses "marker" words and phrases to do the same job.
- Tell the children to work out their birthdays in Chinese and compile a chart showing them with the children writing their own dates

Tell the children that days of the week are easy in Mandarin and that along with moon for month and sun for day, they also need to know the word for star: 星期 star period. Model days of the week 星期一，二,三。。。天 and with the children work out how to say "today is…; tomorrow is….; yesterday was…"

Fig. 1   Time—Sun, Moon and Stars (Trapp 2014: 53–54)

train/bus). In terms of meaning, a simple dictionary search reveals a considerable range, either alone or in combination, including rapid, quick, speed, rate, soon, almost, to hurry, clever, sharp, forthright, plain-spoken, pleased and pleasant (Trapp 2013: 3).

This specificity of Mandarin is in line with what Brooks (1968: 204) discusses in his work, that when learning a foreign language, the meaning of a word is the personal and societal life to which it refers to. In Mandarin, contextualising words and phrases, and sentence structure, take the roles which, in general, cases, tenses, genders, singulars and plurals play in other languages and carry a different message and meaning according to context. English speakers are familiar with the idea of one word having several different meanings, but in Mandarin this is at the very heart of understanding the language and the culture.

There seems to be unanimity amongst researchers in education that culture should be an integral part of language teaching (Byram 1989, 1997a, b, Kramsch 1993, 2001; Zarate 1993; Abdallah-Pretceille 2003; Dervin and Suomela-Salmi 2010, Piller 2011, Dervin and Liddicoat 2013). The remit dedicated to cultural aspects in language teaching has steadily grown in the last 20 years and 'learning a language is not only developing a useful professional skill, it is also understanding about the context and the motives that lie behind communication' (Quist 2000: 137 as cited in Dervin and Suomela-Salmi 2010). As highlighted in the previous quotation, learning a language for the sake of communication is not enough. Culture and raising cultural awareness should be at the heart of teaching and learning. Lu (1991) also goes a step further and discusses that teaching culture should assist students to improve cross-cultural language competency. Therefore, we can assert that the purpose of communication cannot be fulfilled without the appropriate knowledge of culture.

However, when exploring related literature on culture in the language classroom the concept of culture seems to be ambiguous and 'is still in need of a clear, commonly agreed definition' (Dervin and Suomela-Salmi 2010). We can at least distinguish two ways in which we might categorise 'culture'. Is it what Lawes calls 'ethno-culture' 'focusing on daily life, customs and traditions which are more relevant and accessible to young people' (Lawes 2007: 87) or is it 'enrichment culture' (ibid), meaning 'a result of a society's development over centuries encompassing geography, history, political systems, social institutions and all forms of art'? (Dervin and Suomela-Salmi 2010: 143)

A plausible way forward would be not to label culture either as ethno-culture or as enrichment culture, but as a broader social concept that constantly evolves and is alive according to existing conditions (Zhao 1992). This aspect of culture as a live and evolving organism clearly reflects the equally evolving culture and multi-cultures represented in the language classrooms in England. It also emphasises the necessity to share a culture whereby the young learners can make links with their own individual cultures and to be given the opportunity to '...reflect about different cultures [allowing] space for cultural understandings to increase' (Race 2015: 12).

The process of construction of intercultures is achieved, according to Dervin and Liddicoat (2013: 7), through interaction and through different 'methods such as participant-observation, self-reflexive essays, role-plays, simulations and even sojourns abroad' that have been used for allowing learners to develop what Byram (1997a, b) calls *'intercultural communicative competence'*: a process achievable by a number of *savoirs*. He defines the first *savoir* as the 'knowledge of social groups and their products and practices in one's own and in one's interlocutor's country, and of the general processes of societal and individual interaction' (Byram 1997a, b: 58). *Savoir-comprendre* is defined as 'the ability to interpret a document or event from another culture, to explain it and relate it to documents or events from one's own' (Byram 1997a, b: 61). *Savoir-apprendre/faire* is the 'skill of discovery and interaction: ability to acquire new knowledge of a culture and cultural practices and the ability to operate knowledge, attitudes and skills under the constraints of real-time communication and interaction' (ibid). *Savoir s'engager* is 'the ability to evaluate, critically and on the basis of explicit criteria, perspectives, practices and products in one's own and other cultures and countries' (Byram 1997a, b: 63). Finally, *savoir-être* is 'the curiosity and openness, readiness to suspend disbelief about other cultures and belief about one's own' (Byram 1997a, b: 57). On the basis of this conceptual definition of intercultural competence, the role of the teacher in the Chinese foreign language classroom is to teach the skills, processes and the knowledge required to understand the target language country and culture the pupils are studying and also teach the pupils how to critically evaluate their own culture. This can be achieved, according to Byram (1997a, b), not only through an awareness of each other's cultures but also through the teaching of language and communication, hence the concept 'intercultural communicative competence', interpreted as language and culture functioning together at all levels with the view to achieve intercultural understanding.

THE TEACHING AND LEARNING OF CHINESE IN THE PRIMARY SCHOOL CLASSROOM: CHALLENGES AND SOLUTIONS

With the above theoretical framework in mind, we shall aim to discuss the challenges faced in the classroom in relation to the interpretation of culture and the teaching of Chinese characters. We will attempt to offer a new programme of study and a suggestion to adopt new strategies in the teaching of characters and presenting culture. We have established that Chinese characters carry meaning and, equally, elements of culture according to context. In order to simplify the process of language acquisition and meaning for young learners used to the Roman alphabet, teachers in England currently use the Romanisation system pinyin as part of the process of acquiring vocabulary (Zhang and Zhu 2007). The challenge faced subsequently, is that characters are overwhelmed by pinyin in the process of acquiring new vocabulary, and an over reliance on pinyin seems to be observed especially in the process of practising pronunciation at the early stages (Shu et al. 1993).

In addition, the current standard explanation of the four tones of Mandarin Chinese—a high flat tone, a rising tone, a falling and rising tone and a falling tone—to learners of Chinese as a foreign language is that they represent four different ways of saying the same sound; in fact, not only is this inaccurate, it also again introduces an unnecessary extra layer of complexity. The sounds *mā má mǎ mà* actually represent four different sounds in their own right, with the tone being an integral part of the phoneme, not an additional element. Pinyin with tone marks is, of course, a valuable aide-memoire, but it should not be the primary point of access into learning correct pronunciation (Trapp 2013: 3).

A suggestion would be to relegate pinyin at primary level to the role of 'prompt' rather than a first reference and the principal association the learner makes is between character and sound, allowing for a firmer foundation of correct pronunciation by putting emphasis on hearing and reproducing and not recording (ibid). Young learners have no difficulty hearing and reproducing Mandarin Chinese sounds including their tonal value without deconstructing them, and it is this ability that should be harnessed (ibid). Another fundamental tool would be the consistent use of colour-coding for tone in introducing new characters. Thus, *all* new characters that are read in the first tone are red, second tone brown and so on. This method also provides another strategy for character recognition and memorisation (ibid). The incorporation of a visual cue into the presentation of new vocabulary serves to reinforce oral/aural learning without pinyin diluting the immediacy of the characters non-phonetic representation of sound.

Directly related to this in the field of character learning discussed above is the relevance of teaching the structure of characters; understanding of this structure is an important link in the process of understanding Mandarin as a whole (Trapp 2013: 3). Although characters have evolved into a far more complex writing system than their primarily pictographic origins as 甲骨文 (oracle bone script) in the Bronze Age Shang Dynasty, a few survive in contemporary usage unchanged (王 *wáng* king). Others have become increasingly stylized with the passage of time, but still retain the essence of their pictographic origin (马*mǎ* horse; 龟*guī* tortoise). Some simple rebuses such as 上/下 (*shàng/xià* above/below) have continued in use through the millennia as their immediacy could not be improved. A classroom investigation of this part of character development has proved an effective way of engaging young learners with the basic concept of Chinese characters. A relatively small number of characters are 会意字*huìyìzì* compound ideograms such as 好*hǎo* where the ideograms for woman and child are combined to form a character meaning 'good'. Around 90 % of characters in current usage, however, are the 形声字 *xíngshēngzì* phono-semantic combination characters formed by the two elements of radical and phonetic. (ibid) Although the phonetic component is no longer any reliable guide to contemporary pronunciation, the radical remains often a useful indicator of the category of meaning the character carries. Whilst native Chinese speakers acquire their character vocabulary as whole units through constant exposure, breaking characters down into these 'building blocks' provides an analytic key for non-native learners of all ages (ibid). Equally important, approaching the learning of characters in this way directly supports understanding of the conceptual nature of Mandarin Chinese in both written and spoken form.

Conclusion

In this chapter we have strived to demonstrate the impact of the sustained activities of the UCL IOE CI in London in regards to the secondary and—most importantly for this chapter—in the primary sector. The newly designed programme of study for KS2 Mandarin is an exciting new opportunity for further growth and expansion of research in the teaching of Mandarin Chinese. We also hope that we have demonstrated that the new programme of study is crafted by theoretical underpinnings in mind, based on principles of culture and intercultural understanding. However, it is too early formally to assess the efficacy of the KS2 programme of study, but it has been in use across the country by both qualified language teachers and Chinese language assistants. Informal feedback from training undertaken with these groups has indicated both understanding of and support for its approach and the flexibility it provides for integration with other materials. In training specifically undertaken with UK teachers new to Mandarin Chinese, the inclusion of the element of intercultural understanding was seen as essential. One of the most important functions it also seems to perform is to encourage native speaker teachers, particularly those on one or two year placements from China, to look beyond the traditional and somewhat stereo-typed concepts of Chinese culture incorporated in their training, and draw on more personal experience and interests; a process that draws teachers' '... attention to both salient and subtle differences between different cultural groups when intercultural differences are systematically examined and cautiously interpreted' (Zhu Hua 2014: 199).

REFERENCES

Abdallah-Pretceille. (2003). *Former et éduquer en contexte hétérogène. Pour un humanisme du divers.* Paris: Anthropos.

Brooks, N. (1968). Teaching culture in the Foreign Language classroom. *Foreign Language Annals, 1*(3), 204–217.

Byram, M. (1997a). Cultural studies and foreign language teaching. In S. Bassnett (Ed.), *Studying British cultures: An introduction* (pp. 53–65). London: Routledge.

Byram, M. (1997b). *Teaching and assessing intercultural communicative competence.* Clevedon: Multilingual Matters.

Byram, M. (1989). *Cultural studies in Foreign Language education.* Clevedon: Multilingual Matters.

Carruthers, K. (2012). The teaching and learning of Chinese in schools: Developing a research Agenda to support growth, Conference paper, IOE Confucius Institute for Schools.

Dervin, F., & Liddicoat, A. J. (Eds.). (2013). *Linguistics for intercultural education: Introduction* (pp. 1–25). Amsterdam, NY: John Benjamins Publishing Company.

Dervin, F., & Suomela-Salmi, E. (Eds.). (2010). *New approaches to assessing language and (inter-)cultural competences in higher education* (pp. 157–174). Frankfurt, Germany: Peter Lang.

Department for Education (DfE). (2013). The national curriculum in England, key stage 1 and Key stage 2 framework document, pp. 193–196. Retrieved May 30, 2014, from https://www.gov.uk/government/uploads/system/uploads/attachment_data/file/260481/PRIMARY_national_curriculum_11-9-13_2.pdf

Department for Education (DfE). (2014). National archives. Retrieved May 30, 2014, from http://webarchive.nationalarchives.gov.uk/20130802151147/

https://www.education.gov.uk/schools/teachingandlearning/curriculum/ primary/

Kramsch, C. (1993). *Context and culture in language teaching.* Oxford: Oxford University Press.

Kramsch, C. (2001). *Language and culture.* Oxford: Oxford University Press.

Lawes, S. (2007). Cultural awareness and visits abroad. In N. Pachler & A. Redondo (Eds.), *A practical guide to teaching Modern Foreign Languages in the secondary school* (pp. 87–92). London: Routledge Falmer.

Lu, B. (1991). Discussion of the theoretical question of teaching Chinese as a foreign language (Duiwai hanyu jiaoyu de lilun yanjiu wenti cuyi). *Language Teaching and Linguistic Studies, 1*(1), 61–68.

Piller, I. (2011). *Intercultural communication.* Edinburg: Edinburg University Press.

Quah, D. (2010). The Global Economy's Shifting Centre of Gravity. *LSE,* October 2010. http://econ.lse.ac.uk/~dquah/p/GE_Shifting_CG-DQ.pdf

Race, R. (2015). *Multiculturalism and education* (2nd ed.). London: Bloomsbury.

Rodin Valley School. (2015). Curriculum template year 7 French. Retrieved June, 2016, from http://www.rodingvalley.net/wp-content/uploads/2015/07/Curriculum-Template-Year-7-French.pdf

Shu, H., Zeng, H. M., & Chen, Z. (1993). Xiaoxue dinianji ertong liyong pinyin xuexi shengzici de shiyan yanjiu (Research on using Pinyin in learning vocabulary by junior primary school children). *Psychological Development and Education, 1*, 18–22.

Trapp, J. (2013). Rational for IOE IC primary Mandarin Programme of Study, HSBC Global Education Programme. Retrieved June, 2016, from https://ciforschools.files.wordpress.com/2014/01/rationale-for-ioe-ci-primary-mandarin-programme-of-study.pdf

Trapp, J. (2014). IOE IC primary Mandarin Programme of Study, HSBC Global Education Programme. Retrieved June, 2016, from https://ciforschools.files.wordpress.com/2014/01/new-pos1.pdf

Trapp, J. (2016). IOE IC primary Mandarin Programme of Study, HSBC Global Education Programme (revised version). Retrieved June, 2016, from https://ciforschools.wordpress.com/teaching-materials/primary-schemes-of-work/

UCL Institute of Education (IOE) Confucius Institute (CI) for Schools. (2014). Retrieved September, 2016, from https://ciforschools.wordpress.com/primary-mandarin-chinese/

Zarate, G. (1993). *Représentations de l'étranger et didactiques des langues.* Paris: Didier.

Zhang, Q., & Zhu, J. L. (Eds.). (2007). *Yu Wen (Language). Year 1–6.* Nanjing, China: Jiangsu Education Publishing House.

Zhao, Z. (1992). On social culture (Jiaoji wenhua suotan). *Language Teaching and Linguistic Studies, 4,* 96–114.

Zhu Hua. (2014). 'Exploring intercultural communication: Language in action', Part III, chapter 11: Theories of culture: A fundamental question (pp. 186–198). London: Routledge.

Fotini Diamantidaki is a lecturer in Languages in Education for the post graduate certificate in education (PGCE) in Languages and other teacher education routes at the University College London (UCL) Institute of Education. Her research interests involve the integration of literature in the language classroom in combination with the use of Internet and digital technologies as well as the integration of world languages into the curriculum, including the growth of Mandarin teacher education in England. Teacher education pedagogy, cultural and intercultural understanding in classroom contexts are fundamental strands to her research interests.

Katharine Carruthers is Director of the UCL Institute Of Education (IOE) Confucius Institute for Schools and Pro-Vice-Provost (East Asia) for University College London. She has played a leading role in promoting and developing the study of Mandarin Chinese and China across the curriculum in schools in England. This work has been facilitated by the establishment of the IOE Confucius Institute and 45 Confucius Classrooms, in partnership with Peking University and Peking University High School. Katharine is an experienced teacher and examiner of Chinese. Her research interests centre around teaching and learning of Chinese as a foreign language in schools, the notion of intercultural competence in Chinese and UK schools and globalisation and language policy. Katharine is well-known nationally and internationally for her work.

School Activism: The Meanings of Political Participation of Young Migrants in Italian Schools

Federico Farini

INTRODUCTION

While entering into a secondary school in a deprived area of Modena in Italy, an affluent city yet on the verge of a still unforeseen economic crisis, I was overwhelmed by excitement and fears. It was my first experience as a professional researcher, the task being to interview young migrants, promoting narratives about their social networks in and out of the school. Previous experiences suggested to me that adolescents might be reluctant in narrating personal experiences; however, human interaction often surprises expectations: I cannot remember a single interview being anything else than an intelligent and provocative discussion on education, politics and peer groups. The researcher and the students were sharing and co-constructing personal narratives through multicultural dialogue, while learning that social research is an opportunity to have our voices heard. This chapter presents the results of that research with young migrants. All of the research took place in Italy between 2006 and 2014, which saw the

F. Farini (✉)
University Campus Suffolk, Ipswich, UK

© The Author(s) 2018   87
R. Race (ed.), *Advancing Multicultural Dialogues in Education*,
DOI 10.1007/978-3-319-60558-6_6

rise and fall of xenophobic political parties and a continuing debate around migration and inclusion in different social contexts.

THE RESEARCH AND METHODS

Data consists of young migrants' narratives, promoted and collected in 62 focus group and 118 individual interviews. The participants in the research projects were 17–20 years old at the moment of data collection and resident in Italy for more than one year. An exception is represented by the researcher, an Italian citizen in his late twenties and early thirties during the timeframe of the interviews. The first research project was part of a social intervention, *Intendiamoci* (2006), aimed to promote young peoples' (migrant and Italian) perspectives on their social networks and experiences in multicultural classrooms, using photographs taken by them as the starting point of personal narratives. Although the research was not specifically focused on political participation, the narratives produced revealed the importance of political activism for young migrants attending vocational programmes in the City of Modena. *Intendiamoci* consisted of 8 focus groups and 21 individual interviews that took place in classrooms.

The second research project was an evaluation of another social intervention, COMICS (Children of Migrants Inclusion Creative Systems), funded by the European Commission within INTI04 Call for Projects (Farini and Iervese 2006). COMICS aimed to promote participants' social and political participation, using visual art as a medium for young migrants' expression. The evaluative research was aimed to measure the impact of the project through the promotion and analysis of young migrants' narratives. The sample consisted of 12 focus groups and 24 individual interviews at the youth centres where COMICS activities were undertaken.

Similarly to COMICS, the third research project was interested in young migrants' narratives, to explore their semantic of political participation. The research project entitled *Ri-Generazioni* (*Re-Generations* 2008–2011) was supported by the Scandicci Town Council (Tuscany) and consisted of 18 focus groups and 48 individual interviews, taking place in youth centres managed by the Scandicci local authority. As for *Intendiamoci*, the fourth research project was not primarily interested in political participation; rather, it aimed to explore self-narratives of young people who, at the moment of the interviews, were not employed, in education or in training. However, data produced in the research 'A socio-cultural analysis of risk, trust and affectivity in young people groups' (*Risk/Trust* 2012–2014) showed that political engagement was an important aspect of young migrants' narratives. The data was produced through 24 focus groups and 25 individual interviews, again taking place in youth centres in the Region Emilia-Romagna.

Two different non-probabilistic sampling methods were used in the research projects. The first one was *purposive sampling*, which was used for the two evaluations of social interventions. Both evaluative studies were therefore limited only to young people who were involved in the projects. The second sampling method was *convenience sampling*, used in two studies targeted at young people within delimitated areas. For those research projects, subjects meeting the selection criteria (employment status and age for one research, age only for the other) were approached in collaboration with local social services, and their inclusion was dependent on their willingness to be interviewed. Notwithstanding different aims, the four research projects share similar methodology, consisting of the promotion of young people's narratives to support a phenomenological description of their semantics of social participation. Narrative analysis is an extension of the interpretive approaches within the social sciences. Narratives lend themselves to a qualitative enquiry in order to capture the rich data within stories. Narrative analysis takes the story itself as the object of study; thus the focus is on how individuals or groups make sense of events and actions in their lives through examining the story they produce (Riessman 1993, 2008). This approach to study is not new to qualitative sociology. Sociology has had a history of ethnographic study including the analysis of personal accounts. However, with ethnography it is the events described and not the stories created that are the object of investigation: language is viewed as a medium that reflects singular meanings.

Under the narrative movement and criticisms of positivism, the question of textual objectivity has been challenged by social constructionism (Gergen 1997), encouraging many to approach narratives as social constructions, which are social in the sense that they are exchanged between people. As such, life stories are a linguistic unit involved in social interactions and are therefore cultural products in their content and form (Linde 2001). Language is therefore seen as deeply constitutive of reality, not merely a device for establishing meaning. Stories do not reflect the world out there, but are constructed, rhetorical and interpretive (Riessman 1993), lending themselves to a phenomenological analysis.

Linde's (2001) concept of life stories as cultural products and Riessman's (1993) interactive rhetoric inform the methodology of all four research projects, allowing an approach to interviews as a (multi)cultural product of a dialogue co-constructed and continuously re-interpreted by the researcher and the participants. The narrative approach to the analysis of interviews applied in the four investigations hereby presented is posited to have the ability to capture social representations 'in the making'. Narrative analysis is well suited to study subjectivity and identity largely because of the importance given to imagination and the human involvement in constructing a story, allowing an analysis of how culturally contingent and historically contingent the terms, beliefs and issues narrators address are (Rosenwald and Ochberg 1992; Gill 2001).

Participant narratives across all four research projects were promoting dialogical forms of communication, acknowledging that participants in social research actively to construct meanings and social practices, influencing the cultural and social situations in which they are involved (James et al. 1998; Baraldi and Iervese 2012). Inspired by Mercer and Littleton's (2007) research on dialogic teaching, dialogic research is defined here as that in which all participants make substantial and significant contributions and through which thinking or themes are promoted to move forward, and through which researcher and participants mutually encourage each other to participate actively. Dialogic research requires facilitation of interaction, in which the researcher is an organiser of participation, and mutual learning (see Holdsworth 2005). Facilitative dialogic research is a specific form of social research based on methodologies of facilitation.

The practice of facilitation emphasises the production of different perspectives, in displaying and managing predefined assumptions, doubts, divergent interpretations, different stories, experiences and unpredicted emotions. Facilitation enhances and manages different perspectives. In interactions generated by social research, facilitation makes it possible to coordinate and manage active participation and relationships and promote mutual learning-outcome through post-activity feedback and reflection.

Results and Discussion

Narratives produced by young migrants converge in suggesting the criticism of the idea of cultural identity as an 'essential' identity, something given and fixed (Hofstede 1980; Ting Toomey 1999). The researches presented in this contribution support a different theoretical claim, underpinned by social constructivism, advancing the idea that cultural identity is negotiated in public discourse and interaction (Baraldi 2009; Holliday 2011; Piller 2011; Zhu Hua 2014). Data collected in the four social research projects invites us to consider political participation as a crucial context of the construction of cultural identity through social practices.

In this chapter, an English rendition of the original narratives in the Italian language will be provided, aiming to reproduce participants' linguistic choices and style. Excerpts from the intercultural dialogue co-constructed by the researcher and the participants will be used to support the discussion of data. In line with its methodological premises, this chapter approaches personal narratives as constructed through multicultural dialogue, that is, a social *process* rather than an *object*. For this reason, the discussion that will follow should not be understood as an attempt to distil some cultural characteristics of young migrants as a social group; rather, the aim of the chapter is to discuss how personal narratives contribute to the negotiation and co-construction of multicultural identities.

MARGINALISATION IN THE EDUCATION SYSTEM

Participants' narratives emphasise the importance of agency in the construction of the meaning of their social experiences. Agency is observed when individual actions are not considered as determined by another subject (James 2009; James and James 2008, Baraldi 2015), although the concept of agency implies that individuals '... interact with the social conditions in which they find themselves' (Moosa-Mitha 2005: 380), acknowledging limitations imposed by social constraints (Bjerke 2011; James 2009; James and James 2008; Moosa-Mitha 2005; Valentine 2011; Wyness 2014). Agency and its social conditions are visible in social interactions (Bae 2012; Baraldi 2014; Bjerke 2011; Harre and van Langenhove 1999), where agency can be observed in the availability of choices of action and the agent's possibility to exercise a personal judgement and to choose according to it (Dahlberg and Moss 2005; Markstrom and Hallden 2009; Moss 2009).

In the data sets considered, participants' narratives present a situation of limited agency in the education system. This is not surprising, as a tradition of sociological research on education points out that education is interested in standardised role performances, rather than agency (Parsons and Bales 1955; Sinclair and Coulthard 1975; Mehan 1979; Vanderstraeten 2004; Farini 2011; Walsh 2011; Luhmann 2012). The following excerpt is taken from the *Intendiamoci* research; a student from a migrant background is sharing a narrative that represents a form of categorisation.

Modena, Intendiamoci, December 2006 School is the most difficult thing, because if you have problems, then you see that they really expect you to have problems; before you start because you come from a different place. A bad assignment and you are in need of support, but this is not the same for Italian students. They are told to study more, not that they need support, in a way that it is up to them, not up to support they receive, which is somehow more respectful.

Irrespectively of their individuality, migrant students are categorised as members of a problematic group; such membership informs their position in the education system and the interpretation of their contributions. The language used to convey the narrative, and in particular the distinction of respect or lack of respect indicates that the student perceives the ethnic-based categorisation as a negation of his agency.

Tilly's (1998) idea that inequality becomes embedded in any organisational structure may help in further analysing this interesting aspect of participants' narratives. Tilly (ibid.) elaborates an inventory of causal mechanisms through which categorical inequality is generated and sustained. Tilly (ibid.) argues that certain kinds of social structural relations are solutions to problems generated within social systems, for instance the problem of trust. Educational interaction creates, through selective events, categorical forms of inequality. Durable, categorical distinctions make it easier to know who to trust and who to exclude, and categorical inequalities become stable features of organisation, enhancing the stability of educational relationships. In education, inequality among individual performances and goal attainment is a structural feature of social relationships and an expected output of the system. Tilly (1998: 15) distils the core explanation of categorical inequality to three positions:

1. Organisationally installed categorical inequality reduces risks. Categorical inequalities sustain in the risky choice to accord or not trust. This is a claim about the effects of categorical inequality on the stability of organisational relationships: the former stabilises the latter.
2. Organisations whose survival depends on stability therefore tend to adopt categorical inequality. This is a selection argument: the functional trait, categorical inequality, is adopted because it is functional.

3. Because organisations adopting categorical inequality deliver greater returns to their dominant members and because a portion of those returns goes to organisational maintenance, such organisations tend to crowd out other types of organisations.

For educational organisations the limitation of risk offered by institutional distrust frees resources for the attainment of curricular goals via the exclusion of categories of students. In educational situations, categorical distinctions stabilise social relationships, but also positions of marginalisation (with regard to migrant students, see Devine 2013). Institutional trust and institutional distrust may be understood as consequences of the operations through which educational organisations reproduce themselves. The two following excerpts illustrate Tilly's (1998) theory: categorical inequalities contribute to the stabilisation of marginalisation.

Piacenza, Risk/Trust, June 2013 I feel that teachers genuinely want migrants to succeed, but they are anxious because they have this idea that migrants have problems and it is enough to be a bit slower that they run around asking for help and you are not seen as the same as others anymore. But maybe you just need time. This makes it hard ... you may learn Italian but you do not feel like part of the school as the others. Also because when it is said that you need support no one can see what you can do already: you become a preoccupation.

Scandicci, Ri-Generazioni, May 2009 I used to study at the Liceo (selective school comparable to Grammar School in England), *this is what my parents fancied, I suppose. They had that idea that Liceo is for future medical doctors. However, after a single month teachers told me 'fine if you stay with us to listen, but maybe it is better to look for a different school'. This was because it was decided that I was not going to pass. They said that I was showing issues but I think that really the issue was because I am a migrant and they are quick to see you as a failure after just one bad month, because this is what they expect you to do, to fail because you are like that. I was determined to achieve, leaving was no choice of mine.*

The narratives promoted in the research presented here introduce another form of marginalisation that does not concern the educational careers of migrant students but their access to contexts of personal affective relationships, which is an important aspect of the school experience.

The following expert taken from the COMICS research can support a discussion of this form of marginalisation.

Modena, COMICS, January 2008 (Focus Group)

Josie: *I am doing quite well at school, well I am getting better, but still I feel isolated and unhappy.*
Researcher: *Do people exclude you?*
Josie: *No one really does, the system does. They push you back as they think that you are not quite there with guys of your age because of the language, basically.*
Researcher: *Push you back?*
Josie: *Back to a classroom with children that are younger, even three years younger. They are CHILDREN. Of course they do not fancy you and you think they are a bit boring, so to speak. You feel quite alone for the many hours you spend at school.*
Rita: *You may develop language while doing easy stuff with children, but you are left behind with friendship. I feel embarrassed with friends outside, I have only children's antics to share, after a while it is not funny.*

Research suggests that classrooms are contexts of peer-relationships based on affectivity and personal choices that can be therefore observed as expressions of agency (Patrick et al. 2007; Farini 2008; Baraldi and Iervese 2014). Participants' narratives clearly present a semantics of the classroom as a context of peer-socialisation and expression of agency. However, they experience unfavourable conditions for developing interpersonal relationships at school due to educational strategies aimed to support academic achievement, but detrimental for their inclusion in the peer groups.

Removed from their age group at school (*being pushed back*, in the vocabulary of Italian school practices), young migrants experience reduced opportunities for agency: personal affective relationships are simply not viable with much younger classmates. The pedagogical strategy deployed to allow young migrants to familiarise themselves with the education system and to develop linguistic competence at a slower pace supports a process of marginalisation from what participants see as the 'proper peer groups'; such marginalisation can be understood as a latent function of the manifest functions (support of development) of education. As suggested by Deleuze and Guattari (1987), enlightened practices can deny the dignity of self-determination, objectivising certain subjects.

FROM MARGINALISATION TO THE INVENTION OF NEW FORMS OF INCLUSION: SCHOOL ACTIVISM

Participants' narratives concerning inclusion in the political system develop around their distrust in the concrete possibility of agency, connected to their citizenship status. It is possible to utilise the concept of agency (presented in the opening paragraph of the previous section) as a conceptual tool to understand the position of young migrants. While young migrants can make political autonomous choices, such choices are not visible in the political system, due to a limited access to political rights. This prevents their preferences to make a difference. Using Bateson's (1972) vocabulary, the informative value of young migrants' internal difference (their political preference) for the political system is nullified by exclusion from political rights. This short excerpt from the COMICS research illustrates the divergence between personal engagement and lack of agency due to citizenship status.

Modena, COMICS, February 2008 Politics is like football for me, I pick my team, I watch, I get angry if a team I hate wins, but I will be never good enough to play, because I am not good enough, I am no citizen.

Taylor's (1989) historical account of the conceptualisations of human value may support a discussion on the above excerpt, which represents a common form of representation in participants' narratives. According to Taylor (ibid.), in hierarchical societies human value was ranked against the proximity to the owner of the land. Examining the transition from feudal societies to societies based on trade in Western and Southern Europe, Taylor (ibid.) observes a semantic evolution, where human value is a function of dignity, which is taken to be both the possession of and what it is owed to each and every individual, regardless of the conditions of their birth.

However, human value as a structural form does not disappear in trade societies; in order to differentiate grades of human value, the universal and inclusive principle of dignity is coupled with the selective and exclusive principle of 'level of development', which is measured according to separateness from others, self-governance and independence from the claims, wishes and command of others. While Taylor (ibid.) suggests that the function of the combination of development and dignity is to detect a shared quality among aristocracy and bourgeoisie that would otherwise be separated by degrees of honour, such coupling has been the catalyst for semantics of categorical distinction: development is associated with general historical movement (savage against civilised), personal development (child against adult), gender (female against male), ethnicity (black people against white people, white people of the south against white people of the north).

The coupling between dignity and development is still accepted in the public discourse only regarding generational order, although being the object of criticism, particularly from the area of childhood studies (Wyness 2014; Leonard 2016). However, its underpinning structure, that is, the coupling between the inclusive principle of dignity and an exclusive principle, still generates social semantics. An example of this consists in the coupling between dignity and assumed limited school readiness in migrant students (Herrlitz and Maier 2005; Grant and Portera 2011) or in the coupling between agency and citizenship status within legal and political systems. The following expert is taken from the *Ri-Generazioni* research, part of a narrative shared by a migrant young man.

Scandicci, Ri-Generazioni, May 2010 I think that if rights are also about what you can potentially do, maybe you won't but you are not prevented, I mean offering you possibilities, I do not have rights. Or I have less than Italians in Italy. I cannot vote or I can dream of changing the town but I cannot really as I will never be a candidate. Unless I change myself and become Italian in the passport, but this would be like changing to have rights that others have for what they are.

A discussion of the narratives represented by the above excerpt may develop from the ideas that while dignity generates inclusive and universal human rights, citizenship generates exclusive and conditional personal rights (Mattheis 2012). The multicultural dialogue co-constructed by the researcher and the participants indicates that young migrants position themselves at the centre of the paradoxical coupling between dignity and citizenship. The two excerpts shown below, from 2006 to 2013, suggest the persistence of marginalisation and inequality in young migrants' narratives concerning their political participation.

Modena, Intendiamoci, December 2006, Focus Group

Nicu: *At the end of the day I am not really anyone while I feel quite secure about who I am and what I like.*
Researcher: *What do you mean?*
Nicu: *I am not Romanian, well I am but I do not live like one, I live like an Italian, but I am not.*
Amadou: *I am really into politics, I just do not understand the guys who do not care, which is stupid because it is like one who does not care about his body and illness, illness and politics that affect your life. I spend lots of time watching all the debates and shows with politicians and when I go to the Internet Café it is not only a movie but also political news, and international. But while I think it is serious stuff, then I also realise that it is not, because I cannot do much with all of my information, I cannot vote or being a candidate. So it is like a game really if you cannot be of it, and I am not sure if am not wasting my time as the guys who play with NES or Playstation.*
Paulo: *I made up my mind a lot of time ago about politics but I cannot choose in practice, I have no choice but I would know what to choose.*

Cesena, Risk/Trust, June 2013 My idea is that one thing is the passport, another thing is who you are. Because of the passport I am still a guest, a kind of visitor, but I do not feel like one. What are my interests when being heard and to do things here, so I think I am not the data in the passport but the person in the photograph, who wants to be part but cannot as others can. It is a struggle.

These narratives suggest that young migrants do not experience the negation of their human rights, but the exclusion from 'personal rights', and therefore the exclusion from some social domains. The conditional access to personal rights is exemplified by the exclusion from political rights. While the semantics of rights is based on the dogmatic of human dignity (Teubner 1988, 2010), human dignity that does not presuppose human essence; on the contrary, it is the individuality of persons that is constructed in the social sphere by help of rights. This statement may help to conceptualise the connection advanced by young migrants' narratives, between categorical inequalities (exclusion from political rights) and marginalisation in situations of limited agency. However, this is only a possible outcome of categorical inequalities. Another possible outcome is that the excluded groups construct forms of oppositional solidarities. This is suggested by the excerpt below, from the COMICS research.

Modena, COMICS, March 2008 I was feeling isolated and really sad for a while, and angry because I was feeling I was not listened to at school and not be quite like the others outside. It has been quite bad recently; because of the elections I really wanted to be heard but I knew I am no citizen of Italy. Then I see the French guys get out in the street, for the right to a decent job. They are not really touched because they are still students, but they want to make a difference for the people in the here and now. And I realised that you do not need to vote to do it. When it was the students' strike I just joined the guys of the strike because here is not different from France. I do not feel out of place when we have a meeting. I want to join a Union because it is what you want for the future that matters not where you come from.

The excerpt introduces a social process emerging from many narratives that can be discussed by making use of the concept of *unintended consequence*. Merton (1957) analyses types and determinants of unanticipated consequences of purposive action. For Merton (ibid.) the functions of a social practice are its 'observable objective consequences'. Manifest functions are those outcomes that are intended and recognised by the agents concerned; latent functions are those outcomes that are neither intended nor recognised. Although the distinction between manifest and latent functions has been the object of critical review (Campbell 1982, Portes 2000; Farini 2012), the concept of unintended consequences can help understanding participants' narratives. Categorical forms of inequality set in motion a pattern of contradictory effects. Participants' narratives suggest that the exclusion from political rights generates political participation and the access to contexts where fluid identities are constructed and negotiated in multicultural dialogue. *School activism* describes the process of re-inclusion in the political system, based on trust commitments and the development of multicultural personal relationships.

The previous section discussed how participants' narratives indicate that the construction of categorical inequalities in education activates a vicious circle between institutionalised distrust and marginalisation (Luhmann 1988). The effects of marginalisation extend to trust in peer-relationships due to strategies to support young migrants' academic achievement. In particular, removing young migrants from their age group at school and placing them in a younger cohort prevents the construction of person-centred relationships and trust based on affectivity. For Luhmann (ibid.), while trust enlarges the range of possible actions in a social system, distrust restricts this range in that it requires additional premises for social relationships which protect interactants from a disappointment that is considered highly probable. When distrust is established, building trust appears very difficult because the interaction is permeated by trust in distrust.

Although presenting conditions of distrusts and marginalisation, participants' narratives also introduce a counter-process of trust building, based on school activism. In particular, the intercultural narratives collected during the four researches relate school activism to Kelman's (2005) model of trust building. Kelman (ibid.) analyses conditions of radical distrust and building trust in workshops involving Israeli and Palestinian representatives trying to reach peaceful agreements. Kelman (ibid.) argues that in these workshops trust was built through successive approximations of increasing degrees of commitment, starting from the building of a feeble temporary trust (*working trust*) not committing participants to anything beyond the solution of specific problems. Two excerpts help illustrating this process, taken from the COMICS research and *Ri-Generazioni*.

Modena, COMICS, November 2008 There is a lot to do, because you know we are not many, and you do want as many students as possible attending the debate but also that they understand the meaning of it, not only the free time to smoke and drink. I got friends almost without speaking, just doing things which made sense to all. And another thing is that I understand and master the meaning of my actions and I feel this is reckoned as they trust me as I trust them. I have showed skills and trustworthiness.

Scandicci, Ri-Generazioni, May 2010 What I am excited about all those strikes and protest in the street to save the school against privatisation is that I am not 'someone in deficit' anymore. I am not the struggling one to be helped, but I can help with my thoughts and practical actions. Actually, I was not a friend with any of the guys in the political group. I was working with them before befriending them. You walk in the streets with people you do not know well, but also you know them well in the sense that they share what you want for the future. Of course, then you become friendly with some, actually a good friend and there is something more than befriending someone at the disco. Fun is part of the friendship but really it is what you want from the future that makes you feel closer politically and in a personal sense.

In Kelman's (2005) model, working trust and interpersonal relationships can merge, but only at a later stage of the interaction. Interpersonal closeness is not the basis of (working) trusting commitment. However, interpersonal closeness may follow working trust. The two excerpts represent a diffused aspect of the narratives collected over almost ten years: forms of school activism are the context for the development of working trust through political participation and involvement in activities with peers. Working trust creates the presupposition for trust based on affectivity. Data suggest that working trust supports the visibility of political choices and the development of personal relationships.

Conclusion

Rather than a small-scale reproduction of political rights they are excluded from, young migrants' involvement in political activities in schools is the context for the development of working trust, built on mutual interests and orientated to specific limited objectives. The final series of excerpts illustrates this point:

Piacenza, Risk/Trust, June 2013, Focus Group

Michail: *I met my girlfriend while preparing the solidarity march for Greek students. But this is not because I joined the group looking for girls, it just happened.*

Giga: *This is something that you* (the researcher) *make me think about. Why the same people see you as a failure at school and give you responsibilities in the (political) group? My idea is that here you are known for what you do. You are what you really do, not what you are supposed to be.*

Toni: *We all know that the problem at school is that they look for the easy solution. If I come from Albania and don't do well, this is because I need to adapt quicker. Maybe there are other reasons, the same as Italians who struggle more than me. But you are another struggling Albanian.*

Giga: *I think it was the same for his girlfriend who is Italian and because they work together for the political group, she saw he is not an unfortunate.*

Working trust may be the foundation of personal relationships, adding a new dimension to the semantics of political participation of young people. This new dimension consists in (re)-inclusion based on dialogue, a genuinely social process beyond the centrality of individual agency emphasised by previous research (Percy-Smith 2010; Tholander 2011).

Modena, Intendiamoci, December 2006 I think that soon everyone who lives in the country will be able to vote for a candidate, which makes sense as we all live and share issues and hopes with Italians. But this is not really the point, I understand now. I used to hate Citizenship Education, because it is about rights I do not have. But I understand now and the guys and the workshops and the professor from the University coming and taking about anarchism helped...the thing is not having rights, citizenship is about doing it, doing the citizen. This is what I am, a 'maker', we all are.

Modena, Risk/Trust, June 2013 I cannot be happier than when I am not a Moroccan anymore. It is like being born again, and I think it is the same for the Italian guys there and here. Not you are because you come from but you are something different each time, you are the cause you are fighting for.

Young migrants experience marginalisation in the education system and in the political system. 'School activism' describes a situation where movements and campaigning are contexts of active political participation of young migrants. School activism is an example and the context of the development of trusting relationships with peers, where fluid hybrid identities are negotiated and co-constructed around the person through multicultural dialogue.

Young migrants' narratives present a link between educational practices and a concept of cultural identity as an 'essential' identity, given and fixed (Hofstede 1980; Ting Toomey 1999). The same narratives show that cultural essentialism can generate important problems of intercultural communication, in particular problems of ineffective educational treatment of cultural identity. These problems can become particularly relevant during adolescence, an age in which the construction of identity may be seen as challenging (Fail et al. 2004). However, young migrants' narratives do not only concern processes of marginalisation; they also present school activism as the dialogical construction of cultural identities, through the negotiation of cultural difference in interaction (Holliday 2011; Piller 2011; Nederveen Pieterse 2004; Zhu Hua 2014). Migrant and non-migrant, young people are 'makers', makers of cultural hybridisation through multicultural dialogue.

REFERENCES

Bae, B. (2012). Children and teachers as partners in communication: Focus on spacious and narrow interactional patterns. *International Journal of Early Childhood, 44*(1), 53–69.

Baraldi, C. (Ed.). (2009). *Dialogue in intercultural communities: From and educational point of view.* Amsterdam, Philadelphia: John Benjamin.

Baraldi, C. (2014). Children's participation in communication systems: A theoretical perspective to shape research. *Soul of Society: A Focus on the Live of Children and Youth, 18*(18), 63–92.

Baraldi, C. (2015). Promotion of migrant Children's epistemic status and authority in early school life. *International Journal of Early Childhood, 47*(1), 5–25.

Baraldi, C., & Iervese, V. (Eds.). (2012). *Participation, facilitation, and mediation: Children and young people in their social contexts.* London/New York: Routledge.

Baraldi, C., & Iervese, V. (2014). Observing Children's capabilities as agency. In D. Stoecklin & J. M. Bonvin (Eds.), *Children's rights and the capability approach: Challenges and prospects* (pp. 43–65). Dordrecht: Springer.

Bateson, G. (1972). *Steps to an ecology of mind: Collected essays in anthropology, psychiatry, evolution, and epistemology.* San Francisco: Chandler.

Bjerke, H. (2011). It's the way to do it: Expressions of agency in child-adult relations at home and school. *Children & Society, 25*(2), 93–103.

Campbell, C. (1982). A Dubious distinction: An inquiry into the value and use of Merton's concepts of manifest and latent function. *American Sociological Review, 47*(1), 29–43.

Dahlberg, G., & Moss, P. (2005). *Ethics and politics in early childhood education.* London: Routledge.

Deleuze, G., & Guattari, F. (1987). *A thousand plateaus: Capitalism and schizophrenia.* Minneapolis: University of Minnesota Press.

Devine, D. (2013). Valuing children differently? Migrant children in education. *Children and Society, 27*, 282–294.

Fail, H., Thompson, J., & Walker, G. (2004). Belonging, identity and Third Culture Kids: Life histories of former international school children. *Journal of Research in International Education, 3*(3), 319–338.

Farini, F. (2008). Paths of hybridization through the invention of new cultural forms. In W. Gottwald, M. Klemm, & B. Schulte (Eds.), *KreisLäufe— CircularFlows. Kapillaren der Weltkultur—Capillaries of World Culture* (pp. 155–171). Muenster: LIT.

Farini, F. (2011). Cultures of education in action: Research on the relationship between interaction and cultural presuppositions regarding education in an international educational setting. *Journal of Pragmatics, 43,* 2176–2186.

Farini, F. (2012). Affectivity, expertise, and inequality: Three foundations of trust in education—Reflections on presuppositions, (Unintended) consequences, and possible alternatives. In A. Mica, A. Peisert, & J. Winczorek (Eds.), *Sociology and the unintended: Robert Merton revisited* (pp. 155–167). Frankfurt: Peter Lang.

Farini, F., & Iervese, V. (2006). La ricerca qualitativa. In B. Pezzotta (Ed.), *Children of migrants inclusion creative systems project* (pp. 157–191). Modena: Comune di Modena.

Gergen, K. J. (1997). Who speaks and who replies in human science scholarship? *History of the Human Sciences, 10,* 151–173.

Gill, P. B. (2001). Narrative inquiry: Designing the processes, pathways and patterns of change. *Systems Research and Behavioral Science, 18*(4), 335–344.

Grant, C. A., & Portera, A. (Eds.). (2011). *Intercultural and multicultural education: Enhancing global interconnectedness.* London/New York: Routledge.

Harre, R., & van Langenhove, L. (Eds.). (1999). *Positioning theory.* Oxford: Blackwell.

Herrlitz, W., & Maier, R. (Eds.). (2005). *Dialogue in and around multicultural schools.* Tubingen: Niemeyer.

Hofstede, G. (1980). *Culture's consequences.* London: Sage.

Holdsworth, R. (2005). Taking young people seriously means giving them serious things to do. In J. Mason & T. Fattore (Eds.), *Children taken seriously: In theory, policy and practice.* London: Jessica Kingsley Publishers.

Holliday, A. (2011). *Intercultural communication and ideology.* Thousand Oaks/ London: Sage.

James, A. (2009). Agency. In J. Qvortrup, G. Valentine, W. Corsaro, & M. S. Honig (Eds.), *The Palgrave handbook of childhood studies* (pp. 34–45). Basingstoke: Palgrave.

James, A., & James, A. (2008). *Key concepts in Childhood studies.* London: Sage.

James, A., Jenks, C., & Prout, A. (1998). *Theorizing Childhood.* Oxford: Polity Press.

Kelman, H. (2005). Building trust among enemies: The central challenge for international conflict resolution. *International Journal of Intercultural Relations, 29,* 639–650.

Leonard, M. (2016). *The sociology of children, childhood and generation.* London: Sage.

Linde, C. (2001). Narrative and social tacit knowledge. *Journal of Knowledge Management, 5*(2), 160–170.

Luhmann, N. (1988). Familiarity, confidence, trust: Problems and alternatives. In D. Gambetta (Ed.), *Trust: Making and breaking cooperative relations* (pp. 94–107). Oxford: Department of Sociology University of Oxford.

Luhmann, N. (2012). *Theory of society.* Stanford: Stranford University Press.

Markström, A., & Hallden, G. (2009). Children's strategies for agency in preschool. *Children & Society, 23*(2), 112–122.

Mattheis, C. (2012). The system theory of Niklas Luhmann and the constitutionalization of the World society. *Goettingen Journal of International Law, 4*(2), 625–647.

Mercer, C., & Littleton, K. (2007). *Dialogue and development of children's thinking.* London: Routledge.

Mehan, H. (1979). *Learning lessons.* Cambridge: Harvard University Press.

Merton, R. K. (1957). *Social theory and social structure.* Glencoe: Free Press.

Moosa-Mitha, M. (2005). A difference-centred alternative to theorization of children's citizenship rights. *Citizenship Studies, 9,* 369–388.

Moss, P. (2009). *There are alternatives! Markets and democratic experimentalism in early childhood education and care.* Working Paper 53. The Hague: Bernard Van Leer Foundation.

Nederveen Pieterse, J. (2004). *Globalization & culture.* Lanham: Rowman & Littlefield.

Parsons, T., & Bales, R. F. (1955). *Family, socialization and interaction process.* Glencoe: Free Press.

Patrick, H., Ryan, A., & Kaplan, A. (2007). 'Early adolescents' perceptions of the classroom social environment, motivational beliefs, and engagement. *Journal of Educational Psychology, 99,* 83–98.

Percy-Smith, B. (2010). Councils, consultation and community: Rethinking the spaces for children and young people's participation. *Children's Geographies, 8*(2), 107–122.

Piller, I. (2011). *Intercultural communication: A critical introduction.* Edinburgh: Edinburgh University Press.

Portes, A. (2000). The Hidden Abode: Sociology as analysis of the unexpected. *American Sociological Review, 65,* 1–18.

Riessman, C. K. (1993). *Narrative analysis.* Newbury Park: Sage.

Riessman, C. K. (2008). *Narrative methods for the human sciences.* Los Angeles: Sage.

Rosenwald, G. C., & Ochberg, R. L. (Eds.). (1992). *Storied lives: The cultural politics of self-understanding.* New Haven: Yale University Press.

Sinclair, J., & Coulthard, M. (1975). *Towards an analysis of discourse: The English used by teachers and pupils.* Oxford: Oxford University Press.

Taylor, C. (1989). *Sources of the self: The making of the modern identity.* Cambridge: Harvard University Press.
Tilly, C. (1998). *Durable inequality.* Berkeley: University of California Press.
Teubner, G. (1988). *Autopoietic law: A new approach to law and society.* Berlin: de Gruyter.
Teubner, G. (2010). Constitutionalising polycontexturality. *Social and Legal Studies, 19,* 327–341.
Tholander, M. (2011). Student-led conferencing as democratic practice. *Children and Society, 25,* 239–250.
Ting Toomey, S. (1999). *Communication across cultures.* New York: The Guilford Press.
Valentine, K. (2011). Accounting for agency. *Children & Society, 25,* 347–358.
Vanderstraeten, R. (2004). The social differentiation of the educational system. *Sociology, 38*(2), 255–272.
Walsh, S. (2011). *Exploring classroom discourse: Language in action.* New York/London: Routledge.
Wyness, M. (2014). *Childhood.* London: Polity.
Zhu Hua. (2014). *Exploring intercultural communication: Language in action.* London/New York: Routledge.

Federico Farini received his PhD in Sociology of Intercultural Relations from the University of Modena and Reggio Emilia, where he worked as a researcher in Sociology of Education. From 2013 to 2015 he was lecturer in education at Middlesex University, where he was a founding member of the Centre for Educational Research and Scholarship. In 2015 he joined the University of Suffolk as senior lecturer in Sociology of Early Childhood. Federico has published books, chapters and articles and edited books in Italian, English and Slovenian language. In 2014 he was elected as vice-president of the International Sociological Association Research Committee 25, 'Language in Society'.

Greek Roma in Higher Education: Perceptions and Experiences of Educational Success

Panagiota Gkofa

INTRODUCTION

The purpose of this chapter is to discuss the perceptions, constructions and experiences of educational success of some Greek Roma who have entered higher education. Children from Roma communities are amongst the lowest academic achievers in many European countries (Symeou et al. 2009) and the same is true in Greece. In contrast to the usual emphasis on the educational disadvantage of Greek Roma, my study examined cases of Greek Roma who entered university. Informed by the theoretical framework of Pierre Bourdieu, this chapter intends to examine how some Greek Roma who have entered higher education describe educational success and the extent to which they consider themselves to be successful. This chapter begins with contextualising Roma's education in Greece. The next section draws on literature on educational success to provide an understanding of the terminology used. This is followed by the theoretical framework of my research. Next, the methodological approach followed in my doctoral study, which provided the data used in this chapter, is

P. Gkofa (✉)
King's College, University of London, London, UK

R. Race (ed.), *Advancing Multicultural Dialogues in Education*,
DOI 10.1007/978-3-319-60558-6_7

presented. The perceptions, constructions and experiences of educational success of some Greek Roma who have entered higher education are discussed in this chapter to provide a better understanding of Roma's educational success in Greece and contribute to advancing multicultural dialogues in education more widely.

Contextualising the Roma and Their Education in Greece

In the Greek national context, the Roma are Greek citizens but not officially recognised as a national or linguistic minority group (Kostadinova 2011). Thus, little reliable data about the Roma in Greece has been collected (Dragonas 2012). It is estimated that there are around 230,000 Roma in Greece; most are familiar with and use their community language, Romani (Nikolaou 2009). Many Roma in Greece are settled residents and are traders (Markou 2008). In Greece, the Roma are frequently reviled and discriminated against.

As far as their education is concerned, Roma students experience high dropout rates (Mavrommatis 2008; Kostouli and Mitakidou 2009), low performance, higher levels of non-completion compared to their Greek (non-Roma) peers and hostility coming from educators and peers (Nikolaou 2009). Dragonas (2012) has documented the ways in which they continue to experience forms of segregation in educational settings, such as being educated in separate classes inside the mainstream school or allocated to schools which, in some cases, end up with a Roma-only intake. However, there are some Roma students who have progressed in education, against the odds, and thus, I refer to them using the term 'educational success'.

Educational Success: Terminology

In the field of sociology of education, a growing interest in the experiences of students deemed to be educationally successful has emerged worldwide (Gewirtz and Cribb 2009). Yet there are relatively few accounts that compare different conceptions of educational success. Hoskins (2010) had collected and analysed a variety of sources that dealt with the meaning of success. She concluded that success can be viewed as an unfolding and continuous process. She argued that success is frequently conceptualised as a road to be travelled, a journey with the promise of arriving at a destination with the realisation of achievement (Leatz 1993, cited in Hoskins 2010). Success is also characterised as the fulfilment of individual goals. In contrast, for Jones (2004, cited in Hoskins 2010), success is not a destination but an ongoing process. Hoskins (2010) also detailed the view of occupational success often evident in management literature as being portrayed as a ladder, characterised by achieving a series of goals or meeting certain criteria. For instance, Sturges (1999), in her study of how managers describe what career success means to them, identified (a) external criteria (in material terms, such as position in the hierarchy and level of pay), (b) internal criteria for success (e.g. feelings of accomplishment, enjoyment and achievement) and (c) intangible criteria (influence and personal recognition). Thus, there are different ways of understanding the concept of success and educational success. However, there is a common factor presented in most attempts to describe educational success: the notion of achievement of a goal.

Based on research into academic/educational success, the following features emerge as signals of educational success: entrance/attendance at highly rated educational institutions (Power et al. 2003; Byfield 2008; Reay et al. 2009; Ingram 2011; Wright 2011), passing milestone exams (Ingram 2011), high performance (Power et al. 2003; Rhamie 2007; Rollock 2007a, b; Archer 2008; Reay et al. 2009; Ingram 2011; Wright 2011), better achievement compared to others (e.g. peers and parents) (Power et al. 2003), promise/perspective of future progression (Power et al. 2003; Ingram 2009) and self-improvement (Rollock 2007a, b; Archer 2008). These features are summed up in Fig. 1.

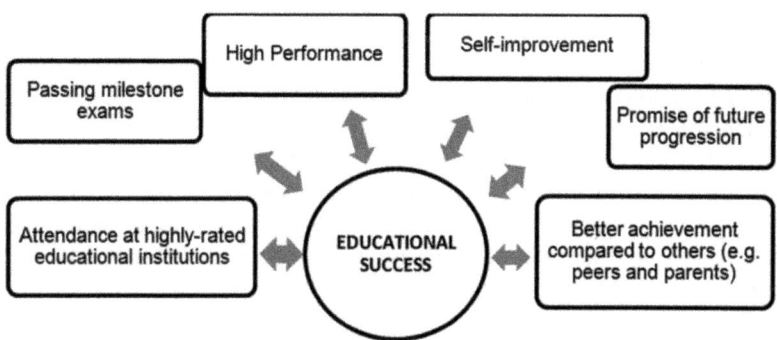

Fig. 1 Features of the concept of educational success

In my study, I take Roma's entrance to higher education as a marker of educational success as only a few Roma have achieved this 'against the odds'. My description of success as access to higher education is informed by the criterion of passing or failing milestone exams, because students enter Greek higher education on the basis of the results of the national (Panhellenic) exams at the end of high school. Moreover, my approach was affected by the high symbolic value of higher studies in Greece; the long-standing belief in upward social mobility through education is well-established in Greek society (Sianou-Kyrgiou and Tsiplakides 2011) because, for many decades, higher education has been the means to improve occupational conditions and social-class positions (Livanos 2010; Themelis 2013).

Theoretical Underpinnings

The role attributes such as class, culture and familiarity with the system play in students' educational progression have been discussed as forms of capital by Pierre Bourdieu (2004). 'Economic capital' refers to money and property rights (Bourdieu 2004). The financial resources of the participants are significant, because, in many European countries, the Roma live in poverty (Symeou et al. 2009) and the same is true in Greece where the income of the majority Roma households is below the poverty line (EC 2009).

In Bourdieu's theory, the concept of 'cultural capital' is key in explaining academic success. 'Cultural capital' refers to the long-lasting dispositions of the mind and body of the students (embodied state), their access to cultural goods, such as pictures, books and instruments (objectified state) and their educational qualifications (institutionalised state). Moreover, the relationships of 'mutual acquaintance and recognition' (Bourdieu and Wacquant 1992, p. 119) an individual or a group has with others are also considered by Bourdieu, under the term 'social capital', as influencing educational progression. In my study, social capital relates to the (Roma and non-Roma) social networks of the participants and also the education values in circulation in these networks.

'Habitus' is another central concept when examining educational success, because it 'underlies the structuring of school experiences' (Bourdieu 2006, p. 87). Habitus:

> ... is an objective basis for regular modes of behaviour, and thus for the regularity of modes of practice... Agents who are equipped with it will behave in a certain way in certain circumstances. (Bourdieu 1990, p. 77)

Habitus is primarily structured by early experiences in the family (Bourdieu 2006) and thus 'reflects the social position in which it was constructed' (Reay 2004, pp. 434–435); however, it is continually restructured by other contexts. Therefore, habitus can transcend the social conditions of its production (Reay 2004). The possibility of one's habitus' transformation is crucial for understanding how some participants succeed in education 'against the odds'. In this chapter, I use 'capital' and 'habitus' in order to better understand the participants' perceptions and experiences of educational success.

METHODOLOGY

Twenty Greek Roma who have entered higher education were interviewed for the purposes of my study (see Table 1). These participants are a 'hard to reach' group (Trevor and Newburn 2001) because no official data about

Table 1 Research participants

Name	Gender	Age	Type of studies	Occupation
Alcmene	F	25	Philology	She gives Greek language lessons—Mediator (programme for Roma's education)
Antigone	F	25	Political Sciences	Mediator (programme for Roma's education)
Athena	F	35	Nursing	Nurse
Demosthenes	M	20	Engineering	Student
Electra	F	20	Balkan, Slavic and Oriental Studies	Student
Hector	M	25	Finance	Military Service
Hippocrates	M	50	Medicine	Doctor
Ifigeneia	F	35	Law	Politician
Iphicles	M	25	Engineering	Student
Ismene	F	25	Finance	She works at an employment agency
Jason	M	30	Translation	Student—Mediator (programme for Roma's education)
Laertes	M	30	Law	Lawyer
Miltiades	M	40	Molecular Microbiology	He works for a pharmaceutical company abroad

(*continued*)

Table 1   (continued)

Name	Gender	Age	Type of studies	Occupation
Nestor	M	55	Sociology	He is conducting his PhD in Roma issues; involved in Roma programmes
Paris	M	20	Accounting	Student—Mediator (programme for Roma's education)
Patroclus	M	25	Accounting	Student
Pericles	M	25	Social Administration	Student
Pylades	M	20	Social Anthropology	Student
Theaetetus	M	35	Theology	Priest-Monk
Theagenes	M	20	Engineering	Student

Roma students are collected by any Greek higher institutions. Gatekeepers (such as NGOs, Roma organisations, academics at Greek universities, people working at the Greek Ministry of Education) facilitated my contacts with potential participants. Finally, I accessed these participants through snowballing techniques, 'from one case to the next' (Flick 2009, 110). The audio-recorded interviews were transcribed into text (in Greek; all participants spoke Greek fluently). A process of thematic coding and analysis was followed (Strauss and Corbin 1998). This chapter presents the data related to the participants' perceptions and experiences of success.

DESCRIPTIONS OF EDUCATIONAL SUCCESS

'Educational success' appeared to be understood by the participants of my study in multiple ways. Although I started my research with an initial perspective that the participants have 'made it', the participants' views were quite different. In particular, only eight participants (8/20) explicitly recognised themselves as successful.

'Objective' and 'Relative' Indicators

In many studies which examine issues related to educational success, passing specific exams or a student's achievement in a significant examination serves as a starting point for characterising a student as educationally successful (Rollock 2007a; Archer 2008; Ingram 2009; Ingram 2011).

A similar rationale was adopted by the majority of the participants of my study who related educational success with high achievement in the nationwide exams taken at the end of high school and with entering higher education. Twelve out of twenty participants understood educational success in relation to access to higher education. For example, Jason said 'entering university is undoubtedly an achievement of success'.

However, some participants introduced 'relative' indicators when describing the educational success achieved by Roma students reflecting an understanding of educational success as 'better achievement compared to others (e.g. peers and parents)' (Power et al. 2003). These participants highlighted the difficulties that Roma students still face in Greek schools, such as the high numbers of student dropout and lower attainment levels than their peers (Nikolaou 2009; Kostouli and Mitakidou 2009), in order to describe Roma's entrance to university as educational success. Although, according to Demosthenes, entering university is not a noteworthy success as, nowadays, this is achieved by the majority of secondary school students, when referring to Roma, higher studies are taken as evidence of educational success because Roma people who study "are an exception to the rule" (*Demosthenes*). Iphicles followed a similar rationale explaining that higher education constitutes success for the Roma, as this is unusual for most of them. Electra had found it strange that journalists wanted to interview her about her entrance to university because she had never felt she had achieved anything exceptional. However, she realises that non-Roma people consider her achievement as evidence of success as the fact that she entered university indicates that there are other options for Roma children. According to Pylades, as long as most Roma drop out, even school attendance is an indicator of educational success.

Hippocrates emphasised the role of locality in Roma's success. First, he took access to higher education as an 'objective' indicator of educational success. However, he recognised the 'relative' character of success in relation to each local context taking into account assets of Roma's capital—economic, cultural and in some cases social—in specific locales. For example, he argued that in areas where Roma live in good conditions (high economic capital), completion of compulsory education would not have been regarded highly enough in order to characterise a Roma as successful because local conditions (such as housing and good financial situation) enable higher levels of educational progression. However, according to Hippocrates, in other Roma locales, where the economic (and also cultural and social) capital of the Roma is low, even completion of primary school might constitute success.

Ifigeneia followed an understanding of educational success in terms of promise/perspective of future progression (Power et al. 2003; Ingram 2009) and self-improvement (Rollock 2007a, b; Archer 2008). She explained that in order to be realistic, she considers the completion of compulsory education as evidence of educational success for Roma pupils. She hopes that, some years into the future, she could describe the educational success of Roma in terms of completion of high school with some promising rates of Roma entrance to university. Ifigeneia sees success for Roma, in the main, as their following predominant non-Roma patterns in terms of their occupation:

> Successful Roma are those who get qualified to become hairdressers, plumbers, electricians ... those who are qualified enough to exercise a profession different than selling [fruits] in the street market...

Alcmene took the above argument further by explaining that she also regards those Roma graduating from technical high schools—and not only those who enter university—as educationally successful. She noted that these Roma are successful because their training enables them to become qualified electricians and mechanics and get better jobs (compared to the jobs most Roma have) with higher earnings. In this context, it seems understandable why both Laertes and Pericles characterised Roma entering university as an 'excess of educational success'.

Educational Success Seen as Internal Cultivation

The way the participants linked higher studies with educational success was complex. Some participants introduced a 'utilitarian' rationale which sees higher studies/educational success as a means to achieve professional success, applying external criteria, such as position in the hierarchy and earnings, to describe success (Sturges 1999). For example, Nestor regarded a university degree as evidence of success which helps a person's professional pathway.

However, internal criteria, such as feelings of accomplishment, enjoyment and achievement (Sturges 1999), were also deployed by some participants. Six participants described educational success in terms of a person's internal cultivation. For example, Alcmene explained that it is not the higher certificate that makes somebody educationally successful; it is the 'way of thinking which starts to change (during higher studies) and the critical stance you start to gain'. Electra eloquently noted that 'educationally successful is the person who is internally educated and is able to internally educate the others'. Moreover, Patroclus, Nestor, Theagenes and Alcmene explicitly linked the concept of educational success with 'intangible criteria' (Sturges 1999): 'recognition' in terms of gaining respect and 'influence' in terms of inspiring others or offering help to others, mainly inside the Roma community.

This 'intangible' approach to educational success (Sturges 1999) was expressed by almost all the participants when they referred to their personal pathways. In particular, most participants try to help other Roma in active ways through participating in political parties, volunteer organisations, Roma educational programmes, small-scale local interventions or even through their professions (e.g. Hippocrates, who is a doctor, offers his services to Roma patients for free). Moreover, they aspire to serve as positive examples for younger Roma as their entrance in higher education seems noteworthy and potentially helpful to others inside the Roma community. As Alcmene commented:

> Roma's success stories can help Roma's education because these Roma serve as positive examples; they show that Roma's success can be achieved. Because there is the opposite opinion frequently presented ... 'We are Roma. Are we going to study? Are we going to attend school? These are non-Roma things'...(But I am saying) and so what? ... Where is the difference? (Education) is a road that we can all enter. There is nothing to hold somebody back ...

Alcmene's argument regarding the possibility of Roma's educational success is confirmed by studies which have started to examine contexts where the Roma have experienced some educational success. For instance, Bhopal and Myers (2009) talked of the inclusive ethos as well as some school inclusionary processes and examples of 'good practice' in primary and secondary schools for Roma students in the UK. Moreover, Kende's (2007) research with Roma university students in Hungary and Abajo and Carrasco's (2004, as quoted in Bereményi and Carrasco 2015, p. 154) study on the Roma in Spain have examined examples of Roma's educational success.

On the basis of the participants' perceptions presented above, I could argue that, although 'objective' elements, such as access to higher education, appear significant, educational success is not a clear-cut one-dimensional concept. In some cases, traditional patterns which are considered to predominate in the Roma community as a part of Roma's habitus (e.g. gendered attitudes) seem to play a role in the way meaning is given to the concept of success by the participants. The participants' understandings of educational success vary, despite the fact that they are all positioned as being 'educationally successful' in my study because they have entered higher education.

FEELINGS OF SUCCESS

The twenty Roma in my sample were selected as cases of educationally successful Roma as they had all entered higher education. Eight participants described themselves as successful because they studied at university. For example, Hippocrates said: 'Simply the fact that I studied Medicine is a success (per se)'. A similar rationale was followed by Nestor who was conducting his doctoral research on Roma's history in Greece during the period of my fieldwork. These participants' understandings of educational success echo the conceptualisation by Leatz (1993, cited in Hoskins 2010) where success is frequently conceptualised as a road to be travelled, a journey with the promise of arriving at a destination with the realisation of achievement; these participants feel they have already arrived at 'success'.

In contrast to these eight participants, ten participants did not perceive themselves to be successful and two participants did not comment on this topic of 'feeling successful'. Ifigeneia and Alcmene do not construct themselves as successful, thinking that their educational progression has been 'normal'. These two females' narratives indicate that their family habitus is key in explaining their educational success. For Ifigeneia this was because she had never lived in a 'camp', although she considers her parents successful because they have managed to 'dodge' the traditional Roma lifestyle. Ifigeneia emphasised her father's family's intergenerational role in championing Roma's rights and her grandfather's vision to educate his grandchildren. As a result, in Ifigeneia's family, educational progression was presented as the only available option. Although Alcmene, too, saw her educational progression as something 'normal', she recognises that others see her educational progression as 'better achievement compared to others (e.g. peers and parents)' (Power et al. 2003) because, according to her, 'only few Roma students make it and enter higher education' when most Roma pupils underperform and drop out (Nikolaou 2009; Kostouli and Mitakidou 2009).

Miltiades, Hector, Theagenes, Electra and Ismene noted that they are following a pathway towards success but there are more things they need to do in order to feel successful. For example, Miltiades longs to establish his own pharmaceutical company, while Electra and Hector said they will feel successful if they manage to continue into postgraduate studies in their fields. Ismene mentioned that she wishes to study for a Master's degree and work in the field of education. These narratives show, in the main, an approach to educational success as an ongoing process (Hoskins 2010) where more goals and criteria need to be met. However, Ismene highlighted moments of success she had already experienced such as her entrance to university and her graduation day which, according to her, consist significant steps of the success ladder (Hoskins 2010).

On the basis of the above, I argue that the way the participants of my study perceive themselves as 'successful' appears to be complex. Although entrance to higher education is recognised as evidence of 'objective' success, 'subjective' elements of success are presented as significant in the way some participants construct themselves as successful or not (e.g. prestigious studies, hierarchical promotion). Some participants seem not to feel successful as they think success requires more achievements (e.g. postgraduate studies, getting a good job); in these cases, the participants' rationale seems to be informed by an understanding of educational success in an intermittent and phased way related to seeing success as a process. Furthermore, feelings of 'being successful' seem to be influenced by culture-/ethnicity-related discourses as, in some cases, the success achieved is seen in relation to what usually happens in the Roma community. Regardless of the extent to which the participants perceive themselves as successful, 'being regarded as successful by others' (Roma and non-Roma) appears of importance as well.

ACHIEVING EDUCATIONAL SUCCESS AND 'OTHERING'

Regardless of how the participants feel about their educational progression and success, being identified as Roma by others—both Roma and non-Roma in Greece—affects the way the participants have been treated in some cases. For some participants, educational success had been accompanied by some forms of rejection coming from parts of the Roma community. Thus, educational success came at a 'price'; regardless of how they describe their individual sense of belonging, other Roma find that they are not 'proper Roma' anymore. In Electra's case, the cost of her educational progression was the loss of her Roma female peers. Indicatively, Electra noted:

> If I had followed (my Roma female friends' lifestyle), e.g. wake up at 12 o'clock, not attend school, enjoy my coffee and go around, I would not have achieved what I did... Thus, I preferred to stay alone without friends rather than stay uneducated...

Athena reported that she is not regarded as a 'proper Roma' now that she is educated. Although she follows a mainstream lifestyle, she is neither considered Greek by the non-Roma Greeks nor Roma by the Greek Roma. This is how Athena described her experience:

> In our city, they call me 'Rakli'. In Romani language, 'Rakli' means the non-Roma female. For the Roma, I am not a Roma ... I am not like them ... because I am educated. However, I feel Roma ... In practice, I belong to two worlds, a Roma world and a non-Roma world but none of them has accepted me ... For the Roma I am the non-Roma and for the non-Roma I am the Roma.

Patroclus' and Pericles' stories highlighted some of the difficulties they faced when they attended the mainstream lower high school in their area after having graduated from a segregated Roma school in their camp. Pericles said:

> Our non-Roma classmates used to treat us (the Roma) in a different way ... They did not socialise with us during the school breaks, they did not talk to us, they did not share the same desk with us, they did not want to go out with us ... When we were on a school trip, they did not even want to take photos with us ...

These accounts reflect that the Roma are still reviled and experience forms of social exclusion in Greece (Dragonas 2012; Georgiadis and Zisimos 2012). Moreover, they show that experiences of non-acceptance by the Greek dominant community can hamper Roma's educational success. So much so, that Athena eloquently reflected that:

> If I had a second life, I do not know if I would study again ... We, the Roma, do not only have to face the difficulties related to school and homework. In addition, we have to confront those ironic comments and contemptuous eyes; all these things that hurt.

In this context, it is unsurprising that feelings of antipathy had often been revealed when the participants attempted to build relationships with non-Roma partners. Ismene confessed that she was dating a Greek non-Roma man at university who disappeared when she told him she was a Roma.

Roma identity recognition can still work in oppressive ways regardless of any educational success. Following Fordham and Ogbu's (1986) work, I have argued elsewhere that the Roma cultural frame of reference is still seen by (some non-Roma) Greeks as not only oppositional to the Greek identity but also as inferior (Gkofa 2017). This is eloquently highlighted by the following event of discrimination Pericles recently experienced:

> I had to e-mail my essay by the deadline given ... I was back home and here, we do not have an Internet Antenna receiver ... Thus, I went to an Internet café in order to submit my essay ... but I was not allowed to enter the Café because many cafés do not welcome Roma clients ... I knew that this shop does not welcome the Roma, but I thought that I would be accepted because I am a university student ... However, I was kicked out ... I called the police ... and if I had signed a complaint report, the owner would have been sent to court ... I finally submitted my essay at the police station and thus I managed to be on time ... I have never talked to anybody about this event before ... I did not even dare to report that event to my professors at university ... I was afraid they might look down on me...

In summary, higher studies play a role in the way the participants represent themselves as successful or not. However, discriminatory practices against the Greek Roma frequently influence the way the participants are treated regardless of any educational success achieved (Gkofa 2017).

GENDER AND EDUCATIONAL SUCCESS

In the literature, patriarchal attitudes regarding the role of Roma women in Greece are well-documented (Dragonas 2012). For example, Greek Roma girls usually stay at home and are not expected to progress at school, confronting multiple forms of discrimination related to their being women and their being Roma (Antonopoulou 2011). Gender issues were also repeatedly reported by almost all the participants (19/20) as influencing the educational success of Roma. The participants reported experiencing different expectations according to their gender. For example, Electra argued that Roma boys are frequently treated as being 'superior' to Roma girls who appear to occupy a subordinate position. Ismene noted that the man is the 'head' in every setting while Roma females learn the role of 'housekeeper' from early on.

In contrast to the gendered discourses to which most participants referred, the family attitudes towards education and sex/gender appeared of great importance in the educational success of my female participants highlighting the role of family habitus in educational success (Bourdieu 2006). Ifigeneia argued that it is not a matter of sex/gender but it is the parents and their expectations that influence children's progression, both their sons' and daughters':

> Parents play the most significant role (in their children's progression); it is their persistence, their vision, their goals which matter the most.

In Ifigeneia's family context, educational progression had been presented as the only available option for her. Somewhat unusually, it had been her grandfather's vision to educate all his grandchildren. Athena highlighted the fact that her parents believed that their daughter would be able to access a better future through education—emphasising external criteria of success (Sturges 1999), the exchange value of education and her family's will for upward mobility—to the extent that they used to make sacrifices in order to ensure she had all the school materials she needed.

So, even though there are always some different expectations, it is the kind of gendered regimes which matters the most. In Alcmene's and Electra's local area, a Roma Female Association is active in fighting for Roma children's education. The positive attitudes towards education and some small-scale educational interventions in this area might have promoted an 'ethos' which facilitated their progression when coupled with their families' positive attitudes towards education (Bourdieu 2006). In Bourdieusian terms, my female participants' familial positive attitudes towards education 'matched' the field of education and enabled their progression (Bourdieu 2006). In addition, there is a university near the area where they live and so they can continue to live at home while studying.

In summary, the participants highlighted the ways in which traditional gendered regimes still influence many Roma females' educational trajectories. However, according to the participants, the gap related to sex/gender differences is gradually being narrowed. In my female participants' cases, sex/gender had not served as a barrier against their educational success. The key factor documented as having facilitated their educational progression had been the positive family attitudes towards education as well as the family's high aspirations for educational success. These Roma participants and their families resisted some of the traditional gendered patterns that limit the emancipation of Roma girls and women, such as early marriages. In Bourdieusian terms, the family habitus as well as assets of high economic capital and cultural capital and in some cases social capital played a crucial role in my female participants' progression (Bourdieu 2006). Moreover, where they lived facilitated the educational progression of my female participants.

Taking into account that, in general, gendered inequalities still influence women's educational lives in Greece (Deliyianni-Kouimtzi and Frosi 2008), it is evident that the Greek Roma educated female participants in my study all constitute exceptional cases inside the unusually exceptional group of Roma who successfully navigated their way through higher education. Even though gendered perspectives are still evident in these female participants' stories (such as the 'feminised' subjects studied at university), the participants' stories show that change is occurring in relation to the gendered attitudes and practices of Roma. Thus, these Roma females seem to be 'change bearers' and education is involved in this change.

CONCLUSION

This chapter has critically examined the perceptions, constructions and experiences of educational success of twenty Roma in Greece who have entered higher education 'against the odds'. Educational success was not understood in a single way by the participants. Higher studies were frequently seen as an 'objective' indicator of success reflecting the value university studies have traditionally held in Greece (Livanos 2010; Sianou-Kyrgiou and Tsiplakides 2011; Themelis 2013). However, 'relative' aspects, internal and intangible criteria (Sturges 1999) also informed the way educational success was perceived. Indeed, educational success was presented as a complex construction not easily understood, described and explained, echoing other studies' findings, such as Hoskins' (2010).

Moreover, some participants presented themselves as successful while others did not. This chapter has highlighted the way Roma are still frequently 'othered'—regardless of any achievements or educational success. Although, in some cases, Roma's acceptance by the dominant Greek community seems to be accomplished when educational success is achieved, the significant events of exclusion against some of the participants underline the continuance of anti-Roma prejudice in Greek society (Dragonas 2012; Georgiadis and Zisimos 2012). Thus, some Roma choose not to talk about their Roma background as 'being Roma' may be seen by the non-Roma as a demeaning aspect of their identity and also as oppositional to 'being Greek' (Gkofa 2017). However, educational success itself may sometimes result in participants being 'othered' even by (non-educated) Roma who do not regard some of the participants as 'proper Roma' anymore.

The chapter has also demonstrated that gender regimes have influenced the participants' experiences of educational success. Briefly put, sex/gender frequently intersects with Roma background making Roma females more 'vulnerable' to discriminatory practices within both the Roma and the mainstream Greek (non-Roma) community which still impede Roma females' educational success (Antonopoulou 2011; Dragonas 2012). However, the women in my sample appear as 'pioneers' showing that change is occurring in relation to Roma's gendered attitudes and that education gets and needs to get involved in this change. Therefore, it can be argued that as regards Roma's educational success, education contributes to achieving social change and social transformation (Apple 2008).

REFERENCES

Antonopoulou, V. (2011). Study on "Combating the isolation of Roma women and girls and promoting their empowerment. Invisible lives – Roma women in Greece, Steering Committee for Equality between women and men (CDEG). Retrieved May 13, 2014, from http://www.coe.int/t/DGHL/STANDARDSETTING/EQUALITY/03themes/gender-equality/CDEG_2011_17_Roma_en.pdf

Apple, M. (2008). Can schooling contribute to a more just society? *Education, Citizenship and Social Justice, 3*(3), 239–261.

Archer, L. (2008). The impossibility of minority ethnic educational 'success'? An examination of the discourses of teachers and pupils in British secondary schools. *European Educational Research Journal, 7*(1), 89–107.

Bereményi, B. Á., & Carrasco, S. (2015). Interrupted aspirations: Research and policy on Gitano education in a time of recession, in Spain. *Intercultural Education, 26*(2), 1–12.

Bhopal, K., & Myers, M. (2009). Gypsy, Roma and traveller pupils in schools in the UK: Inclusion and 'good practice'. *International Journal of Inclusive Education, 13*(3), 299–314.

Bourdieu, P. (1990). *In other words: Essays towards a reflexive sociology* (trans: Adamson, M.). Cambridge: Polity.

Bourdieu, P. (2004/1986). The forms of capital. In S. Ball (Ed.), *The Routledge falmer reader in sociology of education* (pp. 15–29). London: Routledge.

Bourdieu, P. (2006/1977). *Outline of a theory of practice*. Cambridge: Cambridge University Press.

Bourdieu, P., & Wacquant, L. (1992). *An invitation to reflexive sociology*. Cambridge: Polity Press.

Byfield, C. (2008). *Black boys can make it: How they overcome the obstacles to university in the UK and USA*. Sterling, VA: Trentham Books Limited.

Deliyianni-Kouimtzi, V., & Frosi, L. (2008). Introduction. In V. Deliyianni-Kouimtzi, S. Ziogou-Karastergiou, & L. Frosi (Eds.), *Φύλο και Εκπαιδευτική Πραγματικότητα στην Ελλάδα: Προωθώντας Παρεμβάσεις για την Ισότητα των Φύλων στο Ελληνικό Εκπαιδευτικό Σύστημα* [Gender and Educational Reality in Greece: Promoting Gender Equality Interventions in the Greek Educational System] (Chapter 1). Athens: Research Centre for Equality Issues (ΚΕΘΙ). Retrieved June 20, 2014, from http://www.kethi.gr/index.php?option=com_content&view=article&id=149%3A2008-12-18-09-53-35&catid=35%3A-2008&Itemid=23&lang=el

Dragonas, T. (2012). *Roma mothers and their young children*. Country Report. Greece: Bernard Van Leer Foundation (Unpublished Report).

European Commission. (2009). *The Greek Roma issue: Spatial and social exclusion and integration policies* (Peer Review Integrated Programme for the Social Inclusion of Roma) (Host Country Report). Retrieved May 5, 2012, from www.peer-review-social-inclusion.eu

Flick, U. (2009). *An Introduction to Qualitative Research* (4th ed.). London: Sage.

Fordham, S., & Ogbu, J. U. (1986). Black students' school success: Coping with the "burden of 'acting white'". *The Urban Review, 18*(3), 176–206.

Georgiadis, F., & Zisimos, A. (2012). Teacher training in Roma education in Greece: Intercultural and critical educational necessities. *Issues in Educational Research, 22*(1), 47–59.

Gewirtz, S., & Cribb, A. (2009). *Understanding education: A sociological perspective*. Cambridge: Polity.

Gkofa, P. (2017). Being Roma–being Greek: Academically successful Greek Romas' identity constructions. *Race Ethnicity and Education, 20*(5), 624–635.

Hoskins, K. (2010). *Senior female academics in the UK academy: A classed and gendered exploration of success*. PhD thesis, King's College London, London.

Ingram, N. (2009). Working-class boys, educational success and the misrecognition of working-class culture. *British Journal of Sociology of Education, 30*(4), 421–434.

Ingram, N. (2011). Within school and beyond the gate: The complexities of being educationally successful and working class. *Sociology, 45*(2), 287–302.

Kende, A. (2007). Success stories? Roma university students overcoming social exclusion in Hungary. In H. Colley (Ed.), *Social inclusion for young people: Breaking down the barriers* (pp. 133–144). Strasbourg: Council of Europe.

Kostadinova, G. (2011). Minority rights as a normative framework for addressing the situation of Roma in Europe. *Oxford Development Studies, 39*(2), 163–183.

Kostouli, T., & Mitakidou, S. (2009). Policies as top-down structures versus as lived realities: An investigation of literacy policies in Greek schools. In S. Mitakidou, E. Tressou, B. B. Swadener, & C. A. Grant (Eds.), *Beyond pedagogies of exclusion in diverse childhood contexts: Transnational challenges* (pp. 47–63). New York: Macmillan.

Livanos, I. (2010). The relationship between higher education and labour market in Greece: The weakest link? *Higher Education, 60*(5), 473–489.

Markou, G. (2008). Η προσπάθεια ανάπτυξης μιας εθνικής πολιτικής για την οικονομική και κοινωνική ένταξη των Τσιγγάνων [The attempt to develop a national policy for economic and social inclusion of the Roma]. In S. Trubeta (Ed.), *Οι Ρομά στο σύγχρονο ελληνικό κράτος: Συμβιώσεις – Αναιρέσεις – Απουσίες* [The Roma in the Modern Greek State: Symbiosis – Denegation – Absence] (pp. 153–188). Athens: Kritiki.

Mavrommatis, G. (2008). Παιδιά Ρομά στο ελληνικό δημόσιο σχολείο [Roma children in Greek public school]. In S. Trubeta (Ed.), *Οι Ρομά στο σύγχρονο ελληνικό κράτος: Συμβιώσεις –Αναιρέσεις –Απουσίες* [The Roma in the Modern Greek State: Symbiosis – Denegation – Absence] (pp. 199–223). Athens: Kritiki.

Nikolaou, G. (2009). Teacher training on Roma education in Greece: A discussion about the results of INSETRom experience in two Greek schools. *Intercultural Education, 20*(6), 549–557.

Power, S., Edwards, T., Wigfall, V., & Whitty, G. (2003). *Education and the middle class.* Buckingham: Open University.

Reay, D. (2004). Education and cultural capital: The implications of changing trends in education policies. *Cultural Trends, 13*(2), 73–86.

Reay, D., Crozier, G., & Clayton, J. (2009). 'Strangers in paradise'? Working-class students in Elite Universities. *Sociology, 43*(6), 1103–1121.

Rhamie, J. (2007). *Eagles who soar: How black learners find the path to success.* Stoke-on-Trent: Trentham Books.

Rollock, N. (2007a). Legitimising black academic failure: Deconstructing staff discourses on academic success, appearance and behaviour. *International Studies in Sociology of Education, 17*(3), 275–287.

Rollock, N. (2007b). Why black girls don't matter: Exploring how race and gender shape academic success in an inner city school. *Support for Learning, 22*(4), 197–202.

Sianou-Kyrgiou, E., & Tsiplakides, I. (2011). Similar performance, but different choices: Social class and higher education choice in Greece. *Studies in Higher Education, 36*(1), 89–102.

Strauss, A., & Corbin, J. (1998). *Basics of qualitative research: Techniques and procedures for developing grounded theory* (2nd ed.). Thousand Oaks, CA: Sage.

Sturges, J. (1999). What it means to succeed: Personal conceptions of career success held by male and female managers at different ages. *British Journal of Management, 10*(3), 239–252.

Symeou, L., Luciak, M., & Gobbo, F. (2009). Teacher training for Roma inclusion: Implementation, outcomes and reflections of the INSETRom project. *Intercultural Education, 20*(6), 493–496.

Themelis, S. (2013). *Social change and education in Greece: A study in class struggle dynamics.* New York: Palgrave Macmillan.

Trevor, J., & Newburn, T. (2001). *Widening access: Improving police relations with hard to reach groups.* London: Home Office, Research, Development and Statistics Directorate, Policing and Reducing Crime Unit.

Wright, B. (2011). I know who I am, do you? Identity and academic achievement of successful African American male adolescents in an Urban Pilot High School in the United States. *Urban Education, 46,* 611–638.

Panagiota Gkofa has recently completed her PhD research in Education Research (Sociology of Education) at King's College London (UK). Her doctoral study investigated the educational success of some Roma university students in Greece. Her research interest is in the sociology of education and education policy. In particular, she is interested in the issues related to social justice and equality, school exclusion and educational success, issues of class, race, gender, teachers' development, and school curriculum.

A Dialogic Model of Education

Fatih Isik and Omer Sener

INTRODUCTION

Fethullah Gülen is a contemporary Turkish Muslim scholar who resides in the USA. He is the inspiration behind the Hizmet movement, a civil society movement which opens schools and dialogue organisations across the globe. Gülen has written more than 60 books on topics ranging from Sufism, dialogue, belief and spirituality to responsibility. He comes from the Sunni Hanafi tradition within Islam, while promoting dialogue, democracy and human rights and strongly opposing terrorism and violence. Schools inspired by Gülen operate across the globe following the curricula of the educational system of each country. What makes these schools distinctive is they have been inspired by Gülen and his ideas of dialogue, representation (*temsil*) and moral values. Therefore, although the schools are not directly founded by or linked to Gülen, they consider Gülen as an inspiration.

GÜLEN'S PHILOSOPHY OF EDUCATION

Gülen proposes a holistic and humanistic philosophy of education. His view of education can be worked out tracing back to his understanding of human nature. He defined education as a "perfecting process through

F. Isik (✉) • O. Sener
The Dialogue Society, London, UK

© The Author(s) 2018
R. Race (ed.), *Advancing Multicultural Dialogues in Education*,
DOI 10.1007/978-3-319-60558-6_8

127

which we earn in the spiritual, intellectual, and physical dimensions of our beings, the rank appointed for us as the perfect pattern of creation" (Gülen 2006, p. 67). Education is a dynamic and developmental process of perfection, a journey from potential humanity (*ahseni takvim*) to true humanity (*insan-ı kamil*) (Gülen 2005b, p. 112). The holistic qualities in Gülen's notion of human nature reflect his approach to education. Gülen conceives a comprehensive model of education that satisfies body, mind and heart. That is to say, his model of education aims to foster development of intellect, habits, feelings and values. Gülen (ibid.) views education as inherently valuable since it is human to learn and seek understanding. Education also has an instrumental value in that through education people acquire skills to socialise and live as a community. Finally, it has a global value since it provides ventures to establish dialogue with different cultures. All these considered, different aspects of education according to Gülen will be now highlighted under four sub-headings: humanistic, spiritual, social and global.

HUMANISTIC AND SPIRTUAL PERSPECTIVES

Gülen (2006, p. 67) holds that education is both the fundamental purpose and the main duty of human life. He argues that the main aim of human beings in this life is to seek understanding of the physical and metaphysical world (ibid.). Education is essentially the effort of searching for such understanding. Gülen regards education as a necessity of being human. People are truly human as long as they learn, teach and inspire others. He finds it questionable whether people who are ignorant or do not feel the need to renew themselves to set an example are truly human and claimed that "Those who neglect learning and teaching should be counted as dead even though they are living" (Gülen 2006, p. 72). Education, in a nutshell, is attributed an ontological and existential meaning in which human beings are modified as learners.

   Gülen believes that only such comprehensive education, which satisfies all aspects of human(ity), can help develop the whole individual, which later will result in the cultivation of a "golden generation", "representatives of the understanding of science, faith, morality, and art who are the master builders of those coming after us" (Gülen 2005c, p. 128). This highlights a very significant attribute of Gülen's educational vision, raising a "golden generation". It is modified as "a generation of ideal universal individuals who love truth, who integrate spirituality and knowledge, who work to benefit society" (Gülen 1998a). They are also called as possessing two wings (*zül-cenaheyn*). As a bird can fulfil its potential best with the use of two wings, a person can attain human potential and moral perfection with the integration of spirituality and science (in the next section Gülen's idea of reconciling spirituality with science is discussed in more detail). The golden generation is commonly referred to as a normative ideal of Gülen's educational vision in the cultivation of an intellectual and moral generation (Williams 2007; Çobanoğlu 2012; Yavuz 2013).

Gülen also believes the goal of education is more spiritual rather than material. The end of education is taking the potential human (*ahseni takvim*) to the level of the universal human (*insan-ı kamil*) while creating a sense of love manifesting itself as love for humanity, love for knowledge and love for the truth as well as tolerance and compassion as noted by Michel (2010). Gülen (1996, p. 16) criticised modern educational ventures for ignoring non-material values such as profundity of ideas, clarity of thought and depth of feeling and cultural appreciation and proposes that they should also be incorporated. Spirituality is the source of systematic thinking and reflection (*tefekkür*), zeal for research and inquiry (*tecessüs*), passion for the eternity and feeling of anguish (*ızdırap*) (Gülen 1998b).

SOCIAL PERSPECTIVE

Another key point in Gülen's educational philosophy is the social dimension. Gülen attributes education a social mission. So, as well as being naturally human, and inherently valuable, education also becomes a social investment. As the future of a nation is dependent to the coming generations, people who are worried about their future need to invest as much as they can into the education of their children (Gülen 2006, p. 71). If the younger generation is neglected and left vulnerable to the influence of social ills, such nations are prone to endanger their identities and suffer cultural and political failure. For Gülen, the troubles in today's society in Turkey reflect the short-sightedness of administrators which can be traced back to the policies and implementations of the ruling elite 25 years ago (Gülen 2006, p. 72). Correspondingly, to extrapolate about the next generation, today's education needs to be taken into account. Gülen (2005a, p. 44) argued that "Those who wish to predict a nation's future can do so accurately by analyzing the education and upbringing given to its young people".

Great social problems can be overcome through sound education. The elementary problems of today's world, especially in underdeveloped and developing countries, according to Gülen (2004, p. 198), are ignorance, poverty and racism. As a solution he postulated that "Ignorance can be defeated through education, poverty through work, and the possession of capital, and internal schism and separatism through unity, dialogue, and tolerance" (Gülen 2004, p. 199). Amongst these, however, education forms the most important tool. Since any problem ultimately condones to human beings, education makes the most efficient investment (Gülen 2006, p. 87). On the other hand, masses can be kept under control simply by starving them of knowledge (Ünal and Williams 2000, p. 22). Tyranny could be prevented only through education and such universal education paves the way for social justice (ibid.). Mutual understanding, tolerance and respect for human rights in society can only be achieved through such education.

GLOBAL PERSPECTIVE

In the same fashion, education has a global and international dimension. It helps to create dialogue and builds bridges between different cultures especially in an age when the world is socio-politically imagined like a "global village". Gülen, aware of such evolution, said that: "Thanks to rapid developments in transportation and communication, the world has become a global village. Nations are exactly like next-door neighbours" (Gülen 2006, p. 84). This is detailed more in an interview with Sevindi (2002) when Gülen implied:

> In a world becoming more and more globalized, a world where telecommunication and transportation systems are increasingly making us all like people in the same house, people will feel constrained to get to know each other more closely.

Gülen (2004, p. 197) trusted that "a unified mosaic of nations and countries" can be formed. The metaphor of a mosaic illustrates a celebration of different cultures and values and different nations habituating together by sustaining their own characteristics. Accordingly, a focus on national characteristics and values is an essential aspect of Gülen's educational philosophy. Gülen does not see any contradiction with one's national identity and building a global identity.

Inspired from the sayings of Rumi, Gülen's dialogue model proposes that one foot is kept firmly at the centre as the other goes around 72 nations, meaning people of all nations, like the movement of a compass (Gülen 2006, p. 86). So, it is possible to preserve national identity along with mingling with other cultures and creating a shared global culture with them. Robinson (2009, p. 205) explained this as a formation of the plural self:

> When faced by the postmodern world, Gülen does not retreat behind the walls of religion, but rather engages directly with plurality and diversity, partly because his action based philosophy enables him to see the Muslim as a plural self: Muslim and Turkish, citizen, professional, business person and so on.

Gülen provides a model of plural identity also as a precaution to overcome likely threats of globalism and postmodernism. Establishing dialogue with others while respecting plurality and managing plural identities becomes an obligation particularly in this age as a consequence of globalisation (Gülen 2006). Gülen, as a Muslim scholar, responds to the challenges posed by globalisation through application of the mechanism of *ijtihad,* the flexibility that is permitted by Islam through reinterpretation of authentic sources to find answers for changing circumstances. As a scholar engaging in *ijtihad,* Gülen creates a global platform to engage in dialogue through a universal medium, which is education. With the example of Hizmet schools, Islam manages to engage with the global via the representation of universal human values.

AN EXAMPLE OF HIZMET SCHOOLS

Gülen's approach to moral development and education has its own practical implications. There are educational institutions in a wide range that have been inspired from Gülen's worldview, commonly known as Hizmet schools. Over a thousand schools from pre-school to higher education levels in over 150 countries have been established over the last three decades. There are also alternative educational facilities such as prep schools, supplementary schools, language schools and community centres in these countries. Although all of these schools are opened by people inspired from Gülen, the concept of Hizmet schools mostly refers to the official week-day schools in primary and high school (college) levels.

Hizmet schools are different from the Montessori type of international schools or the Hyde Schools in the USA in that they do not have a set framework, policies, mission or vision statements that they all pursue commonly (See Gauld (1993) for Hyde Schools, and Montessori (2008) for the Montessori method). Although they might take other Hizmet schools as a model in their establishment or transfer and exchange their experience, these schools are independently managed. There is no formal relationship between them except when they are part of a chain run by an educational charity trust (Aslandoğan and Çetin 2006, p. 53). It is not easy to identify their affiliation with Fethullah Gülen since it is neither officially explained nor stated on their websites (Hendrick 2013, p. 104). When questioned directly about their link, affiliation with Gülen's ideals is acknowledged, while relationships with other Hizmet schools are described with a lack of any *organic* connection (Hendrick, op. cit.). This is in line with Gülen's depictions in an interview with Gündem (2005):

> If a movement has started to produce its own models, and people have started to admire it, following in its steps, and devoting themselves to this cause, making it their ideal, or if they have accepted it as mafkura (lofty ideal), in the words of Ziya Gokalp, then the person who seems to be at the front of this movement would not even be aware of what is happening most of the time. People would do similar things here and there even if they didn't know anything about each other because they don't have any organic connection and because they have not been introduced to each other. But they are connected together by the bonds of a very serious thought and a lofty ideal.

Gülen's explanations confirm Hendrick's observations. Gülen also clarifies his own link with Hizmet schools and other activities of the Hizmet movement. Describing the 'lofty ideals' as an ambiguous reality, Hendrick (2013, p. 103) characterised the movement as "... fluid and adapting organization of autonomous actors and institutions". Regarding their structure, experiential field study with a particular focus on sample schools can provide better understanding for these schools. Since it is not the central focus of this chapter, this study will be limited to other researchers' views and observations. Although they might be different and independent from each other, there are certain common characteristics that most Hizmet schools share. This can certainly be ascribed to their shared "lofty ideal" inspired by Fethullah Gülen.

ACADEMIC FOCUS ON SCIENCE

Hizmet schools invariably follow the national curriculum of the country they are in even when private schools are exempt from such a requirement (Woodhall 2005). They usually teach in multi-language: positive sciences in English and social sciences in locally dominant or required language(s); they also teach Turkish. There is a special emphasis on science, language, information technology and sport. However, this means relatively less focus on social sciences such as humanities, literature, history and geography as well as arts (Mohamed 2007, p. 564). One of the most remarkable aspects of Hizmet schools is a vigorous attention for teaching science and the creation of a competitive spirit through Science Olympiads (Kocabaş 2006; Arslan 2009). They have strong scientific orientations supported with modern and up-to-date equipment in science and computing laboratories (Woodhall 2005; Mohamed 2007). Science Olympiads create a platform for Hizmet schools to acknowledge their achievements. All Hizmet schools encourage their students to attend science competitions in different areas such as physics, biology, chemistry, mathematics, computing and ecology. Students undergo a very competitive process within their own schools to be eligible to attend these competitions. And if they succeed in national competitions they represent their schools and country in continental and international level Science Olympiads.

A unique educational tradition that fosters participation into these competitions has been created by the early examples of Hizmet schools. Whatever curriculum those schools follow, Science Olympiads have been incorporated into that. Competitions that have provided a ground for strongly science-oriented education in Hizmet schools. Representation of school in regional, national and international levels followed with achievements endorses self-efficacy of students along with feelings of belonging to a specific school community (Aslandoğan and Çetin 2006, p. 53). Project-based science in a competitive environment makes the study of science more relevant to everyday life. This relates to Gülen's (2011a) theory of knowledge that reveals itself through action. Gülen (2004, p. 206) argues that "Knowledge limited to empty theories and unabsorbed pieces of learning … arouses suspicions in minds and darkens hearts, is a 'heap of garbage' around which desperate and confused souls flounder". Actions when repeated develop *ma'rifa*, which means a deeper level of cognition harnessed with love (Ünal and Williams 2000, p. 373). Spiritual values such as a desire for knowledge, research and truth can be developed in a context where culture of knowledge reigns.

Arslan (2009, p. 1) called this process of integration of spiritual values (here understood as Islamic values of vicegerency and responsibility of human beings for the rest of the creation and a God-centric view of creation and scientific phenomena) into the study of science as "pious science". However, she unpacked this concept to involve teaching science with an Islamic discourse. This is how, she thought, Islam and science is combined in Hizmet schools (ibid.). This integration does not necessarily suggest "a full integration of both fields in every sense but envisions re-framing the concepts and practices of science with an Islamic discourse" (Arslan 2009, p. 30). This can be achieved "by persistently relating the concepts, findings and theories of science to (Sunni) Islam, and by explaining them in reference to the 'meaning' of creation and life on earth" (Arslan 2009, p. 28). This explanation sounds reasonable especially in view of Gülen's discourse of telling us about scientific issues in his books and sermons. However, Arslan (2009) does not offer any more details about how this is achieved in a secular curriculum with secular textbooks of science in a Hizmet school context. Therefore, we think Gülen's discourse needs to be distinguished from the practice in Hizmet schools. It is hard to imagine teachers in Hizmet schools always rephrasing the content of each and every science textbook in an Islamic manner. It also leaves the question of how their students can get international success in science competitions. It is even less likely to consider this to be true in the schools abroad regarding their pluralistic nature. Nevertheless, "pious science" makes more sense in explaining teachers' approach to the study of science motivated by a quasi-religious discourse (Arslan 2009, p. 32).

Further research is needed to uncover whether vigorous focus on science in Hizmet schools manages to develop spiritual values such as a desire for research and truth, along with profundity of ideas, depth of feeling and clarity of thought as promoted by Gülen. Based on her fieldwork, Arslan (2009, p. 470) concluded that Hizmet school methodology does not really encourage scientific curiosity and independent study; rather science is studied under disciplinary and controlled practice. Olympiad students that Arslan (2009) observes in her study do not organise themselves according to their likes; rather, they are closely guided and monitored by their supervisors. Moreover, in an atmosphere where competition becomes a culture, the study of science tends to be conceived in a *fetishised* way. As a result, the meaning of learning gets lost while success as an outcome turns into a value.

ALTRUISTIC TEACHERS

Teachers are the most indispensable actors in a Hizmet school model. Although there are teachers outside the movement in a Hizmet school, teachers from the movement reflect the ideal of Gülen and the Hizmet movement. They act altruistically and quite similar to the portrayal of an ideal teacher according to Gülen. They care for the needs of their students attentively. And they model good behaviour for their students. In other words, teachers from Hizmet schools are the representatives of the movement, who have adopted the ideals promoted by Gülen and the Hizmet movement. They help to create a culture of the movement by modelling good morals in a secular school setting.

Teachers from the movement are expected to work altruistically without any worldly expectations. Teachers who leave Turkey move to a country mindful of likely hardship and adversities. Bülent, one of the Hizmet teachers working abroad, shared this spirit in an interview by Tittensor (2010):

> It is dedication because it's another environment, you know, it's difficult to be in an environment with foreign people, and without your family, without your friends, many friends are here you know, it's much more valuable, a lot more valuable.

Teachers are motivated to teach in schools abroad with a sense of a religious activity, which is promoted by Gülen as an alternative pilgrimage and migration (*hicret*) (Gülen 2010, 2011b). They leave their homeland with an altruistic spirit compromising family, friends and a professional career as idealised by Gülen (Ergene 2008, p. 179):

> Sacrifice is one of the important characteristics of a person who teaches others. Those who do not or cannot risk sacrifice from the start cannot be a person of cause. People who do not have a cause cannot be successful. Yes, those who are ready to leave at one stretch whenever necessary, their wealth, life, family, position, fame etc … things which many people desire and put at the purpose of life—that their cause eventually reaches peaks is certain and inevitable.

In these perceptions, teaching becomes a mission (Tittensor 2014; Arslan 2009). Teachers from the Hizmet movement perceive teaching as a way of serving humanity, a form of *hizmet*. Being a teacher becomes a way of living, a life philosophy that governs their lives.

Caring Teacher–Student Relationship

Such devotion is also evident in the relationship with students. Students feel more secure since they know that their teacher will take an extra mile when they need more support. In an interview with *The Star* in Australia, one of the graduating students explained this as follows:

> It is very easy to communicate with our teachers, and whenever we need help they are more than happy to give us anything we need. It takes a lot of pressure off the students when they know they are working hand in hand with their teachers. (Maher 2007)

Yusuf Doğer, a graduate student of Işık College Upfield Campus in Australia, received the top VCE score in 2008. He also expressed similar impressions in an interview with *The Hume Leader* newspaper, also based in Australia:

> Our teachers stayed back after school and held special classes [on weekends]. The teachers helped motivate us so much, I know if it was not for them I would not have gotten such a high score. (Samut 2009)

For Hizmet teachers, being a teacher does not only mean a professional life, but becomes a lifestyle. Students are prioritised sometimes even in spite of their own personal commitments as a student in a Hizmet school explained:

> As the students stated, this young male teacher used to be in contact with them "24 hours a day". They could call him at "any time during the day, for any kind of problem" they had. They told me: "He used to call and ask where we were. If we told him that we were in the city centre, he would meet us there right away. There was a girl he was mad about, I swear, he wouldn't go and see her, but would hang out with us". (Arslan 2009)

Hizmet teachers dedicate their time and efforts for the school and students without much financial return. They usually work 6 days a week without a strict notion of working hours and have a 4-week holiday per annum (Woodhall 2005).

Maintenance of Altruist Dynamism

Tönbekici (2011) highlighted teachers' selfless devotion in Hizmet schools in Uganda, and attracted attention to the dynamic behind this which cannot be justified with any *catch phrases* (slogan). According to Gülen, it is altruism (*adanmışlık*) and sacrifice for a cause that is *hizmet* (Ergene 2008). Although teachers' dynamism contributes significantly to schools, their individuality and individual success are suppressed by the identity and achievements of the community (Arslan 2009, p. 447). Hendrick (2013) explained the motivation of people working for the Hizmet movement as rational as it might be altruistic. However, especially regarding Hizmet teachers working abroad, I believe they have more altruistic motives than rational. This altruistic dynamism might sometimes be neglected by administration. As an English teacher who worked in Kazakhstan and Kyrgyzstan said in an interview with Tittensor (2010): "Many teachers there couldn't get any salary for months. We worked there for three hundred dollars [a month] at the time, and we couldn't get the salaries in time after ten months or so." Melih Yalçıneli worked in Yamanlar *Koleji* for 8 years without any promotion and did not receive financial support when he took students abroad for Science Olympiads (Arslan 2009, p. 445). Altruistic spirit is a distinctive source of dynamism of Hizmet schooling; nonetheless this might fade away if teachers' altruism is tested and their efforts are not appreciated as a more common practice.

CONCLUSIONS

In conclusion, we would like to point out one of the difficulties of writing about these schools, namely, their heterogeneity. In other words, the diversity amongst the schools needs to be taken into consideration. Although they have been inspired from the same ideals, they usually act flexibly to meet local needs and requirements. For instance, they adopt the curriculum and the system endorsed by the local or national authority. This is the case for all Hizmet schools, from schools in European countries (including continental Europe and the UK) to schools in Africa and Southeast Asia and other parts of the world. The schools are generally funded and administered locally, while in Central Asian and Balkan countries, they rely on Turkish contributors more because of the weakness of civic initiatives in those areas (Yavuz 2013). We also noted that although the schools are successful in teaching science and in scientific Olympiads, they run the risk of 'fetishizing' scientific research by focusing on competition and a competitive spirit. Finally, it should be reasserted that the schools emphasise altruism and there should be a balance established between altruism and a lack of expectation of the teachers and appreciation of the outstanding work of the teachers.

It is important to note that this chapter began to be written before 15 July 2016, when a failed coup took place in Turkey, claiming the lives of hundreds of people across Turkey. Because this chapter is on the education philosophy of Gülen, and the post-coup purge against Hizmet volunteers is still unfolding, we decided to limit ourselves to the topic at hand, and urge our readers to refer to other articles written on the subject. However, we briefly note here that although there is still no evidence of involvement of Gülen and the Hizmet movement other than "confessions" by army personnel under severe torture, the Turkish Government has alleged that the coup was orchestrated by the group. As a result of this accusation, all Hizmet-inspired schools in Turkey have been closed down and their staff have been sacked from their jobs. The fact that since this purge, it has become ever more important for Hizmet-inspired people to continue their work in education, dialogue and humanitarian work across the globe, promoting dialogue, human rights and universal values while emphasising their unchanging stance against violence and any form of terrorism.

REFERENCES

Arslan, B. (2009). *Pious science: The Gülen community and the making of a conservative modernity in Turkey.* Ph.D. thesis, University of California.

Aslandoğan, Y. A., & Çetin, M. (2006). The educational philosophy of Gülen in thought and practice. In R. A. Hunt & Y. A. Aslandoğan (Eds.), *Muslim citizens of the globalized world: Contributions of the Gülen movement* (pp. 31–54). New Jersey: The Light.

Çobanoğlu, Y. (2012). *Altın Nesil'in Peşinde: Fethullah Gülen'de Toplum, Devlet, Ahlak, Otorite* [In pursuit of golden generation: Community, state, morals and authority for Fethullah Gülen]. İstanbul: İletişim Yayınları.

Ergene, M. E. (2008). *Tradition witnessing the modern age: An analysis of the Gülen movement.* İstanbul: The Light.

Gauld, J. (1993). *Character first: The Hyde School difference.* San Francisco: ICS Press.

Gülen, M. F. (1996). *Towards the lost paradise.* London: True Star.

Gülen, M. F. (1998a, July). *Düşünce Kaymaları* [Slips of Thought]. *Sızıntı, 15*(172).

Gülen, M. F. (1998b, March). *Varlığın Mânâ Buudu* [Spiritual Dimension of Beings]. *Sızıntı, 20*(230).

Gülen, M. F. (2004). *Toward a global civilization of love and tolerance.* New Jersey: The Light.

Gülen, M. F. (2005a). *Pearls of wisdom.* New Jersey: The Light.

Gülen, M. F. (2005b). *The statue of our souls*. New Jersey: The Light.

Gülen, M. F. (2005c). *The messenger of god: Muhammad*. New Jersey: The Light.

Gülen, M. F. (2006). *Essays-perspectives-opinions*. New Jersey: The Light.

Gülen, M. F. (2010). *Kalb İbresi* [Index of the heart]. İzmir: Nil Yayınları.

Gülen, M. F. (2011a). *Cemre Beklentisi* [Waiting for radiations of warmth]. İstanbul: Nil Yayınları.

Gülen, M. F. (2011b). *Yenilenme Cehdi* [Enthusiasm for renewal]. İstanbul: Nil Yayınları.

Gündem, M. (2005). *11 Days with Fethullah Gülen: An analysis of a movement with question and answers* (5th ed.). İstanbul: Alfa.

Hendrick, D. J. (2013). *Gülen: The ambiguous politics of market Islam in Turkey and the World*. New York: New York University Press.

Kocabaş, Ö. (2006). *Scientific careers and ideological profiles of science Olympiad participants from Fethullah Gülen and other secondary schools in Turkey*. MA Thesis, Middle East Technical University.

Maher, C. (2007). *Işık girls are top of class*. Melbourne: Star.

Michel, T. (2010). *Gülen's pedagogy and the challenges for modern educators*. Retrieved May 12, 2012, from http://www.fethullah-Gulen.org/academic-papers/Gulen-pedagogy.html

Mohamed, Y. (2007). *The educational theory of Fethullah Gülen and its practice in South Africa*. In I. Yılmaz et al. (Eds.), *The Muslim world in transition* (pp. 552–570). Leeds: Leeds Metropolitan University Press.

Montessori, M. (2008). *The Montessori method*. Chicago: BN Publishing.

Robinson, S. (2009, December 5–6). *Virtues, spirituality and public life: The contribution of Fethullah Gülen*. Proceedings of the East and West Encounters: The Gülen Movement, Los Angeles.

Samut, K. (2009). *Işık tops study list*. Melbourne: Hume Leader.

Sevindi, N. (2002). *Fethullah Gülen ile Global Hoşgörü ve New York Sohbeti* [Global Tolerance and New York Interview with Fethullah Gülen]. İstanbul: Timaş.

Tittensor, D. (2010). An alternative pilgrimage: Gülen teachers doing Hizmet abroad. In A. Ünsal (Ed.), *The significance of education for the future: The Gülen model of education*. Jakarta: State Islamic University.

Tittensor, D. (2014). *The house of service: The Gülen movement and Islam's third way*. Oxford: Oxford University Press.

Tönbekici, M. (2011). Uganda'daki Türkiye (Turkey in Uganda) Vatan. Retrieved June 5, 2013, from http://haber.gazetevatan.com/ugandadaki-turkiye/415098/4/yazarlar

Ünal, A., & Williams, A. (Eds.). (2000). *Fethullah Gülen advocate of dialogue*. Fairfax: The Fountain.

Williams, I. (2007). A station above that of angels: The vision of Islamic education within pluralistic societies in the thought of Fethullah Gülen—A study of contrasts between Turkey and the UK. In İ. Yılmaz (Ed.), *Peaceful coexistence*. London: Leeds Metropolitan University Press.

Woodhall, R. (2005). *Organizing the organization, educating the educators: An examination of Fethullah Gülen's teaching and the membership of the movement.* Islam in the contemporary world: The Fethullah Gülen movement in thought and practice, Rice University, Houston, Texas.

Yavuz, M. H. (2013). *Towards an Islamic enlightenment: The Gülen movement.* New York: Oxford University Press.

Fatih Isik obtained his BA and MA degrees in English Teacher Education from Bilkent University and has completed his PhD at Leeds Beckett University. Fatih's areas of interest include moral character education, social and moral development and citizenship.

Omer Sener is a researcher and freelance writer who holds a PhD in Cultural Studies and Literary Criticism. His research interests include ethnicity, multiculturalism and cultural narratives. He is particularly interested in intercultural dialogue and dialogue as an academic concept across disciplines.

Generation Global: A Global Dialogue Programme for Young People

Ian Jamison

The Tony Blair Faith Foundation provides people with practical tools to address religious extremism, prejudice and violence, and to help build open-minded and pluralist societies (this is explored in detail, with examples of the Foundation's work in the 2015 Impact Report). An important part of the Foundation's work since its inception in 2009 has been its global school dialogue programme; 'Generation Global' (Prior to June 2016, the Programme was called 'Face to Faith'. For clarity, I will refer to the current title throughout). This programme provides teachers in schools around the world with a robust and replicable pedagogy that enables them to cultivate the key skills of dialogue for their students, as well as facilitating opportunities to connect directly with their global peers (through videoconferencing and an online community) in order to practice those skills. A more detailed overview of the programme may be found at the Generation Global Website at http://generation.global/. The outcome of this is that students learn directly from one another, thus working effectively to break down their prejudices, building the critical thinking skills to develop resilience against extremist narratives, whilst simultaneously contributing to producing a generation of open-minded

I. Jamison (✉)
Tony Blair Faith Foundation, London, UK

141

young people who are at ease with difference. Since 2009, our records show that the programme has worked with over 2450 schools in over 30 countries, training over 9000 teachers, supporting nearly 250,000 students to engage in global dialogue in over 2400 videoconferences, and through an online community that has supported up to 30,000 registered students.

When the programme was first established, the intention was to provide young people with opportunities to dialogue directly with their global peers in order to break down barriers of misunderstanding and prejudice, and help students learn to navigate the diversity of the increasingly complex global community. As the programme has developed over time, that key experience of global dialogue still lies at its heart, but is now approached and understood in a more profound and urgent way. In the years that the programme has been operating, the world has been struck by increasing waves of violence driven by religious extremism. (The Centre for Religion and Geopolitics Extremism Monitor (2016) identified that, in January 2001, 11 religious extremist groups were recorded as carrying out violent attacks in seven countries. In January 2016, data shows 16 groups killing and kidnapping in 21 countries, with a total of 1673 fatalities.) In the light of this growth, the development of an open-minded understanding of 'the other' while learning to live peacefully with diversity can no longer be viewed as 'bolt on additions' to a core experience of education. If governments are going to satisfactorily address the scourge of extremism, then quality education, that helps young people cultivate higher order critical thinking skills, the practice of respectful dialogue, as well as the opportunity to explore and understand the diversity of the world in which they live, will be critical in driving this forward. In their literature review of the Education and CVE field, Ghosh et al. assert that:

> Respect for the other is an important value in a diverse society. Education that includes knowledge of the other involves a moral and ethical position and is not merely a cognitive function. The opportunity to question and challenge through dialogue, and to relate learning to lived experiences, are essential for developing empathy. This form of education, along with the promotion of a counter-narrative, can prepare students to develop the ability to critique extremist ideologies and refrain from succumbing to its sway. (Ghosh et al. 2016)

The Generation Global approach enables young people to develop these key skills and experiences that will help them to build resilience to extremist narratives (or more on education's role in building resilience against extremism by helping them to grow increasingly comfortable with ambiguity (Rose 2015). The idea is that there may not be one single right answer—while at the same time giving them the opportunity to dialogue respectfully in a safe space about the ideas that are important to them. This core idea of giving students a 'voice that may be heard around the world' is one that appeals to many teachers. The focus of Generation Global dialogues is upon faith and belief, values and identity, which are often precisely the areas that people find so difficult to understand about one another and of which many education systems fight shy; they choose to ignore them, believing them to be too difficult.

The underlying importance of using dialogue, and some of the complexity of that approach, as the core of the approach to changing student's attitudes, is clearly outlined in this reflection from a teacher:

> I have learnt to widen the idea I had about teaching and the role of teachers and I have come to share the Foundation's mission according to which if you help the young generations not to be afraid of diversity, to look at the world and its variety without prejudice, we will contribute to create a more stable society free from intolerance and extremism which today seem to be responsible for so much conflict all over the world. Dialogue is seen as the key to achieve a different attitude to the diversity of the world, but we all have experience that dialogue is often an abused word, though the real meaning of this word is unknown to most people. Thanks to this training programme I've had the chance to go deeper into dialogue and into what it really involves. I've learnt that if we want dialogue to take place, the first thing is that all participants must suspend their assumptions and certainties, because they lead only to conflict and polarization and impede true dialogue which should be based on each participant's wish to look at the opinion of others, to listen to what is on someone's mind, to be empathic and to respond to what other people say and feel. Dialogue is not debate either. Yet there is no dialogue if there is no challenge or disagreement. "Without contraries there is no progression", and it is somehow what to be wished for because when there is agreement on everything, it's hard to have true dialogue. All participants should however have a reason for dialogue and feel in an open, safe, comfortable environment where they can speak frankly about their values and opinion. (Class teacher, Secondary School, Italy)

THE MODEL

The Generation Global programme has a simple model to help schools practice global dialogue. The programme has produced a range of classroom materials which teachers can use to develop their students' skills. One of these, the 'Essentials of Dialogue', is the mandatory starting point for all schools taking part. As the name suggests, this material outlines a range of activities which develop the core skills necessary for taking part in successful dialogue. In addition to giving students opportunities to explore key facets of their own identity and cultivate critical thinking and a cultural/religious literacy, the focus is strongly upon developing the skills needed for effective dialogue. Generation Global identifies these as including active listening, confident global speaking (that is a self-aware approach to speaking to an audience that has not shared your life experiences), good 'response' questioning skills, and the practice of 'I language', a critical component of dialogue as it ensures that students take ownership of what they say while simultaneously avoiding generalisations. None of these skills are particularly difficult to acquire individually; experience from teacher workshops suggests that many teachers can identify individual students who are already gifted at some or many of these. The materials are designed, however, to ensure that a full range of students are able to participate, and are strongly based in a collaborative, student-centred pedagogy that seeks to provide teachers with techniques to empower all their students with these skills and experiences.

Having worked through these introductory materials, teachers then chose how their students can practice these skills with their global peers. This can be done either through facilitated videoconferences, which are provided by the programme or through virtual dialogue through the programme's dedicated online community. This experience is then completed through one or more reflection and review sessions, which integrate the experience into the student's learning (Tarrant 2013; Bolton 2014; Pollard et al. 2014; Sellars 2014; Fook et al. 2016). Having completed the 'Essentials of Dialogue' experience, teachers can choose to book their students into additional videoconferences or online dialogues (some of which are on specific topics; such as wealth, charity and poverty or human rights or human trafficking), and some of these topics will offer special guest videoconferences, where expert practitioners and academics are able to support students' learning by sharing their field experiences, and provoke deeper thinking and dialogue.

All these additional options are supported by preparatory materials that teachers can use to develop their students, whilst at the same time continuing to further cultivate their dialogue and thinking skills. The opportunities in the materials for developing thinking are noted in this comment from a school manager who observed some of the lessons:

> I was fascinated and engaged by the content of ideas and discussions in the lessons. So rarely in the course of their school day are students asked to think about concepts and ideas that could change their perspectives on their own lives and on the views and stereotypes that permeate their thoughts and attitudes. I left the classroom thinking about the questions that had been posed … and I suspect that the students would have also left, continuing to muse over the questions too. I was really interested to see how conceptual the lesson content was and how much it challenged the students to address the lazy assumptions that can form. I was also struck by how peaceful and calm the students were in these lessons when compared to how they may behave in others. They seemed more sensitive and open to personal discussion. (Deputy Principal, Secondary School, UAE)

Where possible, the Foundation supports teachers by providing experiential training workshops (recent examples include an introductory workshop as part of the Georgetown University Summer Institute on Experiencing and Teaching about World Religions in Washington, DC, and for a network of schools in Bangladesh); here teachers are introduced to the pedagogy of the programme by working through the experiences themselves. Many teachers, particularly in countries where there is a tradition of teaching in a more didactic style, need this experiential support as they move their practice into a more student-centred approach to learning and teaching (Dilon and Maguire 2011; Mellanby and Theobald 2014; Aubrey and Riley 2016; Bates 2016; Boyle and Charles 2016). Throughout our work with this programme, we've found teachers keen to enhance their own repertoire of pedagogical techniques, a situation that is exacerbated by the paucity of opportunities for CPD for teachers in many countries. At the same time, traditional didactic approaches often have a deleterious effect, embedding a black and white approach to thinking, which can underpin extremist narratives. Recent research by Comerford and El Badawy indicates that:

> Although teachers overwhelmingly emphasise the importance of developing critical thinking skills, a culture of rote learning is obstructing their

development in young people globally. In countries such as Kenya, Egypt and India, this was perpetuated by exam systems that encouraged memorisation of topics over engagement with issues. (Comerford and El Badawy 2016)

Many schools work hard to embed the techniques and approaches more broadly in their curriculum. A good example of this is the experience of our coordinator in Jordan, who has responded to strong local demand by training nearly one thousand teachers, who are not themselves directly taking part in the programme but whose principals have seen such a powerful effect in the classrooms of teachers who are, that they have asked us to provide whole school training. In order to further respond to this demand, an external-facing version of the Essentials of Dialogue, to support schools that are not engaged with the programme to cultivate the skills, is freely available for download from the Foundation's website at bit.ly/e-o-d in English, Arabic or Urdu. The English version is also available on iBooks at http://itunes.apple.com/us/book/id1125961970. This resource has been included as an example of good practice on the DFE 'Educate against Hate' website and will be included on similar platforms hosted by the Club de Madrid and the Brookings Institution.

CHALLENGES AND CONCERNS

Setting up a programme like this, even within one country, would be potentially challenging, and doing so on a global basis means that we've faced a number of particular challenges, including those of limited space in curricula, different patterns of school governance, the particular challenges of talking about faith and belief, and a range of issues to do with technology. I would like to reflect briefly on a few of these, which I hope will be useful for others working in this field.

Limited Curriculum Space

One of the great challenges that we've found in implementing Generation Global is that schools all over the world are under immense time pressure. Most school systems are now bound in tightly with centralised testing regimes and are judged according to their performance against national (and indeed international) comparisons, a process which Professor Robert Jackson laments as the 'PISAfication of education' (Jackson 2015; referring to the OECD 'PISA'international comparative reporting on educational attainment). This inevitably leads to a pressure to teach to the test and ignore everything else, a situation that is often exacerbated by school leaders who are often pressured into making strategic decisions from this basis. There are exceptions to this where teachers still enjoy considerable freedom to select what and how they teach, but these are increasingly rare.

Different Patterns of Governance

School systems around the world approach decision-making in different ways—many schools are at liberty to participate in initiatives that they believe to be beneficial—but many more are strictly governed by centralised administrations. In many countries access to government schools is impossible without the officially sanctioned imprimatur of the ministry.

Talking About Faith and Belief

In many countries, the explicit discussion of issues like faith, belief and identity entirely excluded from the education system and is regarded as far too controversial to be included. Where it is handled, it is genuinely done so from the point of view of inculcating a particular faith tradition. One of the important things to show people is that the dialogues here are age appropriate—students don't get into deep theological discourses, because they are speaking from their own experiences—but what they are able to do is talk freely about the things and ideas that are important to them. The understanding that results may be profound, but the terminology that builds it does not have to be. At the same time, young people only ever represent themselves; nobody is called upon to represent a country, a faith community or even a school—and this is one of the major differences with 'traditional' inter-faith dialogues, which are often rooted in that representational approach, and therefore exclude many young people who are regarded as ill-prepared to be a 'proper representative'. As Ghosh et al. point out, this challenge is part of a larger issue around the extent to which teachers are prepared to deal with difficult or controversial issues:

> Teachers typically avoid discussing controversial issues in the classroom, and countering violent religious extremism is no exception. This is often because it involves too much difficulty and risk requiring teachers to have well thought out and thorough lesson plans that can successfully deliver sophisticated information to the students, rather than merely 'classroom wizardry'. (Ghosh et al. 2016)

Technology

Although our globalised world is closely interconnected through technology, schools are not always places that are on the cutting edge of this. Many teachers also struggle with their own fears about using technology and have local cultures of usage. Schleicher (2016) states that OECD data suggests that 1 in 5 teachers in OECD countries feel that they need further training in using ICT in the classroom. For example, there are some regions of the world where contacting teachers through email will never work—but SMS or WhatsApp groups will generate successful connections; Indonesia is a critical example of this approach.

Some of the greatest challenges have resulted, not from lack of access to technology, but the way that it is controlled in the school. We've worked with some schools in the Middle East and Asia where there is an excellent internet connection, at least to the principal's office and administration. We've worked with others in the UK and the USA, so profoundly defended by firewalls and 'net nannies' that although students all have school email addresses, they can't communicate outside the school and are only allowed to access a small number of websites identified by the schools. In addressing this we've built up a thorough practice of working with the gatekeepers for each school's IT (which may be teachers within the school who are interested, a particular IT specialist in charge of the school or large corporate organisations who provide IT support to a range of schools—many of whom are excited to work on a programme that actually enables them to use IT with their students in a new way.

Fundamentally, all these challenges are about perceived risk: the risk of allowing students to express an opinion, the risk of working on subjects that will not be in exams, the risk of connecting young people to their peers. The mitigation of these challenges lies in helping people to change their perception and to appreciate the enormous benefits, but it's critically important to allow them to do this at their own speed (Beck 1992, 1999, 2005, 2013).

IMPACT

For the last academic year we've been working closely with a team of researchers at the University of Exeter, who have been undertaking an evaluation of the impact of the programme, particularly upon student attitudes. While this is still a work in progress, some initial analysis of the quantitative data has begun. During the survey period (Sept 2015 to May 2016), over 11,000 student survey forms were received electronically, along with detailed information about each school represented, completed by teachers. In addition, teachers provided information about each video-conference event that they prepared their students for. Initial analysis of these responses shows that the measurement instruments used with students (measuring 'dialogic open-mindedness', MDOM and 'Knowledge and Experience of Difference', KED) were very reliable and that at the commencement of the programme, students taking part and those in a control group in each school (who did not take part in the programme) scored similarly on both scales.

The data gathered is complex, exploring cleaned responses from 1200 individuals from 90 schools in 17 different countries at a number of points across the survey period. Because of this, there is no simple story, but we can see that overall, students participating in the programme reported greater increases in MDOM than those who did not take part, but patterns of change were different at both school and country level. Initial findings suggest that a significant amount of the variation in post-event scores is related to school level effects rather than individual student effects, but that these affects are similar across schools in the same country. From a preliminary analysis, factors such as teacher experience, level of qualification and length of training do not appear to statistically affect changes in student scores, but further analysis of this data, including the effect of different types and lengths of preparation for involvement in videoconferences, is currently underway and will be reported elsewhere.

In addition to the Exeter research, we have built up a large amount of qualitative feedback—anecdotal evidence from students, parents and teachers (All quotes in this chapter were submitted in the period 2015/2016; they are also representative of general themes that are more widely reported). I'm going to reflect upon some of the key points that emerge from those, and the starting point for thinking about the impact of this work lies in the critical experience of communication for the students. Sometimes just the experience of being able to communicate with global peers is in itself a source of excitement:

> I am living in Quetta, Baluchistan, which is one of the backward province of Pakistan as far as education and health is concerned. And for girls and female, society is very conservative. Thanks to Generation Global organization for giving me a chance to talk and share my feelings with outside world.

> We girls are not allowed to chat with other people on internet but my parents do not have any objection for me to sit in the video conference and share my views with other people of the world. (Female Student, Quetta, Pakistan)

For many students, however, the experience of direct encounters with their peers can effect powerful changes in attitude towards the other, and this is rooted in the way that the Generation Global experience allows students to personalise the other. All too often our young people learn about the world through sources that, consciously or unconsciously, homogenise people into groups. When people are perceived within groups, then prejudice and othering are both easily cultivated. Through the direct experience of dialogue, young people are able to directly encounter one another, in a safe environment, that enables them to step beyond the ideas promulgated by their media or text books. It may be useful here to refer to Levinas—for whom ethical concern comes as the first element of mutual encounter; the obligation to care for the Other is the a priori state. Levinas refers to the idea of 'the face' (with considerable resonance for 'Generation Global') as the way in which we encounter the Other—"…the encounter with the face—that is, moral consciousness, can be described as the condition of consciousness tout cort' (Levinas 2002: 11). In this short quote, one may find a distillation of three of the most significant elements of Levinas' thought. Firstly, that one meets the Other through an encounter with the face; secondly, that this encounter is, by its very nature, a profound form of ethics; and thirdly, that the primary condition of consciousness itself is ethical concern—'ethics comes first'. I think that this focus reveals some of the power of the videoconference technology—because one is actually able to see the face of the speaker (and indeed we encourage students to think about their body language too), there is a surprising sense of connection. Students, teachers from many countries across the programme, as well as visiting speakers have all commented upon this. Of course, sometimes the technology is imperfect—but the human ability to recognise a face should not be underestimated. Levinas' language of 'the face' is also unconsciously used by this student from the USA discussing the depth of his experience in Generation Global:

> There is so much that goes on in the world that I have not experienced or truly understood despite having seen it all on the news. Actual contact with someone in a certain situation is far more meaningful to me than seeing

someone analyse it on TV. It also puts a face to situations that I would probably otherwise consider distant or unimportant. (Student, USA)

This 'putting a face to the other' is also significant for students' deeper understanding both of the stories that they see on the news, but also of the impact that this has upon young people like themselves. Here a student from the Philippines reflects upon their dialogue with Syrian students from a refugee camp in Jordan, and what they have learned from it, finding inspiration from those difficult stories:

Before this, I constantly complained about how tired I was, especially with my academics and the college entrance tests. I wanted time to rest and be free from stress even for a week. When I got to talk to the Syrian refugees, I realized that all my complaints, my hardships were nothing compared to what they were going through. Just a few days ago, I was complaining about lack of sleep—and here they are—the Syrian refugees who cannot even go to sleep assured with their safety. Their families are torn apart and they are far from their homes. Also, my physical exhaustion was insignificant compared to theirs. They lack comfort, emotional support and security. I learned that there are many people all over the world who are struggling. Their conditions are unimaginable at times, yet here we are, complaining about homework or quizzes. The refugees, at such young age, have gone through so much in their life, yet they still continue to smile and have a positive outlook in life. I learned that we should never give up. (Student, Philippines)

Probably the most interesting examples of this kind of attitude change come where students 'attitudes to the others are sharply focused by their own culture—where prejudicial viewpoints are not merely inculcated at home—and by peers, but also by media and broader society'. I want to concentrate upon two particular examples of this; the first from our coordinator in Quetta, Pakistan. (Local coordinators support the programme in many countries, delivering training, as well as giving schools technical support) ...

...here in Quetta there are many students who were initially were extremist background, and after completing videoconference with Indian students, with American students... for example yesterday we had a video-conference with an American school and I have seen that after completing the video-conferencing, although it was their 1st VC, the whole concept changed in their mind. One student said that during the time he was reflecting that 'before when I was preparing for the videoconference I was thinking so many thing about the US students, but after doing this it was really a different experience for me'.

This concentrates upon the fact that the students here are conducting videoconferences with peers from other societies that are portrayed as antagonistic to the popular culture where they live and that students' perspectives are informed by some very conservative social and religious views (and important to note that, for many students in this region, extremist violence is part of their regular personal life experience). The other half of the story is told by a Religious Education teacher from an urban school in the UK, who told us about her experience of working with

> ...a group of boys who were in such a fixed-mindset about Islam. A deep-rooted ignorance that all Muslims are terrorists and should 'go home'. I contacted [the team] who helped me pair up with a group of students from the Muslim faith who could challenge these prejudices and stereotypes. The change in attitudes these boys had after using the resources about dialogue and participating in VC's was extraordinary—something which is one of the memorable moments of my teaching career.

Similar changes may be seen reported by this Polish student: ' we've learnt today that Islam is not a bad religion, and it's not a religion like what people in Polish television or Polish politics try and tell us', where the ability to critique the influences of surrounding society may be seen.

One of the most critical elements of the dialogical approach is its profound reciprocity. Once students move past seeing the other *en bloc*, as objectified, they enter what Buber describes as the 'I-Thou' relationship. It is a significant existential and authentic relationship between two beings which grants ethical recognition to the Other. Such relationships are seen as significant encounters where some form of mutuality and exchange takes place: 'one should not try to dilute the meaning of the relation, relation is reciprocity' (Buber 1970: 58). This is particularly significant in terms of the Generation Global experience—inasmuch as that it is not merely about learning from or about the other but is also about teaching them—speaking about our own experiences, beliefs and identity. It is always a mutual, reciprocal exchange. This means that students are not passive consumers of information, using one another as resources, but engaged in a vital exchange where they are empowered to feel that they have a voice that can be heard around the world. This is articulated beautifully in this feedback from a Generation Global teacher at an international school in Egypt:

> ...they felt awesome at the end of VC, when they found out they could be persuasive and change for a moment the opinion of their counterparts in US towards Egyptians. There were some very challenging questions from their counterparts which allowed my students to discover themselves more than ever.

The emphasis here is upon what students learned about themselves; not just in reaction to their responses to their interlocutors, but also in terms of their reflections upon the experience. This sense of learning about the self as a result of dialogue is regularly reported by Generation Global teachers, who often go into the programme with the intention of helping their students to learn about the other, but are often surprised that the most profound learning occurs in Students' self-discovery.

In addition to the impact upon students' attitudes to the other, teachers and parents report a number of other changes in their young people. The emphasis upon collaborative student participation in the preparation materials enables many students to grow in self-esteem and develop greater confidence; indeed it is striking how often teachers comment that the student who took a leading role in a videoconference dialogue is one that was previously very reticent about contributing in class. This is noted by both parents (in this case, of a secondary age student in Egypt):

> ... this program gives my daughter self-confidence to talk freely and express her own ideas, it supports the sense of communication between her friends and people from other countries ...

> ... and by students themselves ...

> ... Before attending Generation Global videoconferences, I was nervous and shy. But then I found the real me. Anyway I became tolerant also. My mindset has been changed after attending these VCs. Apart from being confident, this Generation Global organisation made me communicative instead. (Secondary Student, Poland)

From a pedagogical perspective, many teachers have been enthusiastic about the Generation Global materials—not merely in terms of supporting the development of the skills critical for participation in the programme but also in broader terms as well. In many of the countries doing Generation Global (which includes numbers of schools in the USA, Ukraine, Italy, the UK, Israel, Egypt, Palestine, Jordan, the UAE, Pakistan, India, Indonesia, the Philippines and Mexico—as well as individual schools in other countries), teachers often struggle with a very didactic classroom culture. Teachers are seen as the expert who owns the knowledge necessary to pass the exams; teaching is the process by which this knowledge is imparted to students—frequently by copying from the board or reading from an approved text book. There is a great deal of talk about child-centred pedagogies, and the cultivation of critical thinking, but there is very little practical support to help get this into the classroom. The Generation Global materials, particularly the Essentials of Dialogue, give teachers a set of reliable classroom resources that empower them to start cultivating this approach. Where we are able to deliver teacher training workshops, these take teachers through the experiences that we want the students to have; this is not an abstract lecture on pedagogy, but a reflective experience. Once students have started to acquire and practice these skills, it can often have a strong impact on both the culture of the classroom and on students' behaviour. A teacher in a government school in Palestine commented:

> Mostafa was very impulsive in class; he used to talk without permission, cutting speech of teachers and not listening. After we had the lessons of EoD, he became calmer, listens better in class and raises his hands before he speaks! It was a remarkable transformation for us.

Many teachers report similar impact on their students; in Jordan many schools, after seeing the impact on the classrooms of teachers trained in this approach, have approached our coordinator for whole staff training in the pedagogy, as they wish to embed this across the whole school. At the same time, some teachers are suggesting that this impact also extends to the academic attainment of their students; this particular example is from a government school in Palestine:

> … my students have become more motivated since their participation in the program and attending VCs. They have scored 20% more from other 8th Graders in some general math exam and we (the teachers) think the program had a contribution to this positive impact.

The potential for this kind of activity to support lasting change in societies is outlined by Luisito G. Montalbo, Undersecretary in the Office of the Presidential Adviser on the Peace Process (Generation Global has facilitated a number of videoconferences between students in Metro Manila and Mindanao, with dialogue around the Bangsamoro Peace Process):

> Deliberately teaching students the skills to dialogue will help create a strong constituency that expresses, sees and reaches out to persons of different cultural practices and faiths. I endorse this free resource for use, especially by schools in the Philippines, as it can help create a culture of encounter and understanding—seed beds of voices for peace.

THE FUTURE

More and more people around the world are realising the critical importance of helping young people to be prepared for a future in a globalised world; it is becoming a very urgent concern in education systems across the globe. Schleicher's (2016) announcement at the Dubai Global Education Forum that the OECD are preparing to pilot a new metric of 'Global Competence' in PISA 2018, demonstrates how these ideas are truly becoming a significant part of the education landscape. At the same time, an informed and nuanced understanding of the complex role that faith, beliefs and identities play in the globalised world becomes ever more important.

In addition to the rebranding that the programme has undergone, we've been supported to develop an entirely new website—designed from the ground up to support young people from around the world in dialogue, and we are piloting a series of new resources aimed at building on the experience of global dialogue to support teachers who are struggling to deal with many of the difficult questions that their students are increasingly likely to bring into the classroom. This is both by giving them tools from the dialogical approach to create appropriate environments in their classroom, as well as incorporating the cutting edge research of the Centre on Religion and Geopolitics to develop a nuanced understanding of the challenges of Religious Extremism in the contemporary world. If teachers feel that they don't have the tools to help their young people understand the challenges faced by societies around the world, then those young people are likely to seek understanding online, which may be counterproductive in a number of ways.

The Tony Blair Faith Foundation believes that Generation Global has a significant part to play in establishing best practice, and in developing appropriate resources to share freely with others in order to ensure that our common aim, of empowering young people with the skills and attitudes that they need to build a better world, is realised. In the future as well as continuing to develop new materials, we will continue to advocate for access to quality education for all students; a quality education that will emphasise the enormous significance of dialogue and critical thinking. We seek to build partnerships and leverage support to ensure that young people all over the world are able to develop these critical skills, share these empowering experiences, and be prepared to play their part in building a more peaceful future for all.

References

Aubrey, K., & Riley, A. (2016). *Understanding and using educational theories*. London: Sage.
Bates, B. (2016). *Learning theories simplified*. London: Sage.
Beck, U. (1992). *Risk society. Towards a new modernity*. Sage: London.
Beck, U. (1999). *World risk society*. Cambridge: Polity Press.
Beck, U. (2005). *Power in the global age*. Cambridge: Polity Press.
Beck, U. (2013). *German Europe*. Cambridge: Polity Press.
Bolton, G. (2014). *Reflective Practice* (4th ed.). London: Sage.
Boyle, B., & Charles, M. (2016). *Curriculum development*. London: Sage.
Buber, M. (1970). *I and Thou*. New York: Simon and Schuster.
Centre on Religion & Geopolitics Global Extremism Monitor. (2016). Retrieved September 17, 2016, from http://www.tonyblairfaithfoundation.org/religion-geopolitics/reports-analysis/report/global-extremism-january-2016
Comerford, M., & El-Badawy, E. (2016). Schools of thought; education for open minds: The global state of play. *Centre on Religion and Geopolitics*.
Dilon, J., & Maguire, M. (Eds.). (2011). *Becoming a teacher. Issues in Secondary Education*. Maidenhead: McGraw Hill Education.
Fook, J., Collington, V., Ross, F., Ruch, G., & West, L. (Eds.). (2016). *Researching critical reflection*. Abingdon: Routledge.
Ghosh, R., Chan, A. W. Y., Manuel, A., Dilimulati, M., & Babaie, M. (2016). Education and security; A global literature review on the role of education in countering violent religious extremism. Retrieved September 17, 2016, from http://tonyblairfaithfoundation.org/foundation/news/education-and-security
Jackson, R. (2015, June 16). 'The Interpretative Approach' – Presentation at Tony Blair Faith Foundation and McGill University Intensive Training Course on 'Education and Security".

Levinas, E. (2002). I's ontology fundamental? In A. Peperzak, S. Critchely, R. Bernasconi, & E. Levinas (Eds.), *Basic philosophical writings* (pp. 1–11). Bloomington: University of Indiana Press.

Mellanby, J., & Theobald, K. (2014). *Education and learning: An evidence-based approach*. Chichester: John Wiley and Sons.

Pollard, A., Black-Hawkins, K., Hodges, G. C., Dudley, P., James, M., Linklater, H., Swaffield, S., Swann, S., Turner, F., Warwick, P., Winterbottom, M., & Walport, M. A. (2014). *Reflective teaching in schools*. London: Bloomsbury.

Rose, M. (2015). *Immunising the mind*. Retrieved September 17, 2016, from https://www.britishcouncil.org/sites/default/files/immunising_the_mind_working_paper.pdf

Schleicher, A. (2016, March 12). Making education everyone's business. Presentation at Global Education and Skills Forum, Dubai. Retrieved September 17, 2016, from http://www.slideshare.net/OECDEDU/making-education-everybodys-business

Sellars, M. (2014). *Reflective practice for teachers*. London: Sage.

Tarrant, P. (2013). *Reflective practice and professional development*. London: Sage.

Tony Blair Faith Foundation. (2015). Impact report. Retrieved September 17, 2016, from http://www.tonyblairfaithfoundation.org/foundation/news/our-impact-2015

Ian Jamison is Head of Education and Training at the Tony Blair Faith Foundation. Before working for the Foundation, Ian taught Religious Education for 20 years and has experience of innovative subject leadership in a number of schools across the UK. Involved in the Generation Global programme since its inception, Ian has been privileged to train teachers, run workshops and work directly with young people in over 20 countries. Ian has international experience of delivering training on the Pedagogy of Dialogue, working with educators and religious leaders in a number of very challenging situations, and is a passionate advocate of the power of dialogue for empowering people to address challenges and transform their societies for the better.

Success and Multiculturalism in Finnish Schools

Heidi Layne, Fred Dervin, and Rita Johnson Longfor

INTRODUCTION

In June 2015 the main national Finnish newspaper (*Helsingin Sanomat, HS*) (2015a) published an article explaining that girls with a Somali background were guided toward careers in practical nursing in schools, even if they dreamt of a career as medical doctors. The following month (2015b), one Member of Parliament from the far-right "populist" party, The Finns, announced on his Facebook page that multiculturalism was a nightmare in Finland, and in the larger context of Europe. In 2015–2016 the situation with asylum seekers has changed how immigrants are discussed in the media in many European countries. The so-called "refugee crisis" has raised a wave of demonstrations, both rejecting and defending multiculturalism in Finland. Within this context the 3-year Nordic research project entitled Learning Spaces for Social Justice and Inclusion has tried to understand the good practices and success of education from immigrant students' perspectives.

In this chapter we investigate how multiculturalism is problematized through the notion of success in Finnish education. We adopt a critical race theory (CRT) approach (Leonardo 2009; Solorzano and Yosso 2002)

H. Layne (✉) • F. Dervin • R.J. Longfor
University of Helsinki, Helsinki, Finland

© The Author(s) 2018   159
R. Race (ed.), *Advancing Multicultural Dialogues in Education*,
DOI 10.1007/978-3-319-60558-6_10

and apply Ahmed's (2012) research on white institutional antiracism. Whereas in many European countries immigration has become an increasingly conspicuous phenomenon in the post-war period, Finland began to receive immigrants in larger numbers in the 1990s. This demographic change has affected education, although not to a large extent, as the belief that multiculturalism does not concern all educators is still widespread in Finland (Itkonen et al. 2015; Dervin 2015; Dervin et al. 2012). Individuals with diverse backgrounds have, of course, always been present in Finnish education, but only the larger number of immigrants has been perceived as heralding the beginning of multicultural education (research).

This has also impacted on multicultural education policies and practices, where the focus is now on engaging solely children and families from diverse ethnic backgrounds (Riitaoja 2013). The population with an immigrant background has increased from 26,000 in the 1990s to 280,000 in 2012 (Statistics Finland 2012). In recent years, immigration has diversified and temporary migration has also grown. People come to Finland primarily because of family ties, study or work. However, the asylum seeker and refugee situation in 2015–2016 around the world is also changing the demographics in Finland maybe faster than ever. In addition to migration taking place directly from abroad, people who speak other languages than Finnish and Swedish as their home languages also move to the bigger cities like the capital city Helsinki, Tampere (Southern Finland) and Turku (Southwest coast of Finland).

The data for this chapter were collected from schools offering compulsory education in Helsinki and Turku. Helsinki is the capital of Finland with around 73,608 (2013) non-Finnish-, non-Swedish- and non-Sami-speaking residents, which is circa 12% of the whole population. The city of Turku is the fifth biggest city in Finland. In 2012, the number of overseas citizens in Turku was 10,086. The number of residents speaking a language other than Finnish or Swedish as their mother tongue was 15,609 (8.7%). All in all, more than 100 languages are spoken in Turku (see Statistics of Finland; Kumpulainen 2014).

FINNISH EDUCATION: SOME MYTHS AND REALITIES

According to the Finnish Ministry of Education and Culture, one of the basic principles of Finnish education is that all people must have equal access to high-quality education and training. The same opportunities should be available to all citizens irrespective of their ethnic origin, age, and wealth or where they live. Education policies are built on the principle of lifelong learning (National Curriculum for Basic Education (NCBE) 2014). The basic right to education and culture is also recorded in the Constitution. Public authorities must secure equal opportunities for every resident in Finland to get education also after compulsory schooling and to develop themselves, irrespective of their financial standing. Until 2017, education was free at all levels from pre-primary to higher education. Starting in August 2017, non-EU students will have to pay fees for degrees taught in English at university (ICEF Monitor 2016). Adult education may also require payment. In high school the students need to buy their schoolbooks, which sometimes places families facing unemployment or/ and with an immigrant background in a more difficult position.

The Ministry of Education and Culture states that the keywords in Finnish education policy are quality, efficiency, equality/equity and inter-nationalization. The broad perspectives of Finnish education and science policy are in line with the European 2020 Strategy. Decisions on the contents of legislation on education and research are made by the Parliament, based on government proposals. The government and the Ministry of Education and Culture are responsible for preparing and implementing education and science policy.

Basic education is a free 9-year education provided for the whole age groups in comprehensive schools (currently c. 60,000 children). Compulsory schooling starts when a child turns 7 and ends after the basic education syllabus has been completed or after 10 years of schooling. The local or school curriculum is based on a national core curriculum (NCBE 2014). Completing the basic education syllabus does not lead to any qual-ification, but the school-leaving certificate gives access to upper secondary education or to vocational schools. Nearly all children complete their compulsory schooling. Young people who have completed their compul-sory schooling can opt for one extra year. This voluntary education is intended to help and encourage young people to continue their studies at the upper secondary level (Sahlberg and Hargreaves 2011).

The Finnish National Board of Education determines the national core curriculum for basic education (NCBE 2014). It includes the objec-tives and core contents of different subjects, as well as the principles of pupil assessment, special-needs education, pupil welfare and educational guidance. The education providers, usually the local education authori-ties and the schools themselves draw up their own curricula for pre-pri-mary and basic education within the framework of the national core curriculum. Currently the new national curriculum has become active in the autumn of 2016 (NCBE 2016). The new curriculum emphasizes developing schools as learning communities, and promoting the joy of learning and a collaborative atmosphere, as well as encouraging student autonomy in studying and in school life. The learning goals of the transversal competences are described as seven competence areas. This is a new way of combining competence-based and subject-based teaching and learning. Nevertheless, the traditional school subjects live on, though with less distinct borderlines and with more collaboration in practice between them. In the new curriculum, the aim is to shift from the idea of multicultural education toward multilingualism and cultural competencies as well as multi-literacy (NCBE 2014; Paatela-Nieminen and Itkonen 2016).

Basic education is divided into grades. Classes 1–6 are mainly taught by class teachers and classes 7–9 by specialized subject teachers. As a rule, all teachers have a Master's level university degree. Teachers themselves can choose the teaching methods they use in order to achieve the objectives stated in the curriculum. The national core curriculum includes guidelines for choosing the methods. Commercial publishers mostly produce learning materials. The schools and teachers themselves decide on the material and textbooks used. The same applies to the use of ICT. Students who do not master Finnish or Swedish at a mother tongue level need to be provided with Finnish/Swedish as a second language teaching during school hours. Mother tongue teaching is recommended but it takes place outside school hours, and since it is not mandatory according to the current language policies, the quality and resources to provide such teaching varies placing students in unequal positions. Mother tongue teachers often lack a background in education, which also affects the quality of teaching and how it is delivered (Layne 2016).

The Turku School

The school has 900 students with 25% students whose first language is other than the school language (Finnish). It is located in a neighborhood with a large population of what is often considered as people with an immigrant background, although many families have lived there for a long time and their children were born in Finland. This is also socioeconomically considered as a challenging neighborhood with large areas of city housing. The ideology of the school is to be there for the "whole village";

therefore they keep the school doors open all day. The main aim of basic education in this school is in every possible way to support and take care of each student's achievement in their studies. The school mission statement explains that the goal is that each student gets the best possible school report at the end of compulsory education and continues to study. Having this type of active school located in this type of neighborhood adds value to the area. The school works hard in promoting the neighborhood, and tackling issues such as school dropouts, the provision of hobbies and after-school activities available for all.

In this school we also found some teachers with an immigrant background who worked as regular teachers, not just as "mother tongue teachers", outside the normal school hours, which is typical of the Finnish school system. Instead of multiculturalism, this school has shifted their emphasis toward "real multilingualism". When conducting observations at the school, it is really one of the most authentic multilingual schools in Finland and one can hear many languages across the school corridors and in the cafeteria. Children use their mother tongues freely outside the classroom and sometimes inside. Areas of emphasis at the compulsory level include art, media, science and language (Middle Years Programme: MYP).

Teaching in the various subjects may involve the use of a language other than the school's language of teaching, in which case language is not merely the target of teaching and learning, but a tool for learning the content of a subject. In each grade level there is one classroom where teachers utilize the Content and Language Integrated Learning (CLIL) method, where teaching is done 25% in English. The curriculum corresponds both in quantity and content to the general curriculum for basic education (School Based Curriculum, 2014–2015). Every year the school organizes a week during which they promote multiculturalism, solidarity and multilingualism. During the data collection such activities were observed and students were interviewed about them.

After-school club activities are provided to the students outside school hours. The idea for these clubs is to provide opportunities for children to take part in hobbies that would not be economically possible for them otherwise. The planning officer for these club activities was interviewed during data collection. Although the official name of these activities contains "multicultural", they are open to all the children. The planning officer coordinates these club activities in close collaboration with the school, and is also responsible for communicating about the club activities with home. The after-school club activity brochure was translated into nine languages spoken by students in the school.

The need for these club activities has also allowed solving some of the challenges that the school has faced. For instance, young people hang around the school premises after school, which causes some challenges. The school distributed a survey to the students asking them about the kinds of activities they would like to take part in after-school hours. It has not been an easy task to attract the young people who are not used to taking part in hobbies. Yet they have collaborated closely with teachers and parents. They have different kinds of sport clubs, a girls' club, art clubs, cooking clubs and clubs where they build small airplanes. They have also organized multicultural cooking events for families, which have been very successful. Also some Finnish families have taken part in these events. Right now they also have a media club in collaboration with the Finnish National Broadcasting Company. They set as one condition for the projects to happen that students can produce news both in Finnish and in their mother tongues. One purpose of the clubs is also to activate collaboration with the neighborhood.

The school leaders and teachers are to some extent aware of the challenges that the students face in the school. Many teachers had chosen this school because they wanted to be part of this type of learning community. Many teachers in this school hold PhDs in education and have applied their research to school life. Mother tongue teachers have a big responsibility in bridging the families with an immigrant background to school life. They are seen as the "trusted" people. Yet they do not have permanent positions or full time positions in the schools.

Case Helsinki

The school is located in eastern Helsinki, in a modern urban area next to a University campus. The modern school building is also considered part of this campus. The school has a total of 940 students, from pre-school to upper secondary level. It is considered as one of the top performing schools in this region, based on national examinations. The school is also considered as a "successful school" since entry into many upper secondary schools in Finland is competitive with this school requiring an average point of 9.7/10 to be accepted. The educational philosophy of the school is built on teaching students skills and knowledge needed for the future. One of its main emphases is also research in the "natural" school context.

Therefore, the school, in collaboration with the National Board of Education, participates in research in local, national and international projects in general and teacher education (Viiki Teacher Training School n.d.).

In this school we found no immigrant teacher, however, there were immigrant teachers working outside school hours in mother tongue instruction. It was very clear from initial conversations with some school leaders that immigrants or immigrant students are those who speak other languages than Finnish. During the conversations and interviews, it also became clear that some broad notions of multiculturalism or celebrations of different languages are promoted in the school. When conducting the observations, Finnish remained the most widely spoken language in the corridors. The discussion on "immigrant success" in the interviews became very evasive as participants preferred to discuss success in relation to speaking the Finnish language and not in relation to the broader socioeconomic-academic context. Having this type of school where all students are already considered highly successful, based on some objective criteria of success, adds to our overall objective of understanding how these students are supported academically and socially in education. The City of Helsinki, in collaboration with the school, organizes club activities outside school hours for most students. During our interviews most participants reported making use of these social activities as a means to expand their social groups and staying in touch with friends in different schools.

THEORETICAL FRAMING: CRITICAL RACE THEORY AND INSTITUTIONAL ANTIRACISM

A critical race theory in education starts from the premise that race and ethnicity are socially constructed and "a central, rather than marginal factor in defining and explaining individual experiences" (Solorzano and Yosso 2002, p. 24). Leonardo (2009) argues further that admitting to the existence of white privilege is not enough, but understanding the process of white domination is essential (Leonardo 2009, p. 261). In Finnish schools the number of teachers with an immigrant background is still marginal which directly relates to the issue of white dominance in education. This leads to the fact that the narratives of Finnish school life are still dominantly presented from the (white) majority perspective. The main focus of this chapter is to present how the school staff, predominantly white Finnish teachers trained in Finland, discuss the position of immigrant students, their needs and their opportunities in the future.

The idea of critical race theory is used to give a voice to those who are often silenced (Solorzano and Yosso 2002). The counter-narratives in this chapter (silenced voices) are presented through an article from the main national newspaper *Helsingin Sanomat* (*Helsinki News*), which introduces the voices of students with a Somali background and how they are still guided to become practical nurses instead of doctors although their school success and their personal dreams are more related to the field of medicine (see *Helsingin Sanomat*, June 24, 2015). The representative from the Finnish National Board of Education stated in the article (*Helsingin Sanomat*, June 24, 2015) that there is no purposive misguidance or discrimination behind the guidance.

Finnish education is considered to be the "World's best education system" according to the OECD's Programme for International Student Assessment (PISA) (Dervin 2012; Schatz et al. 2015). However, when in December 2012 Finland dropped a few places in the PISA rankings, some researchers tried to find a reason and the blame started to be put on the lower scores of immigrant students who were deemed unable to study properly in Finland because of the "high quality" of the education system and their lack of Finnish language skills (Harju-Luukkainen et al. 2014; see also *Helsingin Sanomat*, August 18, 2015). The *category of the immigrant* is rarely properly defined: at times reference is made towards first-generation immigrants and sometimes to second-generation immigrants. Another article cited in this study deals with the theme of decreasing PISA success of Finnish education and the role of immigrant students in it (*Helsingin Sanomat*, August 18, 2015).

In this chapter we report the results of the research on how teachers and school psychologists discuss the opportunities and success of immigrant students. By silencing certain voices, an image of equal education can be maintained—less successful students over more successful, and good schools over not so highly appreciated schools. Our analysis relies on Ahmed's (2006) institutional level of analysis, whose components are as follows:

- *Admissions* refer to ongoing processes, actions and inactions such as signs stating certain areas as anti-discriminatory zones. The problem with this type of admission is that they lead us to talk about what we have done instead of what we fail to do. Admissions can also be claimed as a collective prejudice, as a claim for race-equality policy and being good at it.

- By *describing diversity* Ahmed (2006) means the type of commitment to diversity that invokes difference but does not act on injustices (equality-diversity).
- *Commitment* may lead to poor recognition. It is easier to claim that we all want justice than to recognize blind spots. In fact, often, antiracist movements lead to "pride" and to "a tick in the box" rather than really affecting the structures that support systems of injustices.
- *Good performance* stands for good practices for equality and diversity. This is actually a step further from ticking the box. It often means producing some kind of "toolkit" to teach about, for example, multiculturalism in school. Being good at writing documents becomes a competency and at the same time an obstacle to acts aiming to fight against, for example, the structures for white nomination (on an institutional level) (Ahmed 2006, p. 110; Leonardo 2009).

Alongside Ahmed's ideas, Leonardo (2009) agrees that admissions (i.e. ongoing actions and inactions) do not necessarily mean ending domination. Leonardo (2009) talks about the challenges of racism seen as an individual act. He also argues that whiteness as domination and a form of structural discrimination is rarely taught about at school or universities (Leonardo 2009, p. 268). The analysis in this chapter focuses on the type of commitment to diversity and multicultural education the teachers, study counselors and other school staff discuss in our data.

DATA COLLECTION AND ANALYSIS

Critical race theory methodology by Solorzano and Yosso (2002), concentrates on multiple voices and especially on giving voice to those that are not normally heard. Moreover, it allows us to address silenced topics. However, the fact that we have interviewed school staff limits us to demonstrate the "silenced" voices in a sense that the school staff mainly represent the "white" Finnish population who speak Finnish or Swedish as a first language (Finland is officially a bilingual country, Finnish and Swedish). Of course we are aware that there are many more dimensions than language (hierarchies) and race to categorize "us" and "others" or the majority vs. minority. The main idea is to present critical issues in relation to how some students are labeled as immigrant students and how are they are constructed in the school context.

The data were collected in the form of interviews. Kvale (1996) writes about two different contrasting metaphors of interviewers' paths—the miner and the traveler. The miner metaphor refers to knowledge as "given", whereas the traveler metaphor to the constructive formation of knowledge. Multiculturalism being such a critical topic in the current state of Europe and Finland, it is difficult to approach the topic with a blank mind (Layne 2016; Phillips 2007; Race 2015; Dervin 2015). Multiculturalism is also a topic that divides people ideologically and politically (Holiday 2010; Breidenbach and Nyiri 2009). Therefore, it is impossible to claim that we the interviewers purely approached the topic as *travelers* starting to construct knowledge from an "empty" blank state of mind. However, the interview questions were open—not strictly structured but more as a framework for what we wanted to know and understand—and constructed in the format of the interview as a travel.

Data was analyzed using the thematic analysis method. The aim of thematic analysis is to attain a condensed and broad description of a particular phenomenon. In thematic analysis the reasoning is often referred to in two different ways: inductive and deductive. Inductive is more data-driven from more general towards theory, and deductive more testing of hypothesis and driven by theory to confirmation of a certain hypothesis (Elo and Kyngäs 2008). When analyzing the data, we did not have a specific hypothesis in mind; however, we wanted to understand better how students are labeled as immigrants and what kind of assumptions and expectations are behind the label. Some social scientists use both methods of reasoning in the analysis and it is fair to say that our analysis is testing both. The analysis below is following Ahmed's (2006) dimensions for institutional antiracism attempts.

Results

The results are discussed in two different sections based on Ahmed's (2006) theories, first describing the diversity talk and then the subject of immigration followed by a section on commitment. The conclusions are combined with the analysis of good practices that were identified during the data collection, but also the vulnerability of such hegemony of good practices. The central theme of the analysis is how the immigrant subject is constructed in both the *teachers' talk and the media*. Related to the *immigrant subject* diversity talk refers to how roots and belonging are constructed for the immigrant subject. *Commitment* refers to the type of action or power structures that are affecting how strongly the commitments are embedded into school communities. *Good practices* are auditable. Being good at writing documents becomes competency and at the same time an obstacle. The danger of good practices is that tasks and practices toward justice are considered as "completed" once "they are completed". Achieving social justice is a process, not a statistic stage that can be achieved (Layne 2016).

Diversity Talk

In public debates immigrants are often discussed as problems, and their children in the Finnish school system as a challenge with insufficient language and cultural skills (Layne and Lipponen 2016; Tuori 2009). However, it is difficult to determine who these immigrants are in the media and in the field of education. How does one fall under the category of the immigrant? The danger is that it takes place under the category of skin color since the learning material used in Finland can still easily give the false image of Finnish children being blond and white and therefore people with different characteristics being depicted as the other. Sometimes immigrant status is determined by a name, a language spoken at home, a social class and by the circulation of generations like first-, second- or third-generation immigrants. In Finland "choosing better schools over the worse schools" has become an art form although we still often hear that the system of school catchment areas is making the school choices fair for all (Kilpi-Jakonen 2012). There is a difference of reputation between a school with a large number of immigrants and international schools (leading also to categories such as immigrants vs. expatriates, the "global elite" and the "global poor"; see Andreotti and Pashby 2013). In policy terms diversity (immigrants) has come to mean inclusion of people who look different in Finland (Puwar 2004, p. 1; Riitaoja 2013).

Finnish teachers described the immigrant students bringing "hassle" with their home culture and also with religious demands. Immigrant students were also referred to as having limited Finnish language and lower school results—without questioning the responsibility of teachers and institutions. Some teachers seem to share quite a limited view on how it is to be a young person in Finland, what is normal and what is not. This may also explain why students with an immigrant background are expected to score lower and be guided toward lower future professions like practical nurses instead of medicine or medical doctor education. The two teachers with an immigrant background emphasized the importance of bilingualism and understanding the family background. They also stated that they discuss in their teaching with the young people about their identity being somewhere in the intersection of Finnishness and something else. In the next section we explain in more detail how the immigrant subject is constructed and reconstructed in the media and in the data.

(Re)Construction of the Immigrant Subject

This section discusses the way in which school staff discussed the category of the immigrant. It is important to mention that the research project from which this study emerged specifically looked into the immigrant subject, so in a way this type of project also takes part in co-constructing and maintaining this problematic category. We were aware of this issue and we discussed and explained how we defined it as students whose home language is other than the school languages. The school staff was aware of the complexity of dealing with the immigrant students and often their response was that they treated the immigrant students as *any students*. However, when the interview progressed there were also special characteristics that were related to the immigrants: *Muslims, different ethnicities, Serb-Croatian, Somali, Refugees, students whose parents have not adjusted to life in Finland and the imagery of students hanging around the school because they have so much domestic work to do at home.*

Language also seems to be one dimension for discussing immigrants. However, the focus is on Finnish language as deficit and teaching Finnish/Swedish as a second language. Teaching Finnish/Swedish as a second language has a strong position in the National School Curriculum compared to teaching the immigrants' home language (see NCBE in Finland, 2014). Home language education is organized outside school hours whereas second language teaching is part of the school curriculum and school hours. It is interesting to note, nevertheless, that the New National Curriculum from 2016 (NCBE 2014) in Finland emphasizes plural-lingualism. Moreover, the emphasis on majority language teaching is often done in the name of intercultural education, an argument which has been challenged by some researchers (López and Tápanes 2011).

From the Finnish teachers' perspective, it was more a discussion on the different expectations between home cultures and cultures amongst youngsters in Finland. Often we forget that the "culture" of young people is also changing, and formed partly by the media (Tuori 2009). Instead of emphasizing the gaps in cultures the teachers with an immigrant background mentioned roots and belonging, and how it is important for students with an immigrant background to know where they come from and the possible reasons for their "forced" migration. One of the teachers with an immigrant background reflected on the conflict that young people may experience with their fragile identities if their parents feel marginalized in the new host society. According to the teacher the parents could volunteer in the school to at least feel like being inside some community, in this case, the school community. At the same time their children could feel that they can be proud of their parents. In the next section we move toward the language policies and implementations in practice as well how school mission statements are taken further in the school practices.

Commitments

Language policies are also strongly tied to commitments in the schools. There are intentions for organizing home language teaching as mentioned in the last section. Language policies position home language teachers in the margins in relation to other school staff. A teacher with an immigrant background was concerned that, sometimes, students have been placed in special education classes because of insufficient language skills in Finnish, or in their own mother tongue instead of a learning disability. The teacher also emphasized the importance of home language teaching taking place as co-teaching during the "normal" classroom teaching instead of extra curriculum activities. By co-teaching we mean that the classroom teacher and home language teacher work simultaneously and together in the classroom. The classroom teacher has the responsibility of teaching the content while the home language teacher confirms that students understand the difficult terms in their home language.

There were also important reflections from a language teacher related to how home language affects the learning of new languages as the following excerpt shows:

> She obviously doesn't understand the tenses in Finnish, I think she knows them better in English than in Finnish, then someone told me that they do not have those tenses in Russian, it works differently so then I went to a girl and said that you are making the mistakes because you speak Russian. (English teacher)

To us as authors, this type of reflection is a sign of multiple layers in relation to multilingualism. This teacher reached out to the student and claimed that some students do master many languages but not necessary the school language, which in this case is Finnish. Trans-languaging methods (Crese and Blackledge 2010; Garcia and Wei 2014) are called upon within the framework of intercultural education. By trans-languaging methods we mean complex social and cognitive activities that employ multiple languages in the classroom, especially those languages spoken as home languages amongst the students in the classroom (Garcia and Wei 2014). The schools that took part in this research employed more the ideology of multilingualism and in the Turku school they applied the CLIL method in each grade level. CLIL is in a way an example of trans-languaging as it means applying "foreign" language to teaching: in our research school, it meant that English and Finnish were used as instructional languages. However, this type of approach does not encourage children to use their home language but it promotes language hierarchies. Moreover the students applied trans-languaging during breaks rather than it being an official method in teaching.

In one of the schools of this study the "commitment" (the mission statement of the school) was to move students further in their education. However, the school counselor stated how parents with an immigrant background often think that all their children will become doctors or lawyers as the following excerpt states:

> Many students with an immigrant background have parents with high expectations that everyone will become doctors or lawyers. And ok, I tell them that if this child has an average score of 6.5 [out of 10], so the child is not qualified for high school education or even if this allows access to some high school, they will not end up as doctors or lawyers. (Study counsellor)

The future of young students may be determined at a young stage as compulsory education finishes at the age of 16 in Finland. Moreover, the teacher with an immigrant background reflected on his personal interest toward understanding better how students with an immigrant background find their own place in the new society, and he finds it important that he can reflect with the students on how he became a teacher. He also emphasizes how students need diverse "role models" in schools.

Conclusions: Performing "Good" Practices

In this study the focus was to understand better the discourses on the opportunities for immigrant students in two Finnish "school communities". Immigrant teachers were breaking the language and "normality" barriers between the lives of "majority students" and "minority students" in the two schools under review. Co-teaching between a home language teacher and a subject teacher/classroom teacher was identified as a "good" practice but, at the same time, it is challenging because the current education policies do not support such activities. Also the home language teachers are in a vulnerable situation as they do not necessarily have any background in pedagogy. We find the presence and involvement of teachers with an immigrant background important. At the same time, the non-existence of "immigrant" teachers in many Finnish schools is a great concern, as is the lack of student teachers with an immigrant background in teacher education and in Finnish Academia in general (Layne 2016).

One important conclusion for this study is to note how relevant it would be for "majority" teachers' professional development to add the voices of their peer colleagues with an immigrant background. Also the "general" storylines about the "wonders" of Finnish education, as well as about the "normal" life of Finnish young people need de- and reconstructing. However, we observed some attempts of authentic good practices such as antiracism workshops that took place in one school during their multilingual celebration week. The workshops were delivered by a not for profit organization and their educators. In the workshop students were discussing Finnishness and otherness. They were also encouraged to share their own experiences of discrimination. Interestingly, the teachers did not take part in the workshops and discussions on that day, but stood aside and listened to the discussions. Earlier research shows that teachers do not tend to recognize racism even though it is part of the daily hidden curriculum in Finnish schools (Souto 2011; Alemanji 2016).

References

Ahmed, S. (2006). Doing diversity work in higher education in Australia. *Educational Philosophy and Theory, 38*(6), 745–768.

Ahmed, S. (2012). *On being included: Racism and diversity in institutional life.* Durham: Duke University Press.

Alemanji, A. A. (2016). *Is there such a thing…?: A study of antiracism education in Finland*. Helsinki: Helsinki University Press.

Andreotti, V., & Pashby, K. (2013). Digital democracy and global citizenship education: Mutually compatible or mutually complicit? *The Educational Forum*, i First. 10.1080/00131725.2013.822043

Breidenback, J., & Nyiri, P. (2009). *Seeing culture everywhere: From genocide to consumer habits*. Seattle: University of Washington Press.

Crese, A., & Blackledge, A. (2010). Translanguaging in the bilingual classroom. A pedagogy for learning and teaching? *Modern Language Journal, 94*(1), 103–115.

Dervin, F. (2012). *La meilleure éducation au monde? Contre-enquête sur la Finlande*. Paris: L'Harmattan.

Dervin, F. (2015). Towards post-intercultural teacher education: Analysing 'extreme' intercultural dialogue to reconstruct interculturality. *European Journal of Teacher Education, 38*(1), 71–86.

Dervin, F., Paatela-Nieminen, M., Kuoppala, K., & Riitaoja, A.-L. (2012). Multicultural education in Finland – Renewed intercultural competences to the rescue? *International Journal of Multicultural Education, 14*(3), 1–13.

Elo, S., & Kyngäs, H. (2008). The qualitative content analysis process. *Journal of Advanced Nursing, 62*(1), 107–115.

Garcia, O., & Wei, L. (2014). *Translanguaging: Language, bilingualism and education*. Basingstoke: Palgrave Macmillan.

Harju-Luukkainen, H., Nissinen, K., Sulkunen, S., Suni, M., & Vettenranta, J. (2014). *Avaimet osaamiseen ja tulevaisuuteen. Selvitys maahanmuuttajataustaisten nuorten osaamisesta ja siihen liittyvistä taustatekijöistä PISA 2012-tutkimuksessa*. Koulutuksen tutkimuslaitos, Jyväskylän yliopisto.

Helsingin Sanomat. (2015a, June 24). *Ulkomaalaistaustaisia tyttöjä ohjataan lähihoitajaksi, vaikka rahkeet riittäisivät lääkäriksi*. HS: Kaupunki. http://www.hs.fi/kaupunki/a1434855331878

Helsingin Sanomat. (2015b, August). *Maahanmuuttajaoppilaiden koulumenestys kantaväestöä heikompaa*. HS: Kotimaa. http://www.hs.fi/kotimaa/a1439862511831

Holiday, A. (2010). *Intercultural communication*. London: Sage.

ICEF Monitor. (2016). Finland introduces university tuition fees for non-EU students. http://monitor.icef.com/2016/01/finland-introduces-university-tuition-fees-for-non-eu-students/

Itkonen, T., Talib, M., & Dervin, F. (2015). 'Not all of us Finns communicate the same way either': Teachers' perceptions of interculturality in upper secondary vocational education and training. *Journal of Vocational Education & Training, 67*(3), 397–414.

Kilpi-Jakonen, E. (2012). Does Finnish educational equality extend to children of immigrants? Examining national origin, gender and the relative importance of parental resources. *Nordic Journal of Migration Research, 2*(2), 167–181.

Kumpulainen, T. (Ed.). (2014). *Koulutuksen tilastollinen vuosikirja. Koulutuksen seurantaraportit.* Helsinki: Opetushallitus.

Kvale, S. (1996). *An introduction to qualitative research interviewing.* London: SAGE.

Layne, H. (2016). *Contact zones in (Finnish) intercultural education.* Helsinki: Helsingin yliopiston opettajankoulutuslaitos, Tutkimuksia. https://helda.helsinki.fi/handle/10138/165072.

Layne, H., & Lipponen, L. (2016). Student teachers in the contact zone: Developing critical intercultural "teacherhood" in kindergarten teacher education. *Globalisation, Societies and Education Globalisation, Societies and Education, 14*(1), 110–126.

Leonardo, Z. (2009). *Race, whiteness, and education.* New York: Routledge.

López, L. M., & Tápanes, V. (2011). Latino children attending a two-way immersion program in the United States: A comparative case analysis. *Bilingual Research Journal, 34*(2), 142–160.

NCBE. (2014). *National core curriculum for basic education in Finland.* Porvoo: Finnish National Board of Education.

NCBE. (2016). *National core curriculum for basic education in Finland.* Porvoo: Finnish National Board of Education.

Paatela-Nieminen, M., & Itkonen, I. (2016). Reading the world as texts: Intertextuality in theory and practice for (art) education. In T. Itkonen & F. Dervin (Eds.), *Silent partners in multicultural education* (pp. 3–27). Charlotte, NC: Info Age Publishing.

Phillips, A. (2007). *Multiculturalism without culture.* Princeton, NJ: Princeton University Press.

Puwar, N. (2004). *Space invaders: Race, gender and bodies out of place.* Oxford: Berg.

Race, R. (2015). *Multiculturalism and education.* London: Continuum.

Riitaoja, A.-L. (2013). *Toiseuksien rakentuminen koulussa. Tutkimus opetussuunnitelmista ja kahden helsinkiläisen koulun arjesta* [Constructing otherness in school: A study of curriculum texts and everyday life of two primary schools in Helsinki]. PhD dissertation, Helsingin yliopisto, Tutkimuksia 346.

Sahlberg, P., & Hargreaves, A. (2011). *Finnish lessons: What can the world learn from educational change in Finland?* New York: Teachers College Press.

Schatz, M., Dervin, F., & Popovic, A. (2015). From PISA to national branding: Exploring Finnish education. *Discourse: Studies in the Cultural Politics of Education.* 10.1080/01596306.2015.1066311

Solorzano, D. G., & Yosso, T. J. (2002). A Critical race counterstory of race, racism, and affirmative action. *Equity & Excellence in Education, 35*(2), 155–168.

Souto, A.-M. (2011). *Arkipäivän rasismi koulussa. Etnografinen tutkimus suomalais-ja maahanmuttajanuorten ryhmäsuhteista.* [Everyday racism in school. An

ethno- graphic study of group relations between Finnish and immigrant youths]
Nuorisotutkimusseura, julkaisuja 110: Helsinki.

Tuori, S. (2009). *The politics of multicultural encounters: Feminist postcolonial perspectives.* Åbo: Åbo Akademi University Press.

Viiki Teacher Training School. (n.d.). Website. http://www.vink.helsinki.fi/index.php?del=0&d=911

Heidi Layne works as a researcher at the Department of Teacher Education and as a Career Counselor at the Career Services in the University of Helsinki, Finland. Currently her research work consists of the Erasmus+-funded research project ROMTEL on Eastern European Roma children's language identity and Nordplus-funded DELA-NOBA research project on language awareness in the school in the Nordic-Baltic context. As a career counselor she has been actively involved in projects developing guidance services from the international students and immigrants perspectives.

Fred Dervin is Professor of Multicultural Education at the University of Helsinki, Finland. He also acts as a head of STEP—Subject Teacher Education Programme in English in the University of Helsinki; he is a Fellow of the RSA (Royal Society for the encouragement of Arts, Manufactures and Commerce), UK, and the RAI (Royal Anthropological Institute), UK. He specializes in language and intercultural education, the sociology of multiculturalism and linguistics for intercultural communication and education. Dervin is also Director of the research Group Education for Diversities (E4D) (http://blogs.helsinki.fi/dervin/).

Rita Johnson Longfor has conducted research on English as a Second Language (ESL) pedagogy and teacher pedagogical development in Cameroon. She is post-doctoral researcher in the *Education for Tomorrow Nordic research project—Learning Spaces for Inclusion and Social Justice: Success stories from immigrant students and school communities in four Nordic Countries* at the University of Helsinki, Department of Teacher Education (Finland). Her current research interest and teaching focuses on topics like intercultural education, student success, diversities in education, inclusion and social justice. Her publications focus on innovative approaches/pedagogies to the study of diversities in teacher education.

The Need for Dialogue in the Strategies to Combat Anti-Semitism and Islamophobia in Contemporary Scotland

Stephen J. McKinney

INTRODUCTION

The post Second World War recognition of a multicultural Britain that includes an increasing number of ethnic and racial minorities has not always acknowledged the importance of religion for individuals, their membership of religious groups and the identities of religious groups (Meer and Modood 2009). These religious groups are not homogeneous, but are diverse, and the historical and contemporary adaptations to life in Britain can be complex. This requires an informed understanding of the religious groups, their position in society and their continued development in society. This understanding is situated within the context of the contrast between the right to private and public expression of religion and the aspirations for a plural, but secular society (Sikka 2010; Allievi 2012). Further, this is situated within a world affected by the impact of what has been described as 'Islamic terrorism' which has led to an invidious, negative stereotyping of Muslims in Britain and in many parts of the world (Meer and Modood 2009). A similar process has occurred for Jewish

S.J. McKinney (✉)
University of Glasgow, Glasgow, UK

© The Author(s) 2018
R. Race (ed.), *Advancing Multicultural Dialogues in Education*,
DOI 10.1007/978-3-319-60558-6_11

communities as Jews in Britain, and other parts of the world, have been held accountable or targeted as a result of events in the Middle East.

In the last few years, there has been a rise in reported levels of anti-Semitism and Islamophobia in Scotland. This has been a source of great concern for the Jewish and Muslim communities in Scotland and appears to contradict perceptions of an inclusive and welcoming multicultural Scottish society (Kidd and Jamieson 2011). This chapter seeks to understand these increases in discrimination from a number of different perspectives. First, the overall religious landscape of Scotland will be examined and this will demonstrate that while adherence to religion is waning, especially Christian religion, the religious minorities are growing or remaining stable. Second, there will be a concise overview of the history of the Jewish and Muslim communities in Scotland. Third, there is a detailed exploration of the rise in anti-Semitism and Islamophobia in Scotland and the relation of this dual rise to events outwith Scotland. This section will discuss the impact of the dual rise on the lives of Jews and Muslims in Scotland and their perception of their contemporary position and safety in Scotland. The next section will highlight a recurring narrative that Scotland has been a safer place for Jews and Muslims than England and Wales. This narrative will be analysed and critiqued and some of the historical evidence concerning anti-Semitism and Islamophobia will be discussed. This will be followed by a close focus on a greater knowledge and understanding of the different aspects of the position of contemporary Jews and Muslims within Scottish society, using Koenig's (2015) four claims for recognition. There will then be a brief discussion of the implications of the infringements of the human rights of the Jewish and Muslim communities. The final two sections will discuss communication and education and emphasise the need for authentic dialogue and present some concluding remarks.

THE RELIGIOUS LANDSCAPE OF SCOTLAND

The census data of 2001 and 2011 demonstrates a rise in non-adherence in religion in Scotland from 33.3% non-adherence in the population in 2001 (27.8% no religion and 5.5% religion not stated) to 43.7% non-adherence in 2011 (36.7% no religion and 7.0% religion not stated) (National Records of Scotland 2013). Much of the decline is due to a 10% decrease in the largest Christian denomination of the Church of Scotland. The second largest Christian denomination, Roman Catholic, remained stable at 15.9%. The total percentage for all denominations of Christianity is 53.8% and Christianity remains the dominant form of religion. All of the minority religions (Buddhist, Hindu, Muslim, Sikh and other religion) constitute very small percentages of the population, but all recorded increases except the Jews who remained stable: Buddhist (0.1% to 0.2%), Hindu (0.1% to 0.3%), Jewish (0.1%), Muslim (0.8% to 1.4%) and Sikh (0.1% to 0.2%).

This chapter will focus on two minority religions: the Jews and Muslims. These have been chosen because the Muslims are the largest minority religious group in Scotland, and the Jews have had a significant impact on Scottish life and culture. They are also the two religious groups that are specifically identified, other than Roman Catholic and Protestant, in the reporting of religiously aggravated crimes in Scotland (Cavanagh and Morgan 2011; Davidson 2016). Further, parallels can easily be drawn between Jews and Muslims in Scotland and in the rest of the UK and Europe. The next section provides very concise histories of the two religious groups in Scotland.

THE JEWISH AND MUSLIM COMMUNITIES IN SCOTLAND

The first records of a Jewish community date from an early community in Edinburgh in 1816 (Phillips 1979). The Jewish community in Glasgow, established in 1823, was to become the largest and most influential community in Scotland (Collins 1993). The Glasgow Jewish community was enlarged in the 1880s by the arrival of Eastern European migrants (Collins 2008). There was another, smaller influx of Jews from Germany in the 1930s, fleeing from National Socialism (Grenville 2010). The total Jewish population of Scotland is 5887. The majority of the Jews in Scotland are concentrated in the Greater Glasgow Area (the city of Glasgow plus adjoining suburbs of East Renfrewshire and East Dunbartonshire) with 897 in Glasgow City and 2399 in East Renfrewshire (Glasgow City Council 2013; East Renfrewshire Council 2017).

There is recorded evidence of a Muslim presence in Scotland in the sixteenth century and the numbers grew very slowly in the eighteenth and nineteenth centuries (Maan 2008). Many of these Muslims were lascars (seamen) (Dunlop 1990). The small Muslim communities in Scotland were enhanced by the arrival of Indian students in the late nineteenth and early twentieth centuries and by migrants from India in the 1920s. The numbers grew significantly in the 1950s as Indian workers were recruited for unskilled and semi-skilled work, especially in the cities. As has been stated, the Census data from 2001 to 2011 indicates that the Muslim population of Scotland grew from 42,600 in 2001 (0.84% of the Scottish population) to 77,000 in 2011 (1.4%) (National Records of Scotland 2013). Just under a half of the Muslims in Scotland (32,117) live in Glasgow constituting 5.4% of the population of the city (Glasgow City Council 2013).

THE RISE IN REPORTED LEVELS OF ANTI-SEMITISM AND ISLAMOPHOBIA IN SCOTLAND

In the twenty-first century, there has been a rise in reported levels of incidences of anti-Semitism and Islamophobia in Scotland and a greater public awareness of these social problems. The rise of reported levels of anti-Semitism and Islamophobia in Scotland can be partly understood within recent trends in the UK, across Europe and in other parts of the world (Bayrakli and Hafez 2016). Some of the more serious and concerted manifestations that have occurred in Europe are responses to terrorist attacks and events in the Middle East (Iganski and Kosmin 2003). These disturbing trends in discrimination are being monitored by the European Parliament and the European Commission (European Parliament Working Group on Anti-Semitism 2016). This has prompted the European Commission to appoint two coordinators to help combat anti-Semitism and Islamophobia (European Commission 2015). This rise in reported crimes in Scotland also has to be understood within the context of the introduction of national figures for religiously aggravated crimes in Scotland in the last 10 years and the increasing amount of detail concerning these crimes that has been reported in the public forum since 2011 (Cavanagh and Morgan 2011). These figures have been dominated by the crimes committed against Roman Catholics and Protestants, and the historical, and well-known, sectarian divisions between Protestants and Catholics, until recently, have attracted much of the focus of the public and academic discussions on religiously aggravated crimes (The Scottish Government 2015).

There has been a very troubling rise in the number of crimes committed against Muslims (from 12% or below of all religiously aggravated crimes from 2012 to 2015 to 23% in 2015–2016) (Davidson 2016). The crimes against Jews have been between 2% and 4% of all crimes for the same period, but are highly significant as the Jewish population is so small in Scotland. Interestingly, the collation of the figures for the religion of those targeted for religiously aggravated crimes is an assessment of the researcher that is based on the description and details of the crime. There are no figures for any of the other minority religions unless they have been categorised under the headings of *Unknown* or *Other*, both of which record either zero percent of all crimes or very low percentages (Davidson 2016).

There are a number of key events that have been the catalysts for the rise in anti-Semitism in Scotland in the twenty-first century. In 2006 there was a reaction to the Lebanon War in various parts of the world, including Australia, New Zealand and many parts of Europe (World Jewish Congress 2006). There was a sharp rise in incidents in the UK during the 33 days of the war in July and August 2006 (132 incidents) (Moss 2006). In Scotland, in late July the ground outside the synagogue in Garnethill, Glasgow, was defaced with the word 'Hizbollah'. This caused considerable outrage as the Garnethill synagogue is a grand Cathedral-style synagogue that was opened in 1879 and is the oldest purpose-built synagogue in Scotland (Collins 1987; Kadish 2015). There was another sharp rise in the UK in July 2014 connected to the conflict in Gaza. In Scotland this led to heightened anxiety in Jewish communities about the increase in anti-Semitism (Scottish Council of Jewish Communities 2015). The impact of the rise in 2014 can be discerned in the contrast between two connected projects and subsequent publications produced in 2013 and 2016: *Being Jewish in Scotland* and *What's Changed about Being Jewish in Scotland?* (Frank et al. 2013, 2016). Frank et al. (2013) highlighted contemporary challenges for Jews living in Scotland: decline in the Jewish population, challenges in maintaining a Jewish lifestyle and geographical isolation for some Jews. There were some anxieties about anti-Semitism but many expressed the view that their experience of living in Scotland was 'largely positive' (McKinney 2016a). Frank et al. (2016) reported some significant changes. In the original report some Jews were cautious about revealing their Jewish identity; in the second report Jews were more likely to conceal their identities and any visible signs that could identify them as Jewish (e.g. the Star of David and the Mezuzah). Jews felt insecure and vulnerable and were concerned about the use of social media as a conduit for anti-Semitism (Frank et al. 2016). There was a general feeling that living in Scotland had become more problematic for Jews (McKinney 2016a).

Similar to the contemporary situation of the Jews in Scotland, there has been a sharp rise in discrimination against Muslims and many of the prominent incidences are connected to events external to Scotland. The reaction to 9/11 in Scotland may not have been as pronounced as it was in England, but Muslims in Scotland felt an increase in hostility and discrimination (Hussain and Miller 2006; Kidd and Jamieson 2011). This was also experienced after the terrorist attack on Glasgow airport in June 2007 and after 7/7 (McKinney 2016b). However, the after effects of the Paris attack on Friday 13 November 2015 probably had the biggest impact on Scottish Muslims. There was a sharp increase in hate crimes against Muslims (or people perceived to be Muslims) and damage to Muslim property being reported to the police (McKinney et al. 2016). The Strathclyde University Muslim Students Association received death threats. There was an arson attack on a mosque in the Bishopbriggs area and offensive graffiti sprayed on a mosque in Cumbernauld. There was a spate of social media abuse directed at Humza Yousaf, a Scottish Muslim MSP, and women in Muslim dress stated that they now feel intimidated when walking in the streets of Glasgow. This last example can be contrasted with previous evidence that revealed that some Muslim women stated that Muslim dress attracted 'unpleasant attention and occasionally discrimination' (Kidd and Jamieson 2011).

Is Scotland a Safer Place for Jews and Muslims Than England and Wales?

There are a number of recurring historical narratives about the position of religious minorities in Scotland and Scottish society, especially the Jewish and Muslim communities. One of the narratives is the idea that Scotland is a safer place for religious minorities compared to England and Wales. This is reflected in the literature on the Jewish and Muslim communities and some recent research into the perspectives of young people from ethnic and religious minorities on security and nationalism. A number of Jewish and Muslim academics and writers and research studies have argued that Scotland and Scottish society are more tolerant towards their communities (Collins 2008; Abrams 2009; Maan 1992, 2008; Kidd and Jamieson 2011; Botterill et al. 2016).

There are a number of possible reasons for holding this view. First, the overall numbers of Jews and Muslims in Scotland are relatively low when compared to England and Wales (there are 263,000 Jews and 2.7 million Muslims, 0.5% and 4.8% of the overall population respectively) and they may not be perceived to pose the same potential threat to national identity (Office for National Statistics 2012). Second, according to some Jewish sources, the Jews were historically respected as religious people, 'people of the book'. The Jews often created their own employment and, historically, especially in the early years of their arrival in Scotland, seldom drew on public social welfare (Abrams 2009; Collins 1990). Third, drawing from analysis of the census results of 2011, the Muslims in Scotland, overall, appear to have enjoyed greater socio-economic success than their counterparts in England and Wales (Elshayyal 2016). The figure for Muslims in Scotland who have never worked is 15.9%, which is much higher than the national average of 3.1% but can also be compared with England and Wales where around a fifth of Muslims have never worked. There is a greater proportion of Muslims in the higher professions in Scotland than in England and Wales, though the figure for the Muslims in Scotland is lower than the Scottish national average. The figures for the Muslim prison population provide the most striking contrast: the Scottish Muslim prison population is 1.8% (slightly higher than the Muslim population of 1.4%), the Muslim population for England and Wales is 13% (considerably higher than the Muslim population of 4.8%). It can be noted that it can be problematic to draw comparisons between Scotland and England and Wales and it is important that these comparisons, while based on the experiences of security and social mobility in Scotland of the two minorities, are not associated with the rhetoric of anti-English prejudice that exists in some parts of Scottish society.

A deeper analysis, however, is required to provide some local historical background to the (apparently) recent rise in anti-Semitism and Islamophobia in the relative safety of Scottish society. There may be a certain amount of conscious or unconscious denial about the full extent of historical anti-Semitism and Islamophobia and some incidents that have not been stressed, have been under reported or have even been 'forgotten' (McKinney 2016c). There are a number of useful examples. At the onset of the Second World War, there was discrimination against the newly arrived German Jews and vandalism of Jewish shops and properties (Kolmel 1987; Braber 2007). There were anti-Jewish riots in the Gorbals, in Glasgow, after the murder of two British servicemen in Palestine in 1947 (Kushner 1996). Frank et al. (2013), while not wishing to exaggerate the problem, provide examples of experiences of anti-Semitism in public spaces, workplaces, schools and universities. The vast majority of Muslims in Scotland are Asian or of Asian descent, though they may define themselves in terms of multiple identities such as Asian Scottish or Asian British (Elshayyal 2016; Bond 2016). This means they can be susceptible to double discrimination where they can be discriminated against because of their religious dress or the colour of their skin, or both (Kidd and Jamieson 2011). There has been strong opposition to the construction of new mosques in more affluent areas of the Greater Glasgow Area (McKinney et al. 2016).

KNOWLEDGE AND UNDERSTANDING OF THE JEWISH AND MUSLIM COMMUNITIES IN SCOTLAND

It is questionable if there is a sufficiently nuanced knowledge and understanding of the historical and contemporary positions of the Jewish and Muslim communities in the public space in Scotland, a nuanced knowledge and understanding that is arguably absent in the rest of Britain and other parts of Europe (Allievi 2012). Koenig (2015) provides some useful lenses, *the four claims for recognition*, that I have adapted and use for a deeper and more nuanced understanding of the contemporary claims for a position in society by these two communities and the impact of anti-Semitism and Islamophobia on these claims. The four claims for recognition are (1) claims for recognition of difference, (2) claims for more autonomy in public spheres, (3) claims for tolerance and (4) call for greater recognition for equal participation in the organisation of the state (McKinney et al. 2016).

The first claim for recognition refers to distinctive dress and other symbols of religious affiliation. This can be celebrated as part of diversity in a multicultural, multi-faith society. At a practical level, it can mean the recognition of some religious needs by public services, such as the availability of kosher food in hospitals for Jews (Frank et al. 2013). It can also mean that there is a freedom to wear religious dress or religious symbols in public spaces. In some parts of the world this can be perceived to be a challenge to the secular character of the state (e.g. the banning of the public display of the Muslim headscarf and other religious symbols in France) (Sikka 2010). In recent years, the claim for recognition of difference has proved, at times, to be the visible means by which members of the Jewish and Muslim communities can be identified as the *other* and exposed to verbal abuse and intimidation. This has occurred in the concrete examples of the intimidation of women in Muslim dress in Glasgow and Jews concealing visible signs of Judaism. In the case of the women in Muslim dress being intimidated, this creates a serious dilemma. The wearing of the hijab for some of these women can be based on a conscious decision rooted in complex reasons of preserving Muslim female identity and modesty but it also allows them to access the public space (Siraj 2011).

The second form of recognition refers to more autonomy in public spaces, including the adaptation of existing buildings or the construction of new buildings for religious purposes. The construction of the two purpose-built—and quite striking—buildings, the synagogue in Garnethill and the mosque in the Gorbals, created highly visible symbols of the presence of the two minorities in the city. The attacks on the synagogue in late July 2006 and the mosque in late 2015 are equally highly visible symbols as they attack the physical presence of the two minorities in the public space in the city of Glasgow. This second form of recognition can also refer to the funding or partial funding of faith schools for religious minorities. There is one Jewish state-funded primary school in East Renfrewshire and there have been various sets of discussions about the possibility of a state-funded Muslim school. The vast majority of the state-funded faith schools in Scotland are Roman Catholic and their continued existence has, at times, been contested on the grounds that they are divisive, that they indoctrinate or inhibit rational autonomy and the rights of children or that they are connected to sectarianism (McKinney and Conroy 2015). The existence of the state-funded Jewish school is very seldom contested and this school does not tend to feature in these debates. There has been a recurring debate about the viability of the creation of a state-funded Muslim school in Glasgow (Hepburn 2016). The debate frequently stalls, and the current heightened levels of Islamophobia and the attacks on Muslim places of worship may create anxieties that a Muslim school would be an identifiable and accessible target.

The third form of recognition refers to a level of tolerance that may lead to a reconfiguration of national identity, for example, the recognition of new religious holidays in the national calendar, or accommodations that allow Jews and Muslims to observe religious holidays. There is a certain amount of accommodation for Jews and Muslims to observe religious events and holidays in Scotland, but there remain challenges for members of these two communities. Frank et al. (2013) provide examples of helpful changes in schedules at universities to allow Jewish students to observe religious holidays. Interfaith groups recommend that Jewish and Muslim children are allowed to observe religious festivals which may include authorised absences from school (Edinburgh Interfaith Association 2015). There are some schools in the Greater Glasgow Area that accommodate special assemblies led by members of the Jewish community for the Jewish children in the school (McKinney 2004). Schools are encouraged to recognise the demands of Ramadan, and many schools provide rest rooms for Muslim children during this month and provide guidance for school staff about the implications for Muslim children and young people who are fasting during the school day. There are some counter examples including disapproval of children being absent from school to observe Rosh Hashanah.

The fourth form of recognition refers to a call for greater recognition for equal participation in the organisation of the state. There is a rich history of Jewish and, more recently, Muslim engagement in public service, political activism and cultural life in Scotland (Collins 2008; Maan 2008). The Jewish communities of Glasgow and Edinburgh have produced some eminent politicians, including Sir Myer Gilpin (first Jewish Lord Provost of Glasgow, 1958) and Members of Parliament, Manny Shinwell (1922), Maurice Miller (1964) and Malcolm Rifkind, 1974 (McKinney and McCluskey 2017). Scotland's Muslims have produced the first Muslim Councillor (Bashir Maan, 1970) and the first Muslim Member of Parliament (Mohammed Sarwar, 1997) in Great Britain (Bonino 2016). These are, of course, members of the political elite, and while this level of civic engagement is to be commended, there are issues around wider participation by members of the Jewish and Muslim communities. There is a need for a greater participation by Muslim women and young people in Scottish civic society. Elshayyal (2016) reports that the Muslim population has the lowest rate of voter registration for any religion. Frank et al. (2016) call for Jewish communities to foster greater links and communication in their local areas.

ANTI-SEMITISM AND ISLAMOPHOBIA AND VIOLATION OF HUMAN RIGHTS

The association between Jews and Muslims in Scotland with acts of terrorism and with actions in the Middle East is highly problematic and raises some serious questions about the protection of their human rights. Human Rights have, of course, been contested in recent years and there has been a move to the possible introduction of a new Bill of Rights in the UK (O'Cinneide 2012). It is interesting to note that the document *Is Scotland Fairer?* produced by the Equality and Human Rights Commission (2015) devotes very little attention to Islamophobia and anti-Semitism and simply states that there are gaps in the evidence about Islamophobia and anti-Semitism in Scotland. This may be explained by the core quantitative data for the report being drawn from 2008 to 2013 and the later publication of more robust evidence about anti-Semitism and Islamophobia. It nevertheless remains useful to explore the ways in which anti-Semitism and Islamophobia in Scotland can be interpreted as violations of human rights.

The exposure to verbal abuse and intimidation and the attacks on religious buildings infringe the freedoms that have been expressed in European Human Rights Legislation. These freedoms were recognised in the United Nations Declaration of Human Rights (1948), subsequent declarations (United Nations General Assembly 1981, 1992) and in the European Convention on Human Rights, article 9 (European Court of Human Rights 2002).

Any unwelcome and hostile advances towards Jews and Muslims in the public sphere is an infringement of the 1992 declaration:

> *Persons belonging to minorities have the right to participate effectively in cultural, religious, social, economic and public life.* (United Nations General Assembly 1992, article 2, 2)

The attacks on the buildings used for religious purposes are attacks on some of the major sites where the two minorities exercise their freedom to assemble for worship or other religious purposes. The 1992 declaration states clearly that persons belonging to minorities:

> *... have the right to profess and practice their own religion...in private and in public, freely and without interference or any form of discrimination.* (United Nations General Assembly 1992, article 2, 1)

As has been seen above, the violations of human rights that have arguably taken place in Scotland have had a direct impact on the Jewish and Muslim communities being able to sustain the four claims for recognition in a consistent manner.

COMMUNICATION, EDUCATION AND DIALOGUE

The Jewish and Muslim communities in Scotland have experienced heightened levels of anti-Semitism and Islamophobia in the last few years. This chapter has demonstrated that anti-Semitism and Islamophobia are not new phenomena to Scotland and that these heightened levels are directly related to events extraneous to Scotland. This has led to anxiety within the Jewish and Muslim communities about their position in Scotland and their personal and collective safety in public spaces. Frank et al. (2016) provide a series of detailed points for action. These are focused on greater clarity about the distinction between local Jews and actions that are committed in Israel, further nuanced in that some Jews may support Israel and Zionism but not the policies and actions of the Israeli government. There are further points for action that relate to religious festivals, an increase in the quantity and quality of education about Judaism (and other religions) and support for Jewish students. There are clear calls for greater education and dialogue. First, there is a need to organise meetings to discuss the Middle East in an open manner and in a safe environment. Second, there should be 'more and better education about Judaism' in schools. This should be extended to other religions. Third, there is a need for more interfaith dialogue. Similarly, Kidd and Jamieson (2011) demonstrates that many of the participants in the research expressed concerns about the negative stereotyping of Islam that demonstrates a lack of understanding about Islam and the need for more education about their religion. Participants in this research strongly expressed the importance of teaching young people about different religions to engender deeper knowledge and understanding. They also advocated that the history of migration to Britain should be taught and the contribution of the migrant communities to society and culture.

At the heart of these calls for greater understanding and education is the need for more dialogue. These dialogues cannot be restricted to interfaith dialogues but include a broader range of participants. These dialogues need to overcome the barriers of stereotyping, labels and categorisation that can inhibit the establishment and progress of dialogue (Keating 2007). This will involve a growing appreciation of the multiplicity of the ways in which people can identify themselves, for example, as Scottish Jews or Scottish Muslims or as British Jews or British Muslims. This further involves understanding of the diversity within the Jewish and Muslim communities whether this is in terms of denomination or ethnicity, for example, Orthodox and Reform Jews and Asian Muslims and Somali Muslims. Those who participate in dialogues, if they are to be engaged in authentic dialogues, must avoid any tendency to ethnocentrism that promotes the ideas of cultural or national superiority (Peters 2012) They should be willing to listen to and understand each other's views, consider alternate viewpoints and be open to changing and modifying their own point of view (Kazepides 2012; Grigoriev et al. 2017).

Schools play a major role in the education about religion, religious and cultural diversity and in the high-profile initiatives to combat all forms of religious discrimination: sectarianism, anti-Semitism and Islamophobia. Despite religion being a part of the core curriculum in all Scottish schools and the opportunities to discuss religion in other subject areas such as social studies, teachers can still lack confidence in discussing issues such as religious intolerance (Hemming 2015; Arshad and Moskal 2016). Other challenges remain at the level of the engagement between Jewish and Muslim children and other young people. While it may not be widespread, some Jewish children in schools where they constitute a small minority conceal their Jewish identities. There can be confusion in the conflation of ethnic and religious identities within the pupil population. There is evidence of misrecognition and repeated misrecognition where children or young people are judged to be Muslim because of their skin colour but are in fact Sikh, Hindu or Christian. This habitual association between skin colour and membership of a particular religious group can prevent a deeper understanding of the diversity of ethnic origins within the Muslim population and within the other religious groups. Some Muslim children and young people have expressed anxieties about being stereotyped and associated with terrorism (Kidd and Jamieson 2011).

Concluding Remarks

This chapter has examined the recent rise in anti-Semitism and Islamophobia in Scotland, contextualising this rise within the history of the Jewish and Muslim communities and local responses to external events (McKinney 2016a, b). The chapter has further examined the rise as a series of violations of human rights that inhibit the four claims for recognition. The chapter has argued for greater levels of communication, education and authentic dialogue for adults and for school children (McKinney 2016c; Mckinney et al. 2016). This has the potential to generate a greater understanding of the links between cultural and religious identity and, within this process, lenses such as the four claims for recognition can be used to enable a deeper awareness of the position of members of the Jewish and Muslim communities in Scottish society and an appreciation of the richness of multicultural diversity in Scotland that includes a recognition of the key role of religious diversity.

REFERENCES

Abrams, N. (2009). *Caledonian Jews, a study of seven small communities in Scotland*. Jefferson: McFarland and Company.

Allievi, S. (2012). Real identities and Islamophobia: Muslim minorities and the challenge of religious pluralism in Scotland. *Philosophy and Social Criticism, 38*(4–5), 379–387.

Arshad, R., & Moskal, M. (2016). *Racial equality and Scottish school education: Ensuring today's young people are tomorrow's confident citizens. IAA Briefing*, Edinburgh-Glasgow.

Bayrakli, E., & Hafez, F. (Eds.) (2016). *European Islamophobia Report*. Retrieved March 26, 2017, from http://www.islamophobiaeurope.com/reports/2015/en/EIR_2015.pdf

Bond, R. (2016). Multicultural nationalism? National identities among minority groups in Scotland's census. *Journal of Ethnic and Migration Studies, 43*(7), 1121–1140.

Bonino, S. (2016). The Jihadi threat to Scotland: Caledonian exceptionalism and its limits. *CTC Sentinel, 9*(4), 27–31. Retrieved March 26, 2017, from http://nrl.northumbria.ac.uk/26620/1/article.pdf

Botterill, K., Hopkins, P., Sanghera, G., & Arshad, R. (2016). Securing disunion: Young people's nationalism, identities and (in)securities in the campaign for an independent Scotland. *Political Geography, 55*, 124–134.

Braber, B. (2007). *Jews in Glasgow 1879–1939*. London: Vallentine Mitchell.

Cavanagh, B., & Morgan, A. (2011). *Religiously aggravated offending in Scotland 2010–2011*. Scottish Government Social Research. Retrieved March 26, 2017 http://www.gov.scot/Resource/Doc/362943/0122956.pdf

Collins, K. E. (1987). *The growth and development of Scottish Jewry 1880–1940, aspects of Scottish Jewry*. Glasgow: Glasgow Representative Council.

Collins, K. E. (1990). *Second city Jewry*. Glasgow: Scottish Jewish Archives.

Collins, K. E. (1993). *Glasgow Jewry: A guide to the history and community of the Jews in Glasgow*. Glasgow: Scottish Jewish Archives Committee.

Collins, K. E. (2008). *Scotland's Jews. A guide to the history and community of the Jews in Scotland*. Glasgow: Scottish Council of Jewish Communities.

Davidson, N. (2016). *Religiously aggravated offending in Scotland 2015–2016*. Scottish Government Social Research. Retrieved March 26, 2017, from http://www.gov.scot/Publications/2016/06/7309

Dunlop, A. (1990). Lascars and labourers. Reactions to the Indian presence in the West of Scotland during the 1920s and 1930. *Scottish Labour History. Society Journal, 25*, 40–57.

East Renfrewshire Council. (2017). *Religion*. Retrieved March 26, 2017, from http://www.eastrenfrewshire.gov.uk/article/5222/Religion

Edinburgh Interfaith Association. (2015). *Faith and young people*. Retrieved March 26, 2017, from http://www.eifa.org.uk/faith-and-young-people/

Elshayyal, K. (2016). *Scottish Muslims in numbers. Understanding Scotland's Muslim population through the 2011 census.* Edinburgh: University of Edinburgh.

Equality and Human Rights Commission. (2015). *Is Scotland fairer?* Retrieved March 26, 2017, from https://www.equalityhumanrights.com/en/britain-fairer/scotland-fairer-introduction/scotland-fairer-report

European Commission. (2015). *EU commission appoints coordinators on combating anti-semitism and anti-Muslim hatred.* Retrieved March 26, 2017, from http://ec.europa.eu/justice/newsroom/fundamental-rights/news/151201_en.htm

European Court of Human Rights. (2002). *European convention on human rights.* Retrieved March 26, 2017, from http://www.echr.coe.int/Documents/Convention_ENG.pdf

European Parliament Working Group on Antisemitism. (2016). Retrieved March 26, 2017, from http://www.antisem.eu/about-us/

Frank, F., Borowski, E., & Granat, L. (2013). *Being Jewish in Scotland.* The Scottish Council of Jewish Communities. Retrieved March 26, 2017, from https://www.scribd.com/document/170489711/Being-Jewish-in-Scotland

Frank, F., Borowski, E., Granat, L., & Hounsom, R. (2016). *What's changed about being Jewish in Scotland?* The Scottish Council of Jewish Communities. Retrieved March 26, 2017, from http://www.scojec.org/resources/files/bjis2.pdf

Glasgow City Council. (2013). *Briefing paper 2011 census-release 2A-results for Glasgow City.* Retrieved March 26, 2017, from http://www.glasgow.gov.uk/chttphandler.ashx?id=16943

Grenville, A. (2010). *Jewish refugees from Germany and Austria in Britain, 1933–1970.* London: Vallentine Mitchell.

Grigoriev, S., Grinshkun, V., Zannoni, F., Krupova, J., Lvova, O., & McKinney, S. J. (2017). *Teoriia i praktika razvitiia tolerantnosti sredstvami polikulturnoi obrazovatelnoi platformy.* Moskovskogo gorodskogo pedagogicheskogo universiteta.

Hemming, P. J. (2015). *Religion in the primary school. Ethos, diversity, citizenship.* London: Routledge.

Hepburn, H. (2016, December 9). New Muslim school would show commitment to parity. *The Times Educational Supplement Scotland.*

Hussain, A. M., & Miller, W. L. (2006). *Multicultural nationalism: Islamophobia, anglophobia and devolution.* Oxford: Oxford University Press.

Iganski, P., & Kosmin, B. (2003). Globalized Judeophobia and its ramifications for British Society. In P. Iganski & B. Kosmin (Eds.), *A new antisemitism? Debating Judeophobia in 21st-Century Britain.* London: Profile Books.

Kadish, S. (2015). Jewish heritage in Scotland. *Jewish Historical Studies, 47,* 179–216.

Kazepides, T. (2012). Education as dialogue. In T. Besley & M. A. Peters (Eds.), *Interculturalism, education and dialogue*. New York: Peter Lang.

Keating, A. (2007). *Teaching transformation. Transcultural classroom dialogues*. Basingstoke: Palgrave Macmillan.

Kidd, S., & Jamieson, L. (2011). *Experiences of Muslims living in Scotland*. Scottish Government Social Research. Retrieved March 26, 2017, from http://www.gov.scot/resource/doc/344206/0114485.pdf

Koenig, M. (2015). Incorporating Muslim migrants in Western Nation States. In M. Burchardt & I. Michalowski (Eds.), *After integration. Islam, conviviality and contentious politics in Europe*. Wiesbaden: Springer.

Kolmel, R. (1987). *German-Jewish refugees in Scotland, aspects of Scottish Jewry*. Glasgow: Glasgow Representative Council.

Kushner, T. (1996). Anti-semitism and austerity: The August 1947 riots in Britain. In P. Panayi (Ed.), *Racial violence in Britain in the nineteenth and twentieth centuries*. London: Leicester University Press.

Maan, B. (1992). *The new scots*. Edinburgh: John Donald.

Maan, B. (2008). *The thistle and the crescent*. Argyll: Argyll Publishing.

McKinney, S. J. (2004). Jewish education and formation in Glasgow: A case study. *Journal of Beliefs and Values, 25*(1), 31–42.

McKinney, S. J. (2016a, September). Being Jewish in Scotland. *Open House*. No. 262.

McKinney, S. J. (2016b). Sectarianism in Scotland. A changing landscape? *Open House*. No. 257.

McKinney, S. J. (2016c). The implications of historical and contemporary anti-semitism in Glasgow and Scotland for global citizenship. *Forum Sociológico (Special Theme: Interculturalidade e Educação), 29*, 27–36. Retrieved March 26, 2017, from https://sociologico.revues.org/1396

McKinney, S. J., Zannoni, F., & Sakaev, V. (2016). The position of minority religious groups in Glasgow, Novellara and Tatarstan. In I. Vieira, C. Urbano, M. Do Carmo Vieira Da Silva, & L. Baptista (Eds.), *Intercultural Dialogue: Learning, Speaking and Sharing. Proceedings of the International Seminar and Study Visit ALLMEET in Lisbon '15*. CICS. Nova-Interdisciplinary Centre of Social Sciences, FCSH-UNL.

McKinney, S. J., & Conroy, J. C. (2015). The continued existence of state-funded Catholic schools in Scotland. *Comparative Education, 51*(1), 105–117.

McKinney, S. J., & McCluskey, R. (2017). Does religious education matter in non-denominational schools in Scotland? In M. Shanahan (Ed.), *Does religious education matter?* (pp. 152–165). London: Routledge.

Meer, N., & Modood, T. (2009). The multicultural state we're in: Muslims, 'multiculture' and the 'civic re-balancing' of British multiculturalism. *Political Studies, 57*, 473–497.

Moss, I. (2006). *Anti-semitic incidents and discourse in Europe during the Israel-Hezbollah war.* European Jewish Congress. Retrieved March 26, 2017, from https://cst.org.uk/public/data/file/6/1/Antisemitic%20Incidents%20 and%20Discourse%20in%20%20Europe%20During%20the%20Israel%20 Hezbollah%20War.pdf

National Records of Scotland. (2013). *Table 7: Religion, Scotland, 2001 and 2011.* Retrieved March 26, 2017, from http://www.scotlandscensus.gov.uk/documents/censusresults/release2a/rel2asbtable7.pdf

O'Cinneide, C. (2012). *Human rights and the UK constitution.* Retrieved March 26, 2017, from http://www.britac.ac.uk/sites/default/files/Human%20 rights%20and%20the%20UK%20constitution%20WEB.pdf

Office for National Statistics. (2012). *Religion in England and Wales 2011.* Retrieved March 26, 2017, from https://www.ons.gov.uk/peoplepopulation-andcommunity/culturalidentity/religion/articles/religioninenglandandwales 2011/2012-12-11

Peters, M. A. (2012). Western models of intercultural philosophy. In T. Besley & M. A. Peters (Eds.), *Interculturalism, education and dialogue.* New York: Peter Lang.

Phillips, A. (1979). *A history of the origins of the first Jewish community in Scotland – Edinburgh 1816.* Edinburgh: John Donald.

Scottish Council of Jewish Communities. (2015). *Record number of antisemitic incidents in Scotland.* Retrieved March 26, 2017, from http://www.scojec. org/news/2015/15ii_cst/report.html

Sikka, S. (2010). *Liberalism, multiculturalism, and the case for public religion. Politics and Religion, 3,* 580–609.

Siraj, A. (2011). Meanings of modesty and the Hijab amongst Muslim women in Glasgow, Scotland. *Gender, Place and Culture, 18*(6), 716–731.

The Scottish Government. (2015, April). *Tackling sectarianism and its consequences in Scotland. Final report of the advisory group on tackling sectarianism in Scotland.* Retrieved March 26, 2017, from http://www.gov.scot/ Publications/2015/05/4296

United Nations General Assembly. (1948). *Universal declaration of human rights.* Retrieved March 26, 2017, from http://www.un.org/en/universal-declaration-human-rights/

United Nations General Assembly. (1981). *Declaration on the elimination of all forms of intolerance and of discrimination based on religion and belief.* Retrieved March 26, 2017, from http://www.un.org/documents/ga/res/36/a36r055. htm

United Nations General Assembly. (1992). *Declaration on the rights of persons belonging to national or ethnic, religious and linguistic minorities.* Retrieved March 26, 2017, from http://www.un.org/documents/ga/res/47/a47r135. htm

World Jewish Congress. (2006). *Attacks on synagogues around the world*. Retrieved March 26, 2017, from http://www.worldjewishcongress.org/en/news/attacks-on-synagogues-around-the-world

Professor Stephen J. McKinney is the leader of the research and teaching group, Creativity, Culture and Faith in the School of Education in the University of Glasgow. His research interests include faith education, sectarianism and education, the impact of poverty on education and the education of minorities. He has published widely and has authored or co-authored over 120 articles, book chapters, research reports and briefings. He is currently the President of the Scottish Educational Research Association and the co-editor of the *Scottish Educational Review*.

Teaching and Learning About Cross-Cultural Encounters Over the Ages Through the Story of Britain's Migrant Past

Marlon Moncrieffe

INTRODUCTION

The Key Stage 2 National Curriculum for History Curriculum (KS2–HC) (DfE 2013a, p. 4) currently instructs teaching and learning the story of Britain's migrant past with an exclusive focus on the lives of White-European minority-ethnic groups of people, that is, Anglo-Saxons and Vikings. Primary school education in England, Wales and Northern Ireland has two Key Stages (KS): KS1 is for children aged between 5 and 7 years old and KS2 refers to children aged between 7 and 11 years old. The next key stages as part of secondary school education are KS3 for children aged between 11 and 14 years old and KS4 for children aged between 14 and 16 years old. In this chapter, I consider how KS2 teachers can look beyond this narrow privilege and instead develop their practice for teaching and learning more inclusively on Britain's multicultural history.

It is the privileged selection of the 'settlement by Anglo-Saxons' and 'Viking raids and invasions' (DfE 2013a, p. 4) which raises my concerns

M. Moncrieffe (✉)
University of Brighton, Brighton, UK

© The Author(s) 2018
R. Race (ed.), *Advancing Multicultural Dialogues in Education*,
DOI 10.1007/978-3-319-60558-6_12

towards the absence of historical moments, stories and legacies of Minority-Ethnic Group Mass Migration and Settlement (MEGroMMaS) in Britain by non-White-European groups of people over the ages. It has influenced my use of auto-ethnography to offer my personal accounts and analysis on a story of Britain's migrant past—The Brixton Riots of 1981 (BBC 2011). My aim is to make connections between human experiences, for teaching and learning about MEGroMMaS through examples of cross-cultural encounters that have occurred in Britain. I apply Rüsen's (2006) and Clark's (2014) notions of historical consciousness as theories of enquiry and reflection to demonstrate how they can be applied through practice to assist with approaches for teaching and learning.

IDENTITY AND HISTORY

My parents were immigrants to Britain from Jamaica in the 1960s. They followed my migrant grandparents who came to Britain from Jamaica in the late 1950s. My parents as young minority-ethnic group Jamaican adults lived between Brixton, London and Birmingham, West Midlands—both widely known as Afro-Caribbean (including Jamaican) migrant and immigrant settlements. My parents eventually settled in Brixton, London. The Jamaican culture and attitudes to life of my grandparents and parents have been passed on to me. It includes my deep sense of pride in the origins of my history and of my being British today. It includes also the everyday choices in things such as the foods I prefer to eat, the books that I prefer to read and the music that I like to hear (Reggae). Today, I retain a clear sense of my Jamaican culture. I know how it influences my identity. However, I recognise that an identity is not fixed, but is fluid and complex (Hall 2013). Life experiences over time can have an impact on identity.

ACCULTURATION

Since my birth in England in the 1970s, I as a minority-ethnic individual have been immersed—perhaps more so than my grandparents and parents—in the dominant British-White-European cultural modes of being in society. My greater experiences of this immersion would be from the compulsory spaces of interaction such as primary and secondary school and college education as a child and teenager. My non-compulsory spaces of interaction such as my choices of work and through my higher education as an adult have me positioned as a minority-ethnic individual amongst a dominant British-White majority of people. I am aware that my British-Black identity is something that has emerged through processes of assimilation and integration (acculturation). Both consciously and unconsciously by its nature, this ongoing process is fused to those customs, beliefs, attitudes and ways of being inherited and passed on to me from my grandparents and my parents. This has led me to an eclectic sense of identity. Although my heritage is Jamaican, I recognise that my identity is not fully Jamaican. Being born in Britain, I hold an identity in between as well. These are identities which I negotiate between informing my world view. I am conscious about how my world view shapes how I frame my being and existence in Britain and the world today. Gilroy (1993) helps to explain my position where he discusses being both European and Black as requiring specific forms of double consciousness. Hall (1997) discusses this as a continuous change of state, representative of the hybrid-ethnic identity. Bhabha (2004) defines the hybrid-ethnic identity as a third space. My hybrid minority-ethnic group identity is influential to my habitus (Bourdieu 1984). I see my habitus as a very powerful trait which I can use as an asset. It is an asset which allows me to move between social and cultural worlds inhabited by a variety of ethnic and cultural groups that I am linked to in Britain and across the world. It shapes my disposition as a teacher and as an educator in the study of MEGroMMaS over the ages.

MINORITY-ETHNIC

As with the minority-ethnic group of people which I am part of through my existence in Britain today, I conceive and apply the term 'minority-ethnic group' to the people whose lives are offered exclusive coverage within the KS2–HC, that is, 'Saxons' and 'Vikings' (DfE 2013a, p. 4). I apply the term 'minority-ethnic group' to those people in the same way that I do for Afro-Caribbean (including Jamaicans) people, in their large waves of arrival to Britain post-World War Two (Winder 2013). I see no congruency whatsoever between the invading eighth century Vikings of the past with Afro-Caribbean migrants to Britain of the twentieth century. This is because the minority-ethnic group of Afro-Caribbean people were not invading Britain after World War Two, although 'invading' was the view of racist White people in Britain, that is, Enoch Powell via his 'Rivers of Blood Speech' (Powell 1968) In fact, Afro-Caribbean people arriving in Britain post-World War Two were British citizens, invited by the British government to come to Britain, to live and to work in the country (Phillips and Phillips 1998; Sewell 1998).

I do not consider the term 'minority-ethnic' to be an anachronism in my notions of Saxons and Vikings. The work of Harke (2011) can support my view where in his evidence and discussion of ethnogenesis, he suggests that as migrants in the fifth century, the Saxons as minority tribes when first arriving and settling in Britain from what we know today as mainland Europe were outnumbered 50:1 by the indigenous population at the time and that it was only through their further immigration and internal migration that they evolved as a larger hybrid group, namely, Anglo-Saxons. Today, a similar pattern of growth and development is evident with Afro-Caribbean people in Britain. In the late 1950s their numbers as part of the population according to Home Office estimates were approximately 115,000 (Winder 2013). The most recent national census carried out in 2011 had numbers of people declaring themselves of Afro-Caribbean descent in Britain (including British-Black) at a figure of '992,000' (ONS 2015, p. 1). This group is outnumbered 45:1 by those '44,186,000' who declared themselves as British-White (ONS 2015, p. 3).

When thinking about the term 'ethnicity', I consider it to be a product of self-recognition and group belief. I see this in line with Weber (1968, p. 389) who refers ethnicity to 'those human groups that entertain a subjective belief in their common decent because of similarities […] customs, migration'. Farley (2000, p. 8) also defines an ethnic group as a 'group of people who are generally recognised by themselves and/or by others as a distinct group, with such recognition based on social or cultural characteristics'. Further, as Aguirre and Turner (1995, p. 2) write: 'When a subpopulation of individuals reveals, or is perceived to reveal, shared historical experiences as well as unique behavioural and cultural characteristics, it exhibits ethnicity'. However, Cornell and Hartmann (2007) offer an alternative perspective, where they discuss ethnicity as the unity of persons of common blood or descent: a people. From these perspectives, I consider that the terms 'minority-ethnic' and 'ethnicity' stems from a product of exclusive self-recognition and group belief which both make direct reference to a unity of people through blood and common descent. Notions of self-recognition, based upon identity, shared values and history relate to the discourses of political nationalism apparent in our current times.

POLITICAL NATIONALISM

The conception of current aims and contents in the KS2–HC originates from a significant political intervention described as a 'war on terror era' by Guyver (2013, p. 65). He discusses New Labour Prime Minster Gordon Brown's political rhetoric in 2006 which placed direct emphasis on the meaning of Britishness as a 'subtle interplay between British identity, British history and British exceptionalism'.

> We should not recoil from our national history—rather we should make it more central to our education. I propose that British history should be given more prominence in the curriculum—not just dates places and names, nor just a set of unconnected facts, but a narrative that encompasses our history. (Brown 2006, p. 1)

Exactly whose British history is being spoken of by Brown is questionable. What is being articulated by Brown is a discourse of political nationalism through the national curriculum for confronting the growth of Islamic extremism amongst some British-Black and British-Pakistani-born people of minority-ethnic groups (Osler 2009). However, when considering this rhetoric against past examples of a home-fought 'war on terror' and extremism stemming British-born people of White-European minority-ethnic groups (e.g. the Irish extremism in association with the IRA during the 1980s and 1990s) it is interesting that political rhetoric concerning the teaching and learning of British history in formal education to combat such earlier extremism is not as apparent as it has been more recently with the notion of Islamic extremism (Lander 2016).

Brown's rhetoric was met with cross-party political consensus. Former Secretary of State for Education Michael Gove (2010) used a more muscular political rhetoric in suggesting that the current approach to teaching British history '... denies children the opportunity to hear our island story' and that the '... trashing of the past had to stop'. Former Prime Minister David Cameron (2011) put it more bluntly by stating 'Multiculturalism has failed and instead fragmented and segregated our society'. From these perspectives have emerged a plethora of national policies for primary and secondary school history education curricula framed by a discourse of monoculturalism and geared towards raising the profile of teaching and learning specifically selected accounts of British-White history, not just in the KS2 primary school curriculum but as part of the KS3 and KS4 secondary school national curriculum (see DfE 2013b). This has led to the emergence of statutory directives on teaching and learning of fundamental British values (DfE 2014). This policy includes teaching the history of British democracy, tolerance and equality (Boronski and Hassan 2015). It is a policy which seems to complement the contents and aims of the KS2–HC that is shaped by a chronological approach to teaching and learning about the story of Britain's past from the Bronze Age to the year 1066. This has resulted in the erasure of multicultural British history (Lander 2016). Explicit use of the word 'migration' for study is not mentioned anywhere in the KS2–HC. The absence of 'migration' as a unit of study in the KS2–HC denies children an explicit opportunity to learn about non-European minority-ethnic groups of people over the ages that have come to Britain. In fact, KS2 children are more than likely to have to wait until they leave primary school to be able to formally learn about broader examples of non-European MEGroMMaS in Britain. The KS3–HC offers guidance for teachers on 'a study of an aspect of social history, such as the impact through time of the migration of people to, from and within the British Isles' (DfE 2013b, p. 5). But teaching and learning of MEGroMMaS in Britain over the ages is not guaranteed as this guidance statement is non-statutory.

METHODOLOGY

I applied auto-ethnography as a method of writing and analysis to my research (Chang 2007, 2008; Hayler 2011). This was to assist with raising cultural consciousness of self and others and to critically evaluate the extent to which lived experiences of MEGroMMaS in Britain could potentially assist in developing approaches to teaching practice in engagement with current KS2–HC directives. My study involved drawing upon the experiences and perceptions of two subjects: my mother and I. We wanted to share our experiences of Brixton 1981 openly and directly with as many people as possible. Our focused reflection through the lenses of our life experiences are at the heart of the writing and analysis of our findings (Hayler 2011).

Our meaning-making process was shaped by a duo-ethnographic conversation (see Lund and Nabavi 2008). This is where we aimed to detect the levels of interconnectedness and verisimilitude from our disparate histories of Brixton 1981: told through our personal narratives and then reformed in our dialogue (Sawyer and Norris 2013). As a dialogic and collaborative form, the duo-ethnographic accounts from my mother and I are stratified, nested auto-ethnographic accounts of Brixton 1981 (Norris and Sawyer 2012; Sameshima 2013). As the theoretical origins of the duo-ethnographic conversation come from phenomenology (see Heidegger 1962; Sartre 1956; Schutz 1962, 1967), it seeks to make explicit those experiences: of individual lives and experiences, the experiences of others or a combination or both for a refined understanding Brixton 1981.

The theoretical framework adopted for capturing experiences of the past through the auto-ethnographical writing in analysis and evaluation stems from the narrative competencies of historical consciousness offered by Rüsen (2006). He discusses this as a theoretical matrix that assists with orientating the past with the present in a manner that bestows on present actuality a future perspective. Harris and Reynolds (2014) interpret this in a similar way: as a process by which people can make connections between the past and the present, which in consequence affects what they believe is possible in the future.

The linguistic form within which historical consciousness achieves its function of orientation is through the telling of a story. My story of Britain's migrant past focuses upon Brixton 1981. It features minority-ethnic Afro-Caribbean and British-Black people—children and grandchildren of the Windrush generation (Winder 2013). It has also been suggested that historical consciousness is both learnt (through the disciplinary skills of history) and innate (in that we recollect) (Clark 2014). In my personal approaches to thinking, talking and writing about Brixton 1981 and in order to make sense of my construction and reconstructions of the past to develop knowing for today and the future, I positioned myself with Clark's (2014) depiction of a historical consciousness that is innate. This is in respect of being personally 'involved' by having personally experienced these moments (Brixton 1981) of British history. My mother is also positioned with an innate sense of historical consciousness, having also experienced the same moments of Brixton 1981 as I did. Historical consciousness as a theory makes central to its analysis the innate personal micro-narratives and experiences of the researcher. Rüsen (2012, p. 45) discusses this analysis as 'a mental procedure by which the past is interpreted for the sake of understanding the present and anticipating the future'.

REFLECTION, DIALOGUE AND ANALYSIS

The minority-ethnic group Afro-Caribbean community and their British-Black children faced continued racist discrimination in Britain when seeking to gain homes and jobs (Winder 2013). Brixton 1981 was a response to the continued and persistent abuse faced from racist White-led gangs including institutions such as the Metropolitan Police Force as recounted by my mother:

> The Afro-Caribbean people were getting fed up with the police stopping and searching a lot of Afro-Caribbean people, so the riot started. That day I was worried about my family who are Afro-Caribbean, so I took a 37 bus with four children. It was only going to Clapham Common as Brixton was a no go area. So I walked around the side roads to get there. On arrival, Brixton looked like World War Three. A lot of shops and building were burnt out, all except one Afro-Caribbean pub. The police cars and fire engines were still outing the fires. When I did get to my mother's house, the riot did not get that far. I had to walk back to Clapham Common to go home (Mother).

My mother discusses how 'the Afro-Caribbean people were getting fed up' with their treatment by the White-British authorities and that it led to the occurrences of Brixton 1981. The 'police stopping and searching' Afro-Caribbean people that she discusses above was 'revenge swamping' by the Metropolitan Police on the Afro-Caribbean community in Brixton, known as 'Operation Swamp 1981' (Gilroy 1992; Phillips and Phillips 1998). It was influenced by the words of Conservative Prime Minister of the time Margaret Thatcher (1978) who was concerned that White Britain was 'being swamped' by 'other' cultural groups due to increased MEGroMMaS in Britain (Phillips and Phillips 1998).

Below, I (writing as an adult) recount my childhood observations:

> We were walking in the aftermath of what I had seen on television the previous day. We walked past cars that had been burnt out, smashed glass on the floor; large cylinder iron dustbins burnt out and left in the road. We walked past windows of shops that had been smashed and boarded up. The streets were emptier of cars and vehicles that usually rushed by on Brixton Road by the red bricked town hall building. As we crossed the highway of Brixton Road and headed towards Coldharbour Lane, I looked to the left to see the police cars and police vans parked in the distance towards Stockwell. Vans and cars were smashed out. The place must have been something like in the

aftermath of a cyclone. We continued through Coldharbour Lane. We approached the market—The Grandville Arcade and it was dead. For me, it always was a low feeling when I saw it closed, but that day was worse. That place was normally the heart of Brixton: busy and bubbling with life. Now, it was lifeless. We walked past more rubbish and debris on the floor. Something had disturbed Brixton and it was what I saw on the television— the fighting between the Police and Black people. We continued towards Loughborough Park to my Nan's.

Riots are discussed by Lea (2005, p. 1) as 'theatres in which grievances of the poor and socially excluded have been played out'. Hobsbawm (1959) suggests that taking the action to rise up against a system on the part of people without any other means of representing their interests, aiming to defend themselves from abuse, attack and harassment of various types, in the quest for freedom, has a long history. Brixton 1981 should then be considered in relation to similar events and times before. For example, the cross-cultural encounters of the 1950s riots in Notting Hill, London, which had racist White-British led gangs in opposition to the migrant and immigrant Afro-Caribbean community (Winder 2013). However, Afro-Caribbean people in their fight for emancipation from White Britain and the vicious transatlantic slave trade of the fifteenth and nineteenth centuries is perhaps more significant in making connections in the history of cross-cultural encounters between the two (Greenwood and Hamber 1980). Some examples of uprisings include the 1816 slave revolt in Barbados against the White-British system; the 1831 revolt in Jamaica known as 'The Baptist War' which challenged the White-British power structures; and the 1865 revolt in Morant Bay, Jamaica, which was a pro-test against poverty and injustices inflicted upon Afro-Caribbean people by the White-British system (ibid. 1980). They are Afro-Caribbean lega-cies and histories which can be related to post-World War Two MEGroMMaS of the Afro-Caribbean community in Britain. They are legacies of the struggle for freedom shaped by a pride in overcoming irra-tional White-British authorities of the past. As Phillips and Phillips (1998, p. 353) write:

> The Caribbean migrants brought with them a determined black nationalism and anti-colonialism all over the globe in the person of Marcus Garvey. The same Caribbean's carried with them folk memories and descriptions of leg-endary rebellions, from the Maroons and Paul Bogle in Jamaica to the series of slave martyrs all over the Caribbean who bore African names—Quashie

(Akwesi), Quackoo (Akweku), Cuffee (Akofi), all leaders of slave rebellions in the Caribbean.

It is perhaps not surprising then that Afro-Caribbean people, as migrants and immigrants, invited to live and work in White Britain and faced with the oppression of racism and poverty that their ancestors fought so hard to defeat, would eventually respond in the way they did through Brixton 1981.

CONTESTED NOTIONS OF BRIXTON 1981

Influential White-British led public service broadcaster, the British Broadcasting Corporation (BBC), applied the word 'riot' in its portrayal of violence and chaos led by the Afro-Caribbean community of Brixton 1981 (BBC 2011). However, Brixton 1981 in its association with the term 'riot' is contested. Fryer (2010, p. 395) writes:

> 'Riot', being a four-letter word, is excellent for headlines; but its use to describe what were in fact uprisings by entire inner-city populations, black and white together, served to obscure the true nature and causes of the events.

The reference to an 'uprising by entire inner-city populations'; and 'black and white together' by Fryer (2010) implies that Brixton 1981 was not just a revolt against inequalities linked with 'race' and 'racism' in Britain stemming from MEGroMMaS, but an occurrence linked to inequalities framed by class divisions and power structures in society. Despite this, Gilroy (1992) maintains Brixton 1981 as being the reaction by the Afro-Caribbean community in their struggle for equality and social justice. It is view which can be equated with Ouseley (2016) who frames Brixton 1981 as the 'Brixton Disturbances' in the 'struggle for race equality'. Lord Scarman was the judge appointed by the Conservative government in power to provide an enquiry in Brixton 1981. Scarman (1981, p. 73) uses and applies the phrase 'Brixton Disorders'. Perhaps what all of the multiple interpretations above would at least agree on is that the Afro-Caribbean community associated with Brixton 1981 stemmed from MEGroMMaS after World War Two and the occurrence was a cross-cultural encounter with White Britain.

INTERACTIVE INTROSPECTION

In developing our knowing about Brixton 1981, my mother and I engaged in a dialogue (duo-ethnographic conversation). This allowed for a significant recollection between us where the reliving of the time is 'made possible by being part of a culture and/or by possessing a particular cultural identity' (Ellis et al. 2011, p. 3). The dialogue allowed for the emergence of epiphanies: new insights and new understandings on a story of British history and of Britain's migrant past.

Mother: *People (Afro-Caribbean people) were standing up for themselves and they said 'Enough is enough!' They were standing up against racism. They (the Police) didn't believe that something like that could have happened. No Police were on guard. There was no shield. The Police were defenceless. They* (the Police) *were stopping and searching people (Afro-Caribbean people) and people (Afro-Caribbean people) got upset. People (Afro-Caribbean people) couldn't get work. They didn't want to be on benefits. Every time they (the Police) see Black people, they think they are thieves.*

Me: *When I was a child, I didn't know the reasons as to why there was rioting. But what I do know now as I have understood things is that rioting, tension... Well what I am going to relate this to I suppose is more contemporary issues. Like for example the most recent riot in London a few years ago, when Mark Duggan (Black man) got shot by the Police* [in Tottenham, North London]. *Is this simply a continuance of what happened 30 years ago, you know...? Police harassment of Black people or do you think things may have improved and developed? Because what I see now in my mind is almost like a chronology of events involving a struggle for Black people that started even before Brixton. The Notting Hill riots of the fifties; more riots in the eighties and recently. Do you think Black people and their history and their struggles here have served to improve their standing in Britain in any way? You know... Has the government done anything to help them? Because there is a clear chronology of struggle.*

Mother: *I don't think so. But I think they try to do things undercover. There is still undercover racism.*

The 'interactive introspection' (Chang 2008, p. 6) within the dialogue above allowed my mother and me to consider, discuss and see how our minority-ethnic group identities have been situated socially and culturally through our experiences of MEGroMMaS in Britain. To some extent in our dialogue, we were applying in developing our understanding and reasoning with what Wright-Mills (1959) has defined as the sociological imagination: a reflective approach to learning about the relations between history and biography within society. This sociological imagination provided us a chance to reflect deeply and critically about our shared life experiences. It enabled us to explore how identity and power are linked intrinsically 'with the relation between individual agency and social structure' (Bathmaker 2010, p. 1).

My mother concentrated her thoughts on the discrimination and oppression faced by 'Black people' at a specific time in British history, whilst I in doing the same but then by making reference to 'a chronology of events involving a struggle for Black people' aimed to make the past and the present link together. However, my mother saw this 'struggle' as something entrenched within British society—racial discrimination towards Afro-Caribbean people that still exists today, but is not as openly visible as it was in the past. From this meaning-making process, there are some levels of congruency in our thinking and understanding. However, this is also coupled with subtle differences in our interpretations, possibly a reflection of our individual sense of identity through our differing levels of experienced acculturation within British society, moulding our respective diasporic imaginations and therefore the different forms of thought, knowledge construction and articulation through differing orientations with historical consciousness. This is indicative of an epistemological space between our thinking and knowing as captured below in our dialogue:

Me: *So how significant do you think the riots not just in Brixton but all over Britain in which Black people were involved are part of British history?*

Mother: *We don't count in British history.*

Me: *But these events have happened in Britain and there has been some reaction from the government via policies, such as race relations acts for racial justice. Even when you think other incidents such as the murder of Stephen Lawrence… interesting that that didn't a cause a riot, but it did create some reaction through the Macpherson inquiry and report, didn't it?*

Mother:	*Sometimes race relations acts work for people and sometimes it doesn't. Do they teach Black history in school?*
Me:	*Is this Black history?*
Mother:	*Yes.*
Me:	*Is this British history?*
Mother:	*A bit of both.*
Me:	*It happened in Britain, so I think it must be British history. What benefit would children all over Britain have by learning about the history of riots like this in Britain?*
Mother:	*Windrush Square (in Brixton) If you are going to call it Windrush Square they should say that this stands for Black people who came over here. And don't forget it was their children and grandchildren who rioted.*

The dialogue between my mother and I allowed an insight on our individual constructions of self, the culture and subcultures that we are part of in Britain and how this relates to the recounting of our past experiences and present conditions. Our dialogues illustrate the subtle spaces between our ways of thinking and knowing. My mother and I articulated through diasporic imaginations marked by both our conscious and sub-conscious experiences of acculturation into British society which we have both encountered (Vertovec 1996). This helped to generate an understanding for making meaning from our experiences and in our relationship to each other. In continuing to advance the development of a consciousness surrounding current notions of our minority-ethnic identity as individuals, my mother and I used our different perspectives of the story of Britain's migrant past for marking our levels of congruent knowing, relating this to any potential consensus we share from interpreting, understanding and in making meaning through our individual reflections and shared dialogue.

CONNECTING AND BELONGING TO THE STORY OF BRITAIN'S MIGRANT PAST

Minority-ethnic group uprisings of the 1980s were not confined to Brixton, London, but were widespread across Britain where Afro-Caribbean communities existed: most notably in St. Pauls, Bristol; Handsworth, Birmingham; Toxteth in Liverpool; Hyson Green, Nottingham; and Moss Side, Manchester (Winder 2013). This broad geographical range across Britain suggests that the 1980s represent a significant theme of British national history that can be retold as a story of cross-cultural encounters as part of Britain's migrant past. However, within the KS2–HC there is no explicit directive or guidance to teach for learning about this aspect of British history. In fact teaching of episodes from British history concerning the struggle for race equality over the ages are absent in the national curriculum for history. Furthermore, KS2–HC policymakers have not presented in the KS2–HC any Black-British people and their stories. It is a very questionable omission. It seems a gap that needs to be filled, especially in current times of accelerated migration to Britain which has created wider a diversity of ethnic and cultural groups and with it, increased xenophobia (Lander 2016; Smith 2016).

Perhaps Brixton 1981 could be viewed as one of many opportunities to learn from the past for teaching and learning on race equality today and in the future. It is an important consideration, as children of minority-ethnic groups such as the British-Black and Afro-Caribbean, on realising an absence of their minority-ethnic groups from the story of Britain's migrant past at school, have questioned and reconsidered their own sense of place and belonging within the national story, feeling distanced from this or indeed distancing themselves from a constructed school curriculum narrative (see Harris and Reynolds 2014; Hawkey and Prior 2011; Grever et al. 2008; Maylor et al. 2007). The research of Grever et al. (2008) discusses minority-ethnic students becoming disengaged and being at odds with conceptions of their identity expressed in nationalistic terms, which as a further effect, can develop and sustain a crisis of identity in association to their national identity and their birthplace. Heath and Roberts (2008) discuss minority-ethnic students' sense of disconnection and a lack of attachment or belonging to nation and national identity and specifically amongst minority-ethnic young Black children born in Britain of Afro-Caribbean parents. Issues of teaching for learning a national story for British history through MEGroMMaS are considered by my mother and me:

Me: *You mentioned Windrush Square. Do you think they (children) should be taught about Windrush as well as the riots? Do you think children should learn about this in school?*
Mother: *Depends how they take it. What do you think?*
Me: *Well, I think it was social struggle in Britain similar to civil rights movements in the USA during the 1960s based on fighting against*

oppression, discrimination and was calling for an immediate change.

Mother: *'Get up! Stand up!' Standing up for their rights and this can be traced back. So yes it could be taught in schools. Do you think many children will want to hear about violence and riots?*

Me: *Well... in primary schools children learn about the Viking invasions and they were a minority-ethnic group of the past who caused violence and bloodshed in their attacks. Whilst Black people in Brixton, you could argue, were standing up for themselves.*

The contents and aims of the KS2–HC direct that KS2 primary children should learn about migrant Vikings (new minority-ethnic groups aiming to establish themselves) in their violent invasions and their struggles with native Anglo-Saxons (majority ethnic group already established) (DfE 2013a, p. 4).

CONTENT CHOICES FOR TEACHING AND LEARNING

It seems that violent cross-cultural encounters in Britain over the ages are a recurrent theme in the story of Britain's migrant past. However, the choices made by KS2–HC policymakers on which episodes of British history are most important for teaching and learning about a story of Britain's migrant past can dictate for KS2 teachers what is considered as worthy of study, which aspects of history should be given the higher status and respect. Therefore, the decision made by KS2 teachers on which minority-ethnic groups lives are most important enough to be remembered and used in the KS2 classroom for learning about the legacies of MEGroMMaS in Britain and the shaping of British history can potentially shape a consciousness in children in terms of historical value. Children will either feel included or excluded from the stories represented by the KS2 teacher.

Words such as 'migration' and 'invasion' have differing connotations and meanings associated with them as Floyd (2004, p. 184) writes:

Terms such as 'migration' and 'invasion' pose complications of their own, the former resonating too much with notions of progress or a destiny manifest, the latter suggesting deliberate and organised military operations on a large scale.

However, these terms can also become discussion points that can enhance historical inquiry in the KS2 primary school classroom or even via Initial Teacher Education (ITE) with questions such as:

- Are there differences between a 'migrant' and an 'invader'?
- How were Vikings viewed: as 'invaders' or as 'migrants'?
- How were Afro-Caribbean people of the Windrush generation viewed: as 'migrants' or 'invaders'?
- How is the past similar or different to the present in terms of cross-cultural encounters in Britain?
- Did Alfred the Great (Saxon ruler) think that England was being 'swamped' by Vikings and their culture? How does it relate to feelings about migration and immigration in Britain today?
- How was the cross-cultural encounter between Anglo-Saxons and Vikings resolved: via Viking acceptance of Saxon world view or via a treaty of tolerance and co-existence?
- How are cross-cultural encounters between White Britain and minority-ethnic groups today best managed: via assimilation to White British culture or by mutual respect for cultural differences and co-existence through multiculturalism?

CONCLUSION

MEGroMMaS in Britain by minority-ethnic group Saxons and Vikings were in a completely different context to my grandparents and parents. Nonetheless, their reasons are similar: for survival and for increase of their wealth. From minority-ethnic group Saxon invasion came further migration, settlement and diaspora which caused a shift in their existence and identity: from 'invader' to 'migrant' to 'settler' to hybridised 'Anglo-Saxon' identity. These shifts are congruent with the more contemporary peoples of migration to Britain such as that of my mother Afro-Caribbean (Jamaican) and me (British-Black). By examining cross-cultural encounters over the ages through the story of migration to Britain and by seeking congruency in experiences and parallels between minority-ethnic groups, the opportunity emerges for teaching and learning about MEGroMMaS through a more connected story of Britain's migrant past over the ages. This can allow for children a deeper understanding of Britain today; its culturally diverse people and its multicultural context.

REFERENCES

Aguirre, A., & Turner, J. (1995). *American ethnicity: The dynamics and consequences of discrimination.* New York: McGraw-Hill.

Bathmaker, A.-M. (2010). Introduction. In A.-M. Bathmaker & P. Harnett (Eds.), *Exploring learning identity and power through life history and narrative research* (pp. 1–11). London: Routledge.

BBC. (2011). *Brixton riots: Archive.* Retrieved August 4, 2016, from http://www.bbc.co.uk/news/uk-13012055

Bhabha, H. (2004). *The location of culture.* London: Routledge.

Bourdieu, P. (1984). *Distinction: A social critique of the judgement of taste.* London: Routledge.

Boronski, T., & Hassan, N. (2015). *Sociology of education.* London: Sage.

Brown, G. (2006). *Who do we want to be? The future of Britishness.* Retrieved February 6, 2014, from http://fabians.org.uk/events/new-year-conference-06/brown-britishness/speech

Cameron, D. (2011). *State multiculturalism has failed. Speech at the 47th Munich Security Conference.* Munich: Hotel Bayerischer Hof. Retrieved February 5, 2011, from http://www.bbc.co.uk/news/yuk-politics-12371994.

Chang, H. (2008). *Autoethnography as method.* Walnut Creek, CA: Left Coast Press.

Chang, H. (2007). Autoethnography: Raising cultural consciousness of self and others. In G. Walford (Ed.), *Methodological developments in ethnography (Studies in Educational Ethnography, Volume 12)* (pp. 207–221). Bingley: Emerald Group Publishing Limited.

Clark, A. (2014). Inheriting the past: Exploring historical consciousness across the generations. *Historical Encounters: A Journal of Historical Consciousness, Historical Cultures, and History Education, 1*(1), 88–102.

Cornell, S., & Hartmann, D. (2007). *Ethnicity and race: Making identities in a changing world* (2nd ed.). Thousand Oaks, CA: Pine Forge Press.

Department for Education (DfE). (2014). *Promoting fundamental British values as part of SMSC in schools: Departmental advice for maintained schools.* London: DfE.

Department for Education (DfE). (2013a, July). *The national curriculum in England Framework Document.* London: DFE.

Department for Education (DfE). (2013b, July). History programmes of study: Key stages 3 and 4. National curriculum in England, *The national curriculum in Britain Framework Document.* London: DFE.

Ellis, C., Adams, T., & Bochner, A. P. (2011). Autoethnography: An overview. *Qualitative Social Research, 12*(1), 1–13.

Farley, J. E. (2000). *Majority-minority relations* (4th ed.). Upper Saddle River, NJ: Prentice Hall.

Floyd, R. (2004). 449 and all that: Nineteenth- and twentieth-century interpretations of the 'anglo-saxon invasion' of Britain. In H. Brocklehurst & R. Phillips (Eds.), *History, nationhood and the question of Britain* (pp. 184–197). London: Palgrave Macmillan.

Fryer, P. (2010). *Staying power: The history of black people in Britain*. London: Pluto Press.

Gilroy, P. (1993). *The black Atlantic: Modernity and double consciousness*. London: Verso.

Gilroy, P. (1992). *There ain't no black in the union Jack*. London: Routledge.

Gove, M. (2010). All pupils will learn our island story. Speech at Conservative Party Conference, Birmingham. Retrieved August 6, 2015, from http://centrallobby.politicshome.com/latestnews/article-detail/newsarticle/speech-in-full-michael-gove/

Greenwood, R., & Hamber, S. (1980). *Emancipation to emigration*. London: Macmillan Education.

Grever, M., Haydn, T., & Ribbens, K. (2008). Identity and school history: The perspective of young people from the Netherlands and England. *British Journal of Educational Studies, 56*(1), 76–94.

Guyver, R. (2013). Landmarks with questions – England's school history wars 1967–2010 and 2010–2013. *International Journal of Historical Learning, Teaching and Research, 11*(2), 59–87.

Hall, S. (1997). The work of representation & spectacle of the 'other'. In S. Hall (Ed.), *Representation: Cultural representations and signifying practices* (pp. 223–291). London: Sage.

Hall, S. (2013). The spectacle of the 'other'. In S. L. Hal (Ed.), *Representation: Cultural representations and signifying practices* (2nd ed., pp. 215–287). London: Sage.

Harke, H. (2011). Anglo Saxon immigration and ethnogenesis. *Medieval Archaeology, 55*(1), 1–28.

Harris, R., & Reynolds, R. (2014). The history curriculum and its personal connection to students from minority-ethnic backgrounds. *Journal of Curriculum Studies, 46*(4), 464–486.

Hawkey, K., & Prior, J. (2011). History, memory cultures and meaning in the classroom. *Journal of Curriculum Studies, 43*(2), 231–247.

Hayler, M. (2011). *Autoethnography, self-narrative and teacher education*. Rotterdam: Sense Publishers.

Heath, A. and Roberts, J. (2008). British Identity: it sources and possible implications for civic attitudes and behaviour. *Economic and Social Research Council On-line Resource*. Retrieved August 6, 2015, from http://www.esrc.ac.uk/my-esrc/grants/RES-148-25-0031/outputs/read/5dfb4628-3a97-44d5-9c05-d9df56f4fd6d

Heidegger, M. (1962). *Being and time*. Oxford: Basil Blackwell.

Hobsbawm, E. J. (1959). *Primitive rebels: Studies in archaic forms of social movement in the 19th and 20th centuries*. London: WW Norton.

Lander, V. (2016). Introduction to fundamental British values. *Journal of Education for Teaching, 42*(3), 274–279.

Lea, J. (2005, May). From Brixton to Bradford: Ideology and discourse on race and urban violence in the United Kingdom. *The Howard Journal of Criminal Justice, 44*(2).

Lund, D. E., & Nabavi, M. (2008). A duo-ethnographic conversation on social justice activism: Exploring issues of identity, racism, and activism with young people. *Multicultural Education, 15*(4), 27–32.

Maylor, U., Read, B., Mendick, H., Ross, A., & Rollock, N. (2007). *Diversity and citizenship in the curriculum: Research review*. London: The Institute for Policy Studies in Education London Metropolitan University.

Norris, J., & Sawyer, R. D. (2012). Toward a dialogic methodology. In J. Norris, R. D. Sawyer, & D. Lund (Eds.), *Duoethnography: Dialogic methods for social, health, and educational research* (pp. 9–41). Walnut Creek, CA: Left Coast Press.

Office for National Statistics (ONS). (2015). *2011 census analysis: Ethnicity and religion of the non-UK born population in England and Wales*. London: Home Office/Office for National Statistics.

Ouseley, H. (2016). *The struggle for race equality*. Retrieved August 4, 2016, from http://www.runnymedetrust.org/histories/index.php?mact=OralHistories,cn tnt01,default,0&cntnt01qid=35&cntnt01returnid=20

Osler, A. (2009). Patriotism, multiculturalism and belonging: political discourse and the teaching of history. *Educational Review, 61*(1), 85–100.

Phillips, T., & Phillips, M. (1998). *Windrush: The irresistible rise of multi-racial Britain*. London: Harper Collins.

Powell, E. (1968). Rivers of blood. Reprinted in *The Daily Telegraph*, 6 November 2007. Retrieved October 31, 2016, from http://www.telegraph.co.uk/comment/3643823/Enoch-Powells-Rivers-of-Blood-speech.html

Rüsen, J. (2006). Historical consciousness: Narrative structure, moral function, and ontogenetic development. In P. Seixas (Ed.), *Theorizing historical consciousness*. Toronto: University of Toronto Press.

Rüsen, J. (2012). Tradition: A principle of historical sense-generation and its logic and effect in historical culture. *History and Theory, 5*(4), 45–59.

Sameshima, P. (2013). Book review: Duoethnography. *Journal of the Canadian Association for Curriculum Studies, 11*(1).

Sartre, J.-P. (1956). *Being and nothingness, an essay on phenomenological ontology*. New York: Philosophical Library.

Sawyer, R. D., & Norris, J. (2013). *Duoethnography: Understanding qualitative research*. Oxford: Oxford University Press.

Scarman, L. G. (Lord) (1981, April 10–12). *The Scarman report: The Brixton disorders*. London: Penguin Books.

Schutz, A. (1962). *Collected papers, Volume 1*. The Hague: Martinus Nijhoff.

Schutz, A. (1967). *The phenomenology of the social world*. Evanston, IL: Northwestern University Press.

Sewell, T. (1998). *Keep on moving: The Windrush legacy: The Black experience in Britain from 1948*. London: Voice Communications Group Limited.

Smith, H. J. (2016). Britishness as racist nativism: A case of the unnamed 'other'. *Journal of Education for Teaching, 42*(3), 298–313.

Thatcher, M. (1978). *TV interview for Granada world in action ("rather swamped")*. Retrieved November 13, 2015, from http://www.margaretthatcher.org/document/103485

Vertovec, S. (1996). Diaspora. In A. Ellis-Cashmore (Ed.), *Dictionary of race and ethnic relations* (4th ed., pp. 89–101). London: Routledge.

Weber, M. (1968). *Economy and society*. Berkerley, CA: University of California Press.

Winder, R. (2013). *Bloody foreigners: The story of immigration to Britain*. London: Abacus.

Wright-Mills, C. (1959). *The sociological imagination*. Harmondsworth: Penguin.

Marlon Moncrieffe is a Senior Lecturer at the School of Education, University of Brighton, UK. He is formerly a primary school Assistant Head teacher. He currently teaches Education Studies on post-graduate and under-graduate courses. His current research is framed by his interests in Key Stage 2 History Curriculum presentation of British history for a sense of identity and nationhood and the potential of critical approaches to practice in engagement with these made by student-teachers.

Multicultural Dialogues in Post-Conflict Music Education Settings

Oscar Odena

INTRODUCTION

The power of music to affect human beings is documented in the scholarly literature. Sounds and music surround our daily lives and we all experience music, actively or passively. For example, marketing research has shown how music is used to alter consumers' mood (Brown and Volgsten 2006) and psychotherapy research has revealed how communication skills can be developed using music with children on the autistic spectrum (Bunt 2012). At the crossroads between music and education, music education research has established itself since the 1950s as a substantive field, evidenced with the indexation of journals in the Thomson Reuters' Journal Citation Reports and the activities of the International Society for Music Education (ISME). Founded in 1954, affiliated to UNESCO and present in 80 countries, ISME is the premiere international organisation for music education. As a former ISME Research Commissioner (2008–2014), I witnessed scholars investigating music activities for other-than-musical purposes, including the development of language and well-being

O. Odena (✉)
University of Glasgow, Glasgow, UK

© The Author(s) 2018
R. Race (ed.), *Advancing Multicultural Dialogues in Education*,
DOI 10.1007/978-3-319-60558-6_13

215

(e.g. Institute of Education 2011; Welch et al. 2010). However, only recently have a handful of researchers turned their attention to the apparent cross-community integration potential of music and music education activities such as orchestras and choirs (e.g. Odena et al. 2016; Phelan 2016). A study of the potential of music education as a tool for inclusion in Northern Ireland indicated that such activities, when avoiding nationalistic tunes, were allowing children from conflicted communities to work together (Odena 2010). As a result of that study I was invited to work at a peace conference in Cyprus with teachers eager to develop activities for Greek- and Turkish-Cypriot children sharing classrooms for the first time in decades (Odena 2009).

TOWARDS PRAGMATIC DEFINITIONS OF INTEGRATION, ETHNICITY AND MULTICULTURAL EDUCATION

The concepts of 'integration', 'ethnicity' and 'multicultural education' appear to be contested in the literature. Scholars favour a variety of definitions depending on their disciplinary traditions and tend to propose ways forward for advancing their disciplines (e.g. Aman 2015; Frankenberg et al. 2016; Race and Lander 2016). Nevertheless, to facilitate the work of practitioners and policy makers across all sectors of society, unambiguous and pragmatic definitions of the above issues are required that can be shared beyond the academy. A definition of integration that fits this requirement is the one advocated by the Integration Building Inclusive Societies interactive online community. Integration Building Inclusive Societies, jointly developed by the International Organization for Migration and the United Nations (UN) Alliance of Civilizations, defines integration as a two way process of adaptation by both the newly arrived and host communities:

> Whereas assimilation focuses on the migrant adopting the culture and identity of the host country, integration is a two way process of adaptation by both migrants and receiving societies. It can be defined as the process by which migrants become accepted into society, both as individuals and as groups. It implies consideration of the rights and obligations of migrants and host societies, and building a dynamic relationship between the two. (Integration Building Inclusive Societies 2016, p. 1)

Integration thus involves a number of dimensions, including:

- Socio-Economic Integration: covering issues such as access to education and training, access to employment and entrepreneurial opportunities and access to services such as housing and health
- Legal and Political Integration: in particular opportunities for political participation and empowerment and anti-discrimination laws
- Cultural Integration: including initiatives linked to public perceptions and attitudes towards migrants, acceptance and promotion of cultural and religious diversity, both among host societies and among newly arrived communities, and harmonious daily interaction (adapted from Integration Building Inclusive Societies 2016, p. 1)

The apparent consensus for integration of leading Western governments and organisations has been characterised in education and music education as a stage prior to a better, more anti-racist education based on a human rights curricula (Arshad 2012; Race in Race and Lander 2016; Bradley et al. 2007). However, integration would appear to be a very good starting point in contexts with a history of armed conflict, because in the absence of integration communities can grow in physical proximity but without interaction—a situation described in Northern Ireland as a 'benign form of apartheid' (Gallagher 2005; Gardner 2016).

In cross-community contexts where different 'national identities' or 'ethnicities' come into contact, the definition of the 'group' is also contested. Depending on their disciplinary approaches scholars offer a variety of understandings of national identity (e.g. Aman 2015; Deux 2006; Gallagher et al. 2008; Gluschankof 2014). For example, drawing on post-colonial theories Aman (2015) proposes that the notion of cultural and national identity is imprecise and artificial:

Nationhood, like borders, is merely an artificial construct—never physical, never embodied, never pure ... Consequently, we find out who we are by a kind of 'ostensive self-definition by negation,' establishing a border between self and other by articulating who we are not; the Other provides the mirror in which we perceive ourselves. (Aman 2015, p. 150)

The above argument resonates with the idea of a transnational identity in constant flux, one that shifts with every migratory movement (Race in

Race and Lander 2016). Dual ethnic categories found in the UK and the USA—such as British-Pakistani or Korean-American—suggest that 'one can simultaneously hold and blend together the ethnicity of origin and the nationality of current citizenship' (Deaux 2006, p. 94). Regardless of how 'artificial' one's sense of ethnic and cultural identity might be, and even though cultures evolve, most individuals do see themselves as belonging to a group or groups. This sense of belonging appears to be shaped by the groups' context, particularly in post-conflict settings in which violent relationships between 'ethnic' groups have affected the day-to-day experiences of individuals. For example, Gluschankof (2014) identifies elements of three music cultures in the transnational identity of Palestinian girls in an Arab-Hebrew school in Israel, that is, global, Arab and Hebrew. The girls' music cultures are evidenced differently across school, friends and family spaces, in a delicate balance resulting from growing up in contested spaces. For the sake of clarity I will use the following definition of 'ethnicity' from the Belfast-based *UNA A Global Learning Initiative on Children and Ethnic Diversity*:

> 'Ethnic' and 'ethnicity' are used generically to refer to all situations whereby groups of people develop distinctive identities based upon any one or more of the following: race, nationality, religion, language, shared history and/or particular form or example of an ethnic group. (Gallagher et al. 2008, p. 10)

Employing a broad definition of ethnicity is key because the usage of the concept and its components varies around the globe. If we narrowed its definition, for example, to skin colour, we would be at risk of not addressing many relevant issues. For instance, a newcomer to Northern Ireland would not see any differences in skin colour between the main 'ethnic' groups, Protestant and Catholic, who nevertheless see themselves as belonging to one or the other by their shared history, culture and religion.

Having defined integration and ethnicity, we arrive at the concept of multicultural education. A term that evolved over time, I would like to highlight the definition found in The Glossary of Education Reform, slightly adapted with the addition of the word *critically*:

> Multicultural education refers to any form of education or teaching that *critically* incorporates the histories, texts, values, beliefs, and perspectives of people from different cultural backgrounds. At the classroom level, for

example, teachers may modify or incorporate lessons to reflect the cultural diversity of the students in a particular class. In many cases, 'culture' is defined in the broadest possible sense, encompassing race, ethnicity, nationality, language, religion, class, gender, sexual orientation, and 'exceptionality'. (adapted from Great Schools Partnership 2013, p. 1)

The incorporation of the histories and perspectives of people from different backgrounds would need to be done critically, to avoid tokenism and, respectfully, to prevent worsening tensions. In any cross-community environment there will be power relations at play which will facilitate or hinder particular types of educational activities. For example, in a context of a majority group hosting newly arrived children there may be a degree of hostility of the host population towards the culture(s) of the newly arrived—a concept described in Western societies as 'White backlash' by Hewitt (2005) and Race (in Race and Lander 2016). And in a post-conflict context with a history of violence different communities may be reluctant to engage at all, unless the proposed activity is implemented with the agreement (and ownership) of all participating communities. Consequently, the nature of the context and type of previous contact with other groups may determine the nature of the 'multicultural education' and multicultural dialogues arising from it: from being inclusive of a number of cultures to actively promoting them.

Music and Music Education as Tools for Integration

After armed ethnic-conflict communities typically grow apart, developing prejudice and alienation towards each other. Europe has a history of ethnic conflict of which Northern Ireland (1960–90s), Cyprus (1960–70s) and Ukraine (2014–) are just some examples. It would appear that opportunities for rebuilding cross-community integration open up one generation after armed conflict, for example, through shared educational activities between Protestants and Catholics in Northern Ireland and Greek- and Turkish-Cypriots in Cyprus. Music education is seen favourably as a tool for such activities on account of their power to overcome socio-cultural barriers. Indeed, agencies around the globe are currently keen to support music education activities to develop reconciliation of divided communities, such as festivals hosted at the UN-controlled buffer zone in Nicosia (European Economic Area and Norway Grants 2009), cross-community choirs in Cyprus (Association for Historical Dialogue and Research 2016;

Bi-Communal Choir for Peace 2016) and Barenboim's West-Eastern Divan Orchestra which promotes the idea of Palestinian-Jewish dialogue through music (Barenboim and Said 2004). Northern Ireland and Cyprus appear to be within a 'window of opportunity' afforded by having had one generation without armed conflict. Focussing research efforts in these two contexts would be of use for other conflicted contexts, in Europe and globally.

Cross-community music and music education activities are often developed ad hoc to address evolving post-conflict realities. As outlined in a recent international review, the available reports to date provide descriptive snapshots of particular activities, with no comparison between contexts and limited use of theory in interpreting the data (Odena 2014a). There is an urgent unmet need to systematically investigate the effects of music education as a tool for cross-community integration to learn to what extent and under which conditions these activities may or may not work. Current practices are under-researched and the handful of studies available tend to focus on single institutions or programmes in non-conflict zones. For instance, a study from Australia describes how drumming and dance workshops are used to cultivate the feelings of belonging of newly arrived children into a specialist secondary school catering for refugees (Marsh 2012). Focussing on interviews and observations, the study discusses the benefits of the activities for the integration of newly arrived children and reports an increase in the children's sense of belonging to the school.

In Portugal, Costa et al. (2014) studied an orchestral project inspired in Venezuela's *Sistema* programme of youth orchestras, which is aimed at promoting social inclusion of teenagers in educational and social vulnerability through collective musical practice. Following initial positive reports by Venezuelan authorities similar orchestral programmes have been developed internationally, some of whose evaluations were discussed at the 2014 ISME Research Commission (Creech et al. 2014). Although commissioned evaluations offer some insights on the possibilities of such projects—see, for instance, Scotland's *Big Noise* evaluation by Harkins (2014)—researchers more often than not base their data collection on facilitated observations by, and interviews with, project promoters and project leaders, as well as on headcounts of participating individuals and institutions. Not surprisingly, their conclusions point to the need for a more systematic approach in further studies in the process of data collection 'in order to construct a more grounded interpretation of such a complex reality' (Costa et al. 2014, p. 75).

A number of social music and music education activities are being organised in post-conflict zones. However, funders appear to be complacent if the activities have good press coverage, which is seen as 'evidence' of programme effectiveness. Examples include the already mentioned festival in Nicosia's buffer zone and Barenboim's West-Eastern Divan Orchestra, which between 2005 and 2015 played in conflict-affected and symbolic locations including Ramallah, Bogota, the Korean Demilitarized Zone and the United Nations.' Barenboim's orchestra regularly tours with young Jewish and Arab musicians promoting the idea of Palestinian-Jewish dialogue through music (West-Eastern Divan Orchestra 2016). Whereas in the above cases of Australia and Portugal the music education activities are designed to facilitate social integration of disadvantaged minority groups, the Divan Orchestra functions as a neutral environment in which classically trained young musicians (not in education vulnerability) can develop respect for each other's communities. Interestingly, the benefits of musical participation for prejudice reduction are highlighted in the literature without a consideration of the levels of integration participants may already possess when joining the activities.

Beyond the positive media coverage the degree to which music education activities result in positive change or act as a 'self-fulfilling prophecy' remains unknown. There are different aims, approaches and contextual factors to consider when examining music education as a tool for cross-community integration. More systematic research on how best to develop multicultural dialogues through music activities in post-conflict contexts is needed because it would help address the challenge of social cohesion in such contexts.

THE NEED FOR RESEARCH IN POST-CONFLICT CONTEXTS

Wars and armed conflicts result in death, injuries, physical and psychological threats that force family relocations and breed prejudice between communities. Nevertheless, children born after the end of an armed conflict, although affected through their family history, experience a more peaceful upbringing and are open to allow their own children to participate in cross-community activities. For example, in Northern Ireland and in

Cyprus, 40 years after their conflicts resulted in over 3700 and 5000 casualties, respectively (McKittrick et al. 2007; Papadakis and Bryant 2012), a window of opportunity is now opening for shared educational activities—for instance, within the auspices of the Shared Education Signature Project (2016) in Northern Ireland and the Association for Historical Dialogue and Research (2016) in Cyprus. Such activities are fraught with challenges due to previous lack of contact between groups. My study in Northern Ireland outlined that to overcome these challenges a number of conditions are needed: participating groups need equal status, ongoing personal interaction and a situation in which individuals work together towards a common goal (Odena 2010). Shared activities in Northern Ireland and Cyprus suggest music education to be a viable medium for conflicted communities to work together, and more comparative research across local settings and internationally would be valuable for other conflicted contexts. Some of the research questions still to be addressed include:

- What are the key practical issues for the actors involved in music education for cross-community integration?
- What are the strategies that seem to be most effective, and are there any facilitating/hindering factors?
- What is their long-term effect (if any) on the participants' attitudes and aspirations?
- How do actors become involved in such activities and what fuels their resilience? What are their background and pedagogy/pedagogies?

In this type of social research, the objective is not to infer causality but rather to explain the development of trends taking into account the complexity of each context. Although the situation in Northern Ireland and Cyprus is now stable, noticeable tensions still exist, for example, in their capital cities. In Belfast tensions abound during the July marching season, and in Nicosia the buffer zone also known as the 'green line' separating North and South areas of Cyprus is still manned by UN peace-keeping forces. Carrying out social research in such settings involves an element of risk because, under the surface of normality, divisions and prejudice have not been fully resolved. Individuals and groups are likely to portray what happened partially and in extreme cases even try to influence researchers through intimidation (after a visit to a West Belfast school in 2008, the Head ordered me a taxi for the return journey: public transport was deemed too risky due to gun feuding between local groups). Trust needs to be gained and access negotiated with local gatekeepers when doing research in post-conflict contexts.

Since the opening of the first border crossing at Nicosia's Ledra Street in 2003 (now one of seven crossings) families from North Cyprus have been increasingly freer to work in the South where salaries are higher. Some Turkish-Cypriot families temporarily residing or regularly crossing to the South, as well as hundreds of families settled in the North are sending their children to schools across the border, which, as part of the EU system, are well regarded (Volkan 2008). Consequently Turkish- and Greek-Cypriot children are sharing classrooms again for the first time since the early 1970s. The lack of quantification of this phenomena means that the urgency of addressing any remaining cross-community tensions is difficult to assess.

In Northern Ireland today, despite the stability brought about by the 1999 Good Friday Agreement, most schools are de facto segregated—only 7% of schools have a balanced intake integrating Protestant and Catholic children (Gardner 2016). As many mainstream political parties in Northern Ireland and Cyprus do not appear to have integration high in their agendas, any cross-community tensions are at best ignored and at worst fuelled by direct action and support of policies that perpetuate segregation. For example, in Cyprus there was an active campaign against reunification prior to the 2004 Annan Plan referendum, and in Northern Ireland, the Democratic Unionist Party campaigned against the Good Friday Agreement (and did not recognise it once democratically approved). In this field, relatively basic questions regarding social tensions' shape and provenance have often been analysed by proxy, via surveys and election results, for example, the Annan Referendum highlighted the north-south Cyprus divide with 65% and 24% support for reunification, respectively.

At the heart of organising cross-community activities lies the idea that intergroup contact, under certain conditions, can be effective in reducing intergroup prejudice and hostility. This theory, also known as contact hypothesis, was first proposed by Allport (1954) and has been recently corroborated by Pettigrew (1998) and Pettigrew and Tropp (2006). The optimum conditions for effective intergroup contact are:

- Equal status of both groups in the contact situation;
- Ongoing personal interaction between individuals from both groups;
- Cooperation in a situation of mutual independence, in which members of both groups work together towards a common goal;

- Institutional support, where there is official social sanction for contact between distinct groups (adapted from Hughes 2007).

Allport (1954, p. 489) observed that 'to be maximally effective, contact and acquaintance programs' would need to 'occur in ordinary purposeful pursuits', avoiding artificiality. Subsequent studies on contact theory highlight that the emotional response during contact is more important than increasing knowledge about the other group and that the above optimum conditions can be perceived differently by participating groups, for instance, when a minority sees the activity as patronisingly unequal (Pettigrew and Tropp 2006). In a more recent reformulation of contact theory, Pettigrew (1998) proposes a sequential model to reduce conflict between communities containing three stages, which might aid to our understanding of the participants' experiences in cross-community activities:

- First stage: the initial contact, where anxiety is likely to be more pronounced and where personal identity and interpersonal interaction are emphasised in an effort to 'de-categorise' the individual
- Second stage: contact is well established, which affords an optimal situation with less anxiety in which the old salient categorisation of belonging to a particular group is highlighted, resulting in weakened prejudices that are generalised beyond the activity
- Third stage: after extended contact, individuals begin to think of themselves as part of a redefined new larger group that comprises all communities. This involves the development of the idea of a new community or a 're-categorisation' of the old ones (adapted from Odena 2010).

While overtly Protestant and Catholic ensembles were not found in first contact situations in the Northern Ireland study, these were present in long established cross-community school settings (Odena 2010). As shown in Fig. 1 the level of past conflict and remaining tensions of the context would need to be taken into account when planning cross-community activities, in addition to the optimum conditions and stages outlined above. Such multidimensional framework would allow the development of deeper theoretical understandings and of activities appropriate to the particular context.

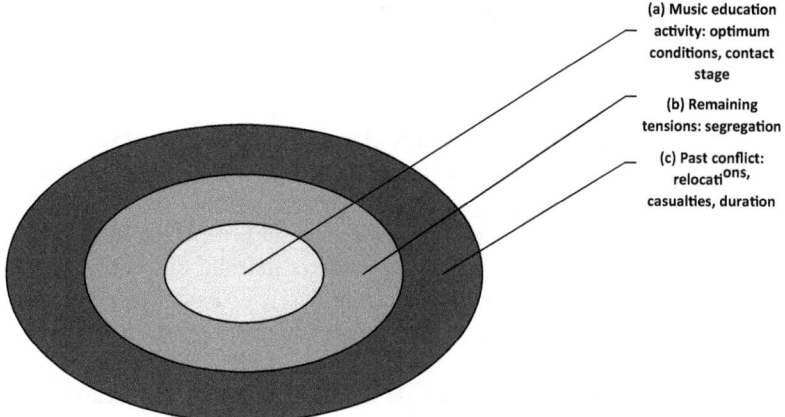

(a) Music education
activity: optimum
conditions, contact
stage

(b) Remaining
tensions: segregation

(c) Past conflict:
relocations,
casualties, duration

Fig. 1 Multiple dimensions for developing music education for integration activities

The participants' future aspirations and attitudes towards cross-community integration, including attitudes towards the musical and cultural expressions of the other community, would need to be considered prior to starting a new programme, school or after-school activity. My work in Ireland and Cyprus suggests the reasons to engage in cross-community activities vary. While some families truly embrace the integration principles behind the activities, others have different motivations, such as their children's development (if quality activities are offered) or their own safety (when cross-community spaces are seen as less problematic, e.g. by mixed couples). This is further complicated by the fact that not only parents but often professionals that work with 'the other' community in such activities may face disapproval and even stigma from extremists in both communities. While, for some, cross-community engagement may have economic aspects (e.g. North-Cypriots working in the South), for others the reason may be to avoid stigma (e.g. children of mixed couples).

When studying already occurring activities, a longitudinal multiple case study design may be most appropriate to shed light on the above issues. At the same time, striving to select comparable settings across Northern Ireland and Cyprus in terms of the level of integration and type of musical activity would allow for cross-country comparison, for instance, selecting cross-community classrooms and out-of-school orchestras and choirs in both countries. The following are some of the contexts that could be considered:

- In Northern Ireland, the music classrooms in the 7% of schools that are part of the integrated school system, existing cross-community music projects and programmes (Odena 2010)
- In Cyprus, educational spaces attended by both communities since the opening of the border and in villages that did not become segregated after partition (Potamia and Pyla), cross-community music projects and festivals operating across the north-south divide

The above settings would provide a unique ground for research. Such study would produce transnational cross-context analysis which could be used by policy leaders and researchers when developing future policy and interventions. Trends across contexts would need to be complemented with rich data at the participants' level, for example, in-depth interviews and 'critical incident charting' (Odena and Welch 2007, 2009). Interviewees on each site could be asked to select memorable experiences that were influential in their educational and work paths, following the bends of an undulating line on a single sheet of paper. This technique is useful in selecting relevant incidents and in allowing participants disclosure of their own thoughts. Critical incident charting is also useful in evidencing the interviewees' backgrounds without asking directly about institutions attended, which can be seen as sensitive in post-conflict contexts. The ideas outlined in critical incident charting may be explored further during interviews, including the range of motivations for practitioners to become involved and for parents to send their children to cross-community settings—to enable access to subjectivities and to understand the meaning of certain acts and choices.

CONCLUSIONS: IMPLICATIONS FOR PRACTICE

As outlined earlier, the characteristics of each post-conflict environment defines what is possible in terms of multicultural education. The resulting main implication is that, unfortunately, there is no magic recipe: any activity would need to be carefully context-bound in terms of the participants' previous contact and expectations and would require a degree of shared design, implementation and ownership by all participating communities.

What I propose below, rather than recipes, are a few principles for the design of pedagogies of multicultural education, which could be adapted for different ages when developing music activities and programmes in and out of school (they could also be adapted for non-musical activities). I hope they are of use for policy leaders, educators and community organisers. These principles are developed from recent publications on using music for integration (Odena et al. 2016), developing creativity and innovative projects (Odena 2012a, 2012b, 2014b, 2014c) and addressing diversity issues in education (Department for Education and Skills 2007; Race and Lander 2016):

1. *Including participants' voices*: school and community educators would need to consider the use of forums, councils or other mechanisms for discussions around identity, belonging and project implementation. Mechanisms need to be in place to ensure participants' voices are heard and acted upon, particularly when activities are aimed at children (Lundy 2007; Leitch et al. 2007).

2. *Harnessing links*: school and community leaders would need to build active links between and across communities, with community cohesion as focus. This may range from electronic links to organising a federation of schools, to links with business and other community groups. Links should be encouraged between all types of schools and groups/programmes, including links between predominantly monocultural and multicultural settings, as well as across segregated groups, to start initial contact as soon as it is feasible, and from an early age.

3. *Harnessing activities*: ideally, cross-community activities would need to be incorporated into regular education courses or into sustained weekly activities, to help avoid tokenism.

4. *Building a positive emotional environment*: participants need to feel capable of taking risks and sense that their contributions are respected. This positive environment can be built and sustained through dialogue between participants and educator with constructive positive feedback and with careful grouping of participants (e.g. pairing newly arrived participants with buddies).

5. *Planning suitable stimulating challenges*: in relation to the participants' developmental stage (so they have a realistic chance of solving it) and in relation to promoting musical activities that have contemporary relevance to them (for instance, inviting participants to come

with their own musical materials, offering alternative tasks or more instruments). Rich and stimulating resources can be used to both initiate and support creative cross-community development. These resources can be musical, visual or spatial, for example, a variety of songs, recordings, slides, films, music software, instruments, body movements and/or dancing (depending on the context and the groups coming into contact).

6. *Facilitating the participants' technical development*: by questioning, prompting and modelling; educators need to set up opportunities for models to be heard (e.g. advanced students, external musicians or themselves). They need to encourage further development of musical ideas, as novice musicians may be satisfied with their work after an initial exploratory phase.

7. *Being sensitive to the participants' time needs:* during their cross-community collaborative processes, flexibly adapting the expectations as their work progresses.

8. *Sharing assessment and developing criteria with participants*: to develop their self-assessment skills and facilitate the emergence of further ideas. For instance, participants may be asked to come up with musical examples (e.g. rhythms, melodies, songs) that match the criteria.

9. *Continuing professional development:* facilitators, music teachers and conductors of cross-community music activities would need continuing professional development to enhance their subject and interpersonal skills. This would assist practitioners to discuss contentious diversity issues without fear and to lead group music activities with increased professional satisfaction.

When using the above principles, the details of what to do and when to do it would need to be developed and agreed with the participants and any other relevant actors in each cross-community context. As contexts evolve (e.g. with new arrivals), multicultural dialogues would need to evolve accordingly and would require leadership, ideally from educators engaged in communities of practitioner-researchers (Odena 2014d) bound by their shared values and commitment.

Multicultural dialogues may be nurtured in seemingly adverse environments, such as Nicosia's buffer zone patrolled by the UN Peacekeeping Force, where rehearsals by the amateur Bi-Communal Choir for Peace are hosted. This cross-community choir's repertoire consists of songs in

'Greek-Cypriot and Turkish-Cypriot dialects as well as newer songs in Greek, Turkish and any other language as long as they send a message of peace, love, solidarity and reconciliation' (Bi-Communal Choir for Peace 2016, p. 1). Turkish-Cypriot and Greek-Cypriot choir members teach each other the correct pronunciation of songs; they have one conductor from each community and regularly perform in towns and villages on both sides of the divide and within the buffer zone. Their experience, which is shown in a documentary by National Geographic (2011), has inspired the recent creation of a children's cross-community choir that also rehearses in the buffer zone (Association for Historical Dialogue and Research 2016). Armed soldiers are still guarding the 'green line' that divides Cyprus and adult memories of forced relocations remain on both sides of the partition. However, children's cross-community activities set in positive emotional environments (principles 2 and 4 above) hosted on a regular basis (principle 3 above), may just provide the space for developing multicultural dialogues as suggested in this chapter. After extended contact, these activities would assist in the emergence of a redefined new larger group comprising all communities in which multicultural dialogues may be the norm rather than the exception.

REFERENCES

Allport, G. W. (1954). *The nature of prejudice.* Reading, MA: Addison-Wesley Publishing.
Aman, R. (2015). The double bind of interculturality and the implications for education. *Journal of Intercultural Studies, 36*(2), 149–165.
Arshad, R. (2012). The twenty-first century teacher needs to engage with race and racism. In R. Arshad, L. Pratt, & T. Wrigley (Eds.), *Social justice re-examined* (pp. 193–207). London: Trentham Books.
Association for Historical Dialogue and Research. (2016). Inter-Communal Children Choir, *News.* [online]. Retrieved October 27, 2016, from http://www.ahdr.info/viewnews.php?nid=252
Barenboim, D., & Said, E. W. (2004). *Parallels and paradoxes: Explorations in music and society.* London: Bloomsbury.
Bi-Communal Choir for Peace. (2016). Brief historical background, *Bi-Communal Choir for peace in Cyprus.* [online]. Retrieved October 27, 2016, from http://choirforpeace.weebly.com/english.html
Bradley, D., Golner, R., & Hanson, S. (2007). Unlearning Whiteness, rethinking race issues in graduate music education. *Music Education Research, 9*(2), 293–304.

Brown, S., & Volgsten, U. (Eds.). (2006). *Music and manipulation: On the social uses and social control of music*. Oxford: Berghahn Books.

Bunt, L. (2012). Music therapy: A resource for creativity, health and well-being across the lifespan. In O. Odena (Ed.), *Musical creativity: Insights from music education research* (pp. 165–181). London and New York: Routledge.

Costa, J. A., Cruz, A. I. S., & Mota, G. (2014). The *Orquestra Geração*—unveiling its complexity. In O. Odena & S. Figueiredo (Eds.), *Proceedings of the 25th International Seminar of the ISME Commission on Research, João Pessoa, Brazil*. (pp. 59–76). Malvern, Australia: International Society for Music Education (ISME). Retrieved October 26, 2016, from https://issuu.com/official_isme/docs/2014_11_10_isme_rc_ebook_final_pp37/1

Creech, A., González-Moreno, P., Lorenzino, L., & Waitman, G. (2014). El Sistema and Sistema-inspired programmes: Principles and practices. In O. Odena & S. Fig ueiredo (Eds.), *Proceedings of the 25th International Seminar of the ISME Commission on Research, João Pessoa, Brazil*. (pp. 77–97). Malvern: ISME. Retrieved October 26, 2016, from http://issuu.com/official_isme/docs/2014_11_10_isme_rc_ebook_final_pp37

Deaux, K. (2006). *To be an immigrant*. New York: Russell Sage Foundation.

Department for Education and Skills. (2007). *Diversity and citizenship curriculum review*. London: DfES.

European Economic Area and Norway Grants. (2009). 'Music, poetry and film jam in Cyprus' UN buffer zone', *News*. [online]. Retrieved October 26, 2016, from http://eeagrants.org/News/2009/Music-poetry-and-film-jam-in-Cyprus-UN-buffer-zone

Frankenberg, E., Fries, K., Friedrich, E. K., Roden, I., Kreutz, G., & Bongard, S. (2016). The influence of musical training on acculturation processes in migrant children. *Psychology of Music, 44*(1), 114–128.

Gallagher, A. M. (2005). *Education in divided societies*. Basingstoke and New York: Palgrave Macmillan.

Gallagher, T., Connolly, P., & Odena, O. (2008). *Joint learning initiative on children and ethnic diversity report of phases I and II*. Belfast: Centre for Effective Education, Queen's University Belfast.

Gardner, J. (2016). Education in Northern Ireland since the Good Friday agreement: Kabuki theatre meets danse macabre. *Oxford Review of Education, 42*(3), 346–361.

Gluschankof, C. (2014). Preschool as a musical-cultural system Palestinian girls dance their worlds in a bilingual (Arab and Hebrew) preschool. In O. Odena & S. Figueiredo (Eds.), *Proceedings of the 25th International Seminar of the ISME Commission on Research, João Pessoa, Brazil*. (pp. 130–147). Malvern: ISME. Retrieved October 26, 2016, from https://issuu.com/official_isme/docs/2014_11_10_isme_rc_ebook_final_pp37/1

Great Schools Partnership. (2013). Multicultural education, *The Glossary of Education Reform*. [online]. Retrieved October 26, 2016, from http://edglossary.org/multicultural-education/

Harkins, C. (2014). *Evaluating Sistema Scotland*. Glasgow: Glasgow Centre for Population Health.

Hewitt, R. (2005). *White backlash and the politics of multiculturalism*. Cambridge: Cambridge University Press.

Hughes, J. (2007). Mediating and moderating effects of inter-group contact: Case studies from bilingual/bi-national schools in Israel. *Journal of Ethnic and Migration Studies, 33*(3), 419–437.

Institute of Education. (2011). *Case study on the impact of IOE research: Music education* [January 2011, booklet, p. 15]. London: IoE University of London.

Integration Building Inclusive Societies. (2016). *Practices*. [online]. Retrieved October 26, 2016, from http://www.unaoc.org/ibis/integration-practices/

Leitch, R., Gardner, J., Mitchell, S., Lundy, L., Odena, O., Galanouli, D., & Clough, P. (2007). Consulting pupils in assessment for learning classrooms: The twists and turns of working with students as co-researchers. *Educational Action Research, 15*(3), 459–478.

Lundy, L. (2007). 'Voice' is not enough: Conceptualising Article 12 of the United Nations convention on the rights of the child. *British Educational Research Journal, 33*(6), 927–942.

Marsh, K. (2012). "The beat will make you be courage": The role of a secondary school music program in supporting young refugees and newly arrived immigrants in Australia. *Research Studies in Music Education, 34*(2), 93–111.

McKittrick, D., Kelters, S., Feeney, B., Thornton, C., & McVea, D. (2007). *Lost lives: The stories of the men, women and children who died as a result of the Northern Ireland troubles*. Edinburgh: Mainstream Publishing.

National Geographic. (2011). The Island of Cyprus, *National Geographic: Islands*. [online documentary series]. Retrieved October 27, 2016, from https://www.youtube.com/watch?v=QBIl7pPU_rU

Odena O. (2009). Using music education as a tool for inclusion. Keynote and workshop. In *Pedagogical institute of Cyprus Intercultural education and peaceful co-existence International Conference*. Larnaca, Cyprus, 11/2009. Retrieved October 26, 2016, from http://eprints.gla.ac.uk/84003/

Odena, O. (2010). 'Practitioners' views on cross-community music education projects in Northern Ireland: Alienation, socio-economic factors and educational potential. *British Educational Research Journal, 36*(1), 83–105.

Odena, O. (Ed.). (2012a). *Musical creativity: Insights from music education research*. London and New York: Routlege.

Odena, O. (2012b). Creativity in the secondary music classroom. In G. McPherson & G. Welch (Eds.), *The Oxford handbook of music education, Volume 1* (pp. 512–528). Oxford and New York: Oxford University Press.

Odena, O. (2014a). Musical creativity as a tool for inclusion. In E. Shiu (Ed.), *Creativity research: An inter-disciplinary and multi-disciplinary research handbook* (pp. 247–270). London and New York: Routledge.

Odena, O. (2014b). Towards pedagogies of creative collaboration: Guiding secondary school students' music compositions. In M. S. Barrett (Ed.), *Collaborative creative thought and practice in music*, pp. 239–251. London and New York: Routledge.

Odena, O. (2014c). Facilitating the development of innovative projects with undergraduate conservatory students. In P. Burnard (Ed.), *Developing creativities in higher music education: International perspectives and practices* (pp. 127–138). Abingdon and New York: Routledge.

Odena, O. (2014d). Some challenges of practice based/centred enquiry. In S. D. Harrison (Ed.), *Research and research education in music performance and pedagogy* (pp. 119–131). Dordrecht: Springer.

Odena, O., Summers, M., Jaap, A., & Rodríguez, A. (2016). *Music for integration research briefing: Exploring the potential of music education for integrating newly arrived children in schools.* Glasgow: University of Glasgow Press. Retrieved October 26, 2016, from http://eprints.gla.ac.uk/121386/

Odena, O., & Welch, G. (2007). The influence of teachers' backgrounds on their perceptions of musical creativity. A qualitative study with secondary school music teachers, *Research Studies in Music Education, 28*(1), 71–81.

Odena, O., & Welch, G. (2009). A generative model of teachers' thinking on musical creativity, *Psychology of Music, 37*(4), 416–442.

Papadakis, Y., & Bryant, R. (Eds.). (2012). *Cyprus and the politics of memory: History, community and conflict.* New York: I. B. Tauris.

Pettigrew, T. F. (1998). Intergroup contact theory. *Annual Review of Psychology, 49*(1), 65–85.

Pettigrew, T. F., & Tropp, L. R. (2006). A meta-analytic test of intergroup contact theory. *Journal of Personality and Social Psychology, 90*(5), 751–783.

Phelan, H. (2016). *Singing and sustainable social integration.* Limerick: Irish World Academy of Music and Dance, University of Limerick. Retrieved October 26, 2016, from https://issuu.com/singingandsustainablesocialintegrat/docs/singing_and_sustainable_social_inte

Race, R. (2016). The multicultural dilemma, the integrationist consensus and the consequences for advancing race and ethnicity within education. In R. Race & V. Lander (Eds.), *Advancing race and ethnicity in education* (pp. 210–229). Basingstoke and New York: Palgrave Macmillan.

Race, R., & Lander, V. (Eds.). (2016). *Advancing race and ethnicity in education.* Basingstoke and New York: Palgrave Macmillan.

Shared Education Signature Project. (2016). *Background information.* [online]. Retrieved October 27, 2016, from http://www.sepni.org/site/homepage.asp?page_area=6459&page_id=0

Volkan, V. D. (2008). Trauma, identity and search for a solution in Cyprus. *Insight Turkey, 10*(4), 95–110.

Welch, G., Preti, C., Himonides, E., & Toni, B. (2010). The musical and other-than-musical benefits arising from music education: An example from the *Progetto Musica Regione Emilia-Romagna*. In G. Mota (Ed.), *Proceedings of the 23rd International Seminar of the ISME Commission on Research. Changchun, China*. Malvern, Australia: ISME.

West-Eastern Divan Orchestra. (2016). *Explore the story*. [online]. Retrieved October 27, 2016, from http://www.west-eastern-divan.org/

Dr. Oscar Odena is Reader in Education at the University of Glasgow, UK. He has held posts at universities including Hertfordshire, Brighton, Barcelona and Queen's University Belfast, where he completed a study on the potential of music education to diminish ethnic tensions. His areas of expertise comprise qualitative research approaches, social inclusion and music education. He was Co-Chair of the Research Commission of the International Society for Music Education (2012–2014). He serves on the boards of four leading journals and the review colleges of the Irish Research Council and the UK Arts and Humanities Research Council

Advancing Australian Multicultural Dialogues in Education

Richard Race

INTRODUCTION

Multiculturalism and multicultural education as sociological ideas still matter both in domestic and international contexts (Gereluk and Race 2007; Eade et al. 2008; Boyle and Charles 2011; Shin 2014). Evidence used in this chapter will demonstrate that the concept of multiculturalism and its practical applications are very much alive rather than dead (Joppke 2017). Moreover, within this context, the chapter sheds light onto the Australian case of multicultural education policy and uses this rather unexplored example to argue that Australia's policy of acknowledging its cultural diversity offers some positive lessons for education policy. Furthermore, the chapter will discuss how Australia has its national values formalised in citizenship policy. This is in contrast to England which gives mere advice on what values should be taught in schools (DSS 2011; DfE 2011, 2014). Australian multiculturalism derives from its cultural diversity with 25% of the population born overseas in the 2011 Census (DIPB 2014). The country has maintained multicultural policies placing a strong emphasis on multicultural education (Watkins and Noble 2013). Although

R. Race (✉)
Roehampton University, London, UK

© The Author(s) 2018
R. Race (ed.), *Advancing Multicultural Dialogues in Education*,
DOI 10.1007/978-3-319-60558-6_14

Australia has not been the first country to apply a multicultural policy, in the wake of the Sydney siege of December 2014 and the death of two captives in a coffee shop, one should appreciate that Australia has been developing and evolving multicultural policies for over 50 years (Markus et al. 2009; Mackay 2011; BBC 2014). In this respect, the Australian case study is appropriate to apply within multicultural education.

The chapter relies on two main sources that give important contextual depth to the Australian case study and this analytical discussion. First, it will use Soutphommasane's (2009, 2013) idea and who currently serves as Australia' Race Discrimination Commissioner. Secondly, the chapter will use the empirical data collected by the Rethinking Multiculturalism/ Reassessing Multicultural Education (RMRME) project on multiculturalism and multicultural education, a three-year Australian Research Council project conducted jointly by the Institute for Culture and Society at the University of Western Sydney, the New South Wales (NSW) Department of Education and Communities and the NSW Institute of Teachers. Each one of the sources above reveals the intricacies of Australian education policy and allows us to reach informed conclusions about whether such a prescriptive multicultural education policy can be applied to English and other international contexts. They also show the deep interest that the Australian case study has and justifies its standing as one of the forefront countries in the world on implementing multicultural perspectives and policy.

In order to position Australian politics, theory and education research into the wider multicultural discourse and dialogues, this chapter begins with an examination of the work of three key multicultural authors. Kymlicka's (2012) theories on multiculturalism bring a greater understanding to the potential of multiculturalism and multicultural citizenship. Parekh's work (2011) discusses the 'multi' over 'mono' culture within the British educational context, whereas Banks (2009) examines and advocates multicultural education practice from an American perspective with international applications. The chapter will then focus on the Australian context. It will discuss Gillard's (2012) multiculturalism statement as a former Australian prime minister, and juxtapose it with political speeches by European leaders that touched upon aspects of multiculturalism in Europe (Race, in Race and Lander 2016). It will then move to Soutphommasane's (2009, 2012) idea of a 'cultural literate dialogue' and use it as a foundation to discuss further specific political contexts and practical solutions that enable both an Australian list of values and Australia's increasing cultural diversity to be taught through the subject of citizenship

(DoIC 2012). Australia's increasing diversity has also been factually underlined in the Census statistics of 2011 (DIPB 2014). Using the sources above, this chapter will highlight a positive picture of both advancing Australian multiculturalism and multicultural education and will suggest lessons concerning multicultural dialogues for the wider international and global community.

KYMLICKA, PAREKH AND BANKS: ADVANCING MULTICULTURALISM AND MULTICULTURAL EDUCATION

Multiculturalism, for Kymlicka, is '… first and foremost about developing new models of democratic citizenship, grounded in human rights ideas, to replace earlier uncivil and undemocratic relations of hierarchy and exclusion …'. Multiculturalism essentially is about constructing new and relevant civic and political relations to overcome social and cultural inequalities. In this way, Kymlicka (1995) recognised that cultural diversity within a state involves the co-existence of different ethnicities and therefore different diverse cultures which involve many national minorities rather than one nation. Kymlicka (1995: 11) defines nation as 'a historical community, more or less institutionally complete, occupying a given territory or homeland, sharing a distinct language and culture. A "nation" in this sociological sense is closely related to the idea of a "people" or a "culture"—indeed, these concepts are often defined in terms of each other'. This notion is important in the Australian context as national values are being taught together with cultural diversity.

Unfortunately, as I have argued before, the concept of immigration has always been seen as political and has been used to promote political interests rather than to acknowledge the cultural, social, economic as well as educational influences of minority groups (Race 2015; Race, in Race and Lander 2016). However, within a multicultural framework, cultural pluralism is essential; a nation exhibits cultural pluralism if

> … it accepts large numbers of individuals and families from other cultures as immigrants, and allows them to maintain some of their ethic particularity … Immigrant groups are not 'nations', and do not occupy homelands. Their distinctiveness is manifested primarily in their family lives and in voluntary associations, and is not inconsistent with their institutional integration … The commitment to ensuing a common language has been a constant feature of the history of immigration policy. (Kymlicka 1995: 13–14)

What I would suggest needs to be continually analysed is how far the state intervenes in relation to individual and family lives and how the boundaries of cultural pluralism are affected by integrationist policy. The danger in Kymlicka's (2012: 15) eyes is '… the proliferation of "civic integration" policies, typically in shaping the form of obligatory language and county knowledge requirements' (Joppke 2012, 2017). These civic integration policies, that is, citizenship tests and identification cards, represent, as Lyon (2009) argues, a phase in the long-term attempts of states to find stable ways of identifying citizens. The multiculturalism-integration debate should remain within the idea of multiculturalism-as-citizenisation, as Kymlicka (2012) suggests, and the obstacles that prevent new modules of multicultural citizenship should be at the very least debated.

Kymlicka (2007: 296–98) suggests further that increasing democratic citizenship must be an international rather than a domestic project which would involve active participation by all citizens in both majority and minority communities. But this idea in itself raises major dilemmas regarding the collaboration of nation states, as well as non-state actors from different regions of the world. Is a multicultural citizenship possible within a globalised world in the twenty-first century (Joppke 2017)? I would suggest that multicultural citizenship can be politically controlled through specific policy which has long-term consequences for individual rights. Kymlicka's (2012) theories relate to this and the control of cultural rights because cultural membership in the state culture involves individual and group choice. Who has the right to choose in relation to assimilation, integration and multicultural existences is a significant issue. Some citizens have more choices than others and some have their right to choose recognised by the state; when thinking of Bourdieu's (2005, 2010; Bourdieu and Passeron 1990) ideas, educated 'middle class' citizens have more cultural capital than others to make social choices (Ball 2003), such as the option of choosing home education rather than school education (Race, in Race and Lander 2016). A possible forum for cultural and social choices will be examined later in this chapter when we examine Soutphommasane's (2009) idea of 'cultural literate dialogue' and the consequences this idea can have for promoting multicultural citizenship.

Kymlicka's work on multicultural citizenship and his ideas on the need to move beyond recognition and tolerance to celebration are also important when considering cultural rights in multicultural education. Such ideas form the basis for supporting the need for advancing curricula based on multicultural citizenship (Race 2012). Consistent with Kymlicka's framework, Parekh (2000: 225–26, 2008, 2011) is also a supporter of a multicultural over a monocultural society and education. The limitations of monocultural curricula are obvious for Parekh, as students' 'intellectual curiosity' is dulled, students' perspectives of their own cultures are getting narrowed, and the opportunity to study cultural difference gets limited. Parekh (2000: 226–27) concludes: 'Monocultural education also tends to breed arrogance, insensitivity and racism ... Monocultural education, then, is simply not good education.' He advocates for the need to express multicultural principles through a multicultural curriculum which subsequently allows for multicultural citizenship to be taught, critiqued and developed. If, as Parekh (2000: 230) claims, '... multicultural education is an education in freedom, both in the sense of freedom *from* ethnocentric prejudices and biases and freedom *to* explore and learn from other cultures and perspectives ...', the issue then becomes how multicultural citizenship is taught within a multicultural educational framework.

Adding an American perspective, Banks (2007) gives us insights into how multicultural education can be developed beyond multicultural citizenship inspired curricula. He highlights the need to change education to make it more contemporary and relevant to students and teachers. Education, Banks (2007: 13) argues, needs to be able to help all students '... to acquire the knowledge, attitudes, and skills needed to function effectively in today's knowledge society. Our schools were designed for a different population at a time when immigrant and low-income youths did not need to be literate or to have basic skills to get jobs and to become self-supporting citizens'. Within a globalised world and with the need for education to highlight cultural diversity within today's knowledge and Information and Communication Technology (ICT) world, the need for more education support for all citizens becomes apparent. For Banks, multicultural education is: '... *an idea or concept, and* [an] *educational reform movement and a process*' (Banks 2014: 1). It is perhaps that idea of process that Banks describes in relation to multicultural education that becomes important—highlighted within the idea of Soutphommasane's (2009, 2012) 'cultural literate dialogue' which will be examined later in this chapter, because you need a multicultural dialogue before you can have a reform movement and consequently a contemporary evolution of the idea of multicultural education.

For him, multicultural education means that all students should have equal opportunities to learn in school. Banks continues: 'Multicultural education ... also assumes that diversity enriches a nation and increases the

ways in which its citizens can perceive and solve personal and public problems.' Banks (2014: 7) supports the idea that education needs to change
for a more multicultural focus and that an effective citizenship education
can help students '… to acquire the knowledge skills, and values needed to
function effectively within their cultural communities, nation-states,
regions, and the global community'. The concept of multicultural education therefore needs to focus on a more culturally diverse and citizenship-
orientated curriculum. Multicultural education can theoretically shape
curriculum delivery, but for these changes to take place, in Banks' words,
an educational reform movement is needed to instigate this change both
in the United States and around the world. In a way similar to Parekh and
Kymlicka, The promotion of more multicultural dialogues is perhaps the
start of that education reform movement. Banks (2014: 23) recognises
that this will not be easy; however, he adds: 'We are living in a dangerous,
confused, and troubled world that demands leaders, educators, and classroom teachers who can bridge cultural, ethnic, and religious borders,
envision new possibilities, invent novel paradigms, and engage in personal
transformation and visionary action.'

Gillard and Soutphommasane: The Australian Values and Cultural Literate Dialogue Debates

In addition to the intense scholarly interest on multiculturalism, politicians
have jumped on the multiculturalism bandwagon. Four political speeches
have touched upon different aspects of the concept. The first three, by
Angela Merkel, David Cameron and Nick Clegg, were delivered in Germany
and England in 2010 and 2011 (see Pillar 2010; Mahamdallie 2011; Race
2015) and covered multicultural but also more integrationist themes. The
fourth speech was a political endorsement of Australian multiculturalism.
Even though Merkel, Cameron and Clegg (Race 2015: 127–133) talked
more tentatively about 'multiculturalism', pointing out advantages and dis-
advantages, in contrast, the then Australian Prime Minister Julia Gillard
positively supported and even promoted a national, multicultural policy.
Gillard (2012) underlined: 'Australia is a multicultural country. We sing
"Australians all" because we are' (DSS 2011: 2). It is worth comparing this
advocacy of multiculturalism to the European speeches: Certainly, Clegg's
support of cultural diversity, the ambiguity of Merkel's position on multiculturalism, and the more monocultural approach by Cameron (Race

2015) did not get as far as Gillard's open support for the concept. One can explain the former Australian prime minister's support on the basis of the history of her state's formation (DIMA, 1997; Commonwealth of Australia, 2003) still, this endorsement is also reflected in Australia's national policy, as explicitly mentioned in the nation state's report on Australia's Multicultural Policy (DSS 2011: 6). The report highlights that it '… is committed to a just, inclusive and socially cohesive society where everyone can participate in the opportunities that Australia offers and where government services are responsive to the needs of Australians from culturally and linguistically diverse backgrounds'. The language used is much more positive towards multiculturalism than any speech or report coming out of Germany or the UK: 'The Australian Government welcomes the economic, trade and investment benefits which arise from our successful multicultural nation' (ibid).

Tim Soutphommasane (2009, 2012) offers an insight into Australian citizenship and multiculturalism. Using the idea of the need for a 'cultural literate dialogue' within the Australian nation (DSS 2011), Soutphommasane applies the ideas of Kymlicka (2007, 2012) in education by stressing the need for increasing multicultural citizenship and active participation by all citizens. Soutphommasane (2012: 188–189) also uses the idea of cultural literacy taken from Hirsh (1987), whereby cultural literacy '… exists between the basic level of knowledge that everyone can be expected to possess and the expert level known only to specialists'. Cultural literacy needs to include people from majority and minority backgrounds within schooling and equip children as Soutphommasane (2012: 189) argues, ' … for participation in a national conversation'. Drawing inspiration from the ideas of Kymlicka and Hirsh, Soutphommasane (2009) develops the idea of 'patriotism' which involves a critical examination of Australian national tradition which forms national identity. This can be achieved, as he argues, through an examination of national values (ibid). There is an interesting comparison here with the political discourse of British values which as a notion is collectively expressed but not officially defined in detail. The nearest to a British values list in English education was within the Teachers' Standards (DfE 2011) and included the following 'fundamental British values': 'democracy, the rule of law, individual liberty and mutual respect and tolerance of different faiths and beliefs'. As well as the Teachers' Standards, Spiritual, Moral, Social and Cultural (SMSC) development was to be promoted in all schools in England (Citizenship Foundation 2014). SMSC is taught through the

Citizenship and Personal, Social and Health Education (PSHE) curricula (Race 2015: 98–108). From November 2014, British values had to be taught through SMSC. The list below describes what understanding and knowledge is expected to be reached by pupils in English schools when promoting fundamental British values:

- An understanding of how citizens can influence decision-making through the democratic process;
- An appreciation that living under the rule of law protects individual citizens and is essential for their wellbeing and safety;
- An understanding that there is a separation of power between the executive and the judiciary, and that while some public bodies such as the police and the army can be held to account through Parliament, others such as the courts maintain independence;
- An understanding that the freedom to choose and hold other faiths and beliefs is protected in law;
- An acceptance that other people having different faiths or beliefs to oneself (or having none) should be accepted and tolerated, and should not be the cause of prejudicial or discriminatory behaviour; and
- An understanding of the importance of identifying and combatting discrimination.

(DfE 2014)

The advisory list above describes what is expected and should be taught in all subjects in relation to British values, not only citizenship and PSHE. In contrast, the Department of Immigration and Citizenship (DoIC 2012) below defines more extensively a social and cultural list of Australian national values through citizenship. The Department of Immigration and Citizenship records the following Australian values:

- Parliamentary democracy
- The rule of law
- Living peacefully
- Respect for all individuals regardless of background
- Compassion for those in need
- Freedom of speech and freedom of expression
- Freedom of association
- Freedom of religion and secular government

- Equality of the individual, regardless of characteristics such as disability and age
- Equality of men and women
- Equality of opportunity

(DoIC 2012: 27)

Admittedly, there are similarities between British and Australian values; for example, both value lists refer to democracy and the rule of law. The most important values missing in the above lists in the context of this article is culture. Two more important values which are missing in the above lists are race and ethnicity (Race and Lander 2016). However, one can see that the British values refer more to constitutional principles, such as separation of powers and accountability, whereas the Australian list goes more in depth in relation to Australian values and citizenship.

These values form an important basis to allow Soutphommasane's (2009, 2012) 'cultural literate dialogue' to take place, that is, freedom of speech, freedom of expression and freedom of association. On the other hand, any debate must avoid what Ang (2003) has described as the notion of 'Fortress Australia' which aims to defend the boundaries of Australia within a wider and continuing 'immigration is fear' discourse. As Soutphommasane (2009: 70) notes, 'Cultural anxiety is not just about "race" but, in a more complex and profound way, about space: the space or territory of Australia as a nation'. A 'cultural literate dialogue' has to go beyond the economics of immigration and can take a form of a forum created to discuss the national values list through citizenship. This may complicate the cultural literate dialogue idea; but to be truly multicultural, this complication has to be addressed. Soutphommasane (2009: 74) highlights that ' ... personal identity is also shaped by features such as gender, class and politics ...', terms missing and barely recognisable in the British values list, but interestingly, terms more visible in the Australian values list. In addition, the British values do not give the sense of a society in the same way as the Australian values of compassion and peaceful living. In this respect, the list of British values highlights Sen's (2009) notion of 'plural monoculturalism' whereby cultures within a society can live in isolation from one another. Sen's idea of such a 'community of communities' runs the danger that communities get separated from each other, being actually encouraged to do so through state integrationist policy-making (Sen 2009; Merry 2013). Social participation, as Soutphommasane (2009: 75) correctly highlights, occurs solely within cultural communities but then, when there is no interaction among communities but only between communities and the state, a social reaction can be one of social prejudice and negative stereotyping of particular minorities.

Modern citizenship therefore presupposes a state that guarantees legal rights and to some measure, as Soutphommasane (2009: 76) suggests, equal respect and dignity. Anything less can lead to second-class citizenship or a difference-blind form of citizenship. In addition to this though Soutphommasane's idea also requires individuals to continually engage in an ongoing 'cultural literate dialogue' about their national identity. Soutphommasane (2009: 80) links the idea of 'a cultural literate' citizen to the schools and education policy in the following way: 'This literacy can be achieved in two ways. Historical knowledge and sensibility must be transmitted through education in schools and must involve the teaching of history in the form of a national curriculum.' In addition, those not educated in Australian schools must be given an opportunity to obtain such knowledge through education institutions. Thus, Soutphommasane (2009: 2012) is looking for a national story to be generated through schools and other education institutions, to allow individuals to increase their understandings of Australian national values, that is, patriotism through citizenship. Individuals also need to be 'culturally literate' to understand the social, political and cultural meanings associated within the list of national values (DoIC 2012). So, the implied aim here is to integrate everyone into a national culture, while evolving the national culture through ongoing multicultural dialogue with all social actors. As Soutphommasane (2009: 81) suggests all people must have '… some sense of belonging to a tradition, with all the moral and historical richness that this involves. A national identity is drawn from a culture comprised of a certain vocabulary and set of symbols'. Belonging to a tradition may be used in different ways but should entail the inclusion of everyone in the cultural literate dialogue. However, he cautions that 'a certain vocabulary and set of symbols' may appear culturally exclusive and may close down avenues for a real cultural literate dialogue and lead to a more specific and integrationist focus on the national culture.

The 'cultural literate dialogue' that Soutphommasane (2009, 2012) talks about is particularly important in the increasing culturally diverse Australia, as highlighted in the 2011 Australian census. The census acknowledges demographic issues such as the overseas-born population which was 24.6% of the population in 2011, an increase of 2.7% in 20 years, making a leap from 4.1 million people in 2001 to 5.2 million in

2011 being born overseas (DIPB 2014: vii). The main overseas birth-places as a percentage of the overall population in 2011 were: England (4.2%), New Zealand (2.2%), China (1.5%), India (1.4%), Italy (0.9%) and Vietnam (0.9%) (DIPB 2014: 19). It is worth contrasting the above with the faster-growing overseas birthplaces highlighted in the 2006 census, which were Bhutan, Togo, Nepal, Congo, Rwanda and Saudi Arabia (ibid). The two lists of countries show the complexity of cultural diversity with global movements of immigrants entering Australia from different countries and continents. In addition, the education attainment percent-age of the Australian population with a bachelor degree or higher is 17.2% (DIPB 2014: 63). Interestingly, immigrants registered have a higher per-centage of bachelor degree holders: 21.6% of English people living in Australia have bachelor degrees, China (38.7%), India (54.6%), Vietnam (17.7%), the Philippines (40.5%), Scotland (19.6%), Germany (20.7%), Malaysia (50.2%) and the United States (52.2%) (DIPB 2014: 63–65). This quantitative data shows simply that Australia needs to do much more than merely acknowledge its overseas born; it needs to react to changing cultural requirements with new waves of immigrants coming in from dif-ferent and new counties which is an expression of the fluidity of immigra-tion and cultural diversity. In addition, Australia's immigrants are highly qualified people that allow the state to cope and evolve within an increas-ing globalised world. It is these statistics that need to be socially and cul-turally recognised, but also acknowledged and included in the 'cultural literate dialogue'. As Soutphommasane (2009: 84) highlights, 'A liberal multiculturalism that offers recognition of diversity actually involves mutual accommodation. There is a responsibility on the part of the exist-ing society to accept that its culture will be changed by its new arrivals'. Thus, a 'cultural literate dialogue' needs to accept and acknowledge diver-sity but also moreover be open to cultural change and evolution.

However, it is not only the recognition of cultural diversity with cul-tural changes that is at the core of multicultural policies. Having national values as a reference point for a 'cultural literate dialogue' about the Australian nation can be problematic, when comparing the internationali-sation processes underlined in the Australian 2011 Census (DIPB 2014). As Soutphommasane (2012: 43) underlines, the danger of discussing a national culture is that it '… ends up favouring "core" ethnic and cultural groups over minorities'. It is the opposite of what Soutphommasane (2012) suggested and the claims made by immigrant groups who seek polyethnic rather than national rights. Cultural recognition has to go beyond tolerating different groups and the state has to play a more positive role in ensuring equal treatment for members of minority groups. And this is where and how Soutphommasane (2009, 2012: 54) develops the 'cultural literate dialogue' idea, moving it away in education terms from schooling and history to allow communities to enter into this dialogue at different points to make a claim for recognition: 'It should be emphasised here this process of recognition must involve a *public dialogue,* conducted within democratic forums of debate, between the political community and minority cultural groups.' The 'cultural literate dialogue' needs to move away from nationalism to a cultural dialogue which is more inclusive rather than exclusive. For Soutphommasane (2012) this dialogue should be patriotic but should also acknowledge a culturally diverse rather than a national focus. This can be problematic for two reasons as Soutphommasane (2012: 61–62) accepts: '[Firstly] … Any expression of a national patriotism may collapse into an expression of collective identity, which is biased in favour of a dominant national grouping within the polity. Second, endorsing a national identity appears to leave limited scope for the public recognition of cultural identities: after all, recognition could make it more difficult for a political community to assert a shared culture, language, history and tradition as the basis of citizenship.'

For a patriotic focus to work, all citizens have to see themselves as part of a 'people' when, in this case, the set of Australian values feel as their own (DoIC 2012). How this will be achieved by people born overseas settling in to Australia is of course a challenge. The main issue of Soutphommasane's theory (2012: 69) is whether it is possible to reconcile the tension between patriotism and multiculturalism in the setting of a national community. It is perhaps that term 'national' that provides an insight into the 'tension' created between the national citizen on the one hand and the immigrant on the other. When reassessing multiculturalism, the 'cultural literate dialogue' has to put the Australian national identity and culture at the centre of the debate, while at the same time acknowledging the complexity of diversity, seen as enriching identities rather than entrenching traditional notions of patriotism. The danger when considering Soutphommasane's (2009, 2012) notion of the 'cultural literate dialogue' is that the debate will already be conditioned or institutionalised through schooling, within many subjects including the history and citizenship curricula (Doherty et al. 2012). If one looks more closely, the DoIC (2012) list of Australian national values, although providing opportunities for multicultural recognition, for example, respect for all individual regardless of background, still looks more integrationist than multicultural. The 'cultural literate dialogue' needs to be more international rather than national and less nation focused in a globalised world to be both relevant and contemporary. Recognition can work only if, in this case, a 'cultural literate dialogue' is ongoing and multiple-way focused conversations take place across Australia and between communities, based upon reasoned exchanges involving different representatives from different cultures. However, even this process can become more integrationist rather than multicultural if the focus is on a one-way national dialogue about identities which would potentially favour assimilation, rather than integration or multiculturalism (Modood 2013; Race 2015).

As Soutphommasane (2013: 60) demonstrates, recognition debates can also exclude cultures with parts of them turning to conflict: 'A conflict … is represented by the broad ban that some parliaments in Europe (at the time of writing the French and Belgian Assemblies) have introduced on face covering in public places, ostensibly aimed at the wearing of the burqa/niqab.' But it is the idea of cultural debates and the potential and possibilities of a 'cultural literate dialogue' that needs in itself to be recognised (Soutphommasane 2009, 2012, 2013). The dialogue itself needs to be inclusive, reasoned, reflective and of course multicultural. Difference and diversity need to be acknowledged and more importantly celebrated. This multicultural dialogue needs to avoid national bias which is difficult but by no means impossible when discussing history, citizenship and patriotism. 'If citizens retain the capacity to reflect on their cultural affiliations, this in turn suggests that a national identity will be open to active revision so as not to exclude minority ethnic or cultural groups' (Soutphommasane 2013: 62). The aim, as Soutphommasane (2013: 63) underlines, '… of any democratic deliberation or dialogue is to achieve, as much as possible some consensus or agreement within the political community'.

Advancing Australian Multicultural Dialogues in Education

Soutphommasane's (2009, 2012, 2013) notion of a 'cultural literate dialogue' has been analysed in the context of this chapter to increase our understandings of Australian Multiculturalism and more formal Australian multicultural policy (DSS 2011). There still is, as Kelly et al. (2011) suggest, a lack of clarity of what multiculturalism, and as a consequence what multicultural education actually means in Australia, as well as its usefulness in the twenty-first century. 'Within this context, multicultural education faces questions concerning its relevance, framework and modes of delivery' (Kelly et al. 2011: 1). The project on RMRME aimed to shed light on the challenges posed by increasing cultural complexity in New South Wales (NSW) government schools and their communities in urban and rural areas, and the role education can play in social inclusion. Distributed to all 55,000 teachers in NSW public schools, the RMRME survey was the first large-scale survey of its kind, and it delivered a rich and nuanced dataset. For example, '… when teachers were invited to define their own cultural background, the 5128 survey respondents gave 1155 different kinds of responses … They described themselves with reference to provincial ethnic and "racial" categories with reference to provincial, ethnic and "racial" categories with references [also] to language, faith and geopolitical region; and with reference to a vast range of "Australianness"' (Kelly et al. 2011: 7–8).

The Multicultural Education Survey, conducted as part of the RMRME Project,

> … revealed that NSW public school teachers in 2011 are strongly pro-diversity (94.5%), have a non-assimilatory stance (74.8%) and acknowledge racism as a problem in Australian society (70.1%). The survey also found that teaches are pro-multicultural education (84.0%) and strongly support anti-racism in schools … the RMRME project indicates that teacher attitudes are more strongly pro-diversity than the general Australian population and that teachers are less likely to hold assimilatory views … One interpretation of this data is that schools could be sites of less racism and less intercultural tension than elsewhere is [Australian] society. (Kelly et al. 2011: 11)

What is significant in relation to the RMRME project is that it examined the cultural profiles of NSW public school teachers and found a culturally complex teacher profession. The teaching workforce would be an important part of Soutphommasane's (2009) 'cultural literate dialogue' within Australia. Teachers used for the sample revealed that overall 65 different countries had been involved in their initial teacher training, a remarkable piece of empirical data highlighting the diversity and plurality of teacher's backgrounds in Australia. Even though the vast majority (92.2%) were trained in Australia, '… of the remaining 7.9%, the top four countries respondents nominated were: United Kingdom. (1.2%), India (1.0%), New Zealand (0.9%) and Fiji (0.9%)' (Watkins et al. 2013: 16). As Watkins et al. (2013: 17) continue:

'There is also a clear trend towards with teachers of less than six years' experience who are more than twice as likely at 69.2 per cent to have had some training in this area (excluding English Second Language (ESL) compared with 33.3 per cent for those with more than 25 years of experience). This is an encouraging finding and may reflect the impact of the NSW Initial Teacher's professional teaching standards which, since 2009, have required that initial teacher education programs ensure graduates receive training in aspects of multicultural education'.

Diversity awareness rather than diversity training (Race 2015) seems to be prominent in NSW. As the RMRME survey reports, there seems to be far greater awareness of the NSW Anti-Racism Policy, compared to the Multicultural Education Policy. This may be the result of the extensive training programme associated with Anti-Racism policy and its related procedures that followed its inception in 1992 and its revision in 2005 (Watkins et al. 2013: 39). The creation in 2005 of an Anti-Racism Contact Officer (ARCO) in schools has raised further the profile of anti-racism education in all public NSW schools. The survey results highlight anti-racism awareness of the policy and its implementation across NSW (ibid). It seems that ARCOs are still very much needed in NSW schools: 'When teachers were asked if "racism is a problem in schools", 52.5 per cent agreed, with a large number (29.9%) indicating that they were neutral on the issue and 15.6 per cent disagreeing that it is a problem. This suggests that teachers see racism as more of an issue within the broader Australian community than in schools' (Watkins et al. 2013: 44). The continuation of work carried out by ARCOs in conjunction with continued multicultural education policy would be beneficial in both NSW schools and wider society. Therefore, both anti-racism issues and multiculturalism could be part of a 'cultural literate dialogue' involving the culturally diverse teaching workforce, not only situated in NSW but across all of Australia.

Reassessing multicultural education terminology is also highlighted by the authors of the RMRME survey. Watkins et al. (2013) argue that we should be concerned about terms surrounding multiculturalism and their meanings as they are 'real world problems' that are subject to political and academic debate (Soutphommasane 2012). As the RMRME survey highlights, '... our understandings of words shape our practice, and this is especially important for teaching' (Watkins et al. 2013: 55). The key goal would be to go beyond addressing diverse backgrounds of students as problems or things to be serviced, '... nor [to] celebrate ossified forms of cultural traditions, but to encourage skills and knowledge that are increasingly important for both students and their teachers as they grapple with the cultural and social complexities in the globalised world of the twenty-first century (ibid)'. The report recommends that NSW education requires a specific unit of study within initial teacher education on multicultural education which engages with issues around cultural diversity (Lander, in Race and Lander 2016). This could be another important issue within the cultural literate dialogue involving teachers and headteachers, as well as teacher training and continuing professional development. Another recommendation, as Watkins et al. (2013: 57) highlight of the report is '… leadership training rather than or combined with awareness training which will ensure more effective policy implementation in the area of multicultural education'.

CONCLUSIONS

The idea of reassessing Australian multicultural terms and meanings to stimulate multicultural dialogues (Watkins et al. 2013) is an ongoing continuous exercise which is still of great relevance and has application internationally (Modood 2013). Examining Australian policy and theory in this chapter adds to the existing literature and contributes to ongoing debates on the application of multiculturalism. These debates prove how political multiculturalism is in Germany, England and Australia. Even though all three countries are multicultural, politicians have to appeal to their electorates in different ways. In the Australian case, Gillard is an advocate of Multicultural Australia because she politically had to be multicultural to appeal to her electorate, as is shown by the Multicultural and Settlement Policy (DSS 2011). In contrast, Merkel was rather ambiguous about multiculturalism within a German context as she promotes cultural diversity but acknowledges integration which has appealed successfully to different sections of the German electorate. Cameron promoted more monoculturalism because of his conservative politics within the UK, whereas Clegg took a middle ground, compromising position which leans towards support of multiculturalism. Clegg quotes Parekh (2000) and advocates for cultural diversity, which highlighted a political difference over multiculturalism within the UK Coalition government, 2010–2015 (Race 2015: 127–142).

In this chapter, an examination of Australian multiculturalism and multicultural education and its wider social and political contexts revealed that in contrast to Germany or England, the Australian state took the political decision to address its increasing cultural diversity through being very clear, vocal and positive about its multicultural policy (DSS 2011; DoIC 2012; Gillard 2012). As a consequence, this demonstrated that Australia has more intense multicultural education practice in place because of its culturally diverse policy and wider demographic issues concerning the country (DIPB 2014). The state encourages that multicultural policy is visible at all levels within the Australian state including schools (Watkins and Noble 2013; Watkins et al. 2013) but also within universities with the need to encourage wider domestic participation in bachelor degree and higher qualifications at a time when highly qualified immigrants are making up domestic shortfalls in highly skilled areas (DIPB 2014: 63–65). Soutphommasane's (2009, 2012) idea for a 'cultural literate dialogue' can be part of a wider debate, or a more detailed multicultural dialogue on Australian values (DoIC 2012), if one deals importantly with the dangers of a fall back into a traditional, national value framework dialogue which would benefit 'Fortress Australia' rather than 'Multicultural Australia' (Ang 2003; Vertovec and Wessndorf 2010; Race 2012).

Therefore, when reassessing multiculturalism and multicultural education and using policy evidence and theory from Australia, we can conclude with three points: firstly, Australia needs an evolving Multicultural and Settlement Policy because of its increasing culturally diverse demographic (DIPB 2014). It needs an evolving multicultural dialogue. Secondly, Soutphommasane, (2016a, 2016b, 2017) in his current role as national Anti-Discrimination Commissioner for Australia, provides an interesting if not debatable notion of a 'cultural literate dialogue' which can address, critique and evolve Australian national values, within a multicultural citizenship (Kymlicka 2012) but, if not given the right tools, can as equally regress towards a multicultural backlash (Vertovec and Wessendorf 2010) with more integrationist policy (Race 2014; Pfeffer 2015; Vitikainen 2015). Thirdly, the 'cultural literate dialogue' can be promoted both within Australian schools and among the teaching workforce. However, as Watkins et al. (2013) highlight, multicultural education practice needs parity with anti-racism policy in Australian schools which can benefit wider society. The 'cultural literate dialogue' can theoretically be a means of addressing both multicultural education and anti-racism policy in Australian schools and society.

Australia's case study is important because it instigates comparisons and important lessons for the ongoing debates relating to British values (DfE

2011, 2014). Soutphommasane (2013: 64–71) calls for Britain to have a 'national-culture dialogue' but within this theoretical debate, communities will need to discuss how each one relates to the other within a common national culture. Hirsh (1987) raises an interesting question, that is, how high is cultural literacy in Australian and British communities? Multicultural education within citizenship and SMSC curricula is one means of achieving higher levels of cultural literacy if a 'cultural literate dialogue' is to take place. Moreover, what is clear, as highlighted in this chapter, is that levels of cultural literacy are very high within educated immigrant communities in Australia (DIPB 2014). Furthermore, what is also clear is that both Australia and Britain (a political entity currently containing four countries with four unique cultures)—in the same way as other countries—need more inclusive debates, for example, 'cultural literate dialogues' and multicultural dialogues, which focus on all cultures and not singularly on the nation. This is vital when considering that culture continuingly evolves with new waves of immigration and processes of internationalisation changing ultimately not only national cultures but multicultures (Pathak 2008; Silj 2010; Shin 2014; Modood 2013; Meer 2015; Bash and Coluby 2016; Meer et al. 2016; Osler 2016; Joppke 2017).

References

Ang, I. (2003). From White Australia to Fortress Australia: The anxious nation in the new century. In L. Jayasuirya, D. Walger, & J. Gothard (Eds.), *Legacies of White Australia: Race, culture and nation* (pp. 51–69). Crawley: University of Western Australia Press.

Ball, S. J. (2003). *Class strategies and the education market: The middle classes and social advantage*. London: RoutledgeFalmer.

Banks, J. A. (2007). *Educating citizens in a multicultural society* (2nd ed.). New York: Teachers College Press.

Banks, J. A. (2009). *The Routledge international companion to multicultural education*. New York: Routledge.

Banks, J. A. (2014). *An introduction to multicultural education* (5th ed.). Boston: Pearson Education.

Bash, L., & Coulby, D. (Eds.). (2016). *Establishing a culture of intercultural education. Essays and papers in honour of Jagdish Gundara*. Newcastle-Upon-Tyne: Cambridge Scholars Publishing.

Bourdieu, P. (2005). *The social structures of the economy*. Cambridge: Polity Press.

Bourdieu, P. (2010). *Distinction: A social critique of the judgement of taste*. London: Routledge.

Bourdieu, P., & Passeron, J.-C. (1990). *Reproduction in education, society and culture* (2nd ed.). London: Sage.

Boyle, B., & Charles, M. (2011). Education in a multicultural environment: Equity issues in teaching and learning in the school system in England. *International Studies in Sociology of Education, 21*(4), 299–314.

British Broadcasting Company (BBC). (2014). *Sydney siege: Three dead after commandos storm café*. Retrieved February 22, 2015, from http://www.bbc.co.uk/news/world-australia-30485355

Citizenship Foundation. (2014). *Doing SMSC*. Retrieved March 28, 2015, from http://www.doingsmsc.org.uk/

Commonwealth of Australia. (2003). *Multicultural Australia: United in diversity*. Retrieved October 21, 2014, from https://www.dss.gov.au/our-responsibilities/settlement-and-multicultural-affairs/publications/multicultural-australia-united-in-diversity

Department of Education (DfE). (2011). *Teachers' standards*. Retrieved December 2, 2014, from https://www.gov.uk/government/collections/teachers-standards

Department of Education. (2014). *Departmental advice on promoting basic important British values as part of pupils' spiritual, moral, social and cultural (SMSC) development*. Retrieved February 22, 2015, from https://www.gov.uk/government/publications/promoting-fundamental-british-values-through-smsc

Department of Immigration and Boarder Protection (DIBP). (2014). *The people of Australia: Statistics from the 2011 census*. Retrieved October 21, 2014, from http://www.immi.gov.au/media/publications/statistics/immigration-update/people-australia-2013-statistics.pdf

Department of Immigration and Citizenship (DoIC). (2012). *Beginning a life in Australia*. Retrieved October 21, 2014, from https://www.dss.gov.au/our-responsibilities/settlement-services/beginning-a-life-in-australia

Department of Immigration and Multicultural Affairs (DIMA). (1997). *Multicultural Australia: The way forward*. Retrieved October 21, 2014, from https://www.dss.gov.au/our-responsibilities/settlement-and-multicultural-affairs/programs-policy/a-multicultural-australia/programs-and-publications/a-new-agenda-for-multicultural-australia/message-from-the-minister/what-is-australian-multiculturalism/multicultural-australia

Department of Social Services (DSS)—Settlement and Multicultural Affairs. (2011). *The people of Australia—Australia's multicultural policy*. Retrieved October 21, 2014, from https://www.dss.gov.au/our-responsibilities/settlement-and-multicultural-affairs/publications/the-people-of-australia-australias-multicultural-policy

Doherty, C., Luke, A., Shield, P., & Hinksman, C. (2012). Choosing your Niche: The social ecology of the International Baccalaureate Diploma in Australia. *International Studies in Sociology of Education, 22*(4), 311–332.

Eade, J., Barrett, M., Flood, C., & Race, R. (Eds.). (2008). *Advancing multiculturalism, post 7/7.* Newcastle-upon-Tyne: Cambridge Scholars Press.

Gereluk, D., & Race, R. (2007). Multicultural tensions in England, France and Canada: Contrasting approach and consequences. *International Studies in Sociology of Education, 17*(1–2), 113–129.

Gillard, J. (2012). *Australian Multicultural Council (AMC) Lecture—Address by the Hon Julia Gillard MP, then Prime Minister of Australia.* Retrieved November 30, 2014, from http://www.amc.gov.au/speech/amc-lecture-2/

Hirsh, E. D. (1987). *Cultural literacy. What every American needs to know.* Boston: Houghton Mifflin.

Joppke, C. (2012). *The role of the state in cultural integration: Trends, challenges, and ways ahead.* Retrieved April 30, 2014, from http://www.migrationpolicy.org/research/TCM-state-role-in-cultural-integration

Joppke, C. (2017). *Is multiculturalism dead?* Cambridge: Polity Press.

Kelly, M., Watkins, M., & Noble, G. (2011) *Rethinking multiculturalism. Reassessing multicultural education. International Symposium,* Institute for Culture and Society, University of Western Sydney, 30–31 August 2011, Retrieved October 21, 2014, from http://www.multiculturaleducation.edu.au/wp-content/uploads/2012/02/Book-04.pdf

Kymlicka, W. (1995). *Multicultural citizenship. A liberal theory of minority rights.* Oxford: Clarendon Press.

Kymlicka, W. (2007). *Multicultural Odysseys. Navigating the new international politics of diversity.* Oxford: Oxford University Press.

Kymlicka, W. (2012). *Multiculturalism: Success, failure, and the future.* Retrieved April 30, 2014, from http://www.migrationpolicy.org/research/TCM-multiculturalism-success-failure

Lander, V. (2016). Initial teacher education. The practice of Whiteness. In R. Race & V. Lander (Eds.), *Advancing race and ethnicity in education* (pp. 93–110). Houndmills: Palgrave Macmillan.

Lyon, D. (2009). *Identifying citizens. ID cards as surveillance.* Cambridge: Polity Press.

Mackay, H. (2011). *Advance Australia … Where?* Sydney: Hachette.

Mahamdallie, H. (Ed.). (2011). *Defending multiculturalism: A guide for the movement.* London: Bookmarks Publications.

Markus, A., Jupp, J., & McDonald, P. (2009). *Australia's immigration revolution.* Crows Nest: Allen and Unwin.

Meer, N. (2015). *Citizenship, identity and the politics of multiculturalism. The rise of Muslim consciousness.* Houndmills: Palgrave Macmillan.

Meer, N., Modood, T., & Zapata-Barrero, R. (2016). *Multiculturalism and interculturalism. Debating the dividing lines.* Edinburgh: Edinburgh University Press.

Merry, M. S. (2013). *Equality, citizenship and segregation: A defense of separation.* Houndmills: Palgrave Macmillan.

Modood, T. (2013). *Multiculturalism* (2nd ed.). Cambridge: Polity Press.

Osler, A. (2016). *Human rights and schooling. An ethical framework for teaching for social justice*. New York: Teachers College Press.

Parekh, B. (2000). *Rethinking multiculturalism. Cultural diversity and political theory*. Harvard: Harvard University Press.

Parekh, B. (2008). *A new politics of identity, political principles for an interdependent World*. Houndmills: Palgrave Macmillan.

Parekh, B. (2011). *Talking politics. Bhikhu Parekh in conversation with Ramin Jahanbegloo*. Oxford: Oxford University Press.

Pathik, P. (2008). *The future of multicultural Britain*. Edinburgh: Edinburgh University Press.

Pfeffer, D. (2015). *Group integration and multiculturalism. Theory, policy and practice*. New York: Palgrave Macmillan.

Piller, I. (2010). *What did Angela Merkel really say?* Retrieved March 14, 2014, from http://www.languageonthemove.com/language-globalization/what-did-angela-merkel-really-say

Race, R. (2012). The warning of the integrationist alternative for education and the multicultural backlash. In H. K. Wright, M. Singh, & R. Race (Eds.), *Precarious international multicultural education* (pp. 333–346). Rotterdam: Sense Publishers.

Race, R. (2014). The multicultural Dilemma, the integrationist consensus and the consequence for advancing race and ethnicity in education. In R. Race & V. Lander (Eds.), *Advancing race and ethnicity in education* (pp. 210–229). Houndmills: Palgrave Macmillan.

Race, R. (2015). *Multiculturalism and education* (2nd ed.). London: Bloomsbury.

Race, R., & Lander, V. (Eds.). (2016). *Advancing race and ethnicity in education*. Houndmills: Palgrave Macmillan.

Sen, A. (2009). *The idea of justice*. London: Allen Lane.

Shin, K.-H. (2014). Global interconnectedness and multiculturalism in undergraduate sociology courses in the USA. *International Studies in Sociology of Education, 24*(2), 210–227.

Silj, A. (Ed.). (2010). *European multi-culturalism revisited*. London: Zed Books.

Soutphommasane, T. (2009). *Reclaiming patriotism. Nation-building for Australian progressives*. Cambridge: Cambridge University Press.

Soutphommasane, T. (2012). *The virtuous citizen. Patriotism in a multicultural society*. Cambridge: Cambridge University Press.

Soutphommasane, T. (2013). Multiculturalism as national dialogue. In P. Balint & S. G. de Latour (Eds.), *Liberal multiculturalism and the fair terms of integration* (pp. 54–72). Houndmills: Palgrave Macmillan.

Soutphommasane, T. (2016a, April 8). *The state of our race relations: Speech at the Crescent Institute*. Retrieved April 11, 2017, from https://www.humanrights.gov.au/news/speeches/state-our-race-relations-speech-crescent-institute

Soutphommasane, T. (2016b, October 21). *Global day of dignity speech.* Retrieved April 11, 2017, from https://www.humanrights.gov.au/news/speeches/global-day-dignity-speech

Soutphommasane, T. (2017). *2017 International Day for the elimination of racial discrimination.* Retrieved April 11, 2017, from https://www.humanrights.gov.au/news/speeches/2017-international-day-elimination-racial-discrimination

Vertovec, S., & Wessendorf, S. (Eds.). (2010). *The multiculturalism backlash. European discourses, policies and practices.* New York: Routledge.

Vitikainen, A. (2015). *The limits of liberal multiculturalism. Towards an individuated approach to cultural diversity.* Houndmills: Palgrave Macmillan.

Watkins, M., & Noble, G. (2013). *Disposed to learn. Schooling, ethnicity and the scholarly habitus.* London: Bloomsbury.

Watkins, M., Lean, G., Noble, G., & Dunn, K. (2013). *Rethinking multiculturalism. Reassessing multicultural education.* Project Report Number 1. Surveying New South Wales. Public School Teachers. Retrieved October 21, 2014, from http://www.multiculturaleducation.edu.au/wp-content/uploads/2012/02/RMRME-Report-1-web.pdfm

Dr. Richard Race is senior lecturer in education at Roehampton University, UK. He is author of *Multiculturalism and Education* (2nd Ed.) (London, Bloomsbury, 2015) and co-editor with Professor Vini Lander (Edge Hill University, UK) of *Advancing Race and Ethnicity in Education* (Houndmills, Palgrave Macmillan, 2016). He is currently working on his second monograph, *Integration and Education Policy-Making* (contracted with Palgrave Macmillan). Richard is currently a member of the British Education Research Association Council and remains co-convenor of the Postgraduate Pin within the Society of Research in Higher Education.

Let's Talk About 'Culture' in Multiculturalism: The Case of Early Childhood Policy and Practice

Leena Helavaara Robertson

REFLECTION

In my work with university students, teachers and researchers, and in various contexts, I often nudge discussions towards multiculturalism or diversities—and particularly towards diverse families. Much of my professional work has focused on young multilingual children and their families, communities and schools. I am Finnish and have worked in England as an early years teacher, teacher educator and researcher for many years, so I have a personal interest in this area. In conversations, I often draw attention to different backgrounds, home languages, family situations and life experiences. But just recently I have often been stopped in my tracks. Rather than readily sharing pedagogical ideas about multicultural schools or understandings of multilingual families, very quickly many professionals express astonishing comments about some children. Phrases like 'education is not important in their culture' or 'they are not doing so well in school, because their families do not care about their school progress'

L.H. Robertson (✉)
University of Middlesex, London, UK

© The Author(s) 2018
R. Race (ed.), *Advancing Multicultural Dialogues in Education*,
DOI 10.1007/978-3-319-60558-6_15

seem far too common. These kinds of negative comments are not restricted to teachers in England either; similar views are expressed in informal conversations in other parts of Europe, including Finland, France, Estonia and Romania where my research projects have taken me in the last five years or so. It is also important to acknowledge that these research projects have not specifically focused on children's cultural backgrounds, so the various comments referred to in this chapter have not been formally recorded in my publications either. They have been a by-product of various international meetings (see, e.g. Robertson et al. 2015). When asked for evidence for a family or a whole community not caring about their children's education, the answers become somewhat evasive: 'Well, you know, I mean those parents. Not interested in education. It's just not in their culture.'

In these informal contexts then, the word 'culture' has taken on some new meanings which are hurtful, insidious and plain wrong. In a book such as this, and in advocating multicultural and multilingual dialogues and pedagogies in general, negative statements must be confronted and challenged. The aim of this chapter is to show how the use of 'culture' as a construct has become an acceptable tool to drive a wedge between groups of people and how this discriminatory use has been legitimised in early years policy and normalised in everyday use. I argue that 'cultural' and 'culture' have become bywords for something that is not there when education professionals discuss some children—children who are somehow perceived to be the norm and considered to be 'our' children, and not minoritised. Yet—and very obviously—everyone has a culture, a cultural background (Said 1994; Race 2015). But when teachers draw attention to some children's cultural backgrounds, the culture in question tends to be framed in a deficit model: it requires fixing. It is not good enough for early years settings, schools or policy makers. Teachers rarely draw attention to white, middle-class children's culture, who arrive at school with esteemed cultural capital. The groups of children who are perceived in need of fixing are typically those who are from a working-class background or black, or speak another language at home, or they are from a minority ethnic background, or a Muslim, Gypsy, Roma, Traveller (GRT) or they are recent migrants.

This list is not exhaustive and the labels are problematic: they are complex social constructs to which new meanings are attached as contexts and situations change. Mamdani's (1998, 2002) work is extremely helpful here. He has termed the practice of using 'culture' to justify exclusion and marginalisation as 'Culture Talk' and shows how references to culture and cultural backgrounds serve to uphold boundaries between 'them' and 'us'. At the same time it is critical to locate individual statements in the broader societal context. The current dominant discourses that surround teachers' and policy makers' understanding of 'culture' need to be examined and challenged. I do this by engaging in critical discourse analysis and analyse the use of the term 'cultural' in one of the highly influential and much used early years guidance documents in England, 'The Development Matters in Early Years Foundation Stage (EYFS)' (Early Education 2012). I argue that this document reveals a deep-seated deficit view of minorities, and its view of gender and 'race' is similarly problematic. This document adds to the deficit discourse, normalises it and consequently shapes, maintains and legitimises early childhood professionals' negative views.

I conclude by drawing on critical race theory (Gillborn 2008) and on postcolonial theories and ask why do we still, in twenty-first century Europe, minoritise certain cultures, whilst we do not do the same for others? I argue that we need to recognise that cultures are narratives as Said (1994) so neatly puts it. In any discussion of a culture, we need to ask whose story are we telling? We need to challenge racism in action, and aim to do things differently. It may be more helpful to focus on children's and their families' funds of knowledge (Moll et al. 1992) and their everyday lifeworld experiences (Hogg 2015) rather than frame discussions and planning and assessment around minority cultures.

Culture Talk and Education

When education professionals state that a 'home culture' prevents some children from doing well at school, there are four key issues to address: (1) defining cultures; (2) evidence for cause and effect; (3) agency; and (4) the bigger picture: societal and structural barriers.

My discussion draws on sociocultural perspectives, and this refers to a Vygotskian perspective that recognises that people and their ideas are influenced by their social environment. Vygotsky (1978) argued that children begin to perceive the world not only through their eyes but also through their speech and through the words they use. Likewise early childhood professionals and policy makers see the world of education through the terms and concepts that have become part of their professional practice. Their thinking about multiculturalism, and of different groups of children, is mediated by the language they use. The kind of sociocultural approach that I advocate rejects developmentally appropriate practices (Bredekamp 1991) which are largely constructed by developmental psychologists and focus on a 'universal child' and 'universal' developmental stages. Instead I maintain a firm recognition of the 'social child' and the varied social contexts that surround children and move towards democratically appropriate practices (Kinos et al. 2016). I accept children's social agency at the centre of their own learning.

All practices have semiotic elements, and as Fairclough (2001) noted, all practices are practices of production. Critical discourse analysis (CDA) used here in deconstructing the use of 'culture' in 'The Development Matters in Early Years Foundation Stage (EYFS)' (Early Education 2012) makes explicit the relations of power and dominance. The lives of children are represented through discourses, and these vary according to children's real and imagined cultural, linguistic and socioeconomic backgrounds. According to Fairclough (2001), genres and practices are always networked together, and thereby 'discourse' can be understood as a moment of social practice. A careful analysis of language—and genres such as the policy genre—can help to identify action.

Defining Cultures

In 1870 the British anthropologist Tylor (cited in Avruch 1998: 6) defined 'culture' as 'that complex whole which includes knowledge, belief, art, morals, law, custom, and any other capabilities and habits acquired by man [sic] as a member of society'. Others have noted that culture is a 'fuzzy' concept with blurred boundaries, and with leakages, because group members rarely agree on all of the above. People of the same cultural group will have differences in their attitudes or habits, and yet, individuals often also like to self-identify themselves as belonging to a cultural group because their cultural beliefs and practices show similarities with others', or they show a kind of a 'family resemblance' (Spencer-Oatey 2012).Others may want to withdraw their membership from one group and join another. Others may never be granted a full membership to a group by its more well-established members.

Families' cultures and cultural practices are, nevertheless, important educational considerations. The difficulty arises when 'home culture' is conceptualised from an outsider perspective, and consequently a whole range of unique and very diverse families and cultures are collapsed into a single category, for example, a Muslim or a Somali. This process of reduction (for 'ethnic reductionism', see Baumann 1996) tends to include a selection of elements which then in use are perceived as an essential aspect of that culture (Fuchs 2001; Gillborn 2008; Philips 2012). Food, music, clothing and festivals are pertinent examples of this in early years contexts. Or 'saris, samosas and steel bands'—parts of cultures that are perceived as essential—as Troyna (1987) observed nearly 30 years ago in his discussion of tokenism in the advancement of multiculturalism in schools.

Philips (2012) discusses four distinct meanings of essentialism. The first is the attribution of certain characteristics to everyone subsumed within a particular cultural category; for example, 'African-Caribbean children have a good sense of rhythm and love steel bands'. The second is the way in which those characteristics become a 'natural' aspect of that group ('it's in their genes—they are born with a gift of rhythm') rather than something that is socially created or constructed. The third is the acknowledgement of that collectivity as the subject or object of action ('African-Caribbean boys need more role-models') that presumes a homogenised and unified group. The fourth is the policing of this collective category; in the use of supposedly shared characteristics which cannot be questioned or modified without undermining an individual's right to belong to that group (e.g. ' … but I thought that you would be better suited for music rather than physics because of your culture').

Listening out for specific examples of essentialism reveals entrenched structures of thought that are also surprisingly naïve. And racist. Myths, such as some cultures are 'primitive' whilst others are 'civilised', over time come to be thought of as 'common sense' knowledge. Said's (1979, 1994) work on examining how the 'West' is constructed as 'civilised' and the 'non-West' as the 'other' remains pertinent here because these kinds of binary divisions have developed into accepted discourses. The perception of some children's cultural backgrounds as backward is often accepted as true both in fleeting, informal moments of conversation and in policy discourse. Said (1994: xiv) points out that '… culture is a sort of theatre where various political and ideological causes engage one another'. Applying Charles Dickens (1812–1870), a much-loved and respected author of English literature, Said (1994) asks how is it possible that Dickens is, on the one hand, venerated as one gigantic cultural icon in Britain today, but on the other, Dickens' acceptance of colonial expansion and his view of colonialised others as inferiors are not discussed in the context of his greatness and influence. Why are these two sides of a culture separated? 'Culture conceived in this way can become a protective enclosure: check your politics at the door before you enter' (Said 1994: xiv).

In the context of early years, parents' presumed reluctance to engage with educational matters—because of 'culture'—allows practitioners to shift the attention away from the relationships of power and dominance, and from the failures of the education system (Rostas and Kostka 2014). Some very young children start school as winners. Others as losers.

Culture clashes and wars, and underground, alternative, hipster, heritage, hegemonic cultures—the list goes on—do not exist in a vacuum. Rather they are '… a turbulent system where "order" and "chaos" emerge locally and for the time being' (Fuchs 2001: 4). In one of our recent research studies (Robertson and Drury 2013) in a London nursery school, I interviewed the mother of a 4-year-old girl, Leyla. Initially the school had introduced Leyla to me as an Albanian and with English as an additional language (EAL), but the mother gave the following description of her family's cultural and linguistic background: 'I came from Albania and have been in England for 15 years. Leyla's father is from Somalia and lived in Finland. Our home languages are Somalian, Finnish, Albanian and some Arabic. Me and my husband use English together but I want to learn a bit of Finnish and some Arabic for reading the Quran.' Later Leyla's mother also told me about their Finnish home and how she would love to go and visit their family in Finland soon.

These kinds of descriptions are typical of England today, and increasingly everywhere, and provide examples of Vertovec's (2006) 'super-diversity'. As Vertovec (2006, 2009) demonstrates diversity has further diversified in the last 20 years:

> [Super-diversity] is distinguished by a dynamic interplay of variables among an increased number of new, small and scattered, multiple-origin, transnationally connected, socio-economically differentiated and legally stratified immigrants who have arrived over the last decade. (Vertovec 2006: i)

In Leyla's case it was difficult for her mother to decide what Leyla's first language was because Leyla used different languages for different purposes and in different contexts in her life. They were all 'first' and important. The use of hyphenated nationalities, such as Albanian-Somali, or Somali-Albanian, is one way of saying something about Leyla's ethnicity, but there is more to Leyla than this. In terms of her family's faith, Islam is important, but mother's and father's knowledge of it was not fixed. It was in the process of taking shape and of becoming. In addition, some of the family's lifeworld, languages and practices, also included Finnish and English elements. In sociocultural tradition it is pertinent—and ethical—to recognise that what counts as being an Albanian, Somali, Finnish or English varies from place to place and family to family. If we accept that cultures are narratives, it can—and should—become easy for educational professionals to ask parents and children to tell their story. We need to create space for the families to explain what they deem important in their own everyday cultural lives *and* their backgrounds in order to avoid naïve generalisations and cultural essentialism. Similarly, researchers and policy makers need to take account of families' origins, languages, routes of migration, socio-economic situations, not just in the sense of plurality but also in terms of complexity (Arnaut et al. 2015). Documenting the numbers of languages spoken in homes or schools is a start, but this needs an acknowledgement and analysis of how these languages are used, in what domain, for what purpose and with whom (Robertson and Drury 2014).

EVIDENCE FOR CAUSE AND EFFECT

When one cultural group underachieves in education, is culture the cause, and if so, where is the evidence? In all UK schools, including Leyla's nursery school, detailed information and data are routinely collected for monitoring individuals and different ethnic groups and their educational achievement. The data are largely based on test results (in England these include 6-year-olds' 'phonics screening' tests, 7- and 11-year-olds' SATs tests and 16-year-olds' GCSE examination results), and each school and local area are rated against others. National and governmental statistics are presented each year, and it is possible to track different groups, such as English as an additional language (EAL) and black and minority ethnic (BME) groupings, and their educational attainment from year to year.

There are many inherent problems with this English system of performativity and accountability, and its impact on curriculum and on increased systems of surveillance (such as target setting and school inspections), and subsequent plummeting teacher morale and shortage of teachers. Children's achievement and development are viewed as measurable and they are graded which encourage immediate competition between individual children, teachers and settings. Assessment itself is not fair; when 6-year-olds are tested, some are just 6 years of age and others nearly 7.

Some have been in school longer and have developed the situated knowledge required for appropriate institutionalised participation. The curriculum and its topics are more familiar for some. Some have been taught in small groups and in a familiar language. What is calculated, how statistics are produced (Gillborn 2008) and consequently how they are reported in the media are just as problematic.

In principle, I advocate a change in the overall education system and want to work towards a different kind of accountability, one that is framed in morality and ethics (Biesta 2004) and not in simplistic, quantifiable measures. But because these statistics exist, they have *some* use here, too. They show group by group the long-term patterns of achievement and underachievement in education. Some of the well-established categories used for tracking progress include EAL, BME and GRT. The Runnymede Trust's (2012) evidence demonstrates that various cultural, linguistic and socioeconomic groups' performance in schools is not static. Large populations, for example, of Bangladeshi, Indian and Pakistani children do better in schools now than they did 10 years ago, but this change is not due to a change in family culture. Statistical evidence reveals a complex picture of intersectionality, of social class background, race and gender. Strand's (2015) analysis of UK government's statistics shows that among pupils eligible for free school meals all ethnic minority groups outperformed white working-class pupils at GCSE level and that the gap between the two groups has increased. It also showed that while much concern has focused on white working-class boys, white working-class girls' show low levels of attainment too.

The Department for Education has recently renamed FSM/CLA (i.e. pupils entitled to free school meals and children who are looked after) as 'disadvantaged pupils' (DFE 2016). It is pledging to achieve '... educational excellence everywhere; Every child and young person can access high-quality provision, achieving to the best of his or her ability regardless of location, prior attainment and background' (DfE 2016: 7). According to the plan, this aim will be achieved by ensuring that more schools become 'excellent' as defined by their Ofsted inspections. In this plan there is no specific reference to GRT pupils, who typically have free school meals and, therefore, are included in the disadvantaged.

Historically, in England, Roma pupils have had the poorest outcomes of any ethnic group in terms of attainment, attendance and exclusions (Runnymede Trust 2012; Ofsted 2014). The Roma are the largest minority ethnic group in Europe, around 12 million citizens (Rostas and

Kostka 2014) and the achievement of the Roma pupils is consistently low in all European countries. The level of discrimination and racism they experience in all European countries is also well-documented (EUNP 2012). Tackling discrimination of this scale should be concerned with Roma communities, and not just with the 'disadvantaged'. In fact it seems appropriate to follow Ladson-Billings' (2006) example and accept Roma children's 'achievement gap' as an 'education debt' to Roma families. With this I mean that because the disparities between levels of education between Roma and other groups are stark and serious, they should not only be conceptualised as a gap in attainment but also as a debt. Generations of policy makers, schools and teachers have failed to provide positive educational experiences to Roma children and families. The debt is real.

The myth, that there are some families, communities or cultures that do not care about education, and that this is the cause of a group's underachievement, persists even though there is no evidence that this cause and effect relationship is true (Crozier 2000; Strand 2015). The Runnymede Trust advocates an alternative view:

'A reason for educational attainment differences could be an unconscious bias from teachers, leading them to assume that children of certain ethnic groups are more (or less) likely to misbehave or work hard. There has been concern from a sizeable number of newly trained teachers that their training does not well prepare them for teaching pupils of different ethnicities. Improved teacher training on this issue may improve outcomes' (Runnymede Trust 2012). However, newly qualified teachers cannot change these views and practices by themselves; senior leadership teams, in-service training, teacher educators and policies must also change.

AGENCY

Perspectives shaped by Culture Talk (Mamdani 2002) fail to recognise individuals' agency. All families make their own decisions about what kinds of cultural practices are maintained at home, and when, and for whom. Each family, as an agent, engages with wider social structures. Like many postcolonial writers, Mamdani (2002) questions the ways in which some groups' culture is perceived modern and creative, whilst others' are viewed as premodern and backward. He asks why is it that typically 'Western' commentators tend to present a view of some people having a culture from which they can pick and mix creatively, whereas others are seen as prisoners of their own culture? How is it possible that 'we have' culture, but culture 'has them'?

When teachers meet a new set of Roma parents, for example, do they see a family capable of making choices and engaging with their life in the twenty-first century or do they see a 'backward culture'? Or when they meet a Roma girl, do they see an individual, an expert in her own life, strong and willing to succeed in her world, or a prisoner of her family's culture? There is a disjunction between how individuals and families see themselves and the kind of knowledge that surrounds some families in the 'West' (Mani 1989).

Moll et al. (1992) discuss families' agency in terms of their funds of knowledge. The concept of 'funds of knowledge' refers to the knowledge, resources, competences, values and assumptions, which are historically and culturally situated. They are meaningful to the families, developed through life experiences and within social networks which are flexible, adaptive and active and may involve multiple persons from outside the home. The process is dynamic. González et al. (2005) see families' funds of knowledge as 'thick' and 'multi-stranded'; teachers, on the other hand, often look for familiar cultural signifiers and when not seeing them, perceive the families' funds of knowledge as 'thin' and 'single-stranded' (Robertson and Drury 2014).

BIGGER PICTURE: SOCIETAL AND STRUCTURAL BARRIERS

Many families live precarious lives (Hill et al. 2016), without stable jobs or adequate income and they feel marginalised by society. In some cases oppression of communities has taken place over generations—with others it is more recent. In all cases the current emphasis on families' identities in the context of education has a tendency to hide larger societal and structural barriers in accessing high-quality education. Culture Talk (Mamdani 2002) shifts the attention away from uneven funding and resources, from lack of support, and locates underachievement with the communities themselves rather than as a consequence of societal structures.

Many of the categories discussed above (EAL, GRT, BME) have, for many years, been discussed in relation to 'barriers' that teachers need to overcome in their professional work without adequate systems of support. The use of BME and BAME (black, Asian and minority ethnic) as categories locates the 'barrier' with black people themselves, with their skin colour and ethnicity, without addressing the historical and structural racial discrimination and oppression (Smith 2012). The National Curriculum for primary and secondary schools in England noted that special educational needs, disabilities or EAL may be the cause of a 'barrier to learning' (DfEE 1999: 33). From the onset children with EAL, their families' languages and their multilingualism are perceived as a problem, obstacle, barrier, rather than an individual and collective societal strength. Consequently, children as young as five years of age, are placed in ability groups in which they tend to be 'imprisoned' (Boaler 2005) throughout their school lives. BME children, those from poorer backgrounds and children with EAL are disproportionally represented in 'low ability' groups in primary schools and often irrespective of their individual progress (Robertson 2007).

The myth, that poverty leads to language disorders, weak work ethics with children and adults, and to an inability to plan for the future (Rostas and Kostka 2014), has successfully diverted the attention from the role of the state and its inability to address socioeconomic inequalities. It allows politicians and policy makers—and many practitioners—to blame the victim. In spite of the evidence (e.g. Strand 2015; Crozier 2000) that shows contrary, the myth lives on.

QUESTIONING AND CHALLENGING DOMINANT DISCOURSES

'The Development Matters in the Early Years Foundation Stage (EYFS)' begins with grand assertions:

> Children develop quickly in the early years, and early years practitioners aim to do all they can to help children have the best possible start in life. Children have a right, spelled out in the United Nations Convention on the Rights of the Child, to provision which enables them to develop their personalities, talents and abilities irrespective of ethnicity, culture or religion, home language, family background, learning difficulties, disabilities or gender. (Early Education 2012: 1)

My question here is what is it about this document that builds on and contributes to dominant and negative discourses on ethnicity, culture or religion, home language, family background, learning difficulties, disabilities or gender? I have critiqued elsewhere the above notion of 'best start in life' that permeates current early years policies (Robertson 2015) at the time of 'austerity measures' and when '... the current early years qualifications system is not systematically equipping practitioners with the knowledge, skills and understanding they need, to give babies and young children high quality experiences' (Nutbrown 2012: 5). Many of the answers to my own questions relate to diminishing social and education funding from the state, for example, the lack of language classes for parents new to English, and the substantial increases in children's class sizes. Many of the reception-year pupils (5-year-olds) are now taught in classes of 30 or more pupils; this is one of the largest average primary school class sizes amongst the Organisation for Economic Cooperation and Development (OECD) countries (DfE 2011).

The statutory main document, the 'Early Years Foundation Stage' (DFE 2014), specifies the statutory areas of learning and development for children from birth to 5 years. These are divided into three prime areas— (1) personal, social and emotional; (2) physical development; and (3) communication and language—and four specific areas: (4) literacy, (5) mathematics, (6) understanding of the world and (7) expressive arts and design. Each of the seven areas is further subdivided (see Appendix 1).

'The Development Matters in the Early Years Foundation Stage (EYFS)' is a document that provides non-statutory guidance material that is intended to support practitioners—teachers, nursery nurses, child-minders and so on—in implementing the statutory education requirements. It is widely used as a point of reference in planning and observing children and in assessing their learning. There are ten instances of the word 'cultural' (EYFS, Early Education, 2012: 1–47) (see Appendix 2).

MULTICULTURAL DIALOGUES

Before addressing the specific problems that the ten individual statements raise, it is important to note that there is no rationale put forward for multicultural practice in general. There is no discussion or exploration of the need to develop multicultural practices apart from the rhetorical claim, quoted earlier, of ensuring that all children develop their personalities, talents and abilities 'irrespective' of potential barriers such as cultures (Early Education 2012: 1). There needs to be a general rationale for multicultural education (Banks and McGee Banks 2009; Race 2015) and in my view for the three conceptually different kinds of tasks that must be addressed if the above aim is to become reality:

1. Practitioners need to seek to understand diverse children's and families' cultural backgrounds and their funds of knowledge, and seek to

understand the complexity rather than plurality, and reject essentialism and the various frequent and normalised deficit models.

2. There is a need to ensure that practitioners draw on a variety of cultural practices and funds of knowledge in the development pedagogical practices and this development must be an everyday part of their professional thinking. Not a tokenistic, occasional after-thought.

3. There is a need to recognise that multicultural practices are beneficial for all, and not just for some children whose backgrounds have been minoritised.

LANGUAGE AND GRAMMAR—HOW IS AUTHORITY CONSTRUCTED?

A closer examination of the grammatical structure is illuminating. In all but one example, the recommendations for pedagogy are constructed with the use of imperatives—'discuss', 'plan', 'celebrate'. Imperatives are grammatical constructs that function as commands. They convey an authoritative stance. Number 8 is different: 'In pretend play, imitates everyday actions and events from own family and cultural background, e.g. making and drinking tea.' It does not give an order; rather it reminds practitioners to observe imaginative play as a source of cultural knowledge, such as making a cup of tea. It makes a nod towards recognising that *all* children have cultural backgrounds, but this is not an obligation. It is indicative—and not at all surprising—that this is to take place in the context of play. 'Play' remains one of the cherished, hallowed and often untheorised aspects of early years practice (Wood 2010) and it is worth noting that practitioners are not 'commanded' to use play as a source of cultural knowledge. Play continues to remain aloof and separate from other curricular considerations.

HIERARCHY AND THE SELECTION AREAS—WHOSE SELECTION?

The statements (see Appendix 2) appear to be an ill-conceived, ad hoc list of concerns. It is astonishing that communication and language, one of the prime areas of learning and development, is not deemed suitable for developing cultural understanding. Instead cultures and cultural aspects of teaching are considered to be largely as matter of physical development: four out of the ten statements (numbers 2–5) address physical development and its subsection of health and self-care. No other area has as many examples. Physical development appears to relate to concerns of health, rather than cognition and it is not included in the 'closing the gap' agenda, nor is it discussed when statistical information on school achievement is compiled. There is an internal hierarchy between the seven areas—they do not carry equal weighting.

MODEL MINORITIES—WHY CHINESE?

The example of 'cultural spread' is to be considered within literacy and through different writing symbols (number 6: 'Provide materials which reflect a cultural spread [...] which they are familiar, e.g. Chinese script on a shopping bag.'). It is intended to be an example that benefits children who are familiar with them. Rather than everyone. Languages and ethnicities have their own internal hierarchies in discourse practice. Though the largest minority language group in England is Polish, (Office for National Statistics 2012) the Polish language is not mentioned in this way. Why Chinese? According to Gillborn (2008), some minorities are typically presented as model minorities—Chinese and Indian most commonly in the UK—as they are perceived to be 'hardworking' and therefore successful. Chinese pupils' GCSE results are consistently high (Runnymede Trust 2012). Gillborn (2008) raises questions about model minorities and essentialism and warns that the focus on these is dangerous because it silences other groups who are not successful in the same way. Model minorities are stereotypes that appear to be positive and flattering but the construction of Chinese as one homogeneous group overlooks the diversity within this group (Francis et al. 2009).

CULTURE TALK—WHO WINS? WHO LOSES?

The construction of language, what comes first and what follows and how policy statements are constructed, demonstrates how dominant discourses are maintained. The view that 'other' people have cultural concerns is inherent in all of the ten statements. This is how linguistic and racial dominance can be constructed. Number 1 locates '… cultural differences in attitudes and expectations' with parents who do not yet speak English. From the onset 'culture' signals others, typically migrants as a problem not a local strength or a societal advantage. Number 2 and its focus on '... cultural needs and expectations for skin and hair care' is instantly interpreted by many practitioners as a concern for black skin and black hair. The trajectory of thinking, from cultural concerns of others who are outsiders of 'our' society to positioning black people as others, is deeply worrying. This view that black children have cultural needs which are essentially different from all other children maintains white privilege. This is an example of institutionalised racism and provides evidence on how white supremacy is constructed. It takes place within the words themselves and in the meaning created between the lines.

Number 4 suggests that there are '... cultural attitudes to children's developing independence', which suggests that there are families who do not support their children in developing independence. But independence is a culture-specific construct, and what was typical of many grandparents' generation—playing independently outside without any adult supervision, for instance—may no longer be common place in England. Today a young child playing independently outside without any adult supervision is often perhaps viewed negatively or as a sign of neglect. It is, however, still typical in many other places. What counts as independence in England today is a complex, paradoxical construct.

The majority of young children, within the age-band of 16–26 months, are learning about toilets. The change from nappies, to sitting on a potty, to using toilets and urinals and learning to do this competently and independently in public places as well as in the privacy of the home is a lengthy business for all. However, number 5—'... discuss cultural expectations for toileting, since in some cultures young boys may be used to sitting rather than standing at the toilet'—is primarily concerned with gender and maintaining the supremacy of perceived masculinities. Why is standing at the toilet prioritised and why now for this age group? Why is this document preoccupied with very young boys and their perceived masculinities and why do these masculinities need to be policed? We could also ask what about transgender children—how does this document support practitioners with all children, whatever their gender?

Finally, numbers 7, 9 and 10 call for cultural and religious celebrations and backgrounds to be recognised and storytellers and musicians to be invited to settings. Where this happens as a part of routine-like, everyday practice—rather than occasionally during the Chinese New Year or Black History month—it is a great example of multicultural pedagogy in action. Where celebrations are added on to the existing practice as an after-thought, it raises questions about the practitioners' values. In essence, viewing cultural experiences and expectations as a problem to be fixed, or as something exotic to be celebrated occasionally, emerges from the same starting point and from similar beliefs. Both are part of the same process of 'othering'. Both viewpoints—problems and exotic celebrations—are examples of marginalisation that cumulatively have a tendency to alienate many families and children.

Moving On

If we accept that informal discussions, and careless throw-away comments, and legitimised policies based on Culture Talk are a problem, we need to seek solutions that are political and long term, and local and immediate. We can best promote social justice in early years settings (see, e.g. Scarlet 2016) when we understand and respectfully engage in cognitive conflict. As a profession we must challenge the dominant discourse that positions some children as 'deficient' and others as 'normal', and work towards reconceptualising and reimagining multiculturalism in early years—multi-culturalism that is built on respect and dignity of all and that views societal diversity as the norm.

In our collaboration with diverse families, it is more helpful to focus on families' funds of knowledge and their real, lived and authentic lifeworld experiences, rather than predetermined and essentialist 'minority cultures'. In finding out about funds of knowledge, the voluntary sector (after-school provision and supplementary schools, such as Saturday schools) is a good place to start (Francis et al. 2009; Kenner and Mahera 2012). Early years practitioners have always worked closely with parents, grandparents, child-minders and communities, and they are well placed to open up new conversations about children's lifeworlds, and with their children's supple-mentary school teachers, too. Early years settings are good places for renewing multicultural dialogues.

As Said (1994: 15) reminds us, far from being monolithic constructs constituting a single set of histories, practices, beliefs and experiences, all cultures consist of differences, of foreign and not-so-foreign elements: '... cultures are humanly made structures of both authority and participation, benevolent in what they include, incorporate, and validate, less benevolent in what they exclude and demote'. Cultures have always included more of others, and across national, linguistic and religious borders than policy makers would have us currently believe. Multicultural dialogues are needed in early childhood education and in all aspects of education. The journey of discovery of what each child's everyday culture consists of can be an exciting new way of understanding not only of children in our setting but also what it means to be a human in the twenty-first century.

APPENDIX 1

In the statutory Early Years Foundation Stage policy (DfE 2014)

Areas of learning and development	Aspect
Prime areas	
1. Personal, social and emotional	Making relationships
	Self-confidence
	Managing feelings and behaviour
2. Physical development	Moving and handling
	Health and self-care
3. Communication and language	Listening and attention
	Understanding
	Speaking
Specific areas	
4. Literacy	Reading
	Writing
5. Mathematics	Numbers
	Shape, space and measure
6. Understanding of the world	People and communities
	The world
	Technology
7. Expressive arts and design	Exploring and using media and materials
	Being imaginative

Appendix 2

Example from 'The Development Matters in the Early Years Foundation Stage (EYFS)' (Early Education 2012)

Prime area—personal, social and emotional development: self-confidence and self-awareness

1   Be aware of cultural differences in attitudes and expectations.   22–50 months
    Continue to share and explain practice with parents, ensuring a
    two-way communication using interpreter support where
    necessary. (p. 11)

Prime area—physical development: health and self-care

2   Discuss the cultural needs and expectations for skin and hair care   Birth to
    with parents prior to entry to the setting, ensuring that the needs   11 months
    of all children are met appropriately and that parents' wishes are
    respected. (p. 25)

3   Plan to take account of the individual cultural and feeding needs   Birth to
    of young babies in your group. (p. 25)   11 months

4   Be aware of and learn about differences in cultural attitudes to   16–26 months
    children's developing independence. (p. 25)

5   Discuss cultural expectations for toileting, since in some cultures   16–26 months
    young boys may be used to sitting rather than standing at the
    toilet. (p. 25)

Specific area—literacy: writing

6   Provide materials which reflect a cultural spread, so that children   22–36 months
    see symbols and marks with which they are familiar, e.g. Chinese
    script on a shopping bag. (p. 30)

Specific area—understanding the world: people and communities

7   Celebrate and value cultural, religious and community events and   16–26 months
    experiences. (p. 37)

8   In pretend play, imitates everyday actions and events from own   22–36 months
    family and cultural background, e.g. making and drinking tea.
    (p. 37)

9   Invite people from a range of cultural backgrounds to talk about   30–60 months
    aspects of their lives or the things they do in their work, such as a
    volunteer who helps people become familiar with the local area.
    (p. 38)

Specific area—expressive arts and design: exploring and using media and materials

10 Draw on a wide range of musicians and storytellers from a variety   22–36 months
    of cultural backgrounds to extend children's experiences and to
    reflect their cultural heritages. (p. 43)

REFERENCES

Arnaut, K., Blommaert, J., Rampton, B., & Spotti, M. (2015). *Language and superdiversity*. London: Routledge.

Avruch, K. (1998). *Culture and conflict resolution*. Washington, DC: United States Institute of Peace Press.

Banks, J., & McGee Banks, C. A. (Eds.). (2009). *Multicultural education, issues and perspectives* (7th revised ed.). Hoboken, NJ: Wiley & Sons.

Baumann, G. (1996). *Contesting culture: Discourses of identity in multi-ethnic London*. Cambridge: Cambridge University Press.

Biesta, G. J. J. (2004). Education, accountability, and the ethical demand: Can the democratic potential of accountability be regained? *Educational Theory, 54*(3), 233–250.

Boaler, J. (2005). The 'Psychological Prisons' from which they never escaped: The role of ability grouping in reproducing social class inequalities. *FORUM, 47*: 2&3, 25–134. Retrieved September 2, 2016, from http://www.youcubed. org/wp-content/uploads/psychogicalprisons2005.pdf

Bredekamp, S. (1991). Redeveloping early childhood education: A response to Kessler. *Early Childhood. Research Quarterly, 6*, 199–209.

Crozier, G. (2000). *Parents and schools*. Stoke-on-Trent: Trentham.

DfE (Department for Education). (2011). *Class size and education in England, evidence report*. Retrieved August 24, 2016, from https://www.gov.uk/government/publications/class-size-and-education-in-england-evidence-report

DfE. (2014). *Statutory framework for early years foundation stage, setting the standards for learning, development and care for children from birth to five*. Retrieved August 22, 2016, from https://www.gov.uk/government/publications/early-years-foundation-stage-framework--2

DfE. (2016). *Corporate report. Single department plan: 2015–2020*. Retrieved August 22, 2016, from https://www.gov.uk/government/publications/department-for-education-single-departmental-plan-2015-to-2020/single-departmental-plan-2015-to-2020#educational-excellence-everywhere

DfEE (Department for Education and Employment). (1999). *National Curriculum, the handbook for teachers in England (Key Stages 1 and 2)*. London: QCA. Retrieved September 1, 2016, from http://www.educationengland.org.uk/documents/pdfs/1999-nc-primary-handbook.pdf

Early Education (British Association of Early Childhood Education). (2012). *Development matters in Early Years Foundation Stage (EYFS)*. London: DfE. Retrieved November 30, 2016, from https://www.gov.gg/CHttpHandler.ashx?id=104249&p=0

EUNP (European Union Agency for Fundamental Rights). (2012). *The situation of Roma in 11 member states*. Luxembourg: Publications Office of the European Union.

Fairclough, N. (2001). *Language and power* (2nd ed.). London: Routledge.

Francis, B., Archer, L., & Mau, A. (2009). Language as capital, or language as identity? Chinese complementary school pupils' perspectives on the purposes and benefits of complementary schools. *British Educational Research Journal, 35*(4), 519–538.

Fuchs, S. (2001). *Against essentialism: A theory of culture and society.* Harvard: Harvard University Press.

Gillborn, D. (2008). *Racism and education, coincidence or conspiracy?* London: Routledge.

González, N., Moll, L., & Amanti, C. (Eds.). (2005). *Funds of knowledge, theorizing practices in households, communities and classrooms.* London: Lawrence Erlbaum.

Hill, K., Davis, A., Hirsch, D., & Marshall, L. (2016). *Falling short: The experiences of families living below the Minimum Income Standard.* Joseph Rowntree Foundation. Retrieved November 4, 2016, from https://www.jrf.org.uk/report/falling-short-experiences-families-below-minimum-income-standard

Hogg, L. (2015). Funds of knowledge: A tool for New Zealand teachers to reimagine the lives of minoritized students. *The International Journal of Learner Diversity and Identities, 22*(4), 1–16.

Kenner, C., & Mahera, R. (2012). Connecting children's worlds: Creating a multilingual syncretic curriculum in partnership with complementary schools. *Journal of Early Childhood Literacy, 13*(3), 395–417 (2013). Retrieved September 19, 2016, from http://ecl.sagepub.com/content/13/3/395.abstract

Kinos, J., Robertson, L., Barbour, N., & Pukk, M. (2016). Child-initiated pedagogies: Moving toward democratically appropriate practices in Finland, England, Estonia, and the United States. *Childhood Education, 92*(5), 345–357.

Ladson-Billings, G. (2006). *Presidential address: From education gap to education debt: Understanding achievement in U.S. schools.* Retrieved August 22, 2016, from http://advising.wisc.edu/facstaff/sites/default/files/files/Achievement%20%26%20Educational%20Debt%20Ladson-Billings%20copy.pdf

Mamdani, M. (1998). *Good Muslim, bad Muslim: America, the Cold War, and the roots of terror.* Pretoria: UNISA Press.

Mamdani, M. (2002). Good Muslim, bad Muslim: A political perspective on culture and terrorism. *American Anthropologist, 104*(3), 766–775. Retrieved September 8, 2016, from http://jan.ucc.nau.edu/sj6/mamdanigoodmuslimbadmuslim.pdf

Mani, L. (1989). Multiple mediations: Feminist scholarship in the age of multiple mediations. *Inscriptions, 5,* 1–23.

Moll, L., Amanti, C., Neff, D., & González, N. (1992). Funds of knowledge for teaching: Using a qualitative approach to connect homes and classrooms. *Theory into Practice, 31*(2), 132–141.

Nutbrown, C. (2012). *Foundations for quality, the independent review of early education and childcare qualifications. Final report.* Retrieved August 24, 2016, from https://www.gov.uk/government/uploads/system/uploads/attachment_data/file/175463/Nutbrown-Review.pdf

Office for National Statistic. (2012). *Ethnicity and national identity in England and Wales: 2011.* Retrieved September 19, 2016, from http://www.ons.gov.uk/peoplepopulationandcommunity/culturalidentity/ethnicity/articles/ethnicityandnationalidentityinenglandandwales/2012-12-11

Ofsted. (2014). *Ensuring Roma children achieve in education.* Retrieved August 26, from https://www.gov.uk/government/publications/ensuring-roma-children-achieve-in-education

Phillips, A. (2012). *What's wrong with essentialism?* Retrieved August 21, 2016, from http://eprints.lse.ac.uk/30900/

Race, R. (2015). *Multiculturalism and education* (2nd ed.). London: Bloomsbury.

Robertson, L. H. (2007). Bilingual children's story of learning to read. In J. Conteh, P. Martin, & L. H. Robertson (Eds.), *Multilingual learning stories in schools and communities in Britain* (pp. 41–61). Stoke-On-Trent: Trentham Books Ltd.

Robertson, L. H. (2015). Early years: Young children deserve the best possible start in life. *Forum, 57*(1), 31–34.

Robertson, L. H., & Drury, R. (2013). *Silences within Super-Diversity—Young multilingual children starting school in England.* Paper presented at Language and Super-diversity: Explorations and interrogations, June 5–7, 2013, University of Jyväskylä, Finland.

Robertson, L. H., & Drury, R. (2014). Silencing bilingualism: A day in a life of a bilingual practitioner. *International Journal of Bilingual Education and Bilingualism, 17*(5), 610–623.

Robertson, L. H., Kinos, J., Barbour, N., Pukk, M., & Rosqvist, L. (2015). Child-initiated pedagogies in Finland, Estonia and England: Exploring young children's views on decisions. *Early Child Development and Care. Special Issue: Early Childhood Pedagogy, 185*(11–12), 1815–1827.

Rostas, I., & Kostka, J. (2014). Structural dimensions of Roma School desegregation: Policies in Central and Eastern Europe. *European Education Research Journal, 13*(3), 268–281.

Runnymead Trust. (2012, June). *Briefing on ethnicity and educational attainment.* Retrieved August 23, 2016, from http://www.runnymedetrust.org/uploads/Parliamentary%20briefings/EducationWHdebateJune2012.pdf

Said, E. W. (1979). *Orientalism.* New York: Vintage.

Said, E. W. (1994). *Culture and imperialism.* New York: Vintage.

Scarlet, R. R. (Ed.). (2016). *The anti-bias approach in early. Childhood* (3rd ed.). Melbourne: Multiverse Publishing.

Smith, H. S. (2012). A critique of the teaching standards in England (1984–2012): Discourses of equality and maintaining the status quo. *Journal of Education Policy, 1–22*, 1–22.

Spencer-Oatey, H. (2012). What is culture? A compilation of quotations. *GlobalPAD core concepts*. Retrieved August 22, 2016, from http://go.warwick.ac.uk/globalpadintercultural

Strand, S. (2015). *Ethnicity, deprivation and educational achievement at the age of 16 in England: Trends over time*. London: DfE (Department For Education). Retrieved August 23, 2016, from https://www.gov.uk/government/uploads/system/uploads/attachment_data/file/439867/RR439B-Ethnic_minorities_and_attainment_the_effects_of_poverty_annex.pdf.pdf

Troyna, B. (Ed.). (1987). *Racial inequality in education*. London: Routledge.

Vertovec, S. (2006). *The emergence of super-diversity in Britain*. Centre on Migration, Policy and Society, Working Paper 25, Oxford: Oxford University.

Vertovec, S. (2009). *Transnationalism*. London: Routledge.

Vygotsky, L. S. (1978). *Mind in society: The development of higher psychological processes*. Cambridge, MA: Harvard University Press.

Wood, E. (2010). Developing integrated pedagogical approaches to play and learning. In P. Broadhead, J. Howard, & E. Wood (Eds.), *Play and learning in the early years* (pp. 9–26). London: Sage.

Leena Helavaara Robertson is an associate professor at Middlesex University, London, where she works as the education research degree coordinator and leads the MProf/DProf Education Pathway. Her long-term interests, expertise and publications include culture, multilingual learning and social justice in early years settings and schools; some of her publications draw on her own teaching experiences as a class teacher in and around London. Currently, she is leading two international research projects with international teams of teachers and researchers, one focusing on Gypsy, Roma, Traveller children, which is funded by the European Union (Erasmus+), and the other on child-initiated pedagogies.

Advancing the Dialogue: Naming White Supremacy and Patriarchy as Power Blocs in Education

Shirley R. Steinberg

INTRODUCTION

There is no one way to teach multiculturalism, just as there is no one thing which causes racism, classism, sexism, homophobia, and religious persecution. It is essential to maintain a critical read on all the aspects, which create inequality, and to understand the contextual etymology of each of these constituents. I believe a major mistake in continuing imbalance is to emphasize one *bad guy*. However, as we engage in a discussion to create equity and to decolonize previous assumptions, we must articulate, identify, name, and break down the power blocs (Fiske 1993, 1994) which serve to sustain an inequitable world (Steinberg 2009). Using Fiske's notion of a power bloc, Joe Kincheloe and I organized the notion of critical multiculturalism (Kincheloe and Steinberg 1997), in which we *named* the forces which fight against a democratic and diverse ... a multicultural world. In this chapter, I want to call out the white supremacist and patriarchal power blocs which maintain a dominant cultural stance within an examination of oppression. Make no mistake, I am

S.R. Steinberg (✉)
University of Calgary, Calgary, AB, Canada

© The Author(s) 2018
R. Race (ed.), *Advancing Multicultural Dialogues in Education*,
DOI 10.1007/978-3-319-60558-6_16

not suggesting that race and gender are *the primary factors* in a discussion of diverse and critically multicultural society, but that they are two of the guiding components in governing our abilities to identify what is needed in diversity, multicultural dialogues, and multicultural education. For the purposes of this chapter, I focus on White Supremacy and Patriarchy.

WHITE SUPREMACY: CREATING A NONPRESENCE

The white supremacist power bloc assumes its power from its ability to erase its presence. As the measure of all others, whiteness is unhyphenated, undepicted in "cultures of the world," in no need of introduction, and absent in most multicultural texts and dialogues. Undoubtedly, it is one of the most powerful "nothings" we can conjure. Morrison (1993: 59) refers to the nothingness of whiteness as "… mute, meaningless, unfathomable, pointless, frozen, veiled, curtained, dreaded, senseless, implacable." Again, it is important to specify that the white nothingness we are describing does not imply that white people are not seen as white. Instead, it asserts the inability of individuals to understand exactly what whiteness entails. It is the nature of whiteness and its effects—for example, its status as power bloc, as norm and the privilege it bestows—that are invisible in twenty-first-century Western societies. In the Western white collective (un)consciousness, whiteness has been used not so much to signify a culture but rather the nonpresence of a culture, the absence of a "distasteful and annoying" ethnicity. In this same collective (un)consciousness, Haymes (1996) astutely observes, this white nothingness assumes a superior shadow that transforms it into whiteness as a "transcendental consciousness." Such a higher order of being, Haymes (ibid) continues, involves at some level the privileging of reason over culture. Like the science that grounds white reason, this white consciousness has been so far unable to react upon its own origins, to confront its own particular assumptions (Mcintosh 1995; Frankenberg 1993; Nakayama and Krizek 1995; Morrison 1993; Stowe 1996).

This power of white nothingness reveals itself in everyday life, casual conversations, and political discourses. When a right wing American politician implores his *[sic]* audience to "… take back our cities … take back our culture, and take back our country," the "our" in question signals whites. When the right wing in any country refers to *family values*, they are speaking of a white entity, a white norm missing in non-white homes.

Television reporting of politics refuses to engage questions of whiteness in relation to such public pronouncements. Indeed, schooling and cultural pedagogy in general provide no lessons on the existence, not to mention the effects, of the white power bloc on life in Western culture. Even some forms of academic anti-racist multiculturalism fall victim to the power of whiteness, as they fail to appreciate the ways academic discourse is structured by Western forms of rationality—white reason. Whiteness is further erased in schools by the reticence of many teachers to discuss whites as a racialized group and white racism. Many teachers see value in multicultural education workshops and seminars only if such programs provide new information about minority groups they didn't already know about—the study of privilege(s) makes no sense to them. Many complain that they already know about minority groups such as blacks and Latinos—a comment that grants insight into their theoretical schemas regarding multicultural education.

Faced with teachers who many times are reluctant to speak of whiteness and whose conceptual mapping of multiculturalism induces them to see no value in such a pedagogy, critical multiculturalists have had a terrible task in front of them. Though it will be difficult, critical educators must be intellectually equipped to make a convincing case for the need to expose the white power bloc on the academy. The white power of nothingness must no longer be allowed to tacitly shape the knowledge production and the academic canon of Western schooling. In this context, a critical pedagogy of whiteness produces a counter-history grounded on the deconstruction of a whitewash of racial history. Such a counter-history opens questions for discussion and research—for example, questions about the deracialization of early Christianity; the possible whitening of ancient Egypt with its appropriation of the culture's innovations in writing, medicine, mathematics, and religion into a white European framework; and the bleaching of particular authors of African descent in the European literary canon, including Alexandre Dumas, Spinoza, and Aesop. Such historical whitewashing conveys debilitating messages to contemporary blacks and other non-whites, teaching them to believe that they are intellectually inferior to whites. In addition to the special understandings about black contributions to history, Western white history in particular, counter-historical study engages students in an analysis of the hegemonic process of the white supremacist power bloc (Kincheloe and Steinberg 1997).

Such an analysis is central to a critical diversity, multicultural dialogue and multiculturalism, as it focuses the attention of student and teacher on the subtle ways racism works to shape our consciousness and produce our identity—whether we are marginalized or privileged. Indeed, no matter what one's racial/ethnic background, such a process is complicit in the construction of subjectivity. Indeed, it can be argued that the conversation about education in Western societies has always, at one level, been about whiteness, in the sense that education was geared to make an individual more rational and to separate him (traditionally a male) from the uneducated, unreasonable other. The academic whitewashing of the white power bloc allows the white magic of nothingness to rob non-whites of their culture, contributions, and identities—a historical process that holds significant contemporary consequences. Recognizing these socio-pedagogical dynamics, critical multiculturalism's whiteness education works to produce counter-hegemonic identities among whites and non-whites alike. Such identity production is a crucial step in the development of an anti-racist counter-future that refuses to allow whiteness to continue its role as an oppressive hidden norm (Fiske 1993, 1994; Mcintosh 1995; Sleeter 1993; Tanaka 1996).

As the erased norm, whiteness and the white power bloc hold the peculiar privilege of constituting both the dominant culture and a nonculture. Within this contradiction resides the basis of white power: whiteness can be deployed differently depending on the contextual dynamics it encounters. Students of whiteness can zealously chronicle the workings of whiteness, though not in some complete way, because it is always developing new methods of asserting itself. Our concern here is not to explore white power as it pertains to the Aryan Nation or white militias, although these are very disturbing expressions of white power and merit detailed treatment. Our purpose here in this chapter is to focus more on a mainstream, homespun, "good taste" white power that tacitly shapes everyday life— the white power bloc is nothing if not socially acceptable which provides insight into how the white power bloc shapes the way the social world operates. Dean MacCannell describes an article in the real estate section of the *Los Angeles Times* about the Cahuilla Indians and their ownership of land around Palm Springs. The piece, written by a D. Campbell, describes how the tribe leases land on the reservation to white investors to build condominiums and resorts. The article speaks of the "crazy quilt" legal complexity of the division of land ownership, characterizing it as "half Indian controlled, half free."

The discursive use of "free" emerges unaltered from the white unconsciousness—an unintentional rhetorical device to erase white ownership in particular and the white power bloc in general. In the newspaper article, the Cahuilla are variously described as falling into the "catbird seat," "forty rag-tail Indians," irresponsible in their handling of money, "living in complete isolation from any large group of civilized humans," and "primitive." Such discursive positioning of the Cahuilla puts them in an unusual position as landowners. According to Campbell: (1) even though they live in a money economy that values profit making, the Cahuilla don't deserve to make a profit from their land; (2) maybe white renters should not honor their debts to the Indians because their scale irresponsibility is so pronounced that they probably wouldn't know what to do with the cash once they procured it. While this article was written almost three decades ago, the discourse remains, relating to Black people, immigrants, and refugees. The power of whiteness permeates this article given that the Cahuilla are positioned as the primitive, irrational "other." Without referring overtly to whiteness, the author makes it clear that whiteness is the powerful norm from which judgments about the Indians' unwarranted position can be issued. Speaking from the mountaintop of civilization, the author deploys his or her whiteness as a means of declaring the Indians uncivilized. Readers can discern traces of the white supremacist power bloc's white rationale that justify unequal treatment of those who fall too far from the Enlightenment tree of rationality.

Thus, any analysis of white power should recognize the privileged social position whites occupy. As the advertisement for the luxury cruise line teases its privileged potential customers with the notion that "the rules are different here," we gain insight into the fact that the rules are different for whites, whether they are dealing with irresponsible Indian landlords or attempting to secure a home loan from the bank. White power exists; it may be at times rhetorically or discursively masked, but it is still quite apparent to anyone who cares to look. Whites—and white males in particular—control Western information, corporate boards, unions, police departments, and the higher ranks in the military. There's nothing too complex about these data—the white power bloc rules. Yet, despite this obvious reality, whiteness maintains the ability to erase itself, even at times portraying itself as a position of victimization by a politically correct cadre of multiculturalist zealots. As the dominant culture, whiteness is capable of sophisticated measures of self-justification that work best when social inequities within the power of various groups are hidden from view—inequities from which whites profit unjustly (Jordan 1995; Fiske 1994; Nakayama and Krizek 1995; Merelman 1995).

The white power bloc develops a bag of tricks to mask its social location, making use of disguises, euphemisms, silences, and avoidances. Knowing this, it makes more sense when whiteness uses concepts such as equal opportunity, assuming that the term in no way challenges white supremacy. In this situation whites can speak publicly (in racially mixed groups) about their belief in granting everyone a fair chance at [education] success, but understanding all the while at a tacit level that such assertions are "just talk." In reality they know that whites will always be better qualified—or at least appear better qualified and more comfortable to work with than non-whites. This tacit dynamic of whiteness works because whites continue to hang on to negative stereotypes about non-whites. A majority of American whites believe that African Americans, for example, are more violent, less intelligent, and not as hard working as whites. In this articulation of white power, the reason for white racism toward non-whites is the behavior of non-whites themselves. Of course, African Americans take special blame for such white perspectives, as the horror after all is Africa. In this context, whiteness not only fears Africanism but is particularly terrified by the Africanism within itself. Modernist whiteness, buoyed by its white reason, is afraid of Africa's signification of the instinctual, the libidinal, the primitive (Rubin 1994; Merelman 1995; Gresson 1995).

THE PATRIARCHAL POWER BLOC

A diversity and multicultural focus on patriarchy and the patriarchal power bloc is essential because the focus asserts that gender inequality is a pervasive feature of contemporary society. To invoke patriarchy is to problematize the social construction of gender and gender relations in a way that moves us to consider what constitutes a just and democratic academic curriculum, politics, and social consciousness. Any critical multiculturalist approach to patriarchy must draw upon a critical postmodern feminist theory for academic sustenance. Critical postmodern feminism posits that humans are social constructions—not entities determined by innate, biological, universal characteristics (Yuval-Davis 2006). Such a position should not be taken to mean that biology plays no role in the production of humans or that we can change who and what we are simply by wishing it so. The theoretical position does imply that the potential of humans is far more open-ended than traditionally believed and that we should not blame our dispositions merely on biological or psychological determinism.

Although a critical multicultural analysis of patriarchy relies on critical postmodern feminism, it is very careful (especially when theorists happen to be men) to consider the political dynamics of using feminism as it does. Too often men's engagement with feminism can be perceived to be or actually be an appropriation of such scholarship and political work for purposes not consonant with the feminist project. For example, patriarchal theorizing can serve to return the focus of scholarly attention to men in the process of helping to recover the authority of the patriarchal power bloc. Given this possibility, any attempt to analyze patriarchy must carefully examine the danger of appropriation. Any critical multicultural attempt to analyze masculinity without a humble nod to feminist theory and the help of women in general collapses into traditional patriarchy's male bonding rituals—activities that always involve exclusion of women. The form of patriarchal analysis and political practice delineated here takes place in the presence of and with the collaboration of women (Fox 1988; McLean 1996a; Gore 1993).

In the spirit of this nod to feminist theory, a critical multicultural analysis of patriarchy and the patriarchal power bloc is informed by critical feminism's politics of difference that actually works to subvert traditional notions of gender difference in patriarchal societies. Such a traditional notion of difference divides individuals neatly into males and females and unequally distributes power to men. A critical analysis of patriarchy emulates critical feminism's efforts to subvert this system and to end the exploitation of both women and traditional patriarchy's disowned sons—gay men and non-white men. A critical multicultural analysis of patriarchy begins to rethink notions of gender, subjectivity, and sexuality, setting the stage for a reinvention of masculinity. Operating in this manner, theorists have come to realize that the essentialization of male and female difference precludes the recognition that men who reject dominant notions of patriarchal masculinity and who struggle against race, class, and gender domination are ideologically closer to feminists than are women who unquestionably accept traditional notions of gender difference.

Such understandings hold dramatic implications. Indeed, a critical analysis of patriarchy demands nothing less than a questioning of comfortable assumptions about everything from male/female differences to the gender inscriptions of social institutions and the power relations that sustain them. For example, our theory of patriarchy understands the ways that the Western intellectual tradition has developed in the soil of the patriarchal power bloc. Such a realization doesn't mean that we simply dismiss the entire Western canon, but it does induce us to examine and develop alternatives to the epistemological assumptions that ground the tradition. A key function of our multicultural work—the function that earns it the label "critical"—involves analysis of the ways that power shapes knowledge forms, the definition of truth, and the rules of academic and other cultural discourses. It is easy to trace the ways our three power blocs intersect in this knowledge/truth production process. Western democratic societies and this power dynamic is hard to fathom, bathed as they are in a liberal ideology of equal opportunity, a just world, and egalitarian social relations. Understanding this social tendency, a critical diversity/multicultural analysis of patriarchy works hard to demonstrate the ways society is structured by collective power differences that are constructed along lines of race, class, gender, ethnicity, and sexual preference. If the construction of masculinity and the oppression of women are to be understood, such a process will take place only in the context provided by an analysis of structured power relations (Ebert 1991; Clough 1994; Gore 1993; Hedley 1994; McLean 1996a; Walby 1990; McLean et al. 1996).

Gender in our critical conceptualization is a structural system of power and domination, and masculine identity is a socially constructed agent of this power. The social construction of patriarchy helps shape men's self-interest that, in turn, structures their dominant relationship to women. Unlike more liberal gender perspectives that position male–female relations and gender identities as contained within individuals, a critical analysis of patriarchy sees notions of masculinity implanted throughout powerful social institutions, including education, the welfare establishment, the police, the military, the legal system, the media, etc. Indeed, corporations, colleges, and sports organizations are shaped by the patriarchal power bloc's values of Social Darwinism and success for those who conform. The liberal notion of individualism champions the problematic belief that "personal problems" such as spousal abuse, violence, and misogynistic attitudes can be solved by appeal to individuals. Critical multicultural analysis of patriarchy contends that such problems demand both personal and social solutions. Men's oppressive relationship with women cannot be understood until we expose the ways various social institutions attempt to socialize men and women and shape their gender identities in a manner saturated by patriarchy (McLean 1996b).

Any emancipatory transformation in the attitudes and behaviors of men will take place only in a situation where these social institutions are challenged. Male employees who confront the implicit patriarchal values of the corporation may lose their jobs, and male students who confront the tacit androcentric knowledge of the academy may fail—these are the stark prospects that face those who would challenge the power bloc. Critical scholars of patriarchal power must gain insight into the ideologies and discourses that constitute ever-changing articulations of patriarchy and the ever-shifting nature of the patriarchal power bloc. By ideology we do not mean a misrepresentation of what is "real" in society. Rather, we use the term in a critical theoretical sense define a process involving the maintenance of unequal power relations by mobilizing meaning in a way that benefits the dominant group, the patriarchal power bloc. Thus, a patriarchal ideology in this articulation involves a tacit process of meaning-making and mobilization of affect that induces women to accept a passive view of their femininity and men to embrace unproblematically their gender privilege. All of this takes place in ever-changing ways and in a variety of social venues in a manner that camouflages gender antagonisms. Patriarchal forms of discursive power work through what are often perceived as neutral conduits of language to produce a set of tacit rules that regulate, in the context of gender, what can and cannot be said, who speaks with the blessing of authority and who must listen, and whose social constructions are scientifically valid and whose are unlearned and unimportant. Discursive analysis disputes the traditional assumption that individuals possess stable properties such as attitudes and beliefs. In our patriarchal context, language is viewed as a sociopolitical arena where gender identity is continuously renegotiated.

Understanding how patriarchal power works allows us to gain insight into methods of interrupting oppressive patriarchal practices. It prepares us to understand the pain that many heterosexual white men claimed to experience in the late 1990s without ignoring men's privilege and dominant gender position. These theoretical assertions understand that both masculinity and the patriarchal power bloc are ever mutating as they react to challenges from feminists, gay rights advocates, and other individuals and groups. In the same way, this critical multicultural understanding of patriarchy views masculinity as possessing multiple and ambiguous meanings and different expressions in different contexts. Indeed, masculinity is not the same for all men, and, as a result, our analysis of patriarchy refuses to essentialize or universalize the concept. Operating without the crutch of a universalized masculinity, our patriarchal analysis induces teachers to study the conflicting stories a culture tells itself about men and the ideological and discursive dynamics that help construct and frame these narratives. As we examine these stories, the question we seek to induce various individuals to ask is: What is patriarchy (Hedley 1994; McLean 1996a)? How does patriarchy reinscribe a power bloc in dominant culture?

In many ways asking these questions represents a potential radical act. Naturalized assumptions are opened to analysis and negotiation in an unprecedented manner, and the historical existence of "other masculinities/patriarchies" confronts those who would repress awareness of their reality. In the men's movements that have emerged in the last decades the question, "What is masculinity?" has often been answered with a set of assumptions very different from those embraced by the critical patriarchal theory. Men's movement leaders have often sought a "true masculinity." But a more critical and emancipatory search might involve an analysis of the effects of men's narratives and beliefs about masculinity on both themselves and women; or, in this same spirit, does the adoption of an alternative nontraditional masculinity result in the forfeit of patriarchal privilege? Can a critical theory and pedagogy of patriarchy help men who seek alternative masculinities understand gender power dynamics in a way that induces them to resist complicity with a power bloc noted for oppression of women and gay males and that allows them to reconceptualize patriarchy in a different but still hegemonic manner? In this situation, such men must seek the help and support of women, gay men, and non-white men and their insights for dealing with asymmetrical power relations.

In an educational context, how does a critical multicultural analysis of patriarchy help us teach male students to step away from dominant masculinity and the power bloc that supports it? How do multicultural dialogues in education help us to do this? Educational institutions in this culture unfortunately have rarely considered such questions; in fact, they have traditionally taught boys to embrace a patriarchal masculinity. The patriarchal nature of mainstream education—taught by both male and female teachers as surrogates for absent patriarchs—reproduces unequal gender relations. Such an education teaches young men to join in the power struggle that surrounds dominant notions of masculinity and the sacrifice of humanness that accompanies it. Educational institutions that "make men out of boys" often brutalize young men, use homophobia to induce them to conform to an insensitive masculinity, de-emotionalize them, and train them to physically and emotionally abuse one another. Those young men who do not internalize these messages and gain significant validation for mastery of the masculinity curriculum must live in the shadow of self-doubt and male inadequacy for the rest of their lives. Our critical multicultural analysis of patriarchy and the ever-shifting patriarchal power bloc can help teachers make sense of and intervene in these oppressive pedagogical practices.

DEFINING POWER BLOCS IN A MULTICULTURAL CONTEXT: NAMING POWER

Fiske (1993) used the term "power bloc" to describe the social formations around which power politics operated in Western societies in the late twentieth century. Employing the term as did Antonio Gramsci, the Italian political theorist, and Stuart Hall, the British cultural studies scholar, Fiske argued that power wielders do not constitute a particular class or well-defined social category. The power bloc, he contends, is more like an ever-shifting set of strategic and tactical social alliances. Such alliances are arranged unsystematically whenever social situations arise that threaten the "allies'" interests. Power blocs are historically, socially, and issue(s) specific as they come and go in relation to changing cultural arrangements. Power blocs are often created around social formations involving race, class, gender, or ethnicity in the pursuit of privileged access to particular rights or resources. For Fiske, power "… is a systematic set of operations upon people that works to ensure the maintenance of the social order … and ensure its smooth running" (Fiske 1993: 11). It stands to reason that those individuals and groups who benefit the most from maintenance of this social order align their interests with those of the dominant power system and work to keep it running smoothly. Fiske concludes that the power bloc can be described better by "what it does than what it is."

In this conjugation, the notion of "the people" includes those who fall outside the power bloc and are "disciplined" by it. Falling outside the power bloc does not mean that such an individual has no power; the power such outsiders hold is a weaker power (Fiske labels it a localizing power) than that of the power bloc. Indeed, it is a power that can be cultivated, strengthened, and sometimes successfully deployed. Along lines of race, class, and gender, individuals can simultaneously fall within the boundaries of one power bloc and outside another. While no essential explanation can account for the way an individual will relate to power blocs vis-à-vis their race, class, or gender, such dimensions do affect people's relationship to power-related social formations. In most cases, individuals are fragmented in relation to power. A Black male may be disempowered in relation to the racial category of white supremacy yet may enjoy the political benefits of being a male in a patriarchal power bloc or an upper-middle-class male in the economic power bloc. Thus, individuals move in and out of empowered and disempowered positions. In our critical multiculturalist perspective, such fragmented power-related understandings are central, yet at the same time we maintain a keen sense of awareness of the human suffering caused by life outside of particular power alignments. Critical multiculturalists understand that there is little ambiguity to the pain, degradation, and horror that women experience from gender violence by men acting in complicity with the patriarchal power bloc, or that the poor experience as the result of the economic power bloc's insensitive fiscal politics, or that African Americans experience as a result of the white supremacist power bloc's racism (Evans-Winters and Love 2015).

In these painful examples, a basic aspect of power is starkly illustrated: power produces inequities in the ability of human beings to delineate and realize their material and emotional needs. Teachers and other cultural workers who do not recognize the political dynamic will always be limited in their attempts to understand, provide for, and help empower their marginalized students and clients. The power bloc works consistently to obscure such appreciations; indeed, it labors to fix any violation of its borders by localizing powers. Such violations of the boundaries of power blocs have become common fare in Western societies. Public debates over affirmative action, minimum wage legislation, universal health care, sex and violence in TV and movies, and multicultural curricula all constitute skirmishes at the doorstep of the power bloc. The reaction of the power bloc as expressed in the forceful pronouncements of the conservative monoculturalists indicates a sense of threat; from a racial perspective, it reveals white perception of a challenge to racial supremacy. Conservative multiculturalism, with its monoculturalism, singularity of standards of excellence, and one-truth epistemology, is a quintessential representation of a power bloc that is resisting challenges to its previously unquestioned authority.

Beginning in the late 1990s, one formation of the contemporary power bloc united several groups:

1. Dominant economic and political elites concerned with building good business climates to enhance corporate profits, establishing a neo-liberal power bloc
2. White working-class and middle-class groups who sensed their white privilege under attack by minority groups and who were uncomfortable with what conservative leaders refer to as attacks on traditional values like the family—such threats are perceived as coming from *immoral* African American welfare recipients, LGBTQ community, and feminists
3. Social Darwinist conservatives with free market economic perspectives and guardians of Western cultural values who advocate a return to "standards of excellence" and discipline in schools
4. Upwardly mobile members of the new middle class who were not comfortable with the other groups represented in the power bloc but who joined the alliance because of their desire for professional advancement—such advancement is possible only if they buy into the corporate management procedures and non-controversial identities

These blocs remained strong and collected other willing partners, those bent on an obsession to revive and reinstall whiteness as the dominating factor in governing. Ironically, whiteness was never gone; the arrogance of whiteness has never waned, nor lost power, an essential factor in white supremacy remains the fear of losing control, losing privilege. New groups have been added to the growing list of consolidated power blocs:

5. Self-described Christians, who deem whiteness as a sign of supremacy, indeed, a blessing, and a reason to reclaim lost status
6. Xenophobes who believe that the influx of immigrants and refugees of color will contribute to a pollution of history, dignity, and moral values

While such a power bloc constantly aligned and realigned itself depending on the issues in question, some groups obviously were more predisposed to alliance than others (Fiske 1993). These groups continue to align, indeed reach out, to create strange bedfellows through the auspices of preserving civilization, which, of course, is white. Following the vote for Brexit and the American elections of 2016, it appeared that those who were integral to forming the above power blocs aligned to create the largest global power bloc of hate, reinforcing the need to articulate and define power blocs and those who create and sustain them.

CONCLUSION: THE STUDY OF POWER AND PRIVILEGE

Critical multiculturalism demands that educators of diversity and multiculturalism understand the need for studying power and privilege within a critical multicultural curriculum. Such analysis changes our orientation to multicultural education so that we study not only the effects of oppression on the oppressed, but its impact on the privileged as well. Such a curricular addition is not meant to imply that we abandon the inclusion of the cultural productions of non-whites, women, and the poor—not at all. It does mean that we see all human beings as shaped by race, class, and gender inscriptions of power. In today's world, a critically educated person must be conscious of the way the power dynamics of race, class, gender, and other social dynamics operate to produce an individual's identity and consciousness. In this context, therefore, multicultural education and multicultural dialogues become much more than a detour through diversity and a mere acquaintance with cultures and experiences other than one's own; indeed, critical multicultural awareness is essential.

REFERENCES

Clough, P. (1994). The hybrid criticism of patriarchy: Rereading Kate Millett's sexual politics. *The Sociological Quarterly, 35*(3), 473–486.

Ebert, T. (1991). The difference of postmodern feminism. *College English, 58*(8), 886–904.

Evans-Winters, V., & Love, B. (2015). *Black feminism in education: Black women speak back, up and out.* New York: Peter Lang.

Fiske, J. (1993). *Power plays, power works.* New York: Verso.

Fiske, J. (1994). *Media matters: Everyday culture and political change.* Minneapolis: University of Minnesota Press.

Fox, B. (1988). Conceptualizing patriarchy. *Canadian Review of Sociology and Anthropology, 25*(2), 163–182.

Frankenberg, R. (1993). *The social construction of whiteness: White women, race matters.* Minneapolis: University of Minnesota Press.

Gore, J. (1993). *The struggle for pedagogies: Critical and feminist discourses as regimes of truth.* New York: Routledge.

Gresson, A. (1995). *The recovery of race in America.* Minneapolis: University of Minnesota Press.

Haymes, S. (1996). Race, repression, and the politics of crime and punishment in the bell curve. In J. Kincheloe, S. Steinberg, & A. Gresson (Eds.), *Measured lies: The bell curve examined* (pp. 237–249). New York: St. Martin's Press.

Hedley, M. (1994). The presentation of gendered conflict in popular movies: Affective stereotypes, cultural sentiments, and men's motivation. *Sex Roles, 31*(11/12), 721–740.

Jordan, J. (1995). In the land of white supremacy. In C. Berlet (Ed.), *Eyes right: Challenging the right wing backlash.* Boston: South End Press.

Kincheloe, J. L. (2008). *Critical pedagogy primer.* New York: Peter Lang.

Kincheloe, J. L., Steinberg, S. R., Rodriguez, N., & Chennault, R. (Eds.). (1998). *White reign: Deploying whiteness in America.* New York: St. Martin's Press.

Kincheloe, J. L., & Steinberg, S. R. (1997). *Changing multiculturalism: New times, new curriculum.* London: Open University Press.

Lincoln, Y. (1996). For whom the bell tolls: A cognitive or educated elite? In J. L. Kincheloe, S. Steinberg, & A. Gresson (Eds.), *Measured lies: The bell curve examined* (pp. 127–135). New York: St. Martin's Press.

MacCannell, D. (1992). *Empty meeting grounds.* New York: Routledge.

Mcintosh, P. (1995). White privilege: A personal account of coming to see correspondences through work in women's studies. In M. Anderson & P. Collins (Eds.), *Race, class, gender: An anthology.* Belmont, CA: Wandsworth.

McLean, C., Carey, M., & White, C. (1996). Introduction. In C. McLean, M. Carey, & C. White (Eds.), *Men's way of being* (pp. 1–10). Boulder, CO: Westview.

McLean, C. (1996a). The politics of men's pain. In C. McLean, M. Carey, & C. White (Eds.), *Men's way of being* (pp. 111–128). Boulder, CO: Westview.

McLean, C. (1996b). Boys and education in Australia. In C. McLean, M. Carey, & C. White (Eds.), *Men's way of being* (pp. 65–84). Boulder, CO: Westview.

Merelman, R. (1995). *Representing black culture: Racial conflict and cultural politics in the United States.* New York: Routledge.

Morrison, T. (1993). *Playing in the dark: Whiteness and the literary imagination.* Visalia, CA: Vintage.

Nakayama, T., & Krizek, R. (1995). Whiteness: A strategic rhetoric. *Quarterly Journal of Speech, 81,* 291–309.

Ramalho, T. (2017). *Reading the World: Brazilian Notes for the Not-So-Fine Lines.* Rotterdam: Sense Publishing.

Rubin, L. (1994). *Families on the faultline: America's working class speaks about the family, the economy, race, and ethnicity.* New York: HarperCollins.

Sleeter, C. (1993). How white teachers construct race. In C. McCarthy & W. Crichlow (Eds.), *Race, identity, and reproduction in education* (pp. 243–256). New York: Routledge.

Steinberg, S. R. (2001). *Multi/intercultural conversations: A Reader.* New York: Peter Lang.

Steinberg, S. (Ed.). (2009). *Diversity and multiculturalism reader.* New York: Peter Lang.

Steinberg, S. R., & Kincheloe, J. L. (2009). Smoke and mirrors: More than one way to be diverse and multicultural. In S. R. Steinberg (Ed.), *Diversity and multiculturalism: A reader* (pp. 3–22). New York: Peter Lang.

Stowe, D. (1996). Uncolored people: The rise of whiteness studies. *Lingua Franca, 6*(6), 68–77.

Tanaka, G. (1996). Dysgenesis and white culture. In J. L. Kincheloe, S. R. Steinberg, & A. Gresson (Eds.), *Measured lies: The bell curve examined* (pp. 303–314). New York: St. Martin's Press.

Tilley-Lubbs, G. A. (2016). Knowing Joe through a medium. In M. F. Agnello & W. M. Reynolds (Eds.), *Practicing critical pedagogy: The influences of Joe L. Kincheloe* (pp. 87–98). New York: Springer.

Yuval-Davis, N. (2006). Intersectionality and feminist politics. *European Journal of Women's Studies, 13*(3), 193–209.

Walby, S. (1990). *Theorizing patriarch.* Oxford: Blackwell.

Professor Shirley R. Steinberg is the Werklund Research Professor of Critical Youth Studies at the University of Calgary. She is the executive director of freire-project.org and the author and editor of many books on critical pedagogy, social justice, Islamophobia, urban and youth culture, and cultural studies. Her most recent books include: *Curriculum: Decolonizing the Field* (2016); *Critically Researching Youth* (2015); *Critical Youth Studies Reader* (2014); *19 Urban Questions: Teaching in the City* (2010); *Diversity and Multiculturalism: A Reader* (2009). Her latest books (forthcoming in the autumn of 2017) are *Third Wave Islamophobia* and *From Behind and in Front of the Veil: Women in Dialogue.*

Researching Interrelations of Formal and Informal Learning in Early Adolescence Form a Critical Race Perspective

Anke Wischmann

INTRODUCTION

This chapter considers how different modes of learning in early adolescence are interrelated and at the same time interwoven with racialising and racist practices and structures and how this impacts educational trajectories of young people. My assumption is that in early adolescence when belonging to a group and recognition by peers becomes more important, informal learning for all young people becomes more important and is set in a specific relationship to formal learning. This relationship then depends on the social position of the learner and therefore on powerful social categorisations, in particular 'race', since 'race' or 'migration background' is an important indicator in terms of statistically expected educational achievement (Geißler and Weber-Menges 2009).

To analyse these complex interrelations, firstly, I will introduce the situation in Germany in terms of educational inequalities and the discourses on informal learning in this context. Secondly, I will summarise current

A. Wischmann (✉)
University of Hamburg, Hamburg, Germany

© The Author(s) 2018   295
R. Race (ed.), *Advancing Multicultural Dialogues in Education*,
DOI 10.1007/978-3-319-60558-6_17

research in formal and informal learning relationships, with particular attention to adolescence. Thirdly, I will reflect on the notion of learning and argue that it has to be understood as a relational (Mezirow 1997; Künkler 2011) and situated (Lave und Wenger 1991) process. This understanding of learning is especially important with regard to research design. On this basis, I will present a qualitative study that aims to analyse the interrelation of formal and informal learning from a critical race perspective (Delgado and Stefancic 2000). The central aim is to reconstruct how subjective learning experiences and structural conditions come together in narrations about learning (Souto-Manning 2013). Finally, I will discuss the impact of the study's results for current multicultural dialogues in education.

THE CONTEXT IN GERMANY

Research shows that educational achievement and with it formal learning in Germany is strongly determined by social background, in particular by socio-economic status, gender and the presence of a so-called migration background (Krüger et al. 2011). In 2014, 20% (16.4 million people) of the population had a migration background in Germany. The term 'migration background' comprises various groups of which 35.8% were non-German citizens with a personal experience of migration; 8.2% were non-German citizens with no personal experience of migration; 18.9% were so-called *Aussiedler* (those who came from the former Soviet Union and have German citizenship) (Leung 2005); 11.7% were other German citizens with personal experience of migration; 2.9% who became German citizens but had not experienced migration themselves; and 22.6% were German citizens with no experience of migration (e.g. at least one parent immigrated or was born as a non-German citizen) (Statistisches Bundesamt 2014). The numbers of immigrants and the proportion of country origin changed significantly due to the approximately 1.1 million refugees who arrived in Germany in 2015, nearly 500,000 of whom have already applied for asylum (BAMF 2016).

Hence, migration background does not necessarily refer to a particular phenotype but to geographic and national origin and is often related to some sort of 'Other' ethnicity (Mecheril et al. 2010). Not all, but a relatively high number of students with migration backgrounds, succeed less in school than students without such a background (Geißler and Weber-Menges 2009). Since the first 'programme for international student assessment study' (PISA) (Baumert 2002), it was clear that something had to be done. A flurry of measures and studies were conducted, most of them focussed on language education (Gogolin et al. 2009; Gogolin and Banks 2012). Now a relatively new argument in the German debate is that the recognition of informal learning might be an option to compensate underachievement in formal education as it could foster formal learning (Düx and Sass 2005). I want to question whether this can work by taking structural and institutional racism into account (Gomolla and Radtke 2002).

Interrelation of Formal and Informal Learning in Adolescence

Whereas there is quite a lot of research investigating the relationship between formal and informal learning in adulthood, in particular on the importance of informal learning for the workplace (Watkins and Marsick 1992; Colley et al. 2003; Livingstone 2006), there is much less data on informal learning in adolescence and even less about the interrelation between informal and formal learning (Rauschenbach 2006). However, one can assume that because of the particular situation of adolescents and the specific developmental demands and tasks which structure this phase, adolescent learning on the one hand differs from adult learning (Choy and Delahaye 2005) and on the other hand, serves as a starting point for the differentiation of learning modes and their relationships to each other. While in childhood the most important social spaces and consequently learning contexts are the family and educational institutions, in adolescence other spaces are added and become equally, or even more important. Specifically, these are peer-relations (Krüger et al. 2010; Riese et al. 2012) and (new) media (Drotner et al. 2008). However, there are not only new and more differentiated contexts of learning emerging; the already existing spaces are also changing. Research on adolescence as a crucial phase for identity formation shows that family relations are transformed and the meaning of school alters (Steinberg 2010; Arnett 2013; King 2013). In order to find out more about different modes of learning and their interrelation with each other and intersecting social conditions, we need to look at the adolescents' perspectives and listen to the adolescent learners' voices. However, before I come to the methodological and methodical implications, I will take a closer look at the notion of learning.

LEARNING AS A RELATIONAL EXPERIENCE

Both empirical data on learning and the various theoretical conceptions of learning cannot be adequately represented and sufficiently discussed in this chapter. Nevertheless, I shall localise the following research in terms of its understanding of learning as a situated and relational process that is experienced and sometimes also reflected on by the learning subject. Cognitivist and behaviourist approaches assume that learning is located *within* a person (Shuell 1986; Watson 1998). Even though the contexts might change, learning always functions in the same way and the focus lies on the optimal outcome; the process or mode of learning remains unnoticed as well as how different modes might interact.

I will focus on concepts that understand learning as a socially framed and influenced process, which reflects on the influence of the learning situation as well as on the learner's experience. These include social constructivist approaches (Bruner 1985), socio-cultural theories of learning (Lave and Wenger 1991) and transformative learning (Mezirow and Taylor 2009), which not only reflect on the social condition of learning but also plead for an emancipative understanding of the learner. Learning is part of the development of a critical consciousness, not only a process of attaining knowledge or skill adaptation. In these theories, the learner is an active and autonomous subject, and the focus lies on her agency and ability to potentially transform social structures. However, these approaches have set in as normative pedagogical ideas: learning from their point of view should lead to critical consciousness and should enable people to realise the hegemonic mechanisms of power that form and limit their agency. I want to start at an earlier point and have a look at how learning shows and is experienced *before* critical pedagogical intervention. In other words, how is learning interrelated with power structures and social categorisations that position learners in the first place?

The theory of relational learning (Künkler 2011) focusses on the question of how the learning subject is interwoven in complex relations to others as well as to given social conditions and structures. The learning subject of this concept is not autonomous, but decentred, which means she is fluid and constitutes herself in and through learning. It means furthermore that learning is not necessarily something we can control; it can also happen unwittingly and implicitly in a way we never expected it to happen. This may also imply that even if we plan to learn something particular/specific it may not work, no matter how hard we try. 'Learning would therefore be a process neither outside nor inside the subject, but in *between* (relationships to herself, to the world, and to others), and the process of learning would be characterised by a conditional range—due to the context of the situation as well as the person's experiential horizon—of self and externally determined options to act, which play a crucial role in each learning process' (Künkler 2008, p. 44, the emphasis and the translation is mine).

Hence, learning is always related to the learner and the social conditions and cannot be totally controlled. Consequently, if we talk about different modes of learning, we cannot only refer to formal and informal learning (and also non-formal learning), we also need to take into account the differentiation of explicit and implicit learning. What cannot be considered with this approach are the structural dimensions and categorisations that influence learning, in particular the implications of 'race'. Therefore, I will combine the relational learning theory with an intersecting perspective informed by Critical Race Theory (CRT).

RESEARCHING RELATIONAL LEARNING FROM A CRITICAL RACE PERSPECTIVE

One of the major challenges of qualitative research is to conceptualise the relationship of structure and agency and how it can be captured methodologically and methodically (Rosenthal and Fischer-Rosenthal 2004; Souto-Manning 2013). Since the relational theory of learning (Künkler 2011) is based significantly on post-structural theories, in particular the work of Butler (1997, 2004, 2011) and Foucault (1982), it can be confronted with the argument that it is not only relational but relativistic in terms of structural discrimination (Peters 2001). Instead of playing structural and post-structural theories off against each other, I would suggest to combine both perspectives in a mutually enriching way. Chadderton (2013) argues that this theoretical strategy would be promising, in particular, in terms of researching racial inequalities. By bringing together Butler's work on performativity and CRT (Ladson-Billings and Tate 1995; Delgado and Stefancic 2000; Taylor et al. 2009; Zamudio 2011), it is possible to develop a heuristic framework that recognises the persistence and power of structural inequalities and at the same time avoids an essentialist notion of the (learning) subject.

Whilst the subject is constituted and constrained by subjectivation, she is not wholly determined. Although she is dependent, she also has a certain agency created at the moment of subjectivation (Butler 1997). This is not a sovereign agency, rather the subject has discursive agency: agency within the limits of her subjection. This allows for a more complex understanding of resistance to dominant discourses, and the conditions under which resistance is possible, and indeed, that resistance may not necessarily be conscious or explicit, a factor that tends to be under-theorised in CRT. This notion therefore does not challenge the structural theory that master narratives such as white supremacy define societal relations to a large extent, but it extends and complicates it. (Chadderton 2013, p. 49)

CRT assumes that 'race' does matter, as it is one of the most important categorisations in terms of social differentiation and discrimination (Delgado and Stefanic 2000). Racism as a structural function that is deeply embedded in all social practices and discourses is endemic and has great impact on subjectivation and learning. Even though CRT originated from law studies (Crenshaw 1991) in the first place, it has made its way into the 'nice field of education' (Ladson-Billings and Tate 1995) and has already repeatedly demonstrated that educational inequalities are to a large extent caused by structural, institutional and personal racism (Ladson-Billings and Gillborn 2004). CRT can function as a critical tool that helps to avoid falling into deficit perspectives that tend to focus on the individual instead of the complexity of interrelation between structure and agency. Whilst CRT not only uncovers mechanisms of discrimination and even countereffective mechanisms of privilege, it also enables reflection on white supremacy (Leonardo 2009).

Furthermore, CRT takes into account that 'race' is powerful, but not the only issue in terms of discrimination. Actually, it has been stated from the beginning that different categorisations intersect (Crenshaw 1991), not simply adding to but rather leading to varying positions and hence varying forms of discrimination. Even though there are arguments about which and how many categorisations must be taken into account, there is some kind of consensus that some are omnipresent and relevant for all— though in very different ways (McCall 2005). These are 'race', gender and class. The following study on adolescent learning takes a CRT perspective that presumes that structural racism matters in terms of learning and how different modes of learning are interrelated. How these interrelations function and how they are experienced can only become visible through the voices of adolescents in a case-specific way.

LEARNING IN ADOLESCENCE: A STUDY ON INTERRELATIONS BETWEEN FORMAL AND INFORMAL LEARNING[1]

This innovative study investigates the interrelations between formal and informal learning inter alia as part of powerful differentiating practices in education by considering structural inequalities, in particular 'race', gender and class. One of the most important issues that emerged in the interviews was that of racial discrimination. Half of the adolescents we spoke with had a so-called migration background. When designing the study, I tried to avoid pre-determining conceptions of learning by using an open interview strategy (Schütze 1983; Fraser 2004). So, we were able to generate some narratives that give very interesting insights into practices and ideas of learning in early adolescence and how they interact, and also into the underlying structures that unconsciously affect learning or even determine what learning can be and how it is experienced by the subject.

The study includes 21 narrative qualitative interviews with 11–14-year-olds from different ethnic groups. The interviews were analysed with a narrative analysis (Rosenthal and Fischer-Rosenthal 2004) that enabled us to reconstruct the inherent logic of the interview on the content level as well as on the level of form and structure of speech. I chose two case studies to reconstruct the impact of 'race'.

Sara

First I will introduce Sara, a 12-year-old girl who lives in a small town in northern Germany whose parents immigrated to Germany from Sri Lanka. She is attending seventh grade in a comprehensive school. Her parents work for a large fast-food chain. Sara was born in Germany and grew up in the town where she still lives and where she also went to kindergarten and primary school. The interview with Sara turned out to be very halting since she gave very short answers and seemed to be very cautious of me as interviewer. I chose a very open interview design to enable the interviewees to choose their own direction and I was hoping for narrations that would give insights into their everyday lives. This hope was definitely not fulfilled by Sara; it was actually me who spoke the most.

I will now address the question of how in Sara's case dominant social structures interact with her learning. As Sara did not tell her story straight away, I started asking more concretely about her everyday life and about learning:

> 'I: Mhm. And at school- uhm, let's first have a look at school [S: Mhm.] at school (inaudible) can you tell a little bit about how you learn, like how it happens and in which (.) situations. (..)
>
> S: [coughs] well, (...) that is, uhm, important for me [I: Mhm.] well, to have a proper degree [I: Mhm.], that later on I'll have a proper job [I: Mhm.] and (.) yes I (.) want, uhm, to do something for that, well [laughs] (.) [I: Mhm.]
>
> I: So, for you it is important, to get good marks in school and [S: Mhm.] to achieve good results [S: Mhm.] And, okay, how-, uhm, (.) do you have an idea about your future career? (..)
>
> S: Mhmmm, (.) either a- a kindergarten teacher [I: Mhm.] or a doc-, well, pediatrician.
>
> I: Okay. And so, what is your goal now, that you are aiming for, so, what degree maybe? Or haven't you decided (.) yet?
>
> S: @I don't know yet@'[2]

Here we can see the structure of speech of the whole interview and also the dynamics of the interaction, including powerful attributions by the interviewer, myself. I ask Sara if she would tell me how she learns in a school situation. Hence, I am asking for the process, the performance of learning, and therefore presume *that* learning actually takes place and further that this is able to be articulated by Sara in this very setting. However, Sara does not speak about learning experiences as processes or performances but about something that really matters to her in terms of schooling: to get a proper degree in order to get a proper job. Hence, she focusses on the learning *outcome*, the aim of schooling, and states that she wants to do whatever is needed—yet what that exactly is remains unclear.

I haste to summarise her response and bring in the issue of performance: a good exam implies good marks. Hence, I created a relation that Sara never indicated. Then I ask her to concretise her career plans, whereupon she mentions two professions that differ greatly in term of status and obligations. In Germany, a kindergarten teacher does not require a university degree and abitur (A-levels) are not necessary, whereas to become a pediatrician a university degree is obligatory. What these professions have in common is that their subjects are children, and the (status) discrepancy is only marked by my questioning her degree aspirations here. After that she says, laughingly, that she does not know yet what degree she wants to purchase and study for.

My way of asking shows superiority in terms of possessing 'the right knowledge' about a meritocratic school system. When asked about it, Sara seems to not have the same insight or is not able to point them out. Yet, it becomes clear that she is very aware of her goals, and it could have been my responsibility to make the relations between expectations and goals transparent and with it my own powerful position. But even if the power relations seem to be very obvious in this interaction and ensure that the defining power (Foucault 1982) on my side is reproduced, spaces of resistance and agency also become visible—especially when Sara talks about experiences that she can be sure of are very different to mine:

> 'I: Mm, and uhm (..) can you maybe say something about, well, or can you remember something that maybe happened to you in school that was not so nice? (.) When you were angry, maybe, or sad? (..)
>
> S: Uhum, IIIIII am always called something like black [I: Mhm.] well that is because of my skin colour, [I: Mhm.] *I think to myself* that I (.) am not really (.) black, but that I am actually brown and *that is just how I was born* [I: Mhm.] and can do nothing about it and I can't change it. [I: Mhm.] Yes, [I: Mhm.] but I actually don't care about that, because my teacher said I must stay strong and (.) just not care. [I: Mhm.] Yes.
>
> I: Mhm. And who says something like that? (.)
>
> S: Mmmm (.) a couple of (.) boys for example, (.) a- they do that for fun, they say (.), but I am not sure, if I should believe them.'

I ask Sara if there is something annoying or sad she remembers from school. Thereupon she tells me about the racial ridicule she experiences in school and explains it at the same time, because she can suspect that I do not have these experiences as a 'white' academic woman. At the same time, it becomes clear that these experiences are very important, likely the worst experiences she has had in school. It is not something that happened once; she says that she is called 'something like black', a category that seems to be inappropriate from her perspective, and that it happens all the time (always). She assumes that this designation results from her skin colour, which also seems plausible to me ('Mhm'). However, Sara rejects that being black is the right description. She thinks she is not black at all, but rather brown, which appears to be better from her perspective than being black. Hence, she refers to a hierarchical idea of skin colours or 'races' and gets into a paradoxical position that shows exactly how Butler's concept of subjection works (Butler 1997): By referring to the discourse of racial hierarchies, she reiterates them as a given reality, as a powerful structure; at the same time, she deconstructs the discourse by showing that it is *not* evident at all what kind of skin colour a person has and what that means. Sara resists the prescription 'black' and refuses to identify with it, but she is only able to do so by referring to racist and racialising discourse.

Furthermore, Sara tries to ignore the discrimination by the boys because that is her teacher's advice. Now this is obviously problematic advice because the experience of racism is the worst experience Sara goes through in school; she is not able to ignore it. The strategy of ignoring racial discrimination or colour blindness is highly problematic and leads to a further stabilisation of racial inequalities and therefore works for white supremacy (Leonardo 2002). Sara's case shows clearly how racism works on different levels in Sara's life, in terms of her learning, but also within the interview interaction between her and me. On the other hand, it becomes clear that Sara is at the same time subjected to racist and racialising discourses and questions them by rejecting certain designations and evaluating the motives of racial behaviour: she doubts that the boys are just making fun.

Peter

Peter's case differs greatly from Sara's, but here also racism affects how different modes of learning are related to each other. When the interview took place, Peter was 14 years old. He was born in Russia and came to Germany when he was eight years old. His mother worked as a manager in Russia and is now learning German, but would like to work as manager again. Peter came to Germany with his mother and stepfather, who is a German citizen, a so-called *Aussiedler* (a group that is defined as ethnic German, because their antecedents emigrated from Prussia to Russia in the eighteenth century), who initiated the migration. Meanwhile the stepfather has left the family, including his four-year-old son, Peter's little brother. So, today Peter lives with the little boy and his mother in a flat in a small town in northern Germany. His biological father lives in Russia, and it seems that Peter has little or no contact with him because he does not really know what he is doing:

'Ehm, my father, he is in Russia? [mhm] He works in a car company, don't know exactly, something with cars, I guess. Eh, yes.'

Hence, Peter's father had been left behind by the 'new family' who was then left behind by the 'new' father, who initiated the immigration to Germany in the first place. Peter says nothing more about his stepfather. He just says that his mother is not able to go back to her former profession because she struggles with the German language. Language is a very central issue in Peter's narration, in particular the German language. When the family decided to leave Russia, Peter had already started to learn German. Still, after he arrived in Germany, he was put into a special class for learners of German as a second language, which Peter felt was a waste of time and was discriminatory because he had to repeat one class when he could already speak German. Despite being in this class, he picked up most of his German in everyday life and through media.

> 'Ehm, I think, what I have learned regardless of school is my German. [mhm] Ehm, when my mother and my stepfather had decided to move to Germany. We do learn German now. [mhm][...]And then I started to learn in Russia and when we arrived here, I heard something on TV and then I asked what does it mean and then I went on listening. [mhm] Yes.'

Even though Peter as an eight-year-old was not involved in the decision about the family's migration, he prepared actively by teaching himself the language. The German language is presented as the key to participation and to be successful. Peter wanted to become a manager like his mother when they were still in Russia. Hence, he is focused and school achievement is a very important issue for Peter. School seems to be the main topic in his life. The liveliest and most exciting sequences are connected with school and classroom situations. For example, when he talks about his science class where they did a 'lab license' and could do experiments on their own:

> 'Ehm, well I think the lab license was really exciting! (..) And yes. I wish that we could do something like that more often, because it is really exciting! [mhm] And the chemical reactions are really great! [mhm] So much can happen!'

All other activities are subordinate to school. When asked about learning activities in general or even outside of school, he talks about learning multiplication tables with his grandmother back in Russia, or picking up new English vocabulary while listening to music which would be useful for those corresponding school subjects. Because the mother is, at the moment, unable to participate in the workforce and to continue her former professional career, it is up to Peter and the little brother to pursue the family project of migration.

Applying CRT (Delgado and Stefancic 2000) now allows us to consider the racialised modes or frames of recognition that determine what is recognised as learning at all. This becomes very clear in the case of Peter: He presents himself as a very passionate and successful student. As an eight-year-old, he even prepared himself by learning German on his own before the family actually moved to Germany. After his arrival he *learns* not only that his German is considered insufficient and he is forced to repeat a class (which also leads to boredom in school) but also that his mother's career fails because of her lack of German language skills. Even after about six years in Germany, she is unable to work as a manager again.

Thus, for Peter, learning is always linked to the context of migration and associated attribution- or affiliation-discourses. In Germany in particular the language adaptation discourse is publicly and politically of great interest, especially since it is seen as a key aspect of 'integration': once immigrants speak German (although it remains unclear as to what level of German is acceptable), they would be able to participate in society and therefore to integrate (Esser 2009). Many of the measures that have been implemented to raise school performance of students of migration backgrounds focus on the language issue such as the German as a second language classes that Peter mentions (e.g. Ahrenholz 2010). Peter does not evaluate these measures, he only states that they cost him one year in his school career. Even though he learned German informally, this learning or level of learning was not accepted as appropriate and sufficient. Peter spoke German with me fluently, eloquently and without any accent. What and how Peter learns always has to be seen in his particular situation that is pre-structured by discourses on migration and language in Germany. At first sight, it looks as if Peter is not learning informally at all because school plays such a dominate role in his narration.

A closer look shows that he is learning a lot about practices of discrimination via prescription in German society. Besides this, he, as a 14-year-old, becomes the one who is in charge of continuing the family's project of migration that was originally initiated by his stepfather who is now gone. It can be concluded that in Peter's case, the opportunities to individually create some kind of adolescent moratorium are marginal; I assume that this correlates with restricted space for informal learning. The priorities for Peter are clearly set and it irritates him that school is not as important to all students as it is to him. This is one aspect that distinguishes Peter from Sara: for him the expectations of formal schooling seem to be absolutely clear and he is achieving quite well, especially in STEM subjects.

Nevertheless he is experiencing racial discrimination which is not caused by his skin colour but by his origin. As Ignatiev (2009) showed, what makes racial differences significant is not always and not only a matter of skin colour or any other phenotypical issues but is a result of social power relations and discourses that lead to specific—discriminated or privileged—positions which are related to skin colour. In this case, racism works via language or, more accurately, through the disregard of Peter's informal learning of the German language. He is denied recognition as a learner of German while it is assumed that he needs to learn the language the right way, for example, formally in school. Hence, racial discrimination makes it impossible for Peter to profit from his informal learning. Unlike in the interview with Sara, it was mostly Peter who spoke, and my position as interviewer was therefore less dominant. This does not mean that there was no power gap but it was not as apparent.

Conclusion

Through these two case studies, it became clear that white, middle-class ideas of learning not only dominate formal curricula but also what kind of informal learning is acceptable. Hence, not all informal learning is considered valuable for job qualifications or to enhance formal educational success. On the one hand, it depends on who is learning what under which conditions; and on the other, it relies on who determines what is recognised as 'useful' informal learning. Sara is obviously discriminated because of her 'race' and the social status of her family. Informal learning and formal learning do not really correspond and it seems that the often implicit demands of informal learning are not understandable for her. Structural discrimination shows inter alia through misrecognition Sara faces, for example, by her teacher but also by me, the interviewer. For Sara it is not actually the question of which type of informal learning can be helpful to her but of how to deal with the racism she 'always' experiences. This kind of informal learning must be taken into account to understand Sara's educational needs because it helps her to survive in the school context (Rollock 2012).

For Peter, informal learning seems to hold no importance; it is only the formal learning that leads to academic success that counts. His concern is for the stabilisation of the family's status. However, in Peter's case, structural racism also takes effect when his informally learned language skills are disregarded. Like Sara he recognises the discrimination and rejects its influence. Unlike Sara he is not puzzled by the intransparencies around him; he accepts his underprivileged position and aims to transform it via education. In other words, he sticks to the meritocratic ideal, but he has worked hard for it and he also submitted to the structural forces and repeated a year of school, even though he found it too easy. Hence, what does this study imply for multicultural dialogues in education? I argue that there is a need for research in education to recognise the racialised interrelationship between formal and informal learning (not only in early adolescence), and the way in which it affects educational trajectories. In early adolescence, it appears particularly important because modes of learning are being *learned* in the first place. We need to ask what informal and formal learning means in each case and how they are related to each other.

NOTES

1. This study has been funded by the Max-Traeger-Foundation: Grandnumer MTS-5162-2014. Special thanks go to the students that participated in the study: Julie Cossart, Imke Goßmann, Tobias Rehr and Mathias Schulze.
2. Rules of transcriptions: **bold** = loud; <u>underlined</u> = emphatic; small = softly; [laughs] = remarks, gestures and facial expressions; @...@ = laughing; (...) three seconds break; *italics* = fast.

REFERENCES

Ahrenholz, B. (Ed.). (2010). *Fachunterricht und Deutsch als Zweitsprache* [Subject lessons and German as a second language]. Tübingen: Narr.

Arnett, J. J. (2013). *Adolescence and emerging adulthood*. London: Pearson.

BAMF. (2016). *Das Bundesamt in Zahlen 2015. Asyl* [The Ministry in Numbers: Asylum] Bundesamt für Asyl und Migration. Retrieved from http://www.bamf.de/SharedDocs/Anlagen/DE/Publikationen/Broschueren/bundesamt-in-zahlen-2015-asyl.pdf?__blob=publicationFile

Baumert, J. (2002). *PISA 2000: Die Studie im Überblick. Grundlagen, Methoden und Ergebnisse* [PISA 2002: An Overview. Basics, Methods, and Results]. Weimar: RhinoVerlag.

Bruner, J. (1985). Models of the learner. *Educational Researcher, 14*(6), 5–8.

Butler, J. (1997). *The psychic life of power. Theories in subjection.* Stanford, CA: Stanford University Press.

Butler, J. (2004). *Undoing gender.* New York, NY: Routledge.

Butler, J. (2011). *Bodies that matter. On the discursive limits of "sex".* Abingdon, Oxon, New York: Routledge.

Chadderton, C. (2013). Towards a research framework for race in education. Critical race theory and Judith Butler. *International Journal of Qualitative Studies in Education, 26*(1), 39–55.

Choy, S. C., & Delahaye, B. L. (2005). *Some principles for youth learning.* Annual Conference of the Australian VET research Association (AVETRA). AVETRA. Brisbane, 2005.

Colley, H., Hodkinson, P., & Malcom, J. (2003). *Informality and formality in learning.* A report for the Learning and Skills Research Centre. Leeds: University of Leeds Lifelong Learning Institute.

Crenshaw, K. (1991). Mapping the margins. Intersectionality, identity politics, and violence against women of color. *Stanford Law Review, 43*(6), 1241–1299.

Delgado, R., & Stefancic, J. (2000). *Critical race theory. The cutting edge* (2nd ed.). Philadelphia: Temple University Press.

Drotner, K., Jensen, H. S., & Schrøder, K. (Eds.). (2008). *Informal learning and digital media.* Newcastle: Cambridge Scholars.

Düx, W., & Sass, E. (2005). Lernen in informellen Kontexten [Learning in Informal Contexts]. *Zeitschrift für Erziehungswissenschaft, 8*(3), 394–411.

Esser, H. (2009). Pluralisierung oder Assimilation? Effekte der multiplen Inklusion auf die Integration von Migranten [Pluralization or Assimilation? Effects of Multiple Inclusion on the Integration of Immigrants.] *Zeitschrift für Soziologie, 38*(5), 358–378.

Foucault, M. (1982). The subject and power. *Critical Inquiry, 8*(4), 777–795.

Fraser, H. (2004). Doing narrative research. Analysing personal stories line by line. *Qualitative Research and Social Work, 3*(2), 179–201.

Geißler, R., & Weber-Menges, S. (2009). Migrantenkinder im Bildungssystem: doppelt benachteiligt [Migrant-children in the Education System: Double Discrimination.] *Hessische Blätter für Volksbildung, 4*, 383–391.

Gogolin, I., & Banks, J. A. (2012). First-language and second-language learning. In J. A. Banks (Ed.), *Encyclopedia of diversity in education* (pp. 916–919). Thousand Oaks, CA: Sage.

Gogolin, I., Tajmel, T., & Starl, K. (2009). "Bildungssprache"—The importance of teaching language in every school subject. In T. Tajmel & K. Stahl (Eds.), *Science education unlimited. Approaches to equal opportunities in learning science* (pp. 91–102). Münster: Waxmann.

Gomolla, M., & Radtke, F. (2002). *Institutionelle Diskriminierung. Die Herstellung ethnischer Differenz in der Schule/* [Institutional discrimination. Doing ethnic difference in school]. Wiesbaden: VS Verlag für Sozialwissenschaften.

Ignatiev, N. (2009). *How the Irish became white.* New York, NY: Routledge.

King, V. (2013). *Die Entstehung des Neuen in der Adoleszenz* (2nd ed.). *Individuation, Generativität und Geschlecht in modernisierten Gesellschaften* [The Emergence of the New in Adolescence. Individuation, Generativity, and Gender]. Wiesbaden: Springer VS.

Krüger, H.-H., Köhler, S.-M., & Zschach, M. (2010). *Teenies und ihre Peers. Freundschaftsgruppen, Bildungsverläufe und soziale Ungleichheit* [Teens and their peers. Friends, educational trajectories, and social inequalities]. Opladen: Budrich.

Krüger, H.-H., Rabe-Kleberg, U., Kramer, R.-T., & Budde, J. (2011). *Bildungsungleichheit revisited. Bildung und soziale Ungleichheit vom Kindergarten bis zur Hochschule* [Educational inequality revisited]. Wiesbaden: VS Verlag.

Künkler, T. (2008). Lernen im Zwischen. Zum Zusammenhang von Lerntheorien, Subjektkonzeptionen und dem Vollzug des Lernens [Learning in between. About the relationship between subject-constructions and the process of learning]. In: K. Mitgutsch, E. Sattler, K. Westphal und I. M. Breinbauer (Eds.): *Dem Lernen auf der Spur. Die pädagogische Perspektive* [Tracing Learning. The pedagogical perspective], 33–49. Stuttgart: Klett-Cotta.

Künkler, T. (2011). *Lernen in Beziehung. Zum Verhältnis von Subjektivität und Relationalität in Lernprozessen* [Learning in relations. On the relation of subjectivity and relationality in learning]. Bielefeld: Transcript.

Ladson-Billings, G., & Gillborn, D. (Eds.). (2004). *The RoutledgeFalmer reader in multicultural education.* London: RoutledgeFalmer.

Ladson-Billings, G., & Tate, W. F. (1995). Toward a critical race theory of education. *Teachers College Record, 97,* 47–68.

Lave, J., & Wenger, E. (1991). *Situated learning. Legitimate peripheral participation. Repr.* Cambridge: Cambridge University Press.

Leonardo, Z. (2002). The souls of White Folk: Critical pedagogy, whiteness studies, and globalization discourse. *Race Ethnicity and Education, 5*(1), 29–50.

Leonardo, Z. (2009). *Race, whiteness, and education.* New York, NY: Routledge.

Leung, M. W. (2005). Beyond 'the Dragon' and Chop Suey: Understanding the regulated Chinese labour migration to Germany. In T. Geisen (Ed.), *Arbeitsmigration. WanderarbeiterInnen auf dem Weltmarkt Fuer Arbeitskraft* (pp. 137–157). Frankfurt: IKO Verlag für interkulturelle Kommunikation.

Livingstone, D. W. (2006). Informal learning: Conceptual distinctions and preliminary findings. In: Z. Bekerman, N. C. Burbules und D. Silberman-Keller (Eds.), *Learning in places. The informal education reader,* New York: P. Lang, 203–227.

McCall, L. (2005). The complexity of intersectionality. *Signs: Journal of Women in Culture and Society, 30*(3), 1771–1800.

Mecheril, P., Castro Varela, M., Dirim, I., Kalpaka, A., & Melter, C. (2010). *Migrationspädagogik* [Magration Pedagogy]. Weinheim: Beltz.

Mezirow, J. (1997). Transformative learning: Theory to practice. *New Directions for Adult and Continuing Education, 1997*(74), 5–12.

Mezirow, J., & Taylor, E. W. (2009). *Transformative learning in practice. Insights from community, workplace, and higher education.* San Francisco, CA: Jossey-Bass.

Peters, M. A. (2001). *Poststructuralism, marxism, and neoliberalism. Between theory and politics.* Lanham, MA: Rowman & Littlefield.

Rauschenbach, T. (Ed.) (2006). *Informelles Lernen im Jugendalter. Vernachlässigte Dimensionen der Bildungsdebatte* [Informal Learning in Adolescence. Neglected Dimensions of the Educational Debate]. Weinheim, München: Juventa.

Riese, H., Samara, A., & Lillejord, S. (2012). Peer relations in peer learning. *International Journal of Qualitative Studies in Education, 25*(5), 601–624.

Rollock, N. (2012). The invisibility of race. Intersectional reflections on the liminal space of alterity. *Race Ethnicity and Education, 15*(1), 65–84.

Rosenthal, G., & Fischer-Rosenthal, W. (2004). The analysis of narrative-biographical interviews. In U. Flick, E. von Kardorff, & I. Steinke (Eds.), *A companion to qualitative research* (pp. 259–265). London: Sage.

Schütze, F. (1983). Biographieforschung und narratives Interview [Biographical Research and Narrative Interviews] *Neue. Praxis, 13*, 283–293.

Shuell, T. J. (1986). Cognitive conceptions of learning. *Review of Educational Research, 56*(4), 411–436.

Souto-Manning, M. (2013). Critical narrative analysis. The interplay of critical discourse and narrative analyses. *International Journal of Qualitative Studies in Education, 27*(2), 159–180.

Statistisches Bundesamt. (2014). *Bevölkerung mit Migrationshintergrund—Ergebnisse des Mikrozensus* [Population with migration background—Results of the Micro-census]. https://www.destatis.de/DE/Publikationen/Thematisch/Bevoelkerung/MigrationIntegration/Migrationshintergrund20102201 47004.pdf?__blob=publicationFile

Steinberg, L. D. (2010). *Adolescence* (9th ed.). New York: McGraw-Hill.

Taylor, E., Gillborn, D., & Ladson-Billings, G. (2009). *Foundations of critical race theory in education.* New York: Routledge.

Watkins, K. E., & Marsick, V. J. (1992). Towards a theory of informal and incidental learning in organizations. *International Journal of Lifelong Education, 11*(4), 287–300.

Watson, J. B. (1998). *Behaviorism.* Piscataway, NJ: Transaction Publishers.

Zamudio, M. (2011). *Critical race theory matters. Education and ideology.* New York: Routledge.

Dr. Anke Wischmann is Deputy Professor in Education with an emphasis on socialisation at the University of Hamburg (Germany). Before that she worked as a research fellow at the Universities of Oldenburg and Lüneburg (Germany). She wrote her PhD on processes of self-formation in adolescence under conditions of social inequality. Her research focuses on social justice issues in education by referring to critical theories, post-structural approaches and conducting qualitative research, especially by using biographic and ethnographic methods.

Politics and Policy Changes in Minority Education in China: The Case of XinYang

Fei Yan and Geoff Whitty

INTRODUCTION

The challenge of education for ethnic minorities, no matter in which part of the world, has always been an issue for governments as it is closely related to the ever pressing problems of social equality, social mobility, social cohesion and, more broadly, national identity. The provision of education might be an important way in which ethnic minorities can enhance both their personal and professional skills in the labour market, and consolidate their group identity and political status in broader society. However, it could also be used by the State to establish social control over ethnic minorities by different or even opposite approaches such as assimilationist and some versions of multicultural education. The aim is to form a certain sense of nationhood, to create loyal or patriotic citizens and finally to maintain national unity. In most societies, both these tendencies are in evidence, as is a tension between them.

Although China has often been seen as a homogeneous society with its 1.3 billion members sharing one culture (i.e. Confucianism) and speaking

F. Yan (✉)
Institute of Education, University College London, London, UK

G. Whitty
Bath Spa University, London, UK

© The Author(s) 2018
R. Race (ed.), *Advancing Multicultural Dialogues in Education*,
DOI 10.1007/978-3-319-60558-6_18

313

one language (i.e. Mandarin Chinese) (Hobsbawm 1990, 66). It is actually a multi-ethnic society, with the dominant ethnic Han group accounting for about 91% of the total population and 55 so-called minority ethnic groups (*shaoshu minzu*) accounting for more than 100 million (about 9%) of the total population (Chinese Statistics 2010). Located in China's far north-west corner and bordered by eight countries, Xinjiang, or the Xinjiang Uyghur Autonomous Region (XUAR) as it has officially been called in China since 1955, has a heavily multi-ethnic population. According to the official statistics, Xinjiang is home to 13 native ethnic groups, including 8.2 million Uyghur, 7.7 million Han, and other ethnic groups whose populations range from 5000 (Russian) to 1.4 million (Kazak). Among the 13 ethnic groups, 7 of them are Muslim (including Uyghur), and 5 of them (including Uyghur) speak Turkish dialects. Meanwhile, Mandarin Chinese is widely used among the Han, Hui and Manchu ethnic groups in this region. Therefore, Xinjiang is seen as an especially multicultural and multilingual part of China,[1] although one in which one particular minority ethnic group—the Uyghur—predominates. This chapter focuses on relations between Han and Uyghur peoples, but a full exploration of the possibilities and problems of "multicultural dialogues" in Xinjiang would need to embrace the experiences of all 13 nationalities living in the region.

In recent years, Xinjiang has been experiencing a period of intensive ethnic tension which is evidenced by various "terror" attacks and violent inter-ethnic conflicts.[2] There is no doubt that Xinjiang is now becoming one of the country's most politically sensitive regions, arguably even more so than Tibet. Therefore, Xinjiang has become an important target of China's nation building project. Indeed, since the Communist Party of China (CPC) first governed Xinjiang in 1949, it has adopted different strategies to integrate this land and its people into the Chinese nation.

This chapter first reviews the general strategies adopted by the CPC government to integrate its minority ethnic groups and how these strategies have shifted in accordance with changes of political climate in the central government in Beijing. Four periods are identified in this chapter according to the dominant development strategies adopted by the central government—the Socialist period (1949–1976), the Modernization period (1976–1989), the Patriotic period (1989–2008) and the Paradox period (2008-present).[3] It analyzes how particular education policies were adopted to support the aim of the integration of minority ethnic groups in each of these periods. Important education policies such as "bilingual education" and the "in-land class system"[4] are particularly examined since they are often seen as two of the most important integration policies that have applied in the education system in Xinjiang.

We argue that while these policies are presented as facilitating the integration of minority ethnic groups into Chinese society, in practice they do not always constitute genuinely multicultural education. In our view, this should entail intercultural dialogues that respect the cultural identities of all learners. Such an education also needs to provide them with the knowledge, skills and attitudes necessary to achieve full participation in society, while fostering respect, understanding and solidarity among individuals, ethnic, social, cultural and religious groups and nations (UNESCO 2006). Finally, based on the discussion of policies, this chapter will suggest what might be necessary to achieve genuine multiculturalism in the Chinese education system and potentially reduce ethnic tension in Xinjiang.

THE SOCIALIST PERIOD (1949–1976)

As a political party founded on the ideological base of Marxism-Leninism and further developed by Maoist thought, it became imperative after the foundation of the People's Republic of China (PRC) in 1949 for the CPC to spread its ideology to every part of China in order to legitimize its authority as well as consolidate its power over all people in China including both the majority Han and the ethnic minorities. To the Communist leaders, it seemed the most effective way that a united new China could be built was by unification of all Chinese people around a common Socialist ideology (Chen 1981; Hawkins 1978; Hu 1974). Arguably, it was the first time in Chinese history that a rather civic idea of citizenship was adopted, since at least in theory Communism denies cultural discrimination and promotes equal relations among different ethnic groups in China. Indeed, according to Article 53 of the Interim Constitution of the PRC, a degree of local autonomy in ethnic minority regions was promoted and minority ethnic groups were supposed to have "... freedom to develop their dialects and languages, and to preserve or reform their traditions, customs, and religious beliefs" (Dwyer 2005, p. 7). Based on this spirit, the CPC government aimed to establish "... a new governance and society", designed to promote equal relationships between different ethnic groups including between the dominant Han and the various minority ethnic groups (ibid).

So in the early years of the PRC (prior to 1956), the education policies that were adopted in minority ethnic regions were quite liberal and have thus been considered "admirable" (Dwyer 2005, p. 7), since minorities' local conditions and their distinct cultures were taken into consideration (Bass 1998; Bulag 2002; Hawkins 1983). In fact, the CPC government offered two types of schools in minority ethnic regions such as Xinjiang. These were "nationality schools" (*minxiao*), which not only used the mother tongue of major minority ethnic groups (such as Uyghur and Kazak) as the medium for instruction but also provided specific curricula for minorities, including minority literature, history, and so on, and Han schools (*hanxiao*), where minority ethnic students could learn in a Mandarin environment and study exactly the same curriculum as Han students. Thus, within an overall national education system, minority ethnic students were able to make their own choice of schooling. Meanwhile, Han Chinese students in Xinjiang also had the option to study the Uyghur language as this would help them to work better in the region (Stites 1999). Also, although most textbooks used by ethnic minorities were translated from Han Chinese books, some special working groups were set up to compile textbooks specifically for ethnic minorities in order to respond to their local needs and demands (Bass 1998). Moreover, according to Bass (1998), the minorities' stories, mythological characters and historical figures were introduced in textbook published during this period.

This dual school system also reflected a plural language policy which, to a large extent, guaranteed minority ethnic groups the right to use their mother tongue in schools. In fact, the report of the first national conference on ethnic minority education held in 1951 claimed that "… to ethnic minority groups which have developed their own writing script such as Mongol, Korean, Uyghur, Kazak and Tibetan, all the subjects in primary and secondary schools must be taught in their native language" (Wang 2003, 27). In the early and middle 1950s, local languages were encouraged as mediums of instruction in classrooms in Xinjiang. This language policy was seen as "… responsive to local conditions and arguably one of the more flexible in the world" (Dwyer 2005, xi). It was also claimed that this pluralistic language policy was "… generally well received by ethnic minority groups" (Dwyer 2005, x).

However, things changed dramatically as a result of political struggles in the central Chinese government. During the Anti-rightist Campaign (1957–1958), Great Leap Forward (1958–1960) and the Cultural

Revolution (1966–1976), indoctrination of Maoist political ideology often became a national priority. The promotion of socialist ideology and class struggle led to a rejection of the cultures of different ethnic groups which in turn led to an almost exclusive focus on the idea of "ethnic fusion" (*minzu ronghe*) (Wang 2003, 30). As a result, elements of distinctive minority ethnic cultures, such as values, religions and customs were seen to be against the supposedly culture-free ideology of Communism. They became objects of the "cultural" revolution and were all attacked and seen as needing to be "swept over" (Bass 1998; Hawkins 1978).

It was against this background that education in minority ethnic regions became assimilationist and the cultures of minority ethnic groups were re-interpreted within the education system. Schools for minority ethnic groups (*minxiao*) were forced to use Chinese as the medium of instruction while the previous concessions that allowed culturally specific education for ethnic minorities were now abolished. Accordingly, in the education system, textbooks were rewritten again to consist almost entirely of socialist ideological content (Bass 1998). In fact, characteristics of minority cultures were now typically condemned as "feudal" and were explicitly regarded as "backward and useless" (Wang 2003, 31). As a result of this monocultural and monolinguistic approach to schooling, many ethnic minority students were still "illiterate" even after 6 or 7 years in schools (ibid).

After the death of Chairman Mao in 1976, the CPC became increasingly aware that socialist ideologies alone were not capable of coping with either the aftermath of the devastation of the Cultural Revolution, or the new challenges posed by the need to improve the "material condition" (*wuzhi tiaojian*) of the Chinese people. The CPC therefore embarked on a shift of priority in national strategy, which would re-justify its legitimacy and authority.

THE MODERNIZATION PERIOD (1976–1980s)

After the end of the Cultural Revolution, the most urgent task for the CPC was to redevelop the devastated Chinese economy and to achieve the aim of modernizing China. So in the reform period in the 1980s, economics came to be regarded as rather more urgent than political indoctrination and became the new emphasis of China's development strategy. Economic development, however, as seen by the CPC could only be achieved by high quality human resources. Therefore, the CPC started to re-emphasize education as a means to create experts and mass produce labour (Bass 1998). The aims of education were now to be largely economically orientated and related to productivity and growth of the nation.

The shift in national policy and ideology towards economic growth and the modernization of China under Deng Xiaoping's leadership (1978–1989) also impacted upon the treatment of minority ethnic education in China. In 1981, the "National Conference on Education for Ethnic Minorities" laid down a strategy for readjusting and developing minority ethnic education so that these sectors of society could help meet the industrialization and economic targets of modernization (Bass 1998). Accordingly, some reform measures which were adopted widely across inland China were also implemented in minority ethnic regions. These included the introduction of competitive public examinations (such as the *gaokao*—the national examination for university enrolment); the establishment of "key" schools; the expansion of basic education (at least at the beginning of the reform period); and the boarding school programme, which was particularly promoted because a large percentage of the minority ethnic population lived in rural and remote areas of China (Bass 1998; Hawkins 1983; Murphy 2004).

Moreover, the CPC issued various policies specifically to upskill the minority ethnic labour force. For instance, minority ethnic students were given preferable treatment such as a lower minimum examination score to enter university. In 1984, a special "in-land class" (*neidi ban*) (a kind of boarding school) was established in secondary schools across in-land China for students from Tibet to enjoy free and high quality education (Bass 1998; Postiglione 2009; Zhu 2007).

The decrease of political indoctrination through socialist ideology in this period also relaxed constraints on the cultural expression of minority ethnic groups and provided more space for them to claim distinctive cultural identities. In 1984, two important laws were enacted—the "Nationality Law" and the "Regional Autonomy Law"—both aimed to protect minority ethnic groups' rights to cultural autonomy. Therefore, in many ways, minority ethnic groups' culture and their special needs were acknowledged and respected and it appeared that, during this period, many policies and practices towards minority ethnic groups reflected the spirit of multiculturalism.

This multicultural spirit led to two major changes in education policies in minority regions such as Xinjiang. First, during the 1980s, specific minority ethnic cultures were recognized in the education system, and a local curriculum was initiated to respond to minority ethnic groups' needs (Bass 1998). For instance, traditional minority ethnic literature, which had been previously denounced as "feudal" and "backward", was now reintroduced and taught in schools. Furthermore, several new unified sets of textbooks were also published and distributed in China during the 1980s, which included more specific information about the cultures of local ethnic minorities (Bass 1998; Hawkins 1983). Second, the new policies reaffirmed the right of minority ethnic groups to use their language in the education system. This included the use of their mother tongue as a medium for instruction in schools and the compilation and publication of textbooks in minority languages (ibid).

Therefore, during this period, bilingual education was widely promoted in Xinjiang, and the major model of schooling for minority ethnic students in Xinjiang was to use their mother tongue (such as Uyghur) in the teaching of all subjects in primary and secondary schools except Chinese which was taught as a subject of second language (Wang 2003, p. 46). In other words, minority ethnic students were able to mainly use their mother tongue in schools until they reached university and college levels. Wang (2003) shows that bilingual education in this period was generally welcomed since it helped minority students to become excellent in "… both nationality and Chinese (language and culture)" (*min-han jiantong*)— producing a desired kind of person that the education system was trying to cultivate.

However, the push for the improvement of education quality and the spirit of multiculturalism did not necessarily result in greater equity in education. The rhetoric of "modernization" nevertheless implied an unequal power relationship between Han Chinese and non-Han Chinese groups since the former were regarded as the most advanced in terms of economic development, whereas most non-Han Chinese lived in less developed areas. Therefore, minority ethnic groups were often seen not only as "inferior" compared to the "superior" Han but also as "backward" or as "… vulnerable and in need of help, special consideration and advanced training from their more sophisticated and cultured Han brethren" (Hawkins 1983, 194).

There was thus a tension in the policy between an apparent endorsement of the value of diverse cultures and a clear hierarchy among them, at least in terms of their perceived economic value. Although minority ethnic group identities were no longer largely suppressed in the relatively more tolerant political environment, they found that the "modernization" approach did not "… solve the real problems of educational and economic inequity between China's majority (Han) and numerous minorities" (Hawkins 1983, 200). While the "modernization" project and its related ideologies of "economic development" continue to be a state priority even until the present day, the CPC had to adopt new strategies in order to cope with the increasing resistance from minority ethnic groups.

THE PATRIOTIC PERIOD (1989–2008)

At the end of the 1980s, the rule of the CPC faced a serious threat resulting from a continuing decline of public faith in socialism. In order to regain legitimacy after the huge anti-government demonstration in Tiananmen Square [in 1989], the CPC launched a "state-led systematic engineered project" to promote patriotism. This was referred to as the "Patriotic Education Campaign" (PEC) in official discourse (Zhao 2004, 238). The campaign was intended for all Chinese citizens of all generations, irrespective of their ethnicity or class and was an intensive undertaking by the CPC during the period 1991 to 1994. Thereafter patriotism became one of the fundamental, intrinsic and core values propagated through the Chinese education system (He and Guo 2000; Vickers 2009; Zhao 2004).

Zhao (2004, 219) points out that the teaching goals of the PEC in the education system were achieved particularly through instruction on China's unique "long history, flourishing culture, and glorious tradition", so that students could learn the "idea of the country" (*guojia guannian*) through the cultivation of a strong national consciousness (Hughes 2003; He and Guo 2000; Vickers 2009; Zhao 2004). As a result, there was a shift from the previous domination of a socialist narrative to a nationalist narrative, which now focused more on the distinctiveness of China. Subsequently, not only was there a renewed interest in themes such as "common ancestry" (i.e. the Yellow Emperor) in official and public discourse, but Confucianism which had been heavily attacked during the Cultural Revolution was now regarded as the soul of the Chinese culture and the foundation of the Chinese nation. This helped Chinese people to "… guard the gates against western decadence" (He and Guo 2000).

Meanwhile, in order to cope with the increasing separatist feelings among minority ethnic groups in Tibet and Xinjiang, the CPC government adopted an overriding ideology in order to manage inter-ethnic relations—"minzu tuanjie", meaning "solidarity among nationalities"[5] (Bulag 2002, p. 12). Under this ideology of "solidarity among nationalities", the "multipleness" of China was now replaced by the focus on "oneness". Minority ethnic groups' distinctive cultures, which had been tolerated and even promoted in the education system in the 1980s, were once again denounced since they potentially led to multiple ethnic nationalisms (Zhao 2004). Instead, links between minority ethnic groups and the "motherland" were strongly promoted in order to stimulate national sentiment among non-Han peoples. For example, cultural exchange and trade between Han and minority ethnic groups in history were emphasized, whereas wars and conflicts between them were downplayed in history textbooks produced in this period (Baranovitch 2010). Bulag (2002) also gave the vivid example that forced inter-marriages between Han and minority ethnic groups in history were now celebrated as implicit evidence of blood-links between them although they had been condemned as humiliation of the Han Chinese in the previous period.

Against this background, bilingual education and the in-land class system, both of which aimed to integrate minority ethnic students in Xinjiang, experienced a massive expansion in the 1990s and 2000s (though both of the policies were initiated in 1980s). However, during this period, so-called bilingual education started to move away from a model that prioritized the mother tongue of minority ethnic groups to a model that increasingly encouraged using Mandarin Chinese as the medium of instruction in schools in minority ethnic regions. Indeed, not only did the Chinese Ministry of Education (which was called the Education Commission then) announce a plan to implement a regular "Chinese competence test" (HSK)[6] in all minority schools in 1992, but Chinese instruction now began in the first grade of primary school in Xinjiang (Dwyer 2005, pp. 33–37), much earlier than during the previous period. It seemed to some commentators that the government was aiming to make Mandarin Chinese the primary or sole language for instruction in all schools (Schluessel 2007, p. 257).

In 2000, the CPC also decided to extend the in-land class system to students from Xinjiang. The number of students enrolled for Xinjiang in-land classes has increased steadily from 1000 in 2000 to 5000 in 2007 (Chinese Government 2013). The purpose of this initiative was to improve the quality of education and to produce a more skilled labour force for local economic development. But it should also be noted that this system had become strategically important for minority ethnic education as it also played a significant role in training *patriotic* minority ethnic students. In fact, within the document of Chinese Ministry of Education (MOE), "… carrying on patriotic education" and "cultivating patriotic citizens" were repeatedly mentioned to highlight the idea of "… support the leadership of [the] Communist party, love the socialist motherland and support the unification of the nation and solidarity among nationalities" (MOE 2000).

However, as noted by Bulag (2002), the concept of "minzu tuanjie" (solidarity among nationalities) did not necessarily lead to strong social cohesion and an equal relationship between ethnic groups. Instead, since this "oneness" is largely defined by Han culture and its ideologies, the promotion of unity among ethnic groups inevitably resulted in a hegemonic power relationship between the Han-dominated nation state and non-Han Chinese peoples, as arguably the welfare of the wider nation state was upheld at the expense of the minority ethnic groups. Under the rhetoric of "minzu tuanjie", the minority ethnic groups' demands for equality, cultural dignity, and autonomy were perceived as "futile, and jeopardizing", both to the minority and to the Chinese nation, as claimed by the government (ibid). In other words, although in theory "minzu tuanjie" aimed to establish a harmonized relationship between ethnic groups, in reality it helped the state to establish a unified and even homogenized nation (ibid).

When non-Han Chinese do not accept and embrace this Han version of "Chineseness", then the unity and legitimacy of the Chinese nation is seen to be challenged and threatened (He and Guo 2000). Although, to counter this, the Chinese government has put enormous economic investment into Xinjiang (and into Tibet as well) in recent years, it seems that this approach to integration has not so far reduced resistance from minority ethnic groups which has become even more intensive recently.

The Paradox Period (2008–)

Since 2008, there has been a series of ethnic clashes and so-called terrorist attacks across China, which has exposed the serious problem of ethnic relations in China. The CPC government immediately responded to these incidents by organizing several important conferences and issuing several significant policies and statements. The conference reports and the policies could be interpreted as signalling a shift of governing strategy in unstable minority ethnic regions—from "leap-forward development" (*kuayueshi fazhan*, which focused more on economic development) to "social stability" (*shehui wending*) (CHINA 2014a). This adjustment had the implication that the major focus of the CPC's governance in these regions in future would be on inter-ethnic relations as this would be the key to achieving social stability and social cohesion in such regions. One of the statements pointed out that there is a need to build a "... mutually embedded social structure and community" where different ethnic groups are urged to work on "mutual understanding, mutual studying, mutual tolerance, mutual appreciation and mutual help" (Xinhua 2014). The use of the word "mutually/mutual" here could be read to signal a greater commitment to the spirit of ethnic equality and intercultural dialogues in China in future. Moreover, the National Work Forum on Nationalities, which was held in September 2014, pointed out that any discrimination against minority ethnic groups should be strictly prohibited and corrected (PEOPLE 2014).

Education in particular has been seen as a priority in achieving social stability and cohesion in Xinjiang. Indeed, students from different ethnic backgrounds are now to be encouraged to "... play together, study together and grow up together" (CHINA 2014b). Similarly, during a visit to Xinjiang, President Xi specifically encouraged a Han teacher to learn the Uyghur language in order to teach the students better, an approach that goes beyond prevailing approaches to bilingual education in Xinjiang in recent times. Meanwhile, previous education interventions such as the bilingual education and in-land class system have also experienced a further expansion since 2009. Bilingual education has now been expanded to kindergarten level and it was reported that more than 92% of minority ethnic children in Xinjiang are studying in bilingual kindergartens (Minzuban 2013). The number of students enrolled in the Xinjiang in-land classes reached almost 10,000 in 2015, 10 times more than the year 2000 when the programme was launched (Xinjiang Class 2015).

New education interventions were also introduced at local and central levels. In 2013, the CPC government decided to provide 12 years of free education for children in Kashgar in Southern Xinjiang where Muslim Uyghur are the dominant inhabitants (this is an area also where many "terrorist attacks" took place), compared to only 9 years in most parts of the country (China Daily 2013, p. 8). At the end of 2008 (after the Tibet ethnic clash), the Chinese Ministry of Education (MOE 2008) issued a curriculum guideline to introduce a new school subject called "Education for Solidarity among Nationalities" (*minzu tuanjie jiaoyu*) to be taught in primary and secondary school across China. According to the guidelines, the curriculum was to cover areas from basic knowledge about ethnic groups in China, such as their customs, festivals, cultures and heroes and so on, to more abstract and complex issues such as Marxist theories of ethnic relations and national policies on the issue. More importantly, it was reported that the knowledge of the new curriculum would be included in the "gaokao" (the national examination for university enrolment), which would definitely give the curriculum a significant status and encourage students to study it (MOE 2009).

While the above-mentioned initiatives all show positive signs of movement towards a more equal ethnic relationship and generally reflect the spirit of multicultural dialogue, these encouraging shifts in political rhetoric have to be seen alongside reported crackdowns not only on alleged terrorist activity (BBC 2014) but also on Uyghur cultural practices (Wang 2014). In May 2014, the Chinese government launched a year-long massive and rigorous nationwide campaign to eradicate terrorism and within a month, in Xinjiang alone, the government reported that about 32 "terrorist groups" were destroyed and more than 380 suspects of "terrorists" were arrested (ChinaPeace 2014). In addition, about 21 so-called illegal religious study centres were closed (ibid). In September 2014, IIham Tohti, a Uyghur former lecturer at Minzu University, was jailed for life for allegedly advocating independence for his home province Xinjiang, even though his supporters insisted that he was a moderate critic (ABC News 2014). In January 2015, the city of Urumqi, issued a regulation to prohibit the wearing of Islamic dress (jil bab) and veils (hijab) in public areas (PEOPLE 2015). All these measures constitute stricter regulation of ethnicity and religion at the current time. Meanwhile, it seems that the CPC government believes the reason of rise of the "three powers" (*sangu shili*, i.e. the "terrorist", the "separatist" and the "extremist") in Xinjiang was due to weak awareness of national identity among minority ethnic groups (Leibold 2013). Therefore, there has been an overwhelming emphasis on "a shared national identity" in government policies since then.

As Dwyer (2005, 30) pointed out, the "overarching national identity (Zhongguo ren, "person of China")" may reduce the cultural and linguistic diversity in China and eventually lead to assimilation of minority ethnic groups. It seems that, on the one hand, the current policies appear to promote equal ethnic relationships, while on the other hand, they can be seen to encourage the development of a monocultural and monolingual Chinese nation. Indeed, although there are a few signs of encouragement to Han Chinese to learn minority ethnic languages, bilingual education in

Xinjiang still largely means minority ethnic groups learning Chinese. It seems that in the future the CPC government aims to implement a model of bilingual education in all schools in Xinjiang, which requires all school subjects to be taught through Mandarin except the "Language and Literature" of their own language (Zhu 2013). Indeed, a recent policy from the Xinjiang government plans to send about 3000 officials and civil servants to become teachers in kindergartens in Southern Xinjiang and to help minority ethnic children to learn Mandarin Chinese (Xinjiang Education 2016).The languages of minority ethnic groups are therefore further marginalized in the current educational developments, leading to a deterioration of minority students' skills in their mother tongue. This situation echoes Dwyer's (2005, 10) argument that " ... establishing and fostering national unity required promoting Standard Mandarin Chinese to a dominant position at the expense of all other languages, including other varieties of Chinese".

Similarly, the overwhelming focus on the "nation" may also lead to "suppression" or "dilution" of ethnic identities. Dwyer (2005, 30) noted that there has been increasing use of a new non-ethnic identity, Xinjiang ren ("a person of Xinjiang") in the media in recent years. In fact, not only do many Han Chinese in the region now call themselves "Xinjiang ren", but "... the large increases in the Xinjiang Han population over the last decade have prompted debates over whether the ethnonym Uyghur should be deleted from the administrative toponym 'Xinjiang Uyghur Autonomous Region'" (ibid). Moreover, in their reform proposals for ethnic issues, two prominent scholars, Ma Rong and Hu Angang,[7] advocated the idea of weakening ethnic identity or consciousness and replacing it with "a collective sense of national belonging" (Ma 2009, cited in Leibold 2013, 18) or "a shared sense of civic belonging" (Hu and Hu 2011, cited in Leibold 2013, 21)—both aiming to dilute or remove ethno-cultural identity in future.

This tendency, compared to policies which encourage a more multicultural spirit and equal ethnic relationship, reflects the paradoxical nature of current Chinese governance in minority ethnic regions such as Xinjiang.[8] As the current policies are still at their early stage of implementation, it is too early to conclude whether these various policies will pan out and articulate with each other. However, as Leibold and Chen (2014) have pointed out, neither the encouragement of inter-ethnic contact nor the promotion of a shared national identity "address the underlying yet chronic racism in Chinese society". Indeed, unless such issues of institutional discrimination and inequality within the assumed national framework are widely acknowledged and tackled, the tension within the paradoxical policies will not be resolved easily in future.

Conclusion

This chapter has briefly examined policy changes in minority education in China and how the changes responded to wider shifts in the political climate. The case of Xinjiang was particularly discussed as an example of policy intervention in one of China's most multi-ethnic regions. This demonstrated that the Chinese central government had adopted various ways to integrate its minority ethnic population in different periods. Although in some periods education policies (e.g. language instruction and school choice) tended to embrace the spirit of pluralism and multiculturalism, these policies have themselves not necessarily guaranteed equal ethnic relations and educational equality. Law (2012, 59) also concluded that Chinese minority ethnic education policies merely recruit "ethnic cadres" to support a strategy of "racial sinicization". Dwyer (2005) regard bilingual education in China as really monolingual education in Mandarin Chinese and the in-land classes as essentially assimilationist in effect. Therefore, these policies certainly do not seem to have yet been successful in overcoming inter-ethnic tensions in the region, as evidenced in recent alleged "terror attacks" in Xinjiang itself and other cities in China.

As we have tried to demonstrate, at the core of the problem is the challenge of achieving an appropriate balance between "unity and diversity".[9] Other scholars (Vickers 2006; Zhao 2004) too have suggested that long-standing tensions between various discourses about national and ethnic identity have not really been resolved in contemporary official discourse. Indeed, while China has long been claiming itself as "unitary multi-ethnic nation" (*tongyi de duominzu guojia*), "diversity" has often been seen as potentially threatening to the concept of Chinese nationhood (Dwyer 2005, 30–31). Under the rhetoric of Chinese nationalism, "… reducing hundreds of ethnic histories, identities, and languages to the same simple categories and trajectories was seen by the new central government as crucial in building national unity" (Dwyer 2005, 21). When this focus on nationhood and the whole process of "nationalizing" merges with the culture and ideology of the dominant Han group, there is a risk of "great Han Chauvinism" (*da Hanzu zhuyi*) which heavily promotes Han cultural assimilation (or Sinicization) and therefore seriously damages ethnic and cultural diversity in China (Gladney 1988, 226–227).

Therefore, we would argue that there is an urgent need to re-think "Chineseness", so that the current Han dominant vision of China can be replaced with a new vision of multi-ethnic China. Indeed, it is difficult to envisage genuine education equality among different ethnic groups happening in schools on any significant scale in the absence of wider changes in Chinese society, as it is the wider conception of citizenship in a society that largely defines the nature of nationhood and the position of minority ethnic groups in the national framework. As mentioned before, the CPC established the PRC on the basis of a civic Chinese citizenship predicated on the acceptance of Communist ideology rather than on ethnic background. In theory, then, the Chinese government is anti-racist and promotes equality between ethnic groups in China. This is the doctrine of the 56 nationalities that comprise the Chinese people.

However, some researchers maintain that, in practice, there are elements of racism evident in contemporary Chinese society (Dikötter 1992; Law 2012). According to Law (2012), minority ethnic groups such as the Uyghur and Tibetan peoples suffer from institutional racism. He suggests that the social system in China is Han-centric and that minority ethnic groups are not only culturally marginalized but are also discriminated against economically and politically. It is therefore necessary for scholars and policy-makers to address these wider structural issues and understand better how they affect education.

Although it has sometimes been objected by Chinese politicians that racism itself is a Western concept (Dikötter 1992), building a "unitary multi-ethnic" China must surely involve discussion of apparently "racial" differences, whatever their provenance. It is noted that there has been no distinctively anti-racist phase in policies with regard to minority ethnic education in China.[10] Nor has there so far been much evidence of the influence of critical race theory within Chinese educational studies. This approach, which originated in the USA, recognizes the prevalence of racial inequality in society and seeks to demonstrate the way in which racial inequality is maintained through the operation of structures and assumptions that appear normal and unremarkable (Rollock and Gillborn 2011).

In various parts of the world, discussion of such matters in educational studies and teacher education courses has facilitated a greater awareness of the extent to which the education of diverse ethnic groups is a challenge not just to those involved in the education of minority ethnic students themselves but also to those involved in the education of the dominant group in society (Gaine 1987). In this case, the Han majority in a Chinese context means that changes need to take place not only in the education of minority ethnic groups, nor even just in the education of all nationalities in Xinjiang, but also in the education of students of all nationalities throughout China. Only when this is recognized can genuinely multicultural and intercultural education dialogues in education likely to prove possible in places like Xinjiang.

NOTES

1. Xinjiang is also bordered by eight countries which are the Republic of Mongolia, Russia, Kazakhstan, Kyrgyzstan, Tajikistan, Pakistan, Afghanistan and India. There are significant number of same ethnic groups living in both sides of the border, for example, Kazaks in both Kazakhstan and Xinjiang.
2. More than 10 incidents described as "terror attacks" or "ethnic riots" took place in 5 years up to 2014, and the number has escalated subsequently. In the most serious incident, which occurred on 5 July 2009, almost 200 fatalities were reported. At least as significant are various forms of "everyday resistance" identified by Bovingdon (2010).
3. Periodization is not an exact science and some scholars (Hawkins 1983; Wang 2003) prefer a two-phase periodization with a division in the mid-1970s. We identify some shifts in education policy within these broad periods. Furthermore, different approaches to minority ethnic education often co-exist, and there is sometimes a return to earlier forms as may be happening now.
4. "In-land" normally refers to the region between Chinese western border regions and eastern coast regions where Han are the main residents. The "in-land class" refers to a particular type of boarding school established mainly for minority ethnic students from Tibet and Xinjiang. The difference between a Han boarding school and an in-land class is that, whereas Han children are generally sent to board in the nearest urban centre, "minority" students from Tibet or Xinjiang are sent to board in "Han" regions that are both geographically distant and culturally unfamiliar. It was believed that this system would help the government to overcome the obstacle of a scarcity of qualified teachers in minority regions and, at the same time, reduce the cost since it seemed cheaper to construct new schools in in-land than in Tibet where transportation was not so convenient (Wang and Zhou 2003, p. 97).

5. Although "minzu tuanjie" had always been used in official rhetoric to regulate ethnic relations in China, its use has become more widespread in recent years. In fact, as Bulag (2002) has claimed, "minzu tuanjie" has become an ideological framework that is used to define Han-minority relations.

6. HSK (*Hanyu shuiping kaoshi*) was introduced by the Beijing Language and Culture University in 1990. It was the first standardized text for assessing the Chinese competence of non-native speakers. The test is clearly an imitation of the Test of English as a Foreign Language (TOEFL).The HSK test has been put to use largely for the assessment and "encouragement" of non-native speakers of Chinese (Dwyer 2005, p. 33).

7. Ma Rong is a professor of Peking University and a leading scholar in ethnic relations in China. He has been appealing for ethnic-policy reform for a long period of time but, after the recent series of ethnic clashes, his "once-marginal views are now part of the mainstream conversation with a wide range of academic, policymakers, and other thinkers (across ethnic and ideological spectrums) sharing his concerns with the current approach" (Leibold 2013, p. xii). Hu Angang is the founding director of the Institute for Contemporary China Studies at Tsinghua University, one of China's most influential think tanks. He called for a "second generation of ethnic policies" which has triggered fierce debates about this issue.

8. It should be noted that policies adopted in previous periods also sometimes had the problem of being contradictory. But it is after 2008 that their paradoxical nature becomes so apparent, as shown in this section.

9. A recent western book on minority education in China (Leibold and Chen 2014) echoes some of the themes of our chapter. Its subtitle recognizes that one of the biggest challenges in education for diverse groups within a nation is getting an appropriate balance between "unity and diversity in an era of critical pluralism".

10. Race (2015, pp. 15–30) identifies assimilation, integration, multiculturalism and anti-racism as the main conceptual phases in education policy-making within England and Wales.

References

ABC News. (2014). *Uighur scholar Ilham Tohti loses appeal against life sentence for advocating Xinjiang separatism.* [Online news]. Retrieved January 14, 2015, from http://www.abc.net.au/news/2014-11-21/uighur-scholar-loses-appeal-against life sentence/5910860

Baranovitch, N. (2010). Others no more: The changing representation of non-han peoples in Chinese history textbooks, 1951–2003. *The Journal of Asian Studies, 69*(1), 85–122.

Bass, C. (1998). *Education in Tibet: Policy and practice since 1950*. London: Zed Books in Association with Tibet Information Network.

BBC. (2014). *Xinjiang: Tight security after deadly violence*. [Online news]. Retrieved August 12, 2014, from http://www.bbc.co.uk/news/world-asia-china-28558290

Bovingdon, G. (2010). *The Uyghurs: Strangers in their own land*. New York: Columbia University Press.

Bulag, U. E. (2002). *The Mongols at China's edge: History and the politics of national unity*. Lanham: Rowman & Littlefield.

Chen, H. (1981). *Chinese education since 1949: Academic and revolutionary models*. Elmsford, NY: Pergamon Press.

CHINA. (2014a). *The Central Government made new aim for governing Xinjiang: Social stability and long-term safety* [Online news from the Chinese government official news website]. Retrieved July 7, 2014, from http://news.china.com.cn/2014-05/30/content_32530888.htm

CHINA. (2014b). *Let the Children and youth from different ethnic groups play together* [A speech given by Zhang Chunxian, the chief party secretary of Xinjiang, at "the Mobilization Meeting for the 32th month of education for 'Unity of Nationalities'"]. Retrieved July 7, 2014, from http://news.china.com/domestic/945/20140507/18487454.html

China Daily. (2013). WSJ's lies about Uyghurs, Editorial, *China Daily*, November 6.

ChinaPeace. (2014) *The achievement of anti-terrorism Campaign in Xinjiang*. [Online news from the Chinese official news website]. Retrieved January 14, 2015, from http://www.chinapeace.gov.cn/2014-06/24/content_11124746.htm

Chinese Government. (2013). *Further recruitment for Xinjiang In-land class in 2013* [Online news from the Chinese government official website]. Retrieved December 22, 2013, from http://www.gov.cn/jrzg/2013-08/02/content_2459987.htm

Chinese Statistics. (2010). *Tabulation on the 2010 Population Census of the People's Republic of China* [Online statistical data from the Chinese official website]. Retrieved September 22, 2016, from http://www.stats.gov.cn/tjsj/pcsj/rkpc/6rp/indexch.htm

Dikötter, F. (1992). *The discourse of race in modern China*. London: Hurst & Company.

Dwyer, A. M. (2005). *The Xinjiang conflict: Uyghur identity: Language policy and political discourse*. Washington: East-West Center.

Gaine, C. (1987). *No problem here: A practical approach to education and race in White Schools*. London: Hutchinson Education.

Gladney, D. C. (1988). *Dislocating China: Muslims, minorities and other Subaltern subjects*. London: Hurst & Company.

Hawkins, J. N. (1978). National-minority education in the People's Republic of China. *Comparative Education Review, 22*(1), 147–162.

Hawkins, J. N. (1983). *Education and social change in the People's Republic of China.* New York: Praeger.

He, B., & Guo, Y. (2000). *Nationalism, national identity and democratization in China.* Aldershot and Brookfield: Ashgate.

Hobsbawm, E. (1990). *Nations and nationalism since 1780: Programme, myth, reality.* Cambridge: Cambridge University Press.

Hu, C. T. (1974). *Chinese education under communism.* New York: Columbia University: Teachers College Press.

Hu, A., & Hu, L. (2011). Dierdai Minzu Zhengce [Second Generation of Ethnic Policies]. *Xinjiang Shifan Daxue Xuebao (Zhexue Shehui Kexue Bao), 32*(5), 1–13.

Hughes, C. R. (2003). *Chinese nationalism in a global Era.* London: Routledge.

Law, I. (2012). *Red racisms: Racism in communist and post-communist contexts.* Palgrave Macmillan.

Leibold, J. (2013). *Ethnic policy in China: Is reform inevitable?* Washington: East-West Center.

Leibold, J., & Chen, Y. (2014). *Minority education in China: Balancing unity and diversity in an Era of critical pluralism.* Hong Kong: Hong Kong University Press.

Ma, Rong. (2009). The key to understanding and interpreting ethnic relations in contemporary China. *International Institute of Social Studies (ISS),* November 13.

Minzuban. (2013). *More than 90% minority ethnic children received Bilingual education* [Online news from Chinese website for minority ethnic groups and religious affairs]. Retrieved December 22, 2013, from http://www.mzb.com.cn/html/Home/report/13123897-1.htm

MOE. (2000). *Regulation of the Xinjiang In-land class* [Online official documents issued by the Chinese Ministry of Education]. Retrieved September 22, 2016, from   http://www.moe.gov.cn/s78/A09/mzs_left/moe_752/tnull_1009.html

MOE. (2008). *Guideline for education for solidarity among nationalities in Schools (pilot edition)* [Official documents downloaded from the Chinese Ministry of Education website]. Retrieved September 22, 2016, from http://www.moe.gov.cn/srcsite/A09/s3081/200811/t20081126_77787.html

MOE. (2009). *A notice about carrying on education for solidarity among nationalities in Schools* [Official documents issued by the Publicity Department of the CPC Central Committee, Ministry of Education and State Ethnic Affairs Commission]. Retrieved October 29, 2016, from http://www.moe.edu.cn/publicfiles/business/htmlfiles/moe/moe_2800/200910/52932.html

Murphy, R. (2004). Turning peasants into modern Chinese citizens: "Population Quality" discourse. *The China Quarterly, 177,* 1–20.

PEOPLE. (2014). *The national work forum of nationalities* [Online news from the People's Daily website]. Retrieved January 14, 2015, from http://politics.people.com.cn/n/2014/0930/c1024-25763359.html

PEOPLE. (2015). *Urumqi to prohibit the wearing of religious dresses and veils in public areas* [Online news from the People's Daily website]. Retrieved January 14, 2015, from http://legal.people.com.cn/n/2015/0111/c188502-26363205.html

Postiglione, G. A. (2009). Dislocated education: The case of Tibet. *Comparative Review, 53*(4), 483–512.

Race, R. (2015). *Multiculturalism and education: Contemporary issues in education studies* (2nd ed.). London: Bloomsbury.

Rollock, N., & Gillborn, D. (2011). *Critical Race Theory (CRT)* [Online resource of British Educational Research Association]. Retrieved December 8, 2013, from http://www.academia.edu/1201277/Critical_Race_Theory_CRT

Schluessel, E. T. (2007). Bilingual education and discontent in Xinjiang. *Central Asian Survey, 26*(2), 251–277.

Stites, R. (1999). Writing cultural boundaries: National minority language policy, literacy planning, and bilingual education. In G. A. Postiglione (Ed.), *China's national minority education: Culture, schooling, and development* (pp. 95–130). London: Falmer Press.

UNESCO. (2006). UNESCO guidelines on intercultural education. Retrieved December 22, 2013, from http://unesdoc.unesco.org/images/0014/001478/147878e.pdf

Vickers, E. (2006). Defining the boundaries of "Chineseness": Tibet, Mongolia, Taiwan and Hong Kong in mainland history textbooks. In S. Foster & J. Crawford (Eds.), *What shall we tell the children?: International perspectives on school history textbooks* (pp. 25–48). Greenwich: Information Age Publishing.

Vickers, E. (2009). The opportunity of China? Education, patriotic values and the Chinese state. In M. Lall & E. Vickers (Eds.), *Education as a political tool in Asia* (pp. 53–82). London: Routledge.

Wang, H. (2003). *The history and future development of Bilingual education for China's ethnic minorities.* Master dissertation from the Northwest Normal University in China.

Wang, K. (2014). *Chinese city bans beards, Islamic-style clothing on buses during events* [Online news from CNN]. Retrieved October 30, 2016, from http://edition.cnn.com/2014/08/06/world/asia/china-beard-ban

Wang, C. Z., & Zhou, Q. H. (2003). Minority education in China: From state's preferential policies to dislocated schools. *Education Studies, 29*(1), 85–104.

Xinhua. (2014). *The President Xi Jinping's Important Speech at the 'Second Xinjiang Work Forum at the Central Government* [Online news from the official website of Xinhua news agency]. Retrieved July 7, 2014, from http://www.xj.xinhuanet.com/zt/2014-05/30/c_1110932196.htm

Xinjiang Class. (2015). *The general information about the Xinjiang In-land class* [Online report from the official website of the Xinjiang In-land class]. Retrieved

September 22, 2016, from http://www.xjban.com/xjbxin/hmzc/negb/jbqk/2015/92283.htm

Xinjiang Education. (2016). *Xinjiang launches project on sending cadres to preschools in southern Xinjiang to carry on voluntary teaching* [Online news from the website of Department of Education of the Xinjiang government]. Retrieved November 4, 2016, from http://www.xjedu.gov.cn/xjjyt/jxxw/zhzx/2016/101242.htm

Zhao, S. H. (2004). *A nation-state by construction: Dynamics of modern Chinese nationalism*. Stanford, CA: Stanford University Press.

Zhu, X. J. (2013). *Analysis of Bilingual education in Xinjiang* [Online article written by people from the Xinjiang Bilingual Education Quality Monitoring Center]. Retrieved December 22, 2013, from http://www.sdipgr.com/newscontent.aspx?lid=5&sid=6&nid=91

Zhu, Z. Y. (2007). *State schooling and ethnic identity: The politics of a Tibetan Neidi Secondary School in China*. Plymouth: Lexington Books.

Fei Yan is a doctoral student at the UCL Institute of Education, University College London, UK. His PhD research focuses on the portrayal of minority ethnic groups in Chinese mainstream history textbook. His wider research interests include nationalism in education systems, national identity, citizenship education, education for minority ethnic groups, education policy-making and textbook studies. He is currently offered a post-doctoral research position in Beijing Normal University in China.

Professor Geoff Whitty was director of the Institute of Education, University of London, UK, from 2000 to 2010. He currently holds a Global Innovation Chair in Equity in Higher Education at the University of Newcastle, Australia and a Research Professorship in Education at Bath Spa University, UK. He is a sociologist of education who has written widely on education policy. His latest book is *Research and Policy in Education: Evidence, Ideology and Impact* (UCL IOE Press, 2016). He has been an Honorary Professor at a number of Chinese universities, including Beijing Normal and North-west Normal Universities.

CPI Antony Rowe
Chippenham, UK
2017-11-13 09:42